The Sociology of Risk
and Gambling Reader

The Sociology of Risk and Gambling Reader

Edited by James F. Cosgrave

Routledge
Taylor & Francis Group
New York   London

Routledge is an imprint of the
Taylor & Francis Group, an informa business

Routledge
Taylor & Francis Group
270 Madison Avenue
New York, NY 10016

Routledge
Taylor & Francis Group
2 Park Square
Milton Park, Abingdon
Oxon OX14 4RN

© 2006 by Taylor and Francis Group, LLC
Routledge is an imprint of Taylor & Francis Group, an Informa business

Printed in the United States of America on acid-free paper
10 9 8 7 6 5 4 3 2 1

International Standard Book Number-10: 0-415-95222-0 (Softcover) 0-415-95221-2 (Hardcover)
International Standard Book Number-13: 978-0-415-95222-4 (Softcover) 978-0-415-95221-7 (Hardcover)
Library of Congress Card Number 2005035574

Library of Congress Cataloging-in-Publication Data

The sociology of risk and gambling reader / James F. Cosgrave, editor.
    p. cm.
   Includes bibliographical references and index.
    ISBN 0-415-95221-2 (hardback) -- ISBN 0-415-95222-0 (pbk.)
    1. Gambling--Social aspects. 2. Risk--Sociological aspects. I. Cosgrave, James F.,
1959-

HV6710.S65 2006
306.4'82--dc22   2005035574

Visit the Taylor & Francis Web site at
http://www.taylorandfrancis.com

and the Routledge Web site at
http://www.routledge-ny.com

Dedicated to my mother, Elizabeth,
and to the memory of my father, Lawrence.

Contents

Acknowledgments

I would like to thank the following people for their contributions to, and support for, this reader: David Liu for his friendship and editorial acumen; Thomas Klassen for his collegiality on our ongoing gambling research; Ed Ksenych and Tara Milbrandt for their friendship and stimulating discussions; and Stephen Katz, Ronald Paul, and Rachel Volberg for pointing me in the direction of particular pieces that have been included here. Thanks to Nancy Aitken for joining me in participant observation, Betty Cosgrave for all the gambling-related newspaper articles, Aaron Parrett for his gambling bibliography, and Sytze Kingma, Bill Ramp, and Joyce Goggin for their interest in gambling and social theory. I would also like to thank Pat Cosgrave, Jen Bruce, Jack Wayne, and Althea Prince for the support they provided along the way. My students in various sociology classes at Trent University have suffered my gambling topic affliction, and with them I have been able to work through and develop my concerns. Finally, thanks to Mike Bickerstaff, Stephanie Drew, David McBride, Linda Manis, and Mandy Rice at Routledge for making this project see the light of day.

Editor's Introduction

Gambling, Risk, and Late Capitalism

JAMES F. COSGRAVE

Modern economic development as a whole tends more and more to transform capitalist society into a giant international gambling house, where the bourgeois wins and loses capital in consequence of events which remain unknown to him.... The 'inexplicable' is enthroned in bourgeois society as in a gambling hall.... Successes and failures, thus arising from causes that are unanticipated, generally unintelligible, and seemingly dependent on chance, predispose the bourgeois to the gambler's frame of mind.... The capitalist whose fortune is tied up in stocks and bonds, which are subject to variations in market value and yield for which he does not understand the causes is a professional gambler. The gambler, however ... is a supremely superstitious being. The habitués of gambling casinos always possess magic formulas to conjure the Fates. Paul Lafargue, "Die Ursachen des Gottesglaubens,"* 1906.

—Walter Benjamin

---

* *Die neue Zeit*, 24, no. 1 (Stuttgart, 1906), p 512.

The Arcades Project, 1999

The chief factor in the gambling habit is the belief in luck ... it is to be taken as an archaic trait, inherited from a more or less remote past, more or less incompatible with the requirements of the modern industrial process, and more or less of a hindrance to the fullest efficiency of the collective economic life of the present.

—**Thorstein Veblen**
The Belief in Luck, 1899

Against the background of this growing unawareness and non-knowledge in the wake of the modernization of knowledge, the question of deciding in a context of uncertainty arises in a radical way ... a society based on knowledge and risk opens up a threatening sphere of possibilities. Everything falls under an imperative of avoidance. Everyday life thus becomes an involuntary lottery of misfortune.

—**Ulrich Beck**
Risk Society Revisited, 2000

The Sociology of Risk and Gambling Reader is a contribution to the sociological study of risk and gambling, a response to the variety of gambling forms found in North America and in other countries, which calls for more sustained sociological research. The reader collects an array of interpretations and methods of analysis, motivated by a sociological interest in understanding gambling as both subjective experience and cultural activity, which in its official legalized forms, requires particular forms of state regulation and governance. It also adds to the sociological conversation about gambling by linking recent developments in sociological theory, such as the sociology of risk, "risk society," and governmentality perspectives, with contemporary gambling enterprises. While legalized gambling is often represented now in terms of the "leisure" activity of individuals, such a focus tends to neglect the larger questions concerning the social organization of gambling, which must be considered in relation to political, economic, and globalizing processes (McMillen 1996, 2003). The orientation of the reader is primarily sociological, with some selections from history, cultural theory, and journalism.

The contemporary ubiquity of gambling in its various forms—in North America, primarily a result of state legalization and government promotion for the utilitarian objectives of revenue generation—might be thought about as an institutionalization of contemporary orientations to chance and to risk. In its long history as a cultural activity, the meanings of gambling exceed strictly utilitarian and pecuniary orientations; gambling has long been a popular activity, if often a covert activity, and has been interpreted culturally in non-utilitarian ways: as orientations to the sacred, to providence, to chance, and to luck, as forms of unproductive expenditure and play, as expressions of irrationality, superstition, character, and social status. In terms of its history, then, gambling may be considered in terms of its collective representations (Durkheim 1982, 1992); in late capitalist societies in particular, it may understood as an institutionalizing of orientations to, and venues for the acknowledgment of chance, uncertainty, and ontological insecurity (Giddens 1991; Beck 1992; Reith 2002).

It has been suggested that a sociological understanding of gambling has little in common with sociological reflections on the risk society, which "is best viewed as the recovery and extension of the theory of probability to situations of everyday life" (Ferguson 2002). As Gerda Reith argues in her sociological and historical analysis of gambling and Western culture, *The Age of Chance*, what gambling calls us to consider is the orientation to chance in the activity, and more broadly, the elevation of chance to ontological status in modern society (Reith 2002).

In the context of the contemporary climate of gambling legalization, legitimation, and expansion however, the sociology of risk can also contribute to the institutional analysis of gambling activity. Large-scale commercial casinos, for example, may be considered risk institutions, since here we find nothing left to chance, and the management of risks is essential for economic success. From the role of probability theory in the organization of the various games, to the construction of the spatial environment and the pervasiveness of surveillance in the casino setting, the sociology of risk in its various manifestations provides an opportunity to consider these features, as well as other gambling activities and related institutions. The role of the state in gambling enterprises, as well as the development of gambling markets, may also be analyzed from risk-taking and risk-management perspectives (Kingma 2004). Gambling itself, while marketed in its commercialized forms as a type of leisure activity and entertainment, is a form of risk-taking (Garland 2003) and the understanding of the gambling orientation may be applicable to realms outside those properly defined as gambling venues, such as financial markets.

The idea of the "risk society" is German sociologist Ulrich Beck's formulation of the contemporary period of ongoing "reflexive modernization" that characterizes "second modernity" (Beck 1992) or "world risk society" (Beck, Chapter Two). It is an all-encompassing theoretical construction of the present era. My comments here will consider the relationship of gambling to late capitalism. This will allow reflection on the place of gambling expansion and legitimation in relation to economic order, the role of the state, and consideration of some of the risks present in these developments.

Sociological approaches to gambling seek to move beyond individual-based explanations for the activity. Economic, rational choice, or psychological explanations can contribute to sociological analysis, but here gambling is viewed as requiring analysis that invokes the social, collective, or cultural levels, in order to account for the activity as an institution (Durkheim 1984). Even when considering interpretive sociological approaches such as Weber's, with the emphasis on the meanings actors attach to their actions (Weber 1968), these meanings must be considered as they are generated and situated within cultures, worldviews, and discourses. As such, to situate the variety of gambling experiences and the ways in which these are instituted and oriented to, one must consider gambling activities as cultural institutions that exist within particular social structures (Downes 1976; Geertz 1973; McMillen 1996; Kavanagh 2005). On this point, it is instructive to consider recent theoretical formulations of the place of voluntary risk-taking in contemporary society.

In his recent book exploring the concept of "edgework"—forms of voluntary individual risk-taking—Stephen Lyng (2005) presents what appear to be the contradictory ways in which risk-taking can be conceived; on the one hand, it can be theorized as an escape from the routines of everyday life in rationalized and disenchanted societal contexts (Lyng 2005, 6). On the other, and "(F)ramed in terms of the risk society model, the pursuit of risk becomes more than a response to the central imperatives of modern society. It is itself a key structural principle extending throughout the social system in institutional patterns of economic, political, cultural, and leisure activity" (Lyng, 8). Risk-taking may be considered "an especially pure expression of the central institutional and cultural imperatives of the emerging social order" (Lyng, 5).

By "key structural principle," I take Lyng to be referring to an organizing principle that orients social action, for individuals and institutions, and which is an expression of a particular type of social structure. We might distinguish analytically here between the subjective and objective dimensions of the phenomenon, the structural principle therefore referring to both personal and organizational aspects and orientations. Insofar as such a principle is conceived as orienting actors' actions on a number of levels, the pursuit of risk could be thought to embody or demonstrate a form of cultural self-understanding.

While I am inclined to side with the second formulation of risk-taking, in part because it raises the issue of the changing cultural and institutional imperatives that demonstrate and call for forms of risk-taking, the phenomenon of widespread legalized gambling can be considered from both perspectives. Social theorist Anthony Giddens (Chapter One) argues that risk-management plays itself out in late modernity through the interest in safety and the removal of societal risks. But actors in this social context are also free and encouraged to pursue "cultivated risk." Sociologist Erving Goffman (Chapter Twelve) in his analysis of the place of "action" and "character" in American society says that the avenues for fateful character tests are diminishing:

> Although every society no doubt has scenes of action, it is our own society that has found a word for it. Interestingly enough, we have become alive to action at a time when—compared to other societies—we have sharply curtailed in civilian life the occurrence of fatefulness of the serious, heroic, and dutiful kind. (Goffman 1967, 192–193)

From these perspectives, the embracing of risk and risk-taking may be viewed as a response to rationalization, risk-management, and safety, etc. As such, gambling for individual actors may be thought of as an escape from routine, rationalization, and alienation, while at the same time and "structurally" the contemporary social organization of gambling itself demonstrates (and continues to undergo) rationalization, commercialization, and commodification (Reith 2002).

Gambling is a global growth industry (McMillen 1996, 2003; Eadington and Cornelius 1997) where a form of risk-taking is rationalized, capitalized, and marketed as a form of leisure, entertainment, and "excitement"—in short, colonized by the gaming industry as well as by states. From a sociological perspective, the shift in gambling practices from local to global conditions, through the pressures of commercial colonization (Cosgrave and Klassen 2001; Reith 2002; McMillen 2003), raises questions, not only about the meaning of gambling activities for participants in rationalized, commercial, and anonymous gambling environments, but also about the larger cultural contexts within which legalized gambling enterprises are found.

Within neo-liberal social, political, and economic environments, where we find the downloading of societal risks onto individuals (Beck, Chapter

Two; Baker and Simon 2002) gambling may also be thought of as a form of playing with risk, chance, and uncertainty.* As such, gambling may be viewed in relation to the aforementioned "structural principle," insofar as uncertainty is thought to be a feature of the climate of late capitalist, or risk societies (Giddens 1991; Beck 1992, and this volume). Furthermore, in terms of the social organization of gambling in such societies, gambling (primarily through lotteries, but in some jurisdictions through casinos, video lottery terminals [VLTs], and sports betting), is a method used by states for revenue generation, which raises questions about the political and economic structure of late capitalism and the state's role here. Contemporary debates around the power of the state in a globalizing world have produced competing formulations: on the one hand, the state has been represented as having diminishing power or being in "crisis." On the other, the state has been formulated as demonstrating its adaptive powers (Kingma 1996; Cosgrave and Klassen 2001; Della Sala 2004). But the state's entry into the gambling field as promoter and beneficiary also suggests a different form of state activity:

> It might be argued that the legalization of gambling is a sign of the "enabling" of state activity: after all, it is now regulating a widespread activity and reaping the financial rewards. However, it is doing so in recognition that it does not have the capacity to do otherwise. It also signals that the state does not have the moral authority or the capacity to act in the name of the social. It can intervene in the case of gambling because it does so in the name of promoting individual choice, "entertainment," and freedom. Individuals willingly give their money to the state—they invariably always do—through games of chance because they are assuming their own risks and they no longer have faith in the state mechanism to assume risk collectively. (Della Sala 2004, 23)

Individual gambling in state-run enterprises becomes a form of ("voluntary" but regressive) taxation (Clotfelter and Cook 1989), an expression of the neo-liberal state form, whereby government budgets and social programs come to depend more heavily on the activity. In relation to this, it is pertinent to consider the privatization of risks whereby societal risks are

---

* (Kingma 1997; Reith 2002). In "General Economics and Postmodern Capitalism," Goux (1998) develops some of the affinities between aspects of the work of Georges Bataille and neoconservative writer George Gilder (1981). Gilder includes within capitalism characteristics that Bataille felt were features of precapitalist societies. Such characteristics include the potlatch, the gift, and the irrational (for Gilder, the irrationality of capitalist supply). Pertinent to this discussion is the significance that both claim for chance: for Bataille, it has an ontological value; for Gilder, it must be considered in relation to the uncertainties that contemporary capitalism must orient to (Goux, 205).

being displaced from forms of state welfare and social security onto citizens. This shift may be understood as a transformation in the conceptualization and practice of insurance. According to Tom Baker and Jonathan Simon:

> ... private pensions, annuities, and life insurance are engaged in an historic shift of investment risk from broad pools (the classic structure of risk spreading through insurance) to individual (middle class) consumers and employees in return for the possibility of a greater return. Many annuities and pensions have moved from a "defined benefit" approach, in which the risk of sufficient revenues to pay the promised benefit is on the collective pool, to a "defined contribution" approach, in which the risk of sufficient revenues for a comfortable retirement remains on the individual.... The claim is that embracing risk will provide workers with greater returns with which to enjoy their retirement. (Baker and Simon 2002, 4)

In the United States, private individual accounts for the management of various kinds of social risks are being suggested by the current administration. Such accounts include personal retirement accounts for Social Security contributions and portable health care savings accounts for medical needs. This privatization, however, exposes citizens to greater financial risk, especially in relation to increasingly volatile stock market conditions. The consequence of the transference of risks from the state to the individual is not only greater exposure of individuals to risk, but more speculative market activity, and more gambling behavior in markets (Shiller 2005). Legalized gambling then must be understood as a type of state or governing form that becomes an integral part of budget dispensation and state infrastructure, and which calls for the governing of citizens in relation to this.

While Lyng and his contributors focus on forms of voluntary risk-taking, the notion of a structural principle allows us to consider how state-sponsored gambling and, more broadly, the cultural legitimation of gambling is an expression of this principle at the level of institutions. If, and following Reith, chance is to be thought about in terms of its ontological significance in late modern society, we might also consider how orientations to chance (as both different from, and related to, risk-taking) are responded to by institutions in various ways. Not only has chance been commodified through legalized commercial gambling enterprises, we might also speak of the notion of *governing by chance*, through states' entry into the gambling field and their operation of gambling enterprises (see Neary and Taylor, Chapter Sixteen, for a discussion of the British state's role in the lottery).

Gambling in North America, as well as Europe and Australia, has been throughout its history a popular cultural activity, a prohibited and illegal activity, a regulated activity, and a state-sanctioned and promoted activity. Lotteries have been used by states in the past (for example, Britain, France, and the United States) to finance public projects, but from the late nineteenth through most of the twentieth century, most forms of gambling were illegal. We are now in the midst of an unprecedented global expansion of legitimate gambling opportunities. State-sanctioned gambling, as witnessed within North America today—and in many other countries—provides a different context for understanding gambling activities compared to the sociocultural milieu as recently as the mid-1960s, when sociologists such as Irving Zola and Erving Goffman provided their now classic analyses.

Whether one refers to the contemporary milieu of Western societies as late capitalism, late modernity, postmodernity, or the risk society, present-day gambling activities and behaviors are framed by a different discursive field than that which obtained only forty years ago. The values of the Protestant ethic appear to have been left far behind, and in contrast to its strictures about hard work, saving, and asceticism, social and economic values are organized now around consumption, leisure, and risk-taking. The "self-made man" and the "organization man," types of economic actor who adhered to these earlier strictures, have been replaced by varieties of the risk-taking entrepreneur. In the shift from managerial to investor capitalism we find the financial speculator, the day-trader, the young "dotcom" wizard, the visionary CEO. This risk-taking ethic, however, might be thought as a new type of work, even "hard" work, and can be viewed in Lyng's terms as a form of "edgework" (Smith 2005). It is intriguing to consider how contemporary institutions, whether of leisure or occupational activities, call for, or tacitly support, an ethic of risk-taking (Callahan 2004; Lyng 2005).

Citizens are constantly implored through television advertising to feel the "excitement" of casinos or take their chances on a lottery ticket. Such lottery-marketed slogans as "Imagine the Freedom" and "Earning money is great; winning it is even better" (both slogans for Canada's national lotteries) can be taken as collective expressions of work dissatisfaction or alienated labor. Governments themselves, increasingly involved in gambling enterprises and eager to generate more gambling revenues, capitalize on the undermining of the work ethic equation that work equals reward.

One of the themes developed by both Giddens and Beck in their sociological focus on risk concerns the conditions of uncertainty that characterize contemporary late-modern risk societies. This is demonstrated in both the breakdown of opportunities for, and in the meaning of, gainful employment. Risk societies are no longer "gainful employment societies" (Beck 2003, 6). Alongside the issue of the distribution of gainful employment, sociologists have noted for some time that the undermining of the work ethic itself has long been under way, as the "cultural contradictions of capitalism," consumer culture, and the processes of reflexive modernization give rise to identities no longer grounded on the disciplined social values that support this ethic (Riesman et al. 1950; Bell 1975; Campbell 1987; Giddens 1991; Beck 1992).

Further, gambling is now often promoted and characterized as "gaming"—certainly by vested corporate and governmental interests—as the activity gets constructed and represented as leisure and entertainment rather than as deviance. If governments and states no longer approach gambling as a moral issue, the residues of previous negative interpretations still exist, centered now mostly around the medicalized categories of "problem" and "pathological" gambling. Gambling activities are no longer discursively constructed in religious or moral terms, but in economic, consumerist, and medical terms. It is not that moral discourse around gambling has disappeared; rather, the discourse now centers on the individual's self-governance in relation to gambling.

Legal gambling is acceptable, but one is enjoined by official state gambling agencies to be a "responsible" gambler (Cosgrave and Klassen 2001; Campbell and Smith 2003). This neo-liberal moral discourse then raises the issue of the state's relationship to citizens, and since states promote and capitalize on gambling, critics draw attention to the increased accessibility to gambling, the creation of new problem gamblers, and gambling-related suicides (Branswell 2002; Williams and Wood 2004).

The ubiquity of legal gambling in North America is a result of the rapid legitimation and expansion that has occurred since the mid-1960s. Since then, state-sanctioned gambling has moved beyond lotteries to include a wide variety of gambling opportunities: from sports betting, VLTs, Scratch and Win cards, and Keno, to casino games and expanding variations on these games within casinos. While most forms of Internet gambling are illegal in North America, Internet poker and varieties of sports betting are becoming increasingly popular (McMillen 2003).

At present, the laws surrounding online poker are unclear and can vary from state to state. The issue seems to be how the game is defined and organized, and whether state authorities bother to enforce existing laws (Rose 2004). The growth of Internet poker—a very popular activity on U.S. college campuses—has been spurred on by recent television coverage of poker tournaments, from the *World Series of Poker* to various celebrity poker shows. Las Vegas is getting ample television airtime, not only through the televising of poker matches, but in a number of reality (*Casino*) and dramatic television programs (*Las Vegas*) as well. The Las Vegas mystique shows no signs of abating.

The legalization, legitimation, and expansion of gambling is global in scope as industrialized and developing countries have entered into the gambling field. British laws regarding casino gambling are in the process of being liberalized to allow for large casinos. And casino expansion in the Chinese-controlled island of Macau will soon situate the island as the world's largest casino center. Interestingly, the expansion of casinos there is the result of competition between Chinese casino tycoon Stanley Ho, who has held a monopoly on casino gambling, and American casino owners the Sands, MGM, and gambling entrepreneur Steve Wynn (York 2005). While casinos are established in North America, Australia, New Zealand, South Africa, and countries in Western Europe, casino gambling is being liberalized in parts of Asia and in Eastern Europe. Perhaps the fastest growth in gambling is to be found in Russia, where casinos and slot machines are proliferating due to permissive regulation of gaming licenses (Business Week Online 2004).

In the Canadian context, the development of commercial and chari-table gambling opportunities has taken an interesting form: provincial governments have a monopoly on gambling enterprises so that gambling is run by governments, primarily for revenue purposes, but also for job creation and economic development for depressed towns and border cit-ies. Both medium- and large-scale casinos are designated as (tourist) des-tination casinos, such as in Niagara Falls, Ontario, which has two large casinos, and borders New York state. To reverse the influx of American gambling tourists from Detroit, Michigan, to Windsor, Ontario, which has a large-scale destination casino, the City of Detroit replaced its sole casino with three large-scale casinos. With the expansion of state-spon-sored gambling in Canada, legal forms of private-enterprise gambling, such as horseracing and bingo, were negatively affected. In the province of Ontario, bingo appears to be on the wane with declining revenues, but the flagging horseracing industry has been rejuvenated by the introduction of slot machines into provincial racetracks. This move has generated mil-lions of dollars in revenue for the provincial government and the industry through the conversion of racetracks into "racinos." The development of racinos by private industry is also flourishing in a number of U.S. states (Eadington 2003).

Legalized gambling has also been utilized as a growing economic opportunity for Aboriginal groups in various jurisdictions, as evidenced by the spread of native-run casinos in Canada and the United States. There are currently 411 Indian casinos, operated by 223 tribes in 28 U.S. states (*The Vancouver Sun* 2005). The largest casino in the world, the Foxwoods Resort Casino, is run by the wealthiest Indian tribe in the world, the Mashantucket Pequots, and is located on the Mashantucket Pequot Reservation in southeastern Connecticut. In 2000, the casino averaged 40,000 gamblers each day, and the cumulative contributions from slot machine revenue to the State of Connecticut exceeded 1 billion dollars (Fromson 2003, 244). In 2002, the casino employed 13,000 workers (National Indian Gambling Association). A twenty-minute drive away from Foxwoods is the slightly smaller Mohegan Sun Casino, owned by the Mohegan Tribe.

The development of native casinos has not been without controversy, specifically with regard to the often politically opaque approval and development processes. According to Donald Bartlett and James Steele, "Since 1979, as gambling has boomed, the number of recognized tribes on the U.S. mainland has spiked 23 percent to a total of 337. About 200 additional groups have petitioned the bureau for recognition. Perhaps the most notorious example of tribal resurrection is the Mashantucket Pequots of Connecticut, proud owners of the world's largest casino, Foxwoods. The now billionaire tribe had ceased to exist until Congress recreated it in 1983. The current tribe members had never lived together on a reservation" (2002, 25). Native-run gambling in the United States has almost doubled the take of Nevada's gambling industry, pulling in $18.5 billion as of 2004.

However, while some tribes, like the Pequots, have become extremely wealthy, the majority of Native Americans are not benefiting from casino development (Bartlett and Steele 2002). The politics around the entry of native-run gambling into the (global) gambling field are complex, flagging concerns with tribal self-determination and the politics and construction of identity and community.

The states and governments that sponsor, regulate, and promote gambling are now the gambling "houses"—indeed, they may be considered professional gamblers (Fabian 1990)—and citizens are encouraged to gamble in ever-accessible gambling venues, from convenience stores to nearby racetracks and casinos. The aggressive promotion of gambling in Canadian provinces such as Ontario demonstrates a "stimulatory" interest, which aims not only to consolidate gambling markets but to attract new gambling consumers. Individuals can also gamble in the comfort of their own homes, by logging on to the illegal offshore casino-style web sites, or the sports-betting sites that allow certain kinds of betting not permitted by provincial or state-run forms of sports gambling. It will not be long before governments enter this area in order to regulate and raise revenues from it. But if gambling has come to be legitimated, there are still social conflicts over the issues of casino expansion (both state and privately run), Internet gambling, youth gambling, and problem gambling. With the spread of casino and other forms of gambling, and in particular with the convenience of Internet gambling, gambling has been "spatially decontained"—it remains to be seen what the social consequences of the spread of, and accessibility to, gambling opportunities will be in the long run (Schwartz 2003, 217).

Drawing upon the work of French sociologist Roger Caillois (1962) on the structure of play and games, Robert Herman (1976, 215) hypothesizes, "The greater the sense of physical distance between a player's home and the gambling arena, the more aleatory games (games of chance) are encouraged, and the more mimicry is encouraged, and the more vertigo is encouraged." Further, the "sense of distance from home is very useful in releasing the individual from the bind of conventional responsibilities and controls. Chanciness can then increase in influence" (216). While Herman's hypothesis was a call for more empirical analysis (back in 1967), the relative ease of access to gambling for most North Americans raises sociological questions, not only for its influence on gambling behavior, but also for its broader cultural impacts. One example concerns the consequences of youth gambling, since the current and future generations of youth will be living in a legalized and ubiquitous gambling culture (Derevensky et al. 2003). In a report submitted to the Law Commission of Canada on legalized gambling, the authors note findings from "The Australian Productivity Commission Report" on gambling in Australia: "...The report mentioned that widespread legal gambling negatively impacted on Australian society by creating changes in behavioral norms and social ethics. According to several data sources, when governments promote or facilitate gambling its role of protector of citizens' welfare is compromised and the community's trust in public institutions is diluted" (Campbell et al. 2005, 79–80). Here we find the issue of trust being raised that is a topic of sociological concern in the work of Beck and Giddens. The unintended consequences of gambling legalization and expansion may thus be viewed in relation to Beck's conception of the processes of "reflexive modernization."

Regardless of one's position on gambling's place in contemporary culture, it has come to be a feature of late capitalist societies, an activity that might be said to be representative of everyday life in these societies. The recent liberalization of gambling may be considered to be an activity like others—pornography, recreational drug use, same-sex relationships and marriage—that have come to be more accepted, if not celebrated, as expressions of lifestyle, through social and political processes of de-stigmatization. But gambling might also be thought to be a collective representation of life where orientations to chance and risk become institutionalized (Durkheim 1984; Beck, this volume). Not only do gamblers seek out and orient to chance and risk while gambling, but the expansion of gambling puts governments into risk positions, which then have to be managed. It may be argued that gamblers in state-controlled gambling venues (as well as privately-operated and privately-run venues) are not involved in "risk," but in rationalized forms of gambling whereby the house edge will guarantee their losses. State-sponsored and privately-owned commercial forms of gambling are typically marketed and advertised as forms of entertainment, so there is no real representation of risk. Indeed, in North America, the interest in accruing revenues and profits from gambling have ensured that the representation of risks from gambling—possible financial ruin, problem and pathological gambling, and so on—are downplayed and lag the promotion of gambling. Casinos themselves may be thought as liminal spaces, bound off from the constraints and routines of everyday life, where rational orientations are discouraged and the spending of money is for the purpose of experiencing excitement (Mun 2002). Indeed, rational approaches that aim at the making of money (such as card counting) are frowned upon. It is the irrational or non-rational orientation that is potentially problematic, however—for the gambler who will chase his or her losses (Lesieur 1984), and for the state that must manage the populations "at risk" of developing this type of orientation.

Interestingly, in Lyng's recent collection on "edgework," there is no inclusion of gambling activity as a form of this type of voluntary risk-taking—understandable in the case of programmed or aleatory forms such as slot machines, video lottery terminals, roulette, and lottery play where there is no possibility of skill and mastery. However, high-stakes gambling in agonistic games such as poker, and even illegal forms of gambling, may be thought as edgework and Gerda Reith, in the same volume, makes the case for viewing gambling as such (Lyng 2005, fn. 1, 243). We see in these differing views an expression of tensions that are grounded in the larger culture, between rationalization and risk-taking, between aleatory and agonistic orientations, and how the culture of risk is symbolized through the very institutionalizing of gambling.

We have witnessed many examples of this risk culture through recent major events in financial markets. While participation in such markets is always a condition of financial risk, it is important to distinguish types of risk-taking that are becoming more visible. On the one hand, and more obviously, is the risk-taking of speculative activity, whether by financial institutions or individuals, as well as the more mundane investing risks faced by the "average investor." On the other is risk-taking that is criminal, illicit, or just rule-breaking, and which could be explained variously as demonstrating an instrumental orientation toward the goal of greater profits, an implicit value of some forms of corporate culture, or as a desire for the thrill of risk-taking itself (Goffman, this volume; Katz 1988; Callahan 2004; Lyng 2005; Smith 2005). As such, we might see in the financial markets the "structural principle" of modern society's orientation to risk-taking being played out. The risky trading activities of rogue stock trader Nick Leeson literally "broke the bank"—his high-risk derivatives trading on the Japanese and Singapore futures exchanges single-handedly brought down the Barings Bank of London. The orientation to risk has also been revealed recently through the fraudulent activities of brokerage firms, corporate executives, mutual fund companies, and accounting firms (for example, Enron, Worldcom, Tyco, Adelphia, Bre-X, Merrill Lynch, Nortel, RBC Securities, AGF, AIC, Investors Group, Arthur Anderson, and Lord Conrad Black, to name a handful of North American examples) that have resulted in charges of illegal stock trading, market timing and manipulation, corporate bankruptcies, criminal investigations, and the loss of life-savings of individual employees and shareholders. It bears consideration that risk-taking in its illicit or rule-breaking forms may not only be accidental or incidental in late capitalist corporate and financial cultures (Callahan 2004).

Corporate criminality has been an object of study for sociologists interested in forms of white-collar crime (Pearce and Snider 1995), and in the late 1980s and early 1990s, the United States witnessed the worst financial fraud epidemic in its history through the Savings and Loans crisis. In their analysis of the U.S. government's response to corporate financial crimes, sociologists Kitty Calavita and Henry Pontell argue that the government's massive effort to prosecute the Savings and Loan offenders, in contrast to a significantly less vigorous response to other forms of corporate crime, "can be explained at least in part by the potential for these crimes to decimate a whole financial sector and damage the larger economy" (1995, 212). The prosecution of such crimes, they suggest, is not motivated so much by the interest in punishing crime as it is damage control, designed to preserve the economic system. Illegal risk-taking is more widespread in the corporate world than that reported in the media, and governments appear more interested in investigating fraudulent corporate activity when it appears to blatantly threaten the structure and stability of the capitalist economic system itself (1995, 212).

The recent spate of corporate scandals and the concerns about brokerage firms' and financial analysts' conflicts of interest have raised the issue of whether the "average investor" can trust such "experts" to disclose truthful financial information. Further, and more broadly, there is the "role of certain regulatory agencies in shoring up investor's [sic] faith, minimizing uncertainty and risk, and generally stabilizing the financial system" (Calavita and Pontell, 207).

These issues tie in closely with Giddens' and Beck's discussions of the place of trust in the everyday lives of modern individuals who must rely on expert knowledge and abstract knowledge systems (Chapters One and Two, this volume). And further, the very complexity and sophistication of financial systems today has called for the development of new methods of dealing with market risks, from strategies such as hedging to the use of new types of financial instruments, such as derivatives, which point to the pervasive culture of risk in increasingly globalized markets (Pryke and Allen 2000).

For the average investor as for the market analyst, stock market activities have come to be perceived more strongly in terms of the risks involved, where, as a result, the notion of "investing" itself is challenged. The historical distinction between speculation and gambling, a tenuous distinction promulgated to legitimize certain types of stock market-behavior as morally acceptable and productive, has been overcome (Fabian 1990). The moral basis of the dichotomy—productive speculation vs. unproductive and irrational gambling—no longer holds much force; not only is gambling legitimate business in itself, it is increasingly an important part of state infrastructure, such that gambling is economically productive for the state, notwithstanding debates about the social costs. Where previously chance was viewed in Western societies as a threat to a "rational" capitalistic economic order, the latter expressive of and grounded in Protestant interpretations of the world, today it has been commodified (Reith 2002) as an orientation within late capitalist speculation (Gilder 1981; Goux 1998). In late capitalism—casino capitalism (Strange 1986)—the distinction between gambling and investing is not very clear when speculation and "irrational exuberance" or "despondency" play a significant role in market actions and valuations (Shiller 2000). Recent sociological analyses of stock market trading behavior have provided critiques of rational choice conceptualizations, demonstrating the place of emotion, intuition, and risk-taking in the activity (Knorr-Cetina and Bruegger 2002; Knorr-Cetina and Preda 2004; Smith 2005).

As if to make explicit the gambling that takes place within stock markets, Mark Cuban, billionaire owner of the National Basketball Association

Dallas Mavericks team, is planning a hedge fund that explicitly places bets on sports games and blackjack. The fund will be managed by professional gamblers (Herbst-Bayliss 2004). In a climate of financial risk-taking, however, and in the face of a multitude of financial market scandals, we should not be surprised that high-risk hedge funds are under scrutiny by securities regulators in the United States and Canada. Nevertheless, to quote a television financial analyst, "market uncertainty makes for good gambling opportunities."

Under the conditions of late capitalism, or late modernity, "ontological security"—the social and experiential basis of trust necessary for self-identity and security (Giddens 1991)—cannot be taken for granted when the traditions and institutional moorings that provide for such security undergo dissolution. Due to the processes of reflexive modernization, and the consequent occurrence of detraditionalization and individualization, individuals must actively construct their biographies, and do this, not only by utilizing forms of expert knowledge (Giddens 1991), but by criticizing and acting against such knowledge (Beck 1992) and by ignoring such knowledge (Douglas 1994).

The achieved character of ontological security, and the reflexive possibility of ontological insecurity as a feature of the life-world of late modernity, was brought home spectacularly with the terrorist attacks of "9/11." Directed against the symbols of American capitalism and power, the attacks underscore the unintended consequences of globalization in a world where not everyone celebrates secular consumerist values and ideologies. For sociologists such as Giddens and Beck, such an event might be framed within the processes of (reflexive) modernization, which have global consequences. This particular event also had the outcome of heightening citizens' perceptions of risk, not only of future terrorist attacks—a continuing concern—but also of airline travel and working in tall buildings.

In global financial markets, geopolitical events have significant consequences for market valuations. Some individual and large investors are wary of a risky financial climate, while others see speculative opportunities, even in devastation. World events become priced into a technologically interdependent global market, where millions of transactions, large and small, are processed instantaneously, and where the use of speculative financial instruments such as derivatives exacerbates financial risk.

States, under the conditions of heightened risk perception of terrorist attacks and other types of threat, enact forms of risk management—increased airport security, stricter border controls, greater restrictions on citizens' freedom and privacy—with the unintended social consequences of more, and new, types of risk. Interestingly, as noted by casino historian

David Schwartz, the biometric systems now used for security purposes in airports and elsewhere were first used by the casino industry. According to Schwartz, "Americans who want to live in a more controlled society would do well to spend some time in a casino—because these venues have already realized visual and behavioural surveillance systems that mainstream business and law-enforcement are only beginning to understand" (Schwartz 2003, 216–217).

The television drama *Las Vegas* supports this point, as the show seems to be more about rules, regulations, and surveillance than it is about gambling. Such systems are designed to minimize risk to the casino, primarily the financial risks brought about by cheating, fraud, theft, etc. But as states and social institutions attempt to manage and minimize risks, the state itself, through the sanctioning of gambling, sells risks as desirable or, in some sense, necessary for reward (for example, as payoff or excitement). In neo-liberal societies, not only are risks downloaded onto individuals (Baker and Simon 2002; Garland 2003), but individuals are encouraged to take risks (Lyng 2005). From a governmentality perspective (Foucault 1991; Rose 1993, 1996, 1999; Lupton, Chapter Three; Collins, Chapter Seventeen), it is crucial to consider, not only how states regulate and govern gambling activities, but how individuals must govern their own gambling activities—emotionally, socially, financially, ethically, etc. In some jurisdictions, "responsible gambling" is advocated as a harm prevention measure; this, however, may be viewed as a legitimation strategy used by states to manage the risks related to easily accessible and heavily promoted gambling (Cosgrave and Klassen 2001).

We see through such measures that the risks of gambling require the "responsibilization" of the individual (Rose 1999; Ewald 2003)—this in an environment where the social and moral constraints around gambling are weakened. But responsible gambling must be viewed in terms of its political import: "The responsible gambling paradigm transposes social problems affiliated with excessive gambling into individual problems and depoliticizes them" (Campbell and Smith 2003, 143). The discourse of responsible gambling must be viewed in relation to the normalization of gambling activities, and the building and stabilizing of gambling markets.

Private commercial gambling enterprises and states that have entered into the gambling field market gambling as entertainment ("gaming"), but the risks associated with this type of entertainment do not get the same airtime from governmental gambling agencies. Governments (and private casino operators) often reap large economic benefits from problem gamblers: A recent study of the demographic of gambling revenues in Ontario shows that, of the 4 billion dollars taken in from Ontario residents in 2003, 5 percent of gamblers accounted for 35 percent of the total (Williams and Woods 2004). This raises a number of ethical problems in terms of the state's reliance on this money, but from a criminological perspective also raises questions about where this money is coming from. The individualized framework within which gambling is represented in North America denies its societal contexts and habituses (Bourdieu 1990), contributing to the construction of problematic forms of gambling as personal troubles (Mills 1967).

With respect to the issues of problem and pathological gambling—a field dominated by psychology—Collins's chapter (Chapter Seventeen) demonstrates a sociological approach, governmentality, which focuses on the ways in which categories such as "pathological gambler" are discursively constructed within particular historical and social conditions. The social production of categories and forms of knowledge can be examined as topics in their own right. As such, Collins is interested in the ways in which the "psy sciences" (psychiatry, psychology, and psychoanalysis) "have invented new ways of talking about the person and new means of inspecting the population and the individual." Governmentality is interested in how forms of knowledge contribute to the governing of populations.

The gap that exists in terms of sociological accounts of gambling (see Introduction to Section One) must narrow as sociologists come to grips with, and try to keep pace with, the broad cultural scope and significance of gambling legitimation and expansion. McMillen (1996) notes the lag in feminist analyses of gambling; an interesting area of gambling research now concerns the place of gambling in women's lives. While much research on women and gambling has focused on women "problem gamblers," more sociological and anthropological research is being done on the meaning(s) of gambling activity for women. In relation to the broader field of gambling and gender, some researchers are now focusing on the "feminization of gambling" (Volberg 2003). Included here is an ethnographic piece on female bingo players that focuses on the meanings of the activity for the players, and some of the tensions between their bingo playing and the demands of everyday life.

The readings in this book range from classic sociological pieces such as Goffman's "Where the Action Is," Simmel's "The Adventurer," and Zola's "Observations on Gambling in a Lower Class Setting" to more contemporary pieces concerning the phenomenon of risk. The reader will also find a variety of sociological perspectives and methodological approaches for the study of gambling. Applications of these perspectives are found in Zola (functionalism), Nibert and Neary and Taylor (Marxist analyses), and in the interpretive and interactionist traditions represented by Simmel and Goffman. Along with the sociological pieces on risk (Giddens, Beck, Neary and Taylor), other contemporary social-theoretical approaches are represented, ranging from phenomenology and hermeneutics (Reith) to Bourdieu-influenced (Allen) to governmentality (Lupton and Collins). A supplement to the sociological analyses of gambling is provided with journalistic accounts that represent the life-world of gambling activity—represented in the pieces by Frederick and Stephen Barthelme and David Plotz. There are four sections, which are organized thematically to present to the reader different ways into the subject matters of risk and gambling, and the interest is to have the readings generate thinking on such matters as the relationship of social action to social structure and culture.

While the majority of the readings focus on the social and cultural aspects of gambling, the reader begins with representative sociological formulations of risk. The discussions of risk are important not only for understanding the relationship of the concept to modernization processes and for the self-understanding of late modernity, they also help to provide a framework for thinking about the contemporary social contexts in which gambling is flourishing. The recent focus on the sociology of risk and "risk societies" has coincided, not only with the contemporary prominence of risk discourses, but with the legitimation and expansion of gambling. The sociology of risk may help to shed light on the social fact of gambling within late capitalism. Beck's emphasis on the management of "bads," rather than the production of goods, in risk societies (Beck 1992; Beck, Giddens, and Lash 1994), as well as his emphasis on the uncertainties generated by "reflexive modernization," provides a framework for considering states' roles in gambling implementation as a (global) political-economic phenomenon, the possible outcomes of gambling expansion, and the forms of risk management. With state-sanctioned gambling expansion, for example, the production of goods is viewed in terms of nontax revenue generation, as well as economic stimulation and job creation in jurisdictions where casinos and other forms of gambling are introduced. However, risk products or "bads" are also produced in the form of gambling-related crime—theft, fraud, loan sharking, prostitution, and so on, increased numbers of problem and pathological gamblers, potential state legal liabilities, and other not-yet-apparent risk products. These bads then require risk management in order to facilitate legitimation and possible further expansion. One of the issues Beck deals with is the breakdown of forms of social insurance in the face of societal risks (Beck, Chapter Two). As Mike Neary and Graham Taylor argue (Chapter Sixteen), the move by the state into gambling enterprises is indicative of the problems faced by the welfare state and its inability to "insure" citizens against such risks. The problem of uncertainty as a feature of late modernity raises questions about how this is responded to by institutions and individuals, such that rational, irrational, and nonrational orientations require sociological consideration.

The formulations of risk also provide the reader with theoretical and contextual linkages for thinking about other phenomena discussed in this book, for example, the contemporary orientation to chance, not only in gambling but also in financial markets, the medicalization of particular behaviors and their governance, the place of adventure and play in relation to risk-taking, and the development of the state in relation to cultural practices and globalization processes.

Much has been written utilizing the concept of risk and applying it to a variety of activities, behaviors, and institutions since the analysis and advancement of the concept in the work of Beck (1992, German ed. [1986]) and Giddens (1991). It is important to point out other theoretical strands in the development of risk theory, and the work of anthropologist Mary Douglas on the cultural and symbolic basis of risk understandings and perceptions should be singled out in this regard (1982, 1994). Further, the (post-) Durkheimian tradition in sociology and anthropology, represented in the work of Marcel Mauss (1990), Clifford Geertz (1973), Georges Bataille (1988a, 1988b, 1988c, 1991), Roger Caillois (1962), and others provide resources for understanding gambling as a cultural phenomenon, where such themes as play and unproductive expenditure provide alternative interpretations to utilitarian and rationalistic accounts of social phenomena.

The work of Pierre Bourdieu, which bridges sociology and anthropology, also provides an untapped resource for the analysis of gambling and risk-taking in social life (see Allen, Chapter Nine). His concepts of habitus, fields (of power and cultural production), forms of capital (economic, social, cultural), and symbolic violence can all contribute to the understanding of gambling orientations in particular cultural contexts (Bourdieu 1984, 1990, 1991, 1993; Wacquant 1989). In the contemporary environment of global gambling legalization, legitimation, and expansion, we find that the gambling field is one of social struggles for market dominance, e.g., between states seeking revenues and private gambling enterprises seeking profits, and between these and other groups, such as aboriginal groups entering the gambling field or groups interested in curtailing gambling expansion. Bourdieu's work provides an analytical framework for considering these conflicts and their situatedness within particular cultures and habituses.

As with every collection, exclusions are inevitable; a selected readings list is therefore appended. This guide will be of interest to sociologists and students working in the areas of criminology and deviance, medicalization, social problems, the sociology of the state, leisure and consumption, money and exchange, the sociology of culture, and classical and contemporary theory.

References

Baker, Tom, and Jonathan Simon (2002) *Embracing Risk: The Changing Culture of Insurance and Responsibility.* Chicago: The University of Chicago Press.

Bartlett, Donald L., and James B. Steele (2002) "Special Report—Indian Casinos: Wheel of Misfortune," *Time,* (Canadian edition, December 16), 160, no. 25: 22–34.

Bataille, Georges (1988a) *Guilty,* trans. Bruce Boone. San Francisco: The Lapis Press.

Bataille, Georges (1988b) *Inner Experience,* trans. Leslie Anne Boldt. Albany: State University of New York Press.

Bataille, Georges (1988c) *The Accursed Share,* trans. Robert Hurley. New York: Zone.

Bataille, Georges (1991) *Visions of Excess: Selected Writings, 1927–1939,* ed. Allan Stoekl. Minneapolis: University of Minnesota Press.

Beck, Ulrich (1992, German ed. [1986]) *The Risk Society: Towards A New Modernity.* London: Sage.

Beck, Ulrich (2003) "The Theory of Reflexive Modernization: Problematic, Hypotheses and Research Programme," *Theory, Culture and Society* 20(2): 1–33.

Beck, Ulrich, Anthony Giddens, and Scott Lash (1994) *Reflexive Modernization: Politics, Tradition and Aesthetics in the Modern Social Order.* Stanford: Stanford University Press.

Bell, Daniel (1975) *The Cultural Contradictions of Capitalism.* New York: Basic Books.

Benjamin, Walter (1999) *The Arcades Project,* ed. Rolf Tiedemann, trans. Howard Eiland and Kevin McLaughlin. Cambridge, MA: Harvard University Press.

Bourdieu, Pierre (1984) *Distinction: A Social Critique of the Judgement of Taste.* London: Routledge and Kegan Paul.

Bourdieu, Pierre (1990) *The Logic of Practice.* Cambridge: Polity Press.

Bourdieu, Pierre (1991) *Language and Symbolic Power.* Cambridge: Polity Press.

Bourdieu, Pierre (1993) *The Field of Cultural Production.* New York: Columbia University Press.

Branswell, B. (2002) "Gamblers Try to Collect a Debt to Society," *The Toronto Star,* July 13, p. J.4.

Business Week Online (2004) "Russia: 'Ka-Ching' Go The Slots," www.businessweek.com, December 6.

Caillois, Roger (1962) *Man, Play, and Games.* London: Thames & Hudson.

Calavita, Kitty, and Henry Pontell (1995) "Saving the Savings and Loans? U.S. Government Response to Financial Crime," in *Corporate Crime: Contemporary Debates*, ed. Frank Pearce and Laureen Snider. Toronto: University of Toronto Press.

Callahan, David (2004) *The Cheating Culture: Why More Americans Are Doing Wrong to Get Ahead*. Orlando: Harcourt.

Campbell, Colin (1987) *The Romantic Ethic and the Spirit of Modern Consumerism*. New York: Basil Blackwell.

Campbell, Colin S., and Garry J. Smith (2003) "Gambling in Canada—From Vice to Disease to Responsibility: A Negotiated History," *Canadian Bulletin of Medical Health* 20 (1): 121–49.

Campbell, Colin S., Timothy F. Hartnagel, and Garry J. Smith (2005) *The Legalization of Gambling in Canada*, The Law Commission of Canada, July.

Castellani, Brian (2000) *Pathological Gambling: The Making of a Medical Problem*, Albany: State University of New York Press.

Cosgrave, Jim, and Thomas R. Klassen (2001) "Gambling Against the State: The State and the Legitimation of Gambling," *Current Sociology* 49(5): 1–22.

Della Sala, Vincent (2004) "Les Jeux Sont Fait? The State and Legalized Gambling," Working Paper, 02/04, University of Trento, School of International Studies, Italy.

Derevensky, Jeffrey, Rina Gupta, Karen Hardoon, Laurie Dickson, and Anne-Elyse Dequire (2003) "Youth Gambling: Some Social Policy Issues," in *Gambling: Who Wins? Who Loses?* ed. Gerda Reith, 239–57. Amherst, NY: Prometheus Books.

Douglas, Mary (1994) *Risk and Blame: Essays in Cultural Theory*. London: Routledge.

Douglas, Mary, and Aaron Wildavsky (1982) *Risk and Culture: an Essay on the Selection of Technological and Environmental Dangers*. Berkeley: University of California Press.

Durkheim, Emile (1982) *The Rules of Sociological Method and Selected Texts on Sociology and Its Method*, ed. Steven Lukes, trans. W. D. Halls. New York: The Free Press.

Durkheim, Emile (1992) *Professional Ethics and Civic Morals*, trans. Cornelia Brookfield. London: Routledge.

Eadington, William R. (2003) "Values and Choices: The Struggle to Find Balance With Permitted Gambling in Modern Society," in *Gambling: Who Wins? Who Loses?* ed. Gerda Reith, 31–48. Amherst, NY: Prometheus Books.

Eadington, William R., and Judy Cornelius, eds. (1997) *Gambling: Public Policies and the Social Sciences*. Reno: University of Nevada.

Ewald, Francois (2003) "The Return of Descartes's Malicious Demon: An Outline of a Philosophy of Precaution," in *Embracing Risk: The Changing Culture of Insurance and Responsibility*, ed. Tom Baker and Jonathan Simon, 273–71. Chicago: University of Chicago Press.

Fabian, Ann (1990) *Card Sharps, Dream Books & Bucket Shops: Gambling in 19th-Century America*. Ithaca: Cornell University Press.

Ferguson, Harvie (2002) "Preface: Gambling, Chance and the Suspension of Reality," in *The Age of Chance: Gambling and Western Culture*, xiii–xix. London: Routledge.

Foucault, Michel (1991) "Governmentality," in Burchell, G., C. Gordon, and P. Miller, eds. *The Foucault Effect: Studies in Governmentality*, 87–104. Chicago: Chicago University Press.

Fromson, Brett D. (2003) *Hitting the Jackpot: The Inside Story of the Richest Indian Tribe in History*. New York: Atlantic Monthly Press.

Garland, David (2003) "The Rise of Risk," in *Risk and Morality*, ed. Richard V. Ericson and Aaron Doyle, 48–86. Toronto: University of Toronto Press.

Geertz, Clifford (1973) "Deep Play: Notes on the Balinese Cockfight," in *The Interpretation of Cultures*, 403–53. New York: Basic Books.

Giddens, Anthony (1991) *Modernity and Self Identity: Self and Society in the Late Modern Age*. Stanford: Stanford University Press.

Gilder, George (1981) *Wealth and Poverty*. New York: Bantam Books.

Goux, Jean-Joseph (1998) "General Economics and Postmodern Capitalism," in *Bataille: A Critical Reader*, ed. Fred Botting and Scott Wilson, 196–213. Oxford: Blackwell Publishers.

Herbst-Bayliss, Svea (2004) "Billionaire Plans Gambling Fund," *National Post*, Dec. 3, p. IN1.

Herman, Robert D. (1976) "Motivations to Gamble: The Model of Roger Caillois," in *Gambling and Society: Interdisciplinary Studies on the Subject of Gambling*, ed. William R. Eadington. Springfield, IL: Charles C. Thomas.

Katz, Jack (1988) *The Seductions of Crime: Moral and Sensual Attractions in Doing Evil*. New York: Basic Books.

Kavanagh, Thomas M. (2005) *Dice, Cards, Wheels: A Different History of French Culture*. Philadelphia: University of Pennsylvania Press.

Kingma, Sytze (1996) "A Sign of the Times: The Political Culture of Gaming in the Netherlands," in *Gambling Cultures: Studies In History and Interpretation*, ed. Jan McMillen. London: Routledge.

Kingma, Sytze (1997) "'Gaming Is Play, It Should Remain Fun!': The Gaming Complex, Pleasure and Addiction," in *Constructing the New Consumer Society*, ed. Pekka Sulkunen, John Holmwood, Hilary Radner, and Gerhard Schulze. New York: St. Martin's Press.

Kingma, Sytze (2004) "Gambling and the Risk Society: The Liberalisation and Legitimation Crisis of Gambling in the Netherlands," *International Gambling Studies* 4(1), 47–67.

Knorr-Cetina, Karin, and U. Bruegger (2002) "Traders' Engagements With Markets: A Postsocial Relationship," *Theory, Culture and Society* 19(5–6): 161–85.

Knorr-Cetina, Karin, and Alexa Preda, eds. (2004) *The Sociology of Financial Markets*. Oxford: Oxford University Press.

Lesieur, Henry (1984) *The Chase: Career of the Compulsive Gambler*. Cambridge, MA: Schenkman Books.

Lyng, Stephen, ed. (2005) *Edgework: The Sociology of Risk-Taking*. New York: Routledge.

Mauss, Marcel (1990) *The Gift: The Form and Reason for Exchange in Archaic Societies*, trans. W. D. Halls. London: Norton.

McMillen, Jan, ed. (1996) *Gambling Cultures: Studies in History and Interpretation*. London: Routledge.

McMillen, Jan (2003) "From Local to Global Gambling Cultures," in *Gambling: Who Wins? Who Loses?* ed. Gerda Reith, 49–63. Amherst, NY: Prometheus Books.

Mills, C. Wright (1967) *The Sociological Imagination*. New York: Oxford University Press.

Mun, Wing Phil (2002) "Calculated Risk-Taking: The Governance of Casino Gambling in Ontario," Ph.D. thesis, Graduate Department of the Centre of Criminology, University of Toronto.

National Indian Gaming Association. (2002) www.indiangaming.org.

Pearce, Frank, and Laureen Snider, eds. (1995) *Corporate Crime: Contemporary Debates*. Toronto: University of Toronto Press.

Pryke, Michael, and John Allen (2000) "Monetized time-spaces: derivatives— money's 'new imaginary,'" *Economy and Society* 29(2): 265–84.

Reith, Gerda (2002) *The Age of Chance: Gambling and Western Culture*. London: Routledge.

Riesman, David, Nathan Glazer, and Reuel Denney (1950) *The Lonely Crowd: A Study of the Changing American Character*. Garden City: Doubleday Anchor.

Rose, I. Nelson (2004) "Is It a Crime to Play Poker On-Line," Op-Ed/Editorials, www.thewager.org/editorial.htm.

Schwartz, David G. (2003) *Suburban Xanadu: The Casino Resort on the Las Vegas Strip and Beyond*. New York: Routledge.

Shiller, Robert J. (2000) *Irrational Exuberance*. Princeton: Princeton University Press.

Shiller, Robert J. (2005) "American Casino: The promise and perils of Bush's 'ownership society,'" *The Atlantic Monthly*, March: 33–34.

Smith, Charles W. (2005) "Financial Edgework: Trading in Market Currents" in *Edgework: The Sociology of Risk-Taking*, ed. Stephen Lyng, New York: Routledge.

Strange, Susan (1986) *Casino Capitalism*, Oxford: Blackwell.

The Vancouver Sun (2005) "Indian casinos outstrip Vegas," Feb. 16, p. B2.

Veblen, Thorstein (1899/1953) "The Belief in Luck," in *The Theory of the Leisure Class*. New York: Mentor Books.

Volberg, Rachel A. (2003) "Has There Been a Feminization of Gambling and Problem Gambling in America?" *Electronic Journal of Gambling Issues: eGambling 8*, Feature Article.

Wacquant, Loic (1989) "Towards a Reflective Sociology: A Workshop with Pierre Bourdieu," *Sociological Theory* (7): 26–63.

Weber, Max (1968) "General Definitions of Social Action and Social Relationship," in *Max Weber: On Charisma and Institution Building*, ed. S. N. Eisenstadt. Chicago: The University of Chicago Press.

Williams, Robert, and Robert Wood (2004) *The Demographic Sources of Ontario Gaming Revenue: Final Report*, Ontario Problem Gambling Research Centre.

York, Geoffrey (2005) "Turning Macau Into a Temple for Gamblers," *The Globe and Mail*, Feb. 15, pp. A1, A10.

Sociological Approaches to Risk and Gambling

Introduction

This section begins with sociological formulations of risk from the leading exponents of the risk perspective(s), Anthony Giddens and Ulrich Beck. For both, risk comes to be a defining feature and mode of institutional orientation in high (Giddens) or second modernity (Beck). For Giddens, the achieved characteristics of "ontological security" are brought to the fore for individuals who can no longer rely on the traditional institutional moorings of self-identity that are weakening in high modernity. Individuals, under modern risk conditions, come to rely on abstract systems of expert knowledge in order to find their bearings. High modernity reveals tensions between societal interests in safety and the removal of risks on the one hand, and the valorization of "cultivated risk-taking" on the other. In his formulations of the significance of risk for self-identity, Giddens draws upon Goffmanian concepts such as fatefulness and consequentiality (see Goffman, Chapter Twelve).

For Beck, second modernity (also "world risk society") is character-ized by the processes of "reflexive modernization," whereby the rational assumptions and orientations of modern institutions and their manage-ment—predicated on a "logic of control"—are confronted by the risks pro-duced by these very institutions. Beck's piece seeks to open up the ways in which the societal orientations to, and consequences of, risk are reshap-ing (second) modern institutions and political processes. Beck's analy-sis of the processes of individualization (see Beck and Beck-Gernsheim 2002) resembles Giddens's notion of the "disembedding" of individuals from traditional institutions, which prompts actors to come to define their biographies for themselves (Giddens 1991). A theme that emerges from the analyses of both thinkers concerns the social basis of trust, since uncer-tainty comes to be a defining characteristic in the cultural life of late/sec-ond modernity.

Deborah Lupton provides an introductory article on the governmen-tality approach to risk. This approach, which derives from the later work of Michel Foucault (1991), examines the ways in which individuals and populations are governed in modern society. These modes of governing extend beyond the "formal realm of the state ... and refer in an extended way to the range of practices that seek to regulate individual and collective conduct through various institutions, discourses, rules, norms and prac-tices" (Slater and Tonkiss 2001, 145). From a governmentality perspective, "risk may be understood as a regulatory power by which populations and individuals are monitored and managed through the goals of neo-liberal-ism" (Lupton 87). A feature of neo-liberalism concerns the ways in which individuals are encouraged to govern themselves through practices of self-monitoring and regulation. The governmentality approach is utilized and developed by Collins in his discussion of the governing of the "pathological gambler" (Chapter Seventeen) and could also be further utilized to discuss the governing of non-problem gambling citizens within the contemporary climate of gambling legitimation and expansion in North America and elsewhere. This approach also provides a different way of thinking about risk; where Giddens and Beck speak of social conditions that produce dis-embedding and individualization, governmentality views risks within neoliberal societies as entailing particular governing strategies directed at the conduct of individuals.

In 1976, the authors of a British study of gambling, *Gambling, Work and Leisure: A Study Across Three Areas,* remarked at the beginning of the first chapter, "Gambling as a Sociological Problem," that "there have been remarkably few sociological attempts to account for gambling," and that this constituted a "strange gap in sociological accounting" (Downes et al. 1976, 11). While much social scientific work has been written on gambling since then (see, for example, Eadington 1976, 1997; Clotfelter and Cook 1989; Fabian 1990; McMillen 1996; Castellani 2000; Reith 2003), this gap remains within sociology, considering that legalized gambling has expanded rapidly in Canada, the United States, Australia, Britain, and other countries, particularly since the early 1990s. Gerda Reith's *The Age of Chance: Gambling and Western Culture* and Mikal Aasvad's *The Sociology of Gambling* (2003) signal a burgeoning sociological and cultural interest in the study of gambling, and a strong interest has developed in Australia where gambling is a vital aspect of the culture—McMillen's *Gambling Cultures: Studies in History and Interpretation* (1996) is an excellent multidisciplinary and international contribution. But as McMillen notes, echoing the views of Downes et al., "There ... are significant empirical and theoretical gaps in gambling research which have not been addressed: gambling in modern Asian cultures has rarely been studied; and the theories of signification and power deriving from Barthes ... and Foucault ... and the broad area of women's studies provide fertile sources for further insight and stimulation" (32). The governmentality approach, represented in this volume by the readings of Lupton (Chapter Three) and Collins (Chapter Seventeen), demonstrate Foucault's influence.

While the gap in gambling accounts is narrowing, it continues to persist in analyses from feminist, cultural studies, and sociological perspectives. Notwithstanding the important contributions of *Gambling Cultures* to gambling analysis, the first chapter of the Downes book remains in many ways a benchmark for a specifically sociological analysis of gambling. While much has changed in the culture of legal gambling since the 1970s, the piece nevertheless provides an overview of the major issues involved with gambling as a sociological phenomenon, and draws upon diverse theoretical resources in the account. Particularly interesting is their use of Caillois's and Goffman's work, the latter of which is included here (Chapter Twelve).

References

Aasvad, Mikal (2003) *The Sociology of Gambling.* Springfield, IL: Charles C Thomas.
Beck, Ulrich, and Elisabeth Beck-Gernsheim (2002) *Individualization.* London: Sage.
Clotfelter, Charles T., and Phillip J. Cook (1989) *Selling Hope: State Lotteries in America.* Cambridge, MA: Harvard University Press.
Downes, David, B. P. Davies, M. E. David, and P. Stone (1976) "Gambling as a Sociological Problem," in *Gambling, Work and Leisure: A Study Across Three Areas,* 11–28. London: Routledge and Kegan Paul.
Eadington, William R., ed. (1976) *Gambling and Society: Interdisciplinary Studies on the Subject of Gambling.* Springfield, IL: Charles C Thomas.

Eadington, William R., and Judy Cornelius, eds. (1997) *Gambling: Public Policies and the Social Sciences.* Reno: University of Nevada.

Fabian, Ann (1990) *Card Sharps, Dream Books & Bucket Shops: Gambling in 19th-Century America.* Ithaca: Cornell University Press.

Foucault, Michel (1991) "Governmentality," in *The Foucault Effect: Studies in Governmentality,* ed. Graham Burchell, Colin Gordon, and Peter Miller, 87–104. Chicago: University of Chicago Press.

Giddens, Anthony (1991) *Modernity and Self Identity: Self and Society in the Late Modern Age.* Stanford: Stanford University Press.

McMillen, Jan, ed. (1996) *Gambling Cultures: Studies in History and Interpretation.* London: Routledge.

Reith, Gerda, ed. (2003) *Gambling: Who Wins? Who Loses?* Amherst, NY: Prometheus Books.

Slater, Don, and Fran Tonkiss (2001) *Market Society: Markets and Modern Social Theory.* Cambridge: Polity Press.

CHAPTER 1

Fate, Risk and Security

ANTHONY GIDDENS

Fate, Fatalism, Fateful Moments

To live in the universe of high modernity is to live in an environment of chance and risk, the inevitable concomitants of a system geared to the domination of nature and the reflexive making of history. Fate and destiny have no formal part to play in such a system, which operates (as a matter of principle) via what I shall call open human control of the natural and social worlds. The universe of future events is open to be shaped by human intervention—within limits which, as far as possible, are regulated by risk assessment. Yet the notions of fate and destiny have by no means disappeared in modern societies, and an investigation into their nature is rich with implications for the analysis of modernity and self-identity.

Sweeping though the assertion may be, it can be said with some confidence that there is no non-modern culture which does not in some sense incorporate, as a central part of its philosophy, the notions of fate and destiny. The world is not seen as a directionless swirl of events, in which the only ordering agents are natural laws and human beings, but as having intrinsic form which relates individual life to cosmic happenings. A person's destiny—the direction his or her life is due to take—is specified by that person's fate, what the future holds in store. Although there is an enormous variety of beliefs which could be grouped under these two terms, in most of them the connecting point between destiny and fate is death. In Greek thought, fate (*moira*) was the bringer of doom and death, and was thought of as a great power—more ancient than the oldest gods.[1]

Given the nature of modern social life and culture, we tend now to counterpose fate and the openness of future events. Fate is taken to mean a form of preordained determinism, to which the modern outlook stands opposed. Yet while the concept of fate does have the connotation of a partly 'settled' future, it typically also involves a moral conception of destiny and an esoteric view of daily events—where 'esoteric' means that events are experienced not just in terms of their causal relation to one another, but in terms of their cosmic meaning. Fate in this sense has little connection with *fatalism*, as this term is ordinarily understood today. Fatalism is the refusal of modernity—a repudiation of a controlling orientation to the future in favour of an attitude which lets events come as they will.

A main connecting point between pre-existing ideas of fate and those of the post-medieval period was the concept of *fortuna*, which originally derived from the name of the Roman goddess of 'fortune', and came into uneasy tension with the dominant Christian beliefs. The idea of Divine Providence was clearly a version of fate but, as Max Weber pointed out, Christianity introduced a more dynamic role for human beings on this earth than was characteristic of the traditional religions of Greece and Rome.[2] The goddess was frowned on by the Church, since the idea of 'fortune' implied that one could achieve grace without having to work as God's instrument in the world. Yet the idea of *fortuna* remained important and often outweighed providential reward in the afterlife as a feature of local cultural belief. Machiavelli's use of *fortuna* marked a significant transition between the traditional use of the notion and the emergence of new modes of social activity from which fate is excluded. In *The Prince* he says:

> Many have held, and still hold the opinion that the things of this world are, in a manner, controlled by *fortuna* and by God, that men in their wisdom cannot control them, and, on the contrary, that men can have no remedy whatsoever for them; and for this reason they might judge that they need not sweat much over such matters but let them be governed by fate.... I judge it to be true that *fortuna* is the arbiter of one half of our actions, but that she still leaves the control of the other half, or almost that, to us ... I say that one sees a prince prosper today and come to ruin tomorrow without having seen him change his character or any of his traits ... a prince who relies completely upon fortune will come to ruin as soon as she changes; I also believe that the man who

adapts his course of action to the nature of the times will succeed and, likewise, that the man who sets his course of action out of tune with the times will come to grief.[3]

It is not surprising that the study of politics should provide the initial area within which notions of fate become transformed, for although the propaganda of nations may see them as driven by fate to a specific destiny, the practice of politics—in the modern context—presumes the art of conjecture. Thinking how things might turn out if a given course of action is followed, and balancing this against alternatives, is the essence of political judgement. Machiavelli is celebrated as the originator of modern political strategy, but his work gives voice to some rather more fundamental innovations. He foreshadows a world in which risk, and risk calculation, edge aside *fortuna* in virtually all domains of human activity. There seems to have been no generic word for risk in Machiavelli's time, however; the notion appears in European thought about a century later. (In English until the nineteenth century the word was usually spelled in its French version, as *risqué*. For some while the French spelling continued to be used alongside the new Anglicised word, which was first of all employed with reference to insurance. The term *risqué*, meaning a joke that risks giving offence, still retains the old form.)[4]

The notion of risk becomes central in a society which is taking leave of the past, of traditional ways of doing things, and which is opening itself up to a problematic future. This statement applies just as much to institutionalised risk environments as to other areas. Insurance ... is one of the core elements of the economic order of the modern world—it is part of a more general phenomenon concerned with the control of time which I shall term the *colonisation of the future*. The 'openness' of things to come expresses the malleability of the social world and the capability of human beings to shape the physical settings of our existence. While the future is recognised to be intrinsically unknowable, and as it is increasingly severed from the past, that future becomes a new terrain—a territory of counterfactual possibility. Once thus established, that terrain lends itself to colonial invasion through counterfactual thought and risk calculation. The calculation of risk ... can never be fully complete, since even in relatively confined risk environments there are always unintended and unforeseen outcomes. In milieux from which fate has disappeared, all action, even that which sticks to strongly established patterns, is in principle 'calculable' in terms of risk—some sort of overall assessment of likely risks can be made for virtually all habits and activities, in respect of specific outcomes. The intrusion of abstract systems into day-to-day life, coupled with the dynamic nature of knowledge, means that awareness of risk seeps into the actions of almost everyone.

A more extended discussion of risk, and its relation to self-identity, will be given shortly. First, however, it is necessary to introduce one or two other notions connected with that of fate. We have to say a little bit more about *fatalism*, a term which, as mentioned has more to do with modern social life than with more traditional cultures. Fatalism, as I understand it here, differs from stoicism, an attitude of strength in the face of life's trials and tribulations. A fatalistic outlook is one of resigned acceptance that events should be allowed to take their course. It is an outlook nourished by the main orientations of modernity, although it stands in opposition to them.

Fatalism should be separated from a sense of the *fatefulness* of events. Fateful happenings, or circumstances, are those which are particularly consequential for an individual or group.[5] They include the undesired outcomes faced in what I have termed high-consequence risks, risks affecting large numbers of people in a potentially life-threatening way, but they also figure at the level of the individual. *Fateful moments* are those when individuals are called on to take decisions that are particularly consequential for their ambitions, or more generally for their future lives. Fateful moments are highly consequential for a person's destiny.

Fateful moments can be understood in terms of the broader traits of consequential activities that an individual carries on in day-to-day life and over the course of the lifespan. Much of the daily life, so far as the individual is concerned, is inconsequential, and is not seen to be particularly fateful for overall goals. However, some avenues of activity are usually thought of by the person in question as more generally consequential than others—such as activity carried on in the sphere of work. Consider the phenomenon of 'dead' or 'killed' time, analysed with characteristic brilliance by Goffman.[6] Time that has to be killed is also, interestingly, quite often called 'free' time—it is time which is filled in, in between the more consequential sectors of life. If a person finds she has half an hour between one engagement and the next, she might decide to spend that time pottering around or reading the newspaper until her next appointment, rather than putting the time to 'good' use. Killed time is bounded off from the rest of an individual's life and (unless something unexpected happens) has no consequences for it.

By contrast, many more consequential activities of life are routinised. Most 'time on' activities—whether in the formal or more informal sectors of social life—are not problematic, or are so only in terms of the ordinary management of the tasks concerned. In other words, difficult decisions may often have to be taken, but they are handled by strategies evolved to cope with them as part of the ongoing activities in question. Sometimes, however, a particular situation or episode may be both highly consequential and problematic: it is these episodes that form fateful moments. Fateful moments are times when events come together in such a way that an individual stands, as it were, at a crossroads in his existence; or where a person learns of information with fateful consequences.[7] Fateful moments include the decision to get married, the wedding ceremony itself—and, later, perhaps the decision to separate and the actual parting. Other examples are: taking examinations, deciding to opt for a particular apprenticeship or course of study, going on strike, giving up one job in favour of another, hearing the result of a medical test, losing a large amount in a gamble, or winning a large sum in a lottery. It often happens that fateful moments occur because of events that impinge upon an individual's life willy-nilly; but such moments are also quite commonly engineered, as, for example, when a person decides to get together the whole of her savings and start a business. There are, of course, fateful moments in the history of collectivities as well as in the lives of individuals. They are phases at which things are wrenched out of joint, where a given state of affairs is suddenly altered by a few key events.

Fateful moments, or rather that category of possibilities which an individual defines as fateful, stand in a particular relation to risk. They are moments at which the appeal of *fortuna* is strong, moments at which in more traditional settings oracles might have been consulted or divine forces propitiated. Experts are often brought in as a fateful moment approaches or a fateful decision has to be taken. Quite commonly, in fact, expertise is the vehicle whereby a particular circumstance is pronounced as fateful, as for instance in the case of a medical diagnosis. Yet there are relatively few situations where a decision as to what to do becomes clear-cut as a result of experts' advice. Information derived from abstract systems may help in risk assessment, but it is the individual concerned who has to run the risks in question. Fateful decisions are usually almost by definition difficult to take because of the mixture of the problematic and the consequential that characterises them.

Fateful moments are threatening for the protective cocoon which defends the individual's ontological security, because the 'business as usual' attitude that is so important to that cocoon is inevitably broken through. They are moments when the individual must launch out into something new, knowing that a decision made, or a specific course of action followed, has an irreversible quality, or at least that it will be difficult thereafter to revert to the old paths. Fateful moments do not necessarily mean facing a strong possibility that things will go awry, that is, circumstances with a high probability of losing out. What tends to make the risk environment difficult to confront is rather the scale of the consequential penalties for getting things wrong. Fateful moments disclose high-consequence risks for the individual comparable to those characteristic of collective activity.

The Parameters of Risk

Since risk, and attempts at risk assessment, are so fundamental to the colonising of the future, the study of risk can tell us much about core elements of modernity. Several factors are involved here: a reduction in life-threatening risks for the individual, consequent on large tracts of security in daily activity purchased by abstract systems; the construction of institutionally bordered risk environments; the monitoring of risk as a key aspect of modernity's reflexivity; the creation of high-consequence risks resulting from globalisation; and the operation of all this against the backdrop of an inherently unstable 'climate of risk'.

Preoccupation with risk in modern social life has nothing directly to do with the actual prevalence of life-threatening dangers. On the level of the individual lifespan, in terms of life expectation and degree of freedom from serious disease, people in the developed societies are in a much more secure position than most were in previous ages. In the late eighteenth century in Britain, at that time the most economically advanced society in the world, deadly epidemics which killed hundreds of thousands of people were still commonplace. A proliferation of endemic illnesses had to be endured, even when they were not necessarily fatal. Many had cause to observe:[8]

> The weariness, the fever and the fret,
> Here, where men sit and hear each other groan,
> Where palsy shakes a few sad last grey hairs,
> Where youth grows pale, and spectre-thin, and dies.

Only since the early twentieth century have sufficient statistics been available to chart out with any precision the changes which have affected life-threatening outcomes. A study which took the year 1907 as its point of departure showed that at that time newborn infants 'stepped into a minefield'[9] (although rates of infant mortality had been vastly reduced as compared to a century before). On a chart for 1907, about one in seven died in the first year of life, as contrasted to one in sixty-seven on a 1977 chart taken as a basis for comparison. The list given below records some of the most important risk-reducing advances relevant to health which occurred during the years 1907–77—that is, the years spanning the life of a seventy-year-old in 1977:

Safe drinking water
Sanitary sewage disposal
Hygienic food preparation
Pasteurised milk
Refrigeration
Central heating
Scientific principles of nutrition widely applied
Scientific principles of personal hygiene widely applied
Eradication of major parasitic diseases, including malaria
Rodent and insect control
Continually improved prenatal and postnatal care
Continually improved care of babies and infants
Continually improved care of infectious diseases
Continually improved surgical treatment
Continually improved anaesthesia and intensive care
Scientific principles of immunisation widely applied
Blood transfusion made practical
Organisation of intensive care units in hospitals
Continually expanded and improved diagnostic procedures
Continually improved treatment of cancer
Continually improved treatment of occlusive arterial disease
Planned parenthood made feasible and practical
Improved and legalised methods for interrupting pregnancy
Safety in the workplace widely accepted
Safety belts in cars
Continually improved methods for preserving teeth, vision and hearing
Smoking, obesity, high blood pressure and sedentary life recognised as
    damaging to health[10]

We cannot tell in full how far each of the items on this list has affected the changes highlighted in the 1907–77 comparison, since the full impact of some, or even many, of them may only be felt by subsequent generations. Against such risk-reducing changes, moreover, we have to place a considerable number of negative influences. Two world wars, involving massive destruction of life, have occurred during the lifetime of the 1907 generation. Risk of death or serious injury from car crashes has increased steadily over most of this period. From the 1930s to the late 1960s, this generation consumed many drugs that, by current standards, were inadequately tested before being made available. The members of this generation drank a great deal of alcohol, and smoked millions of tobacco goods, before the toxic effects of these were fully realised; environmental pollution, believed by many medical specialists to increase susceptibility to major diseases of various sorts, has sharply increased; and for much of their lives they have eaten food containing many additives and treated by chemical fertilisers, with consequences for health that are at best unknown and at worst may help produce some of the leading killer diseases.

In terms of basic life security, nonetheless, the risk-reducing elements seem substantially to outweigh the new array of risks. There are various ways in which this can be tentatively assessed. One is by calculating how the 1907 cohort actually fared with how it would have fared if the major known life-threatening risks pertaining in 1907 had continued to prevail through the lifetimes of those born in that year—a speculative calculation, but one that can be undertaken with a reasonable degree of statistical backing. Such a calculation indicates no differential, in terms of survival percentages, up to age twenty. After this age, the curve of actual survival begins to rise above the curve given by the newly constructed data in a progressive way, the more so in the later period.

Comparisons can also be made between the 1907 chart and that of 1977 by contrasting life expectancies of the 1907 group with those predicted for the 1977 generation. These show a substantial divergence, starting from the very first year of life and up to old age, in favour of the 1977 cohort (although, of course, we have no way of knowing fully what additional factors might influence life-threatening risks for that generation in years to come).

Risk concerns future happenings—as related to present practices—and the colonising of the future therefore opens up new settings of risk, some of which are institutionally organised. In relatively minor contexts such settings have always existed, for instance in the culturally widespread case of gambling. Occasionally there have been organised risk environments in non-modern cultures where no equivalent institutionalised forms are found in modern social life. Thus Firth describes an institutionalised type of attempted suicide in Tikopia.[11] It is accepted practice for a person with a grievance to put out to sea in a canoe. Since the waters are treacherous, there is a substantial chance that the individual will not survive the experience; chances of survival are also affected by how quickly others in the community notice and respond to the person's absence. While this risk-taking endeavour clearly bears some affinities with risk-taking in suicide attempts in modern settings, in the second of these the institutionalised element is lacking.[12]

For the most part, however, institutionally structured risk environments are much more prominent in modern than pre-modern societies. Such institutionalised systems of risk affect virtually everyone, regardless of whether or not they are 'players' within them—competitive markets in products, labour power, investments or money provide the most significant example. The difference between such institutionalised systems and other risk parameters is that they are constituted through risk, rather than certain risks being incidental to them. Institutionalised risk environments link individual and collective risks in many ways—individual life chances, for instance, are now directly tied to the global capitalistic economy. But in relation to the present discussion they are most important for what they reveal about how the future is colonised.

Take the stock market as an example. The stock exchange is a regulated market which provides a range of securities (an interesting term in itself) that borrowers issue and savers hold, creating a choice of ways of structuring the risks of both borrowers and savers in their objective of achieving financial gain. It also has the effect of valuing securities in relation to their expected returns, taking into account investors' risks.[13] Savers and borrowers have a variety of financial desiderata. Some savers want to accumulate money in the long term, while others are looking for more short-term gains and may be prepared to take considerable risks with their capital with this end in view. Borrowers normally want money for the long term, but a certain risk of loss on the part of lenders is unavoidable. In the stock market, investors can choose from a range of risks and modes of hedging against them, while borrowers can seek to adjust the terms of their received capital against the risks of the business endeavours for which they utilise it. The stock market is a theorised domain of sophisticated reflexivity—a phenomenon which directly influences the nature of the hazards of saving and borrowing. Thus studies indicate that price–earning ratios seem to be poor predictors of subsequent earnings or dividend growth. Some theories applied in stock market investment take this as evidence that the stock market cannot identify which companies will utilise scarce financial resources most satisfactorily, and calculate risk strategies accordingly. Others hold that retention of earnings, plus other specifiable factors, account for this finding, and adopt correspondingly different strategies. A measure of the reflexive complexity of such a situation is provided by the fact that retention policies themselves are likely to be influenced by the type of theory adopted.[14]

Stock markets, like other institutionalised risk environments, use risk actively to create the 'future' that is then colonised. This is well understood by participants. One of the best illustrations of this is the specific existence of futures markets. All savings and borrowings create possible future worlds through the mobilising of risk. But futures markets mortgage the future in a direct fashion, securing a bridgehead in time that offers a peculiar security for certain types of borrowers.

The reflexive monitoring of risk is intrinsic to institutionalised risk systems. In respect of other risk parameters it is extrinsic, but no less fundamental for life chances and life-planning. A significant part of expert thinking and public discourse today is made up of *risk profiling*—analysing what, in the current state of knowledge and in current conditions, is the distribution of risks in given milieux of action. Since what is 'current' in each of these respects is constantly subject to change, such profiles have to be chronically revised and updated.

Consider 'what we die of'—representing the major risks associated with mortality.[15] Risk profiling of the main life-threatening illnesses shows major differences between the turn of the century and the present-day in the developed countries. By 1940 infectious diseases like tuberculosis, nephritis or diphtheria had dropped out of the top ten causes of death. Deaths attributed to heart disease and cancer moved into first and second place after 1940, where they have stayed. The main reason for this change is thought to be the greater proportion of people living to age fifty or more, but this view is challenged by some who hold dietary and environmental factors responsible. One should note that the concepts used to identify the major causes of death have changed substantially since 1900. What was first generally termed 'intracranial lesions of vascular origin' at the turn of the century became 'vascular lesions affecting the central nervous system' in the 1960s, and has since altered to 'cerebrovascular diseases'. Such changes are more than fads: they reflect alterations in medical outlook towards the pathologies in question.

Some two-thirds of the population over thirty-five years of age in countries with high rates of coronary heart disease, like Britain or the United States, are believed to have some degree of narrowing in their coronary arteries, although not enough to bring about distinct pathological symptoms or changes in an electrocardiogram. Each year, about one person in eighty over the age of thirty-five has a heart attack, although only a certain proportion of these are fatal. Heart disease is more common in men than women, although the gap is closing. In the United States and one or two other countries, after a steady increase for many years, the rate of deaths due to coronary heart disease has begun to drop. There is much debate as to why this is so; it may be due to changes in diet, improved emergency care, a decrease in smoking or greater adult participation in regular exercise. It is generally agreed that lifestyle factors of one kind or another strongly influence the risk of contracting heart disease. There is a good deal of comparative evidence on the issue. Thus Japan has the lowest rate of coronary heart disease of any of the industrialised societies. The children and grandchildren of Japanese immigrants to the United States, however, have rates of the disease comparable to that of the US, not Japan. Yet it is not at all clear what influence diet, as compared to other aspects of lifestyle, has in the aetiology of heart illnesses. France, for example, reports low rates of death from coronary heart disease, although the French diet is high in the substances thought to produce it.

Cancer is not a single disease entity, at least in respect of the risks of death associated with it. From the turn of the century, the different forms of the disease have followed divergent paths. For instance, there has been a steady increase in rates of death from lung cancer since about 1930, the continuation of that increase presumably being due to the delayed effects of the widespread popularity of smoking until about the late 1960s. On the other hand, there has been a steady drop in some other types of cancer. The experts disagree about why this is so. They also disagree about whether or not, or to what degree, diet and environmental factors play a part in the onset of the disease.

The regular and detailed monitoring of health risks, in relation to infor-mation such as that just described, provides an excellent example, not just of routine reflexivity in relation to extrinsic risk, but of the interaction between expert systems and lay behaviour in relation to risk. Medical spe-cialists and other researchers produce the materials from which risk pro-filing is carried out. Yet risk profiles do not remain the special preserve of the experts. The general population is aware of them, even if it is often only in a rough and ready way, and indeed the medical profession and other agencies are concerned to make their findings widely available to laypeople. The lifestyles followed by the population at large are influenced by the reception of those findings, although there are normally class dif-ferences in the altering of behaviour patterns, with professional and more highly educated groups in the lead. Yet the consensus of expert opinion—if there is any such consensus—may switch even as the changes in lifestyle they called for previously become adopted. We might recall that smoking was once advocated by some sectors of the medical profession as a relax-ant; while red meat, butter and cream were said to build healthy bodies.

Medical concepts and terminologies change as theories are revised or discarded. Moreover, at any one time, there is substantial, sometimes radi-cal, disagreement within the medical profession about risk factors as well as about the aetiology of major health hazards. Even with illnesses as seri-ous as coronary heart disease and cancer, there are many practitioners of alternative medicine—some of whom are now taken much more seriously by orthodox medical specialists than used to be the case—who dispute the more mainline positions. The assessment of health risks is very much bound up with 'who is right' in these disputes. For although a risk profile drawn up at any one point in time looks objective, the interpretation of risk for an individual or category of individuals depends on whether or not life-style changes are introduced, and how far these are in fact based on valid presumptions. Once set up, a lifestyle sector—say, the following of a par-ticular diet—may be quite difficult to break, because it is likely to be inte-grated with other aspects of a person's behaviour. All these considerations influence the reflexive adoption by laypeople of risk parameters as filtered through abstract systems. In the face of such complexity, it is not surprising that some people withdraw trust from virtually all medical practitioners, perhaps consulting them only in times of desperation, and stick doggedly to whatever established habits they have formed for themselves.

In contrast to health dangers, high-consequence risks by definition are remote from the individual agent, although—again, by definition—they impinge directly on each individual's life chances. It would clearly be a mistake to suppose that people living in modern social conditions are the first to fear that terrible catastrophes might befall the world. Eschatologi-cal visions were quite common in the Middle Ages, and there have been other cultures in which the world has been seen as fraught with massive hazards. Yet both the experience and nature of such hazardous visions are in some respects quite distinct from the awareness of high-consequence risks today. Such risks are the result of burgeoning processes of globalisa-tion, and even half a century ago humanity did not suffer from the same kind of threat.

Such risks are part of the dark side of modernity, and they, or compara-ble risk factors, will be there so long as modernity endures—so long as the rapidity of social and technological change continues, throwing off unan-ticipated consequences. High-consequence risks have a distinctive quality. The more calamitous the hazards they involve, the less we have any real experience of what we risk: for if things 'go wrong', it is already too late. Certain disasters give a taste of what could happen—such as the nuclear accident at Chernobyl. As with many such issues, experts are not fully in agreement about what the long-term effects of the escaped radiation from that accident might be on the populations of the countries it affected. It is generally thought to have increased the risks of certain types of dis-ease in the future, and of course has had devastating consequences for the people most immediately affected in the Soviet Union. But it is inevitably counterfactual guesswork to estimate what the outcome of a larger nuclear disaster might be—let alone a nuclear conflict, even a relatively small-scale one.

Risk assessment endeavours in the case of high-consequence risks have to be correspondingly different from those concerned with risks where outcomes can be regularly observed and monitored—although these interpretations have to be constantly revised and updated in the light of new theories and information. The thesis that risk assessment itself is inherently risky is nowhere better borne out than in the area of high-consequence risks. A common method used in the attempted calculation of risks of nuclear reactor accidents is the design of a fault tree. A fault tree is drawn up by listing all known pathways to possible reactor failure, then specifying the possible pathways to those pathways, and so on. The end result, supposedly, is a fairly precise designation of risk. The method has been used in studies of reactor safety in the United States and several European countries. Yet it leaves various imponderables.[16] It is impossible to make a confident calculation of the risk of human error or sabotage. The Chernobyl disaster was the result of human error, as was, at an earlier period, the fire at one of the world's largest nuclear stations at Brown's Ferry in the United States. The fire first started because a technician used a candle to check for an air leak, in direct contravention of established procedures. Some pathways to potential disaster might not be noticed at all. They have been missed on many occasions in more minor risk settings, and for high-consequence risks dangers have sometimes been spotted only by retroactive revisions of data and assumptions. This happened in a hypothetical setting when a study by the American National Academy of Sciences was convened to determine the risks to the food supply given an exchange of nuclear warfare of a certain intensity. The panel carrying out the study concluded that the resulting reduction in the earth's ozone layer would not threaten the survivors' food resources, as many crops that would survive in the atmosphere of increased ultraviolet radiation would continue to be cultivated. No one among the panel noticed, however, that the raised radiation level would make it virtually impossible to work in the fields to grow these crops.[17]

High-consequence risks form one particular segment of the generalised 'climate of risk' characteristic of late modernity—one characterised by regular shifts in knowledge-claims as mediated by expert systems. As Rabinowitch observes: 'One day we hear about the danger of mercury, and run to throw out cans of tuna fish from our shelves; the next day the food to shun may be butter, which our grandparents considered the acme of wholesomeness; then we have to scrub the lead paint from the walls. Today, the danger lurks in the phosphates in our favourite detergent; tomorrow

the finger points to insecticides, which were hailed a few years ago as sav-
iours of millions from hunger and disease. The threats of death, insanity
and—somehow even more fearsome—cancer lurk in all we eat or touch.'[18]
That was written some twenty years ago: since then, further contaminated
traces have been found in tuna fish, some types of detergent believed safe
in the early 1970s have been banned, while some doctors now say that it is
more healthy to eat butter than the low-fat margarines which were previously widely recommended as preferable.

The point, to repeat, is not that day-to-day life is inherently more risky
than was the case in prior eras. It is rather that, in conditions of modernity,
for lay actors as well as for experts in specific fields, thinking in terms of
risk and risk assessment is a more or less ever-present exercise, of a partly
imponderable character. It should be remembered that we are all laypeople
in respect of the vast majority of the expert systems which intrude on our
daily activities. The proliferation of specialisms goes together with the
advance of modern institutions, and the further narrowing of specialist
areas seems an inevitable upshot of technical development. The more specialisms become concentrated, the smaller the field in which any given
individual can claim expertise; in other areas of life she or he will be in
the same situation as everyone else. Even in fields in which experts are
in a consensus, because of the shifting and developing nature of modern
knowledge, the 'filter-back' effects on lay thought and practice will be
ambiguous and complicated. The risk climate of modernity is thus unsettling for everyone; no one escapes.

The Active Courting of Risks

Of course, there are differences between risks voluntarily run and those
built into the constraints of social life or into a lifestyle pattern to which
one is committed. Institutionalised risk environments provide some settings within which individuals can choose to risk scarce resources, including their lives—as in hazardous sports or other comparable activities.
Yet the differentiation between risks that are voluntarily undertaken and
risks which affect the individual in a less sought-after way is often blurred,
and plainly does not always correspond to the division between extrinsic and institutionalised risk environments. The risk factors built into a
modern economy, as mentioned before, affect almost everyone, regardless of whether a given individual is directly active within the economic
order. Driving a car and smoking provide other examples. Driving is in
many situations a voluntary activity; yet there are some contexts where
lifestyle commitments or other constraints will make using a car close to a

necessity. Smoking may be voluntarily entered into, but once it is an addiction it has a compulsive character, as does alcohol consumption.[19]

The active embrace of certain types of risk is an important part of the risk climate. Some aspects or types of risk may be valued for their own sake—the elation that may come from driving fast and dangerously resembles the thrill offered by certain institutionalised risk endeavours. Taking up smoking in the face of its known risks to health may demonstrate a certain bravado that an individual finds psychologically rewarding. To the degree to which this is so, such activities can be understood in terms of dimensions of 'cultivated risk' that will be discussed further below. But for the most part, the passive acceptance of the hazards of such practices as driving and cigarette smoking by large sectors of the population has to be interpreted in different terms. Two types of interpretation have commonly been put forward. One is that the large corporations, and other powerful agencies, conspire to mislead the public about the true levels of risk, or use advertising and other conditioning methods to ensure that a substantial proportion of the population engages in these risk-taking habits nevertheless. The other suggests that most laypeople are not sensitive to individually distributed or to deferred risk –even though they often overreact to collective disasters or to risks that are more 'visible'. Both explanations tend to lay considerable emphasis on apparently irrational components of action. Neither explanation seems particularly convincing, although no doubt each points to factors of some importance. The main influences involved probably derive from certain characteristic features of life-planning and lifestyle habits. Since specific practices are ordinarily geared into an integrated cluster of lifestyle habits, individuals do not always, or perhaps even usually, assess risks as separate items, each in its own domain. Life-planning takes account of a 'package' of risks rather than calculating the implications of distinct segments of risky behaviour. Taking certain risks in pursuit of a given lifestyle, in other words, is accepted to be within 'tolerable limits' as part of that overall package.

Individuals seek to colonise the future for themselves as an intrinsic part of their life-planning. As in the case of collective futures, the degree to which the future realm can be successfully invaded is partial, and subject to the various vagaries of risk assessment. All individuals establish a portfolio of risk assessment, which may be more or less clearly articulated, well informed and 'open'; or alternatively may be largely inertial. Thinking in terms of risk becomes more or less inevitable and most people will be conscious also of the risks of *refusing* to think in this way, even if they may choose to ignore those risks. In the charged reflexive settings of high modernity, living on 'automatic pilot' becomes more and more difficult to do, and it becomes less and less possible to protect any lifestyle, no matter how firmly pre-established, from the generalised risk climate.

The argument at this point should not be misunderstood. Much risk assessment proceeds on the level of practical consciousness and, as will be indicated below, the protective cocoon of basic trust blocks off most otherwise potentially disturbing happenings which impinge on the individual's life circumstances. Being 'at ease' in the world is certainly problematic in the era of high modernity, in which a framework of 'care' and the development of 'shared histories' with others are largely reflexive achievements. But such histories often provide settings in which ontological security is sustained in the relatively unproblematic way, at least for specific phases of an individual's life.

Risk, Trust and the Protective Cocoon

The world of 'normal appearances' … is more than just a mutually sustained show of interaction which individuals put on for one another. The routines individuals follow, as their time-space paths criss-cross in the contexts of daily life, constitute that life as 'normal' and 'predictable'. Normality is managed in fine detail within the textures of social activity: this applies equally to the body and to the articulation of the individual's involvements and projects. The individual must be there in the flesh to be there at all,[20] and the flesh that is the corporeal self has to be chronically guarded and succoured—in the immediacy of every day-to-day situation as well as in life-planning extending over time and space. The body is in some sense perennially at risk. The possibility of bodily injury is ever-present, even in the most familiar of surroundings. The home, for example, is a dangerous place: a high proportion of serious injuries are brought about by accidents in the domestic milieu. 'A body', as Goffman tersely puts it, 'is a piece of consequential equipment, and its owner is always putting it on the line.'[21]

… [B]asic trust is fundamental to the connections between daily routines and normal appearances. Within the settings of daily life, basic trust is expressed as a bracketing-out of possible events or issues which could, in certain circumstances, be cause for alarm. What other people appear to do, and who they appear to be, is usually accepted as the same as what they are actually doing and who they actually are. Consider, however, the world of the spy who, in the interests of self-preservation, cannot accept the range of normal appearances in the way that other people usually do. The spy suspends part of the generalised trust which is ordinarily vested in 'things as they are', and suffers tortuous anxieties about what would otherwise be mundane events. To the ordinary person a wrong number may be a minor irritation, but to the undercover agent it may be a disturbing sign that causes alarm.

A feeling of bodily and psychic ease in the routine circumstances of everyday life ... is only acquired with great effort. If we mostly seem less fragile than we really are in the contexts of our actions, it is because of long-term learning processes whereby potential threats are avoided or immobilised. The simplest action, such as walking without falling over, avoiding collisions with objects, crossing the road or using a knife and fork, had to be learned in circumstances which originally had connotations of fatefulness. The 'uneventful' character of much of day-to-day life is the result of a skilled watchfulness that only long schooling produces, and is crucial to the protective cocoon which all regularised action presumes.

These phenomena can be usefully analysed using Goffman's notion of the *Umwelt*, a core of (accomplished) normalcy with which individuals and groups surround themselves.[22] The notion comes from the study of animal behaviour. Animals maintain a sensitivity to a surrounding physical area in terms of threats which may emanate from it. The area of sensitivity varies between different species. Some types of animal are able to sense sounds, scents and movements from many miles away; for other animals, the extent of the *Umwelt* is more limited.

In the case of human beings, the *Umwelt* includes more than the immediate physical surroundings. It extends over indefinite spans of time and space, and corresponds to the system of relevances, to use Schutz's term, which enframes the individual's life. Individuals are more or less constantly alert to signals that relate here-and-now activities to spatially distant persons or events of concern to them, and to projects of life-planning of varying temporal span. The *Umwelt* is a 'moving' world of normalcy which the individual takes around from situation to situation, although this feat depends also on others who confirm, or take part in, reproducing that world. The individual creates, as it were, a 'moving wave-front of relevance' which orders contingent events in relation to risk and potential alarms. Time-space movement—the physical mobility of the body from setting to setting—centres the individual's concerns in the physical properties of context, but contextual dangers are monitored in relation to other, more diffuse sources of threat. In the globalised circumstances of today, the *Umwelt* includes awareness of high-consequence risks, which represent dangers from which no one can get completely out of range.

In the settings of modernity, from which *fortuna* has largely retreated, the individual ordinarily separates the *Umwelt* into designed and adventitious happenings. The adventitious forms a continuing backdrop to the foreground relevances from which the individual creates a textured flow of action. The differentiation also allows the person to bracket out a whole host of actual and potential happenings, consigning them to a realm which still has to be watched over, but with minimal carefulness. This has the corollary that each person in an interaction situation presumes that much of what she does is a matter of indifference to others—although indifference still has to be managed in co-present public situations, in the shape of codes of civil inattention.

In contrast to the paranoiac, the ordinary individual is thus able to believe that moments which are fateful for his own life are not the result of fate. Luck is what one needs when one contemplates a risky action, but it has a broader connotation, too, as a means of relating chance to fatefulness (as good or as bad luck). Since the distinction between what is adventitious and what is not is in practice sometimes difficult to draw, however, serious tensions can arise when events or activities are 'misinterpreted'—as where an event affecting another is held to be contrived where it is not, or vice versa. The discovery of contrivance may easily be cause for alarm—a husband is led to suspect infidelity when he finds that an apparently chance meeting between his wife and an ex-lover was actually less than a chance encounter after all. The presumption of generalised trust that the recognition of adventitious happenings involves concerns future anticipations as well as current interpretative understandings. In most circumstances of interaction, an individual assumes that others co-present will not use their current dealings with him as a basis for acts of malevolence at some future time. The future exploitation of current situations, however, is always an area of potential vulnerability.

The protective cocoon is the *mantle of trust that makes possible the sustaining of a viable Umwelt.* That substratum of trust is the condition and the outcome of the routinised nature of an 'uneventful' world—a universe of actual and possible events surrounding the individual's current activities and projects for the future, in which the bulk of what goes on is 'non-consequential' so far as that person is concerned. Trust here incorporates actual and potential events in the physical world as well as encounters and activities in the sphere of social life. Living in the circumstances of modern social institutions, in which risk is recognised as risk, creates certain specific difficulties for the generalised vesting of trust in 'discounted possibilities'—possibilities that are bracketed out as irrelevant to the individual's self-identity and pursuits. The psychological security that conceptions of fate can offer is largely foreclosed, as is the personalising of natural events in the shape of spirits, demons or other beings. The chronic constitutive intrusion of abstract systems into day-to-day life creates further problems influencing the relation between generalised trust and the *Umwelt.*

In modern social conditions, the more the individual seeks reflexively to forge a self-identity, the more he or she will be aware that current practices shape future outcomes. In so far as conceptions of *fortuna* are completely abandoned, assessment of risk—or the balance of risk and opportunity—becomes the core element of the personal colonising of future domains. Yet a psychologically crucial part of the protective cocoon is the deflection of the hazardous consequences that thinking in terms of risk presumes. Since risk profiling is such a central part of modernity, awareness of probability ratios for different types of endeavour or event form one means whereby this can be achieved. What could 'go wrong' can be pushed to one side on the grounds that it is so unlikely that it can be put out of mind. Air travel is usually calculated to be the safest form of transport in terms of various criteria. The risk of being killed in a plane crash, for the regular commercial airlines, is about one in 850,000 per trip—a figure derived by dividing the total number of passenger trips over a given period of time by the number of air-crash victims during that period.[23] It has sometimes been asserted that sitting in a seat in an airliner five miles above the ground is the safest place in the world, given the number of accidents which occur at home, work or in other milieux. Yet many people remain terrified of flying, and a certain minority who have the opportunity or resources to travel by air refuse to do so. They cannot put out of their minds what it would be like if things *did* go wrong.

Interestingly, some such people are willing to travel on the roads without too much worry, even though they are almost certainly aware that the risks of serious injury or death are higher. The weight of the counterfactual seems to matter a lot in this— horrific though road accidents might be, they perhaps do not evoke quite the same degree of dread as the scenario of an air crash.

Deferment in time and remoteness in space are other factors that can reduce the disquiet that awareness of risk as risk might otherwise produce. A young person in good health might be conscious enough of the risks of smoking, but consign the potential dangers to a time that seems impossibly distant in the future—such as when he or she reaches forty—and thus effectively blot out those dangers. Risks remote from an individual's daily contexts of life—such as high-consequence risks—might also be bracketed out of the *Umwelt*. The dangers they present, in other words, are thought of as too far removed from a person's own practical involvements for that individual seriously to contemplate them as possibilities.

Yet notions of fate refuse to disappear altogether, and are found in uneasy combination with an outlook of the secular risk type and with attitudes of fatalism. A belief in the providential nature of things is one sense in which a conception of *fortuna* crops up—an important phenomenon, and one connected with some basic characteristics of modernity itself. Providential interpretations of history were major elements of Enlightenment culture, and it is not surprising that their residues are still to be found in modes of thinking in day-to-day life. Attitudes to high-consequence risks probably often retain strong traces of a providential outlook. We may live in an apocalyptic world, facing an array of global dangers; yet an individual might feel that governments, scientists or other technical specialists can be trusted to take the appropriate steps to counter them. Or else he feels that 'everything is bound to come out all right in the end.'

Alternatively, such attitudes may relapse into fatalism. A fatalistic ethos is one possible generalised response to a secular risk culture. There are risks which we all confront but which, as individuals—and perhaps even collectively—none of us can do much about. The things that happen in life, the proponent of such an orientation might declare, are in the end a matter of chance. Therefore we might as well decide that 'whatever will be will be', and leave matters there. This having been said, it would be difficult to be fatalistic in all areas of life, given the pressures today which propel us towards taking an active, innovative attitude towards our personal and collective circumstances. Fatalism in specific risk contexts tends to devolve into the more encompassing attitudes of what I have elsewhere called 'pragmatic acceptance' or 'cynical pessimism'. The former is an attitude of generalised coping—taking each day as it comes—while the latter repels anxieties through world-weary humour.[24]

There are many unsought-after events which may puncture the protective mantle of ontological security and cause alarm. Alarms come in all shapes and sizes, from the four-minute warning of Armageddon to a slip on the proverbial banana skin. Some are bodily symptoms or failings, others are anxieties sparked by an anticipated or actual failure of cherished projects, or by unexpected events that intrude into the *Umwelt*. The most challenging situations for the individual to master, however, are those where alarms coincide with consequential changes—fateful moments. At fateful moments, the individual is likely to recognise that she is faced with an altered set of risks and possibilities. In such circumstances, she is called on to question routinised habits of relevant kinds, even sometimes those most closely integrated with self-identity. Various strategies may be adopted. A person may, for whatever reason, simply carry on with established modes of behaviour, perhaps choosing to disregard whether or not these conform well with new situational demands. In some circumstances, though, this is impossible: for example, someone who has separated from his spouse can no longer carry on in the same way as he did while married.

Many fateful moments by their very nature oblige the individual to change habits and readjust projects.

Fateful moments do not only 'befall' individuals—they are sometimes cultivated or deliberately sought after. Institutionalised risk environments, and other more individualised risk activities, provide a major category of settings in which fatefulness is actively created.[25] Such situations make possible the display of daring, resourcefulness, skill and sustained endeavour, where people are only too aware of the risks involved in what they are doing, but use them to create an edge which routine circumstances lack. Most institutionalised risk environments, including those in the economic sector, are contests: spaces in which risk-taking pits individuals against one another, or against obstacles in the physical world. Contests call for committed, opportunistic action in a way that situations of 'pure chance', like lotteries, do not. The thrills that can be achieved in cultivated risk-taking depend on deliberate exposure to uncertainty, thus allowing the activity in question to stand out in relief against the routines of ordinary life. Thrills can be sought through risk-taking of high order, vicariously in spectator sports, or in activities where the actual level of risk to life and limb is small, but where dangerous situations are simulated (such as a roller-coaster ride). The thrill of risk-taking activities, as Balint says, involves several discernible attitudes: awareness of exposure to danger, a voluntary exposure to such danger, and the more or less confident expectation of overcoming it.[26] Funfairs mimic most of the situations in which thrills are sought elsewhere, but in a controlled way that takes away two key elements: the individual's active mastery; and the circumstances of uncertainty which both call for that mastery and allow it to be demonstrated.

Goffman points out that someone who is strongly inclined towards cultivated risk-taking—like the inveterate gambler—is able to discern opportunities for the play of chance in many circumstances which others would treat as routine and uneventful. Spotting such angles, one might add, is a way of turning up possibilities for developing new modes of activity within familiar contexts. For where contingency is discovered, or manufactured, situations which seem closed and pre-defined can again look open. Cultivated risk here converges with some of the most basic orientations of modernity. The capability to disturb the fixity of things, open up new pathways, and thereby colonise a segment of a novel future, is integral to modernity's unsettling character.

We could say, I think, that cultivated risk-taking represents an 'experiment with trust' (in the sense of basic trust) which consequently has implications for an individual's self-identity. We could redefine Balint's 'confident expectation' as trust—trust that the dangers which are deliberately courted will be conquered. Mastery of such dangers is an act of self-vindication and a demonstration, to the self and others, that under difficult circumstances one can come through. Fear produces the thrill, but it is fear that is redirected in the form of mastery. The thrill of cultivated risk-taking feeds on that 'courage to be' which is generic to early socialisation. Courage is demonstrated in cultivated risk-taking precisely as a quality which is placed on trial: the individual submits to a test of integrity by showing the capacity to envisage the 'down-side' of the risks being run, and press ahead regardless, even though there is no constraint to do so. The search for thrills, or more soberly for the sense of mastery that comes with the deliberate confrontation of dangers, no doubt derives in some part from its contrast with routine. Yet it also takes psychological fuel from a contrast with the more deferred and ambiguous gratifications that emerge from other types of encounters with risk. In cultivated risk-taking, the encounter with danger and its resolution are bound up in the same activity, whereas in other consequential settings the payoff of chosen strategies may not be seen for years afterwards.

Risk, Trust and Abstract Systems

The abstract systems of modernity create large areas of relative security for the continuance of day-to-day life. Thinking in terms of risk certainly has its unsettling aspects ... but it is also a means of seeking to stabilise outcomes, a mode of colonising the future. The more or less constant, profound and rapid momentum of change characteristic of modern institutions, coupled with structured reflexivity, mean that on the level of everyday practice as well as philosophical interpretation, nothing can be taken for granted. What is acceptable/appropriate/recommended behaviour today may be seen differently tomorrow in the light of altered circumstances or incoming knowledge-claims. Yet at the same time, so far as many daily transactions are concerned, activities are successfully routinised through their recombination across time-space.

Consider some examples. Modern money is an abstract system of formidable complexity, a prime illustration of a symbolic system that connects truly global processes to the mundane trivialities of daily life. A money economy helps regularise the provision of many day-to-day needs, even for the poorer strata in the developed societies (and even though many transactions, including some of a purely economic nature, are handled in non-monetary terms). Money meshes with many other abstract systems in global arenas and in local economies. The existence of organised monetary exchange makes possible the regularised contacts and exchanges 'at distance' (in time and in space) on which such an interlacing of global and local influences depends. In conjunction with a division of labour of parallel complexity, the monetary system routinises the provision of the goods and services necessary to everyday life. Not only is a much greater variety of goods and foodstuffs available to the average individual than in pre-modern economics, but their availability is no longer governed so directly by the idiosyncrasies of time and place. Seasonal foodstuffs, for example, can often now be bought at any time of the year, and food items that cannot be grown at all in a particular country or region may be regularly obtained there.

This is a colonising of time as well as an ordering of space, since provisioning for the future, for the individual consumer, is rendered unnecessary. In fact, it is of little use to hoard stocks of food—although some might choose to do so in the light of high-consequence risks—for the ordinary business of life in a modern economy that is functioning vigourously. Such a practice would increase costs, since it would commit income that could otherwise be used for different purposes. Hoarding could in any case be no more than a short-term strategy, unless the individual has developed the capacity to furnish his or her own food. So long as the person vests trust in the monetary system and the division of labour, these allow for greater security and predictability than could be achieved by any other means.

As another illustration, consider the provision of water, power for heating and lighting, and sanitised sewage disposal. Such systems, and the expertise on which they draw, act to stabilise many of the settings of day-to-day life—at the same time as, like money, they radically transform them as compared to pre-modern ways of life. In the developed countries, for most of the population, water is available at the turn of a tap, domestic heating and illumination are equally to hand, and personal sewage is quickly flushed away. The organised piping of water has substantially reduced one of the great uncertainties which afflicted life in many pre-modern societies, the inconstant character of water supply.[27] Readily available domestic water has made possible standards of personal cleanliness and hygiene that have made a major contribution to improved health. Constant running water is also necessary for modern sewage systems, and thus for the contribution to health which they have facilitated. Electricity, gas and continually available solid fuels similarly help regulate standards of bodily comfort, and provide power for cooking and the operation of many domestic devices. All these have regularised settings of activity inside and outside the home. Electric lighting has made possible the colonisation of the night.[28] In the domestic milieu, routines are governed by the need for regular daily sleep rather than by the alternating of day and night, which can be cross-cut without any difficulty. Outside the home, an increasing range of organisations operate on a twenty-four hour basis.

Technological intervention into nature is the condition of the development of abstract systems such as these, but of course affects many other aspects of modern social life as well. The 'socialisation of nature' has helped stabilise a variety of previously irregular or unpredictable influences on human behaviour. Control of nature was an important endeavour in pre-modern times, especially in the larger agrarian states, in which irrigation schemes, the clearing of forests and other modes of managing nature for human purposes were commonplace. As Dubos has emphasised, by the modern period Europe was already very largely a socialised environment, shaped by many generations of peasants from the original forests and marshes.[29] Yet over the past two or three centuries the process of human intervention into nature has been massively extended; moreover, it is no longer confined to certain areas or regions, but like other aspects of modernity has become globalised. Many aspects of social activity have become more secure as a result of these developments. Travel, for example, has become regularised, and made safer, by the construction of modern roads, trains, ships and planes. As with all abstract systems, enormous changes in the nature and scope of travel have been associated with these innovations. But it is now easy for anyone with the necessary financial resources casually to undertake journeys that two centuries ago would have been only for the most intrepid, and would have taken much longer to accomplish.

There is greater security in many aspects of day-to-day life—yet there is also a serious price to pay for these advances. Abstract systems depend on trust, yet they provide none of the moral rewards which can be obtained from personalised trust, or were often available in traditional settings from the moral frameworks within which everyday life was undertaken. Moreover, the wholesale penetration of abstract systems into daily life creates risks which the individual is not well placed to confront; high-consequence risks fall into this category. Greater interdependence, up to and including globally independent systems, means greater vulnerability when untoward events occur that affect those systems as a whole. Such is the case with each of the examples mentioned above. The money a person possesses, however little it may be, is subject to vagaries of the global economy which even the most powerful of nations may be able to do very little about. A local monetary system may collapse completely, as happened in Germany in the 1920s: in some circumstances, which at the moment we might not envisage at all, this might perhaps happen to the global monetary order, with disastrous consequences for billions of people. A prolonged drought, or other problems with centralised water systems, can sometimes have more disturbing results than periodic water shortages might have had in pre-modern times; while any prolonged shortage of power dislocates the ordinary activities of vast numbers of people.

Socialised nature provides a telling—and substantively a massively important—illustration of these characteristics. McKibben argues, with great plausibility, that human intervention in the natural world has been so profound, and so encompassing, that today we can speak of the 'end of nature'. Socialised nature is quite different from the old natural environment, which existed separately from human endeavours and formed a relatively unchanging backdrop to them. 'It is like the old nature in that it makes its points through what we think of as natural processes (rain, wind, heat), but it offers none of the consolations—the retreat from the human world, a sense of permanence, or even of eternity.'[30]

Nature in the old sense, McKibben points out, was quite unpredictable: storms could come without warning, bad summers destroy the crops, devastating floods occur as the result of unexpected rain. Modern technology and expertise have made better monitoring of weather conditions possible, and improved management of the natural environment has allowed many pre-existing hazards to be overcome, or their impact minimalised. Yet socialised nature is in some fundamental respects more unreliable than 'old nature', because we cannot be sure how the new natural order will behave. Take the hypothesis of global warming, a phenomenon which, if it is really occurring, will wreak havoc around the world. McKibben concludes that the available evidence supports the view that the 'greenhouse effect' is real, and in fact argues that the processes involved are already too far under way for them to be effectively countered in the short or medium term. He may be right about this. The point is that, at the time of writing at any rate, no one can say with assurance that it is *not* happening. The dangers posed by global warming are high-consequence risks which collectively we face, but about which precise risk assessment is virtually impossible.

Security, Deskilling and Abstract Systems

Abstract systems deskill—not only in the workplace, but in all the sectors of social life that they touch. The deskilling of day-to-day life is an alienating and fragmenting phenomenon so far as the self is concerned. Alienating, because the intrusion of abstract systems, especially expert systems, into all aspects of day-to-day life undermines pre-existing forms of local control. In the much more strongly localised life of most pre-modern societies, all individuals developed many skills and types of 'local knowledge', in Geertz's sense, relevant to their day-to-day lives. Everyday survival depended on integrating such skills into practical modes of organising activities within the contexts of the local community and the physical environment. With the expansion of abstract systems, however, the conditions of daily life become transformed and recombined across much larger time-space tracts; such disembedding processes are processes of loss. It would be wrong, however, to see such loss as power passing from some individuals or groups to others. Transfers of power do occur in such a way, but they are not exhaustive. For instance, the development of professional medicine has led to the 'sieving off' of knowledge and curative skills once held by many laypeople. Doctors and many other types of professional expert derive power from the knowledge-claims which their codes of practice incorporate. Yet because the specialisation inherent in expertise means that all experts are themselves laypeople most of the time, the advent of abstract systems sets up modes of social influence which no one directly controls. It is just this phenomenon that underlies the emergence of high-consequence risks.

Braverman was mistaken to suppose that, in the sphere of work, a one-way process of deskilling occurs. In the workplace, new skills are continually created, and in some part developed by those whose activities are deskilled. Something similar is true in many other sectors of social activity where the influence of abstract systems has made itself felt. The reappropriation of knowledge and control on the part of lay actors is a basic aspect of what I have sometimes termed the 'dialectic of control'. Whatever skills and forms of knowledge laypeople may lose, they remain skilful and knowledgeable in the contexts of action in which their activities take place and which, in some part, those activities continually reconstitute. Everyday skill and knowledgeability thus stands in dialectical connection to the expropriating effects of abstract systems, continually influencing and reshaping the very impact of such systems on day-to-day existence.

What is involved is not just reappropriation but, in some circumstances and contexts, *empowerment*. Coupled to disembedding, the expansion of abstract systems creates increasing quanta of power—the power of human beings to alter the material world and transform the conditions of their own actions. The reappropriation of such power provides generic opportunities not available in prior historical eras. Such empowerment is both individual and collective, although the relations between these two levels is often tangled and difficult to unravel, both for the analyst and for the layperson on the level of everyday life.

The profusion of abstract systems is directly bound up with the panoramas of choice which confront the individual in day-to-day activity. On the one hand, there is often a selection to be made between local or lay ways of doing things and procedures on offer from the domain of abstract systems. This is not simply a confrontation of the 'traditional' and the modern, although such a situation is common enough. As a result of processes of reappropriation, an indefinite number of spaces between lay belief and practice and the sphere of abstract systems are opened up. In any given situation, provided that the resources of time and other requisites are available, the individual has the possibility of a partial or more full-blown reskilling in respect of specific decisions or contemplated courses of action.

Empowerment and Dilemmas of Expertise

Consider, for example, a person with a back problem. What should she do to seek treatment? If she were in Britain, she might go to see a general practitioner under the auspices of the National Health Service. The general practitioner might refer her to a specialist, who may perhaps offer recommendations or provide services which satisfy her. But it could easily happen that she finds that nothing the specialist is able to do offers much help in alleviating the condition. The diagnosis of problems to do with the back is notoriously problematic, and most of the forms of treatment available are controversial both within the medical profession and outside. Some medical specialists, for example, recommend operating on disc ruptures. Yet there are studies indicating that patients with the disc problem concerned are almost as likely to recover without surgery as they are with it. There are large differences between different countries in respect of this issue. Thus the number of patients per thousand for whom operations are recommended for disc troubles in the United States is ten times as high as in Britain, this difference representing, among other things, a variation in generic philosophies of how best to treat back problems between the two countries. If she chooses to inquire further, our patient will discover that within orthodox medical circles there are major differences of opinion about operating techniques, even when an invasive treatment has been agreed on as the best strategy. For instance, some surgeons favour micro-surgery over more established spinal surgical procedures.

Investigating a little more deeply, the patient would discover that a variety of other modes of back therapy, held by their proponents to cover ruptured discs as well as many other transitory and more chronic back conditions, are available. These therapies differ not only in the forms of treatment they offer, but in respect of the interpretations they provide of the causal origins of back pains and pathologies. Osteopathy is based on rather different principles from those followed by chiropractors. Each of these orientations also contains competing schools. Other available forms of back treatment include physiotherapy, massage, acupuncture, exercise therapy, reflexology, systems of postural adjustment like the Alexander Method, drug therapies, diet therapies, hands-on healing—and no doubt other therapeutic methods also. One school of thought holds that the vast majority of back problems, including many of a quite serious nature, have their origins in psychosomatic stress, and should therefore be treated by remedying the sources of stress, rather than concentrating directly on the back itself. According to such schools of thought, psychotherapy, meditation, yoga, bio-feedback techniques and other modes of relaxation, or a combination of these, provide the best means of treatment.

At this point the patient might quite reasonably decide that enough is enough and resolve to inform herself about the nature of her complaint and the vying remedies for it. Many non-technical books about the back are available on the popular market. Most give an interpretation of the general state of medical knowledge about the spine and try to provide an informed guide to the competing therapies available. There is, of course, considerable agreement among otherwise differing authorities about the structural anatomy of the body. It would not take long for the sufferer to master a basic understanding of the structural problems which may affect the back. Reskilling/appropriation would be possible fairly readily in that she could learn about at least the outlines of the different treatments available and how they compare with those suggested by the original specialist. Deciding which to opt for, if any, would be more difficult because she would need to balance off the various claims made by the different approaches. There is no overarching authority to whom she might turn—a characteristic dilemma of many situations in conditions of high modernity.

Yet if such a person takes the trouble to reskill appropriately, a reasonably informed choice can in fact be made. All such choices are not simply behavioural options: they tend to refract back upon, and be mobilised to develop, the narrative of self-identity. A decision to go along with conventional or high-tech medicine, for example, is likely to be only partly a matter of informed choice: ordinarily it also 'says something' about a person's lifestyle. It may mean that an individual is following a fairly pre-established pattern of behaviour, perhaps coupled to certain forms of deference. This might be the case if a person goes to see the general practitioner and then the specialist recommended, and simply follows whatever that specialist suggests, in deference to them both as authoritative members of the medical profession. To opt for a form of alternative medicine, particularly of one of the more esoteric varieties, might signal something about, and actually contribute to, certain lifestyle decisions which a person then enacts.

In most such decisions, conceptions of *fortuna*, fatalism, pragmatism and conscious risk-taking are likely to be mingled together. Since experts so frequently disagree, even professionals at the core of a given field of expertise may very well find themselves in much the same position as a layperson confronting a similar decision. In a system without final authorities, even the most cherished beliefs underlining expert systems are open to revision, and quite commonly they are regularly altered. Empowerment is routinely available to laypeople as part of the reflexivity of modernity, but there are often problems about how such empowerment becomes translated into convictions and into action. A certain element of *fortuna*, or of fatalism, thus allows a person to 'ride along with' a decision which can only be partially warranted in the light of whatever local and expert information is to hand.

Summary: Authority, Expertise and Risk

… [N]o one can disengage completely from the abstract systems of modernity: this is one of the consequences of living in a world of high-consequence risks. Yet, of course, lifestyles and lifestyle sectors can be tailored to navigate a course between the different possibilities offered in a world reconstituted through the impact of abstract systems. Trust may be suspended in some or many of the systems which routinely and more sporadically impinge on the individual's life. It would be very difficult indeed, if not impossible, to withdraw completely from the modern monetary system. Yet an individual could choose to keep whatever assets he had in the form of goods or personal property; and he might have as little to do with banks or other financial organisations as he could. Many possible shadings of scepticism or doubt can be reconciled with a pragmatic or fatalistic attitude towards abstract systems affecting one's life chances.

Others may take lifestyle decisions which propel them back in the direction of more traditional authorities. Religious fundamentalism, for example, provides clear-cut answers as to what to do in an era which has abandoned final authorities: those final authorities can be conjured up again by appeal to the age-old formulae of religion. The more 'enclosing' a given religious order is, the more it 'resolves' the problem of how to live in a world of multiple options. More attenuated forms of religious belief, however, may clearly also offer significant support in shaping significant life decisions.

Most of these dilemmas become particularly acute, or are experienced with special force, during the fateful moments of an individual's life. Since fateful moments, by definition, are highly consequential, the individual feels at a crossroads in terms of overall life-planning. Fateful moments are phases when people might choose to have recourse to more traditional authorities. In this sense, they may seek refuge in pre-established beliefs and in familiar modes of activity. On the other hand, fateful moments also often mark periods of reskilling and empowerment. They are points at which, no matter how reflexive an individual may be in the shaping of her self-identity, she has to sit up and take notice of new demands as well as new possibilities. At such moments, when life has to be seen anew, it is not surprising that endeavours at reskilling are likely to be particularly important and intensely pursued. Where consequential decisions are concerned, individuals are often stimulated to devote the time and energy necessary to generate increased mastery of the circumstances they confront. Fateful moments are transition points which have major implications not just for the circumstances of an individual's future conduct, but for self-identity. For consequential decisions, once taken, will reshape the reflexive project of identity through the lifestyle consequences which ensue.

Hence it is not surprising that at fateful moments individuals are today likely to encounter expert systems which precisely focus on the reconstruction of self-identity: counselling or therapy. A decision to enter therapy can generate empowerment. At the same time, it is important to add, such a decision is not different in nature from other lifestyle decisions made in the settings of modernity. What type of therapy should one pursue, and for how long? ... [I]t is perhaps possible for an individual effectively to reorient his life without the direct consultation of an expert or professional. On the other hand, many therapists hold that without regular contact with a professional counsellor there is no hope of real personal change. A very considerable diversity of therapies, all of which claim to treat an overlapping range of similar problems, now exist. As a measure of the level of disagreement between different schools, we might compare classical psychoanalysis with behavioural therapy based on conditioning. There are many therapists who abide by the basic tenets Freud established for psychoanalysis, and formulate their therapeutic procedures according to them. Yet some proponents of behaviour therapy claim that psychoanalysis is utterly without validity as a mode of therapy. In addition, a variety of subdivisions of psychoanalysis exist, coupled to dozens of other varying schools of thought and technique. The reflexive encounter with expert systems helping to reconstitute the self therefore expresses some of the central dilemmas to which modernity gives rise.

Notes

1. Liz Greene, *The Astrology of Fate* (London: Allen and Unwin, 1984).
2. Max Weber, *The Sociology of Religion* (Boston: Beacon, 1963).
3. Niccolo Machiavelli, *The Prince*, quoted from *The Portable Machiavelli* (Harmondsworth: Penguin, 1979), pp. 159–60.

4. Cf. Torsten Hägerstrand, 'Time and culture', in G. Kirsch et al., *Time Preferences* (Berlin: Wissenschaftszentrum, 1985); Helga Nowotny, *Eigenzeit: Entstehung und Strukturierung eines Zeitgefühls* (Frankfurt: Suhrkamp, 1989), ch. 2.

5. Erving Goffman, *Interaction Ritual* (London: Allen Lane, 1972).

6. Ibid.

7. Goffman does not include the second of these in his discussion of fatefulness, but from the point of view of an individual contemplating his or her life, and how to act from a given point onwards, the acquisition of fateful information forms a crucial conjecture.

8. Quoted from John Keats, 'Ode to a Nightingale', in Roy Porter and Dorothy Porter, *In Sickness and in Health* (London: Fourth Estate, 1988).

9. John Urquhart and Klaus Heilmann, *Risk Watch* (New York: Facts on File, 1984).

10. Ibid., p. 12.

11. Raymond Firth, 'Suicide and risk-taking in Tikopia society', *Psychiatry*, 24, 1961.

12. James M. A. Weiss, 'The gamble with death in attempted suicide', *Psychiatry*, 20, 1957.

13. Peter G. Moore, *The Business of Risk* (Cambridge: Cambridge University Press, 1983), pp. 104ff.

14. R. A. Brearley and S. Myers, *Principles of Corporate Finance* (New York: McGraw-Hill, 1981).

15. Urquhart and Heilmann, *Risk Watch*, ch. 4.

16. Paul Slovic and Baruch Fischoff, 'How safe is safe enough?', in Jack Downie and Paul Lefrere, *Risk and Chance* (Milton Keynes: Open University Press, 1980).

17. P. M. Boffey, 'Nuclear war', *Science*, no. 190, 1975.

18. E. Rabinowitch, 'Living dangerously in the age of science', *Bulletin of the Atomic Scientists*, 28, 1972.

19. Urquhart and Heilmann, *Risk Watch*, p. 89.

20. Goffman, *Interaction Ritual*, p. 166.

21. Ibid., p. 167.

22. Erving Goffman, *Relations in Public*, pp. 252ff.

23. Urquhart and Heilmann, *Risk Watch*, p. 45.

24. Anthony Giddens, *The Consequences of Modernity*.

25. Cf. Charles W. Smith, *The Mind of the Market* (Totowa: Rowman and Littlefield, 1981).

26. Michael Balint, *Thrills and Regressions* (London: Hogarth, 1959). This work is drawn on extensively by Goffman in *Interaction Ritual*.

27. Murray Melbin, *Night as Frontier* (New York: Free Press, 1987).

28. René Dubos, *The Wooing of Earth* (London: Athlone, 1980).

29. Ibid.

30. Bill McKibben, *The End of Nature* (New York: Random House, 1989), p. 96.

CHAPTER 2

Risk Society Revisited

Theory, Politics and Research Programmes

ULRICH BECK

Living in an age of constructivism, the attempt to draw a line between modernity (or as I would prefer to say first industrial modernity) and world risk society (or second reflexive modernity) seems to be naive or even contradictory. Within a constructivist framework no one is able to define or declare what really 'is' or 'is not'. Yet, this does not square with my experience. I cannot understand how anyone can make use of the frameworks of reference developed in the eighteenth and nineteenth centuries in order to understand the transformation into the post-traditional cosmopolitan world we live in today. Max Weber's 'iron cage'—in which he thought humanity was condemned to live for the foreseeable future—is to me a prison of *categories and basic assumptions* of classical social, cultural and political sciences. It is the case that we have to free ourselves from these categories in order to find out about the unknown post-Cold-War-world. Do not get me wrong. I do not consider most of the philosophies and theories (sociologies) of so-called postmodernity to fare any better since they cannot answer very basic questions about how and in what ways everyday lives and professional fields are being transformed. Conventional social sciences, I therefore want to argue, even if they are conducting highly sophisticated theoretical and empirical research programmes, are caught up in a circular argument. By using the old categories (like class, family, gender roles, industry, technology, science, nation state and so on) they take for granted what they actually try to demonstrate: that we still live, act and die in the normal world of nation-state modernity.

Some of the discussions in this volume [*Editor's Note*: References in this chapter to "this volume" or "this book," and references to "Van Loon" are to *The Risk Society and Beyond: Critical Issues for Social Theory* (2000), eds. Barbara Adam, Ulrich Beck, and Joost Van Loon, London: Sage], which accuse me of being a 'realist', therefore, are the result of a misinterpretation of my arguments. What strikes me about them is the inability of constructivist thinking to criticize and renew the frameworks of modern and postmodern sociology. Let me explain. I consider realism and constructivism to be neither an either-or option nor a mere matter of belief. We should not have to swear allegiance to any particular view or theoretical perspective. The decision whether to take a realist or a constructivist approach is for me a rather *pragmatic* one, a matter of choosing the appropriate means for a desired goal. If I have to be realist (for the moment) in order to open up the social sciences to the new and contradictory experiences of the global age of global risks, then I have no qualms to adopt the guise and language of a ('reflexive') 'realist'. If constructivism makes a positive problem shift possible and if it allows us to raise important questions that realists do not ask, then I am content (for that moment at least) to be a constructivist. Having grown up with the constructivist philosophies of thinkers such as Kant, Fichte and Hegel, I find today, especially in the area of sociology of risk, that I do not restrict my analysis to one perspective or conceptual dogma: I am both a realist and constructivist, using realism *and* constructivism as far as those meta-narratives are useful for the purpose of understanding the complex and ambivalent 'nature' of risk in the world risk society we live in.[1]

Let us consider for a moment the current state of European intellectual thought. In 1989 a whole world order disintegrated. What an opportunity for venturing into uncharted terrain, exploring new intellectual horizons. Yet, this opportunity has not been seized. Instead, the vast majority of theorists are still holding on to the same old concepts. Reversal rather than revision seems to be the order of the day: radical socialism, Giddens (1995) suggests, has become conservative and conservatism has become radical. Little has changed: the script of modernity is yet [to] be rewritten, redefined, reinvented. This is what the theory of the world risk society is all about.

At this point, I should emphasize that I do not believe that 'anything goes'. Instead, I argue that we have to be imaginative yet disciplined if we are to break out of the iron cage of conventional and orthodox social science and politics. We need a new sociological imagination, one that is sensitive to the concrete paradoxes and challenges of reflexive modernity and which, at the same time, is thoughtful and strong enough to open up the walls of abstraction in which academic routines are captured.

In this chapter I would like to accomplish three main tasks. First, I wish briefly to reiterate my argument of why the notion of risk society can be introduced as a new conception of a 'non-industrial' society, to ask, what are 'risks'? and to enquire about the reality status of risks using 'constructivism' and 'realism' as a matter of pragmatic choice. Secondly, I want to address the views of some of my critics and in the process offer the reader a discussion of what I see as the theoretical issues which now limit the development of my ideas on risk. Finally, I will highlight some of the theoretical and political avenues I would like to see explored in the near future and identify some issues for comparative study at a European level and beyond.

On the Sociological Concepts of Risk and Risk Society

In the first part of this chapter I would like to gather up into a coherent whole arguments that are dispersed throughout my work on the sociological concepts of risk and risk society. In so doing, I also hope to illustrate, indirectly, what I have learned from the existing criticisms of my earlier work.[2] I have structured these issues into eight major points.

1. Risks are not the same as destruction. They do not refer to damages incurred. If they were, all insurance companies would be made bankrupt. However, risks do threaten destruction. The discourse of risk begins where trust in our security and belief in progress end. It ceases to apply when the potential catastrophe actually occurs. The concept of risk thus characterizes a peculiar, intermediary state between security and destruction, where the *perception* of threatening risk determines thought and action. As a result, I have difficulty recognizing the difference discussed by Scott Lash (Chapter 2 this volume) between the 'risk culture' and my concept of 'risk society'. I do, however, find Lash's discussion valuable in that it highlights the radicalization of the cultural framework of risk by cultural theory and cultural studies. Yet, it seems to me that 'relations of definition' (analogous to Marx's relations of production, see below) in the age of culturally defined risks still make the notion of 'risk society' necessary (see discussion below). So ultimately: *it is cultural perception and definition that constitutes risk.* 'Risk' and the '(public) definition of risk' are one and the same.

This peculiar reality status of 'no-longer-but-not-yet'—no longer trust/ security, not yet destruction/disaster—is what the concept of risk expresses and what makes it a public frame of reference. The sociology of risk is a science of potentialities and judgements about probabilities—what Max Weber (1991) called *Möglichkeitsurteile* (trans. as *judgements about probabilities)*. Risks, then, 'are' a type of *virtual reality*, real virtuality. Risks are only a small step away from what Joost van Loon calls 'Virtual Risks in an Age of Cybernetic Reproduction' (Chapter 9 this volume) and I wholeheartedly agree with his assessment when he writes: 'Only by thinking of risk in terms of reality, or better, a *becoming-real* (a virtuality) its social materialization can be understood. Only by thinking risk in terms of a construction can we understand its indefinitely deferred 'essence'. Risks cannot be understood outside their materialization in particular mediations, be it scientific, political, economic or popular.' (Van Loon, see p. 176). I believe this is the way in which the notions of constructivism and realism, although seemingly incompatible, can complement each other:

> [The] electronic media involved in the BSE [bovine spongiform encephalopathy] crisis connect science, politics and popular consumer culture. In so doing, they render the invisibility of risk, for example, the mutating prions of BSE, visible. They bring them into being through digitalized imagery. We, the consumers of such images, have no means to test the adequacy of such representation, nor do we have to. Their origin is fabricated, manufactured, in laboratories, under microscopes, and further enhanced by computer simulations. Their sources are truly cybertechnological, connecting chemistry, molecular biology, medicine with computer graphics and television broadcasting. Rendering the prion visible as a computer simulation allowed news broadcasts to begin to interpret the uninterpretable (to tell us what BSE and CJD [Creutzfeldt-Jakob disease] actually 'are') and to explain the unexplainable (how a normal piece of protein—whatever that might be—could become a pathological prion). The mere possibility that the pathogenesis might be linked to the banal practice of consuming beef,… further illustrates the force of Benjamin's[3] claim that in an age of mechanical reproduction, all aesthetic experiences may become politicized. (Van Loon, see p. 176)

Van Loon continues:

> The 'becoming-real' of the risk of BSE is directly related to its mediation. Now that 'we' know that there 'are' possible risks, 'we' face a responsibility. This responsibility takes the form of a

decision whether to eat beef and other bovine products or not. Therefore, CJD is no longer exclusively a hazard, as a strain has been identified that can be linked to BSE. Although the calculability of this risk has remained problematic, as a virtuality, it operates in exactly the same way. (see p. 176)

Indeed, 'the sudden accessibility of the "knowledge" of the possible relationship between BSE and CJD has thus transformed a hazard into a risk' (Van Loon, p. 176): we now have a decision to make with consequences for ourselves, our loved ones and possibly the rest of our world.[4]

The sociology of risk reconstructs techno-social praxis, both as abstract potential and in a very concrete sense. Where risks are believed to be real, the foundations of business, politics, science and everyday life are in flux. Accordingly, the concept of risk when considered scientifically (risk = accident × probability) takes the form of the calculus of probability, which we know can never rule out the worst case.[5] This becomes significant in view of the socially very relevant distinction between risk *decision-makers* and those who have to deal with the consequences of the decisions of *others*. In this respect, Niklas Luhmann's (1995) differentiation between risk and danger pointed to the sociologically crucial problem of the acceptance of risk decisions. However, this leaves the central question unanswered: What do the calculus of probability and the social difference between decision-makers (risks) and the affected parties, encompassing ever larger social groups (dangers), mean for dealing with disasters? Who has the legitimate right to make decisions in such cases? Or, more generally, how will decisions on hazardous technologies become capable of legitimation in the future?

Closely associated with this issue is the question of what the 'objectivity' and 'subjectivity' of risks would mean in the first place in the context of 'virtual risk realities'. What is 'rational' and what is 'irrational'? This is certainly one point where a sociology of risk and risk society differs fundamentally from technical and scientific risk assessment (more on this later).

2. The concept of risk reverses the relationship of past, present and future. The past loses its power to determine the present. Its place as the cause of present-day experience and action is taken by the future, that is to say, something nonexistent, constructed and fictitious. We are discussing and arguing about something which is *not* the case, but *could* happen if we were not to change course.

·Believed risks are the whip used to keep the present-day moving along at a gallop. The more threatening the shadows that fall on the present day from a terrible future looming in the distance, the more compelling the shock that can be provoked by dramatizing risk today. This can be demonstrated not only with the discourse on the environmental crisis, but also and perhaps even more emphatically, with the example of the discourse on globalization. For instance, as yet, the globalization of paid labour does not exist to a large extent. Rather, it looms as a threat or, more accurately, transnational management threatens us with it. After all, in Germany for example the exchange of expensive European labour for cheap Asian labour so far only amounts to at most 10% of the labour market and primarily affects the lower wage and skilled groups.[6] The brilliantly staged *risk* of globalization, however, has already become an instrument for re-opening the issue of power in society. By invoking the horrors of globalization, everything can be called into question: trade unions, of course, but also the welfare state, maxims of national policy and, it goes without saying, welfare assistance. Moreover, all of this is done with an expression of regret that it is—unfortunately—necessary to terminate Christian compassion for the sake of Christian compassion.

Established risk definitions are thus a magic wand with which a stagnant society can terrify itself and thereby activate its political centres and become politicized from within. The public (mass media) dramatization of risk is in this sense an antidote to current narrow-minded 'more-of-the-same' attitudes. A society that conceives of itself as a risk society is, to use a Catholic metaphor, in the position of the sinner who confesses his or her sins in order to be able to contemplate the possibility and desirability of a 'better' life in harmony with nature and the world's conscience. However, few sinners actually want to repent and instigate change. Most prefer the status quo while complaining about that very fact, because then everything is possible. Confession of sins and identification with the risk society allow us to simultaneously enjoy the bad good life and the threats to it.

3. Are risks factual statements? Are risks value statements? Risk statements are neither purely factual claims nor exclusively value claims. Instead, they are either both at the same time or something in between, a 'mathematicized morality' as it were. As mathematical calculations (probability computations or accident scenarios) risks are related directly and indirectly to cultural definitions and standards of tolerable or intolerable life. So in a risk society the question we must ask ourselves is: How do we want to live? This means, among other things, that risk statements are by nature statements that can be deciphered only in an interdisciplinary (competitive) relationship, because they assume in equal measure insight

into technical know-how and familiarity with cultural perceptions and norms.[7]

What then is the source of the peculiarity in our political dynamics that allows risk statements to develop as a hybrid of evaluations in the intermediate realm of real virtuality and non-existent future which nonetheless activates present action? This political explosiveness derives, primarily, from two sources: the first one relates to the cultural importance of the universal value of survival. Thus Thomas Hobbes, the conservative theorist of the state and society, recognized as a citizen right the right to resist where the state threatens the life or survival of its citizens (characteristically enough, he uses phrases such as 'poisoned air and poisoned foodstuffs' which seem to anticipate ecological issues). The second source is tied to the attribution of dangers to the producers and guarantors of the social order (business, politics, law, science), that is to the suspicion that those who endanger the public well-being and those charged with its protection may well be identical.

4. In their (difficult-to-localize) early stage, risks and risk perception are 'unintended consequences' of the *logic of control* which dominates modernity. Politically and sociologically, modernity is a project of social and technological control by the nation state. Above all others, it was Talcott Parsons who conceptualized modern society as an enterprise for constructing order and control. In this way, consequences—risks—are generated that call this very assertion of control by the nation state into question, not only because of the globality of the risks (climatic disasters or the ozone hole) but also through the inherent indeterminacies and uncertainties of risk diagnosis. It is interesting to note that Weber (1956) does indeed discuss the concept of 'unintended consequences' in a crucial context, and not least of all because that concept remains related in structure to the dominance of instrumental rationality. However, Weber does *not* recognize or discuss the concept of 'risk', one of whose peculiarities is to have lost precisely this relationship between intention and outcome, instrumental rationality and control.

The construction of security and control of the type that dominated (social) thought and (political) action in the first stage of modernity is becoming fictitious in the global risk society. The more we attempt to 'colonize' the future with the aid of the category of risk, the more it slips out of our control. It is no longer possible to externalize risks in the world risk society. That is what makes the issue of risk so 'political' (in a subversive meaning). In this paradox lies an essential basis for an important distinction between two stages or forms of the concept of risk (which, I feel, should answer some the questions Scott Lash raises with his concept of 'determinate judgement' in opposition to 'reflexive judgement'). In the first stage of modernity (essentially the period from the beginning of industrial modernity in the seventeenth and eighteenth centuries to the early twentieth century) risk essentially signifies a way of calculating unpredictable consequences (industrial decisions). As Ewald (1987) argues, the calculus of risk develops forms and methods for making the *unpredictable predictable*. This is what Lash means by 'determinate judgement'. The corresponding repertoire of methods includes statistical representations, accident probabilities and scenarios, actuarial calculations, as well as standards and organizations for anticipatory care. This meaning of the concept of risk refers to a world in which most things, including external nature and the ways of life as determined and co-ordinated by tradition, continue to be considered preordained (fate).

To the extent that nature becomes industrialized and traditions become optional, new types of uncertainties arise which, following Giddens (1990, 1995), I shall refer to as *'manufactured* uncertainties'. These types of internal risks and dangers presume a threefold participation of scientific experts, in the roles of producers, analysts and profiteers from risk definitions. Under these conditions, many attempts to confine and control risks turn into a broadening of the uncertainties and dangers.

5. Hence, the contemporary concept of risk associated with the risk society and manufactured uncertainty refers to a peculiar *synthesis of knowledge and unawareness*. To be precise, two meanings, namely risk assessment based on empirical knowledge (automobile accidents, for instance) on the one hand, and making decisions and acting on risk in indefinite uncertainty, that is, indeterminacy, on the other, are being conflated here. In this sense the concept of 'manufactured uncertainties' has a double reference. First, more and better knowledge, which most people assess in unreservedly positive terms is becoming the source of new risks. Because we know more and more about the brain functions, we now know that a person who is 'brain-dead' may very well be alive in some other sense (because the heart is still beating, for instance). By opening more and more new spheres of action, science creates new types of risks as well. The current examples are advances in human genetics, which make it possible to blur the boundary between ill people and healthy people because more and more congenital diseases can be diagnosed, even those affecting people who consider themselves healthy based on their own experience (Beck-Gernsheim, 1993, 1995). Secondly, the opposite is equally true: risks come from and consist of unawareness (non-knowledge). What are we to

understand by 'unawareness'? In the unbroken security of a life-world, unawareness is often understood as being *not yet* aware or no longer aware, that is to say, as *potential* knowledge. The problems of unawareness are understood here from its opposite, from knowledge and the (unspoken) certainty in which the life-world resides. In contrast to that, the inability to know is becoming ever more important in this second phase of modernity. I am not referring here to the expression of selective viewpoints, momentary forgetting or underdeveloped expertise, but on the contrary, to highly developed expert rationality. Thus, for instance, the calculus of probability can never rule out a given event, or risk specialists may call each other's detailed results into question because they quite sensibly start from different assumptions.[8]

Against the background of this *growing* unawareness and non-knowledge in the wake of the modernization of knowledge, the question of *deciding in a context of uncertainty* arises in a radical way. If we cannot know the effects of industrial research, action and production -as is already generally the case in the fields of genetic engineering and human genetics—if neither the optimism of the protagonists nor the pessimism of their critics is based on certain knowledge, then is there a green light or a red light for techno-industrial development and mass utilization? Is inability to know a license for action or basis for *decelerating* action, for moratoria, perhaps even inaction? How can maxims of action or of being obliged not to act be justified, given the inability to know?

This is how a society based on knowledge and risk opens up a threatening sphere of possibilities. Everything falls under an imperative of avoidance. Everyday life thus becomes an involuntary lottery of misfortune. The probability of a 'winner' here is probably no higher than in the weekly lottery, but it has become almost impossible *not* to take part in this raffle of evils where the 'winner' gets sick and may even die as a result of it. Politicians such as the British ex-prime minister John Major, who complained about the 'hysteria' of consumers in reaction to the debate over BSE in Europe and the resulting collapse in the beef market, while, at the same time, encouraging people to take part in the national lottery, rendered a particular service to the credibility of politics. At the extreme end of the spectrum two strategies for dealing with 'manufactured uncertainties' are conceivable: if one embraces the view of John Major that only certain knowledge can compel us to act, then one must accept that the denial of risks causes them to grow immeasurably and uncontrollably. There is no better breeding ground for risks than denying them. If one selects the opposite strategy and makes presumed (lack of) knowledge the foundation of action against risks, then this opens the flood gates of fear and everything becomes risky.

Risks only suggest what should *not* be done, not what *should* be done. To the extent that risks become the all-embracing background for perceiving the world, the alarm they provoke creates an atmosphere of powerlessness and paralysis. Doing nothing and demanding too much both transform the world into a series of indomitable risks. This could be called the *risk trap*, which is what the world can turn into in the perceptual form of risk. There is no prescription for how to act in the risk trap, but there are very antithetical cultural reactions (within and outside Europe). Within different boundaries and times, indifference and alarmed agitation often alternate abruptly and radically.[9]

One thing is clear: how one acts in this situation is no longer something that can be decided by experts. Risks pointed out (or obscured) by experts at the same time disarm these experts, because they force everyone to decide for themselves: What is still tolerable and what no longer? They require decisions about whether or not, when, and where to protest even if this only takes the form of an organized, intercultural consumer boycott. These issues raise questions about the authority of the public, cultural definitions, the citizenry, parliaments, politicians, ethics and self-organization.

6. Even the antithesis of globality and locality is short-circuited by risks. The new types of risks are simultaneously local and global, or 'glocal' (Robertson, 1992). Thus it was the fundamental experience that environmental dangers 'know no boundaries' that they are universalized by the air, the wind, the water and food chains, which justified the global environmental movement everywhere and brought up global risks for discussion.

This 'time-space compression' (Harvey, 1989) of the hazards of choices between local and global risks confirms the diagnosis of the global risk society. The global threats have led to a world in which the foundations of the established risk logic are undermined and invalidated, in which there are only difficult-to-control dangers instead of calculable risks. The new dangers destroy the pillars of the conventional calculus of security: damages can scarcely still be attributed to definite perpetrators, so that the polluter-pays principle loses acuity; damages can no longer be financially compensated—it makes no sense to insure oneself against the worst-case ramifications of the global spiral of threat. Accordingly, there are no plans for follow-up care should the worst case scenario occur. In the world of risk society the logic of control collapses from within. So, risk society is a (latent) *political* society.

World risk society theory does not plead for or encourage (as some assume) a return to a logic of control in an age of risk and manufactured uncertainties—that was the solution of the first and simple modernity. On the contrary, in the world risk society the logic of control is questioned fundamentally, not only from a sociological point of view but by ongoing modernization itself. Here is one of the reasons why risk societies can become *self-critical* societies. Different agencies and actors, for example, managers of chemical industries and insurance experts contradict each other. Technicians argue that: 'there is no risk', while the insurers refuse insurance because the risks are too high. A similar debate is currently taking place within the realm of genetically engineered food.

In order to speak of the world risk *society*, it is also necessary for the global hazards to begin to shape *actions* and facilitate the creation of *international institutions*. That there are indeed such impulses can be seen from the fact that the majority of the international environmental agreements were concluded during the past two decades. This border-transcending dynamism of the new risks does not only apply internationally, but also exists inside nation–states, implying that system boundaries no longer function properly either. This can be seen from the fact that risks are a kind of 'involuntary, negative currency'. No one wants to accept them or admit them, but they are present and active everywhere, resistant against all attempts to repress them. A characteristic of the global risk society is a metamorphosis of danger which is difficult to delineate or monitor: markets collapse and there is shortage in the midst of surplus. Medical treatments fail. Constructs of economic rationality wobble. Governments are forced to resign. The taken-for-granted rules of everyday life are turned upside-down. Almost everyone is defenceless against the threats of nature as recreated by industry. Dangers are integral to normal consumption habits. And yet they are and remain essentially knowledge-dependent and tied to cultural perception, be they as alarm, tolerance or cynicism.

7. Let us now return to the realism-constructivism debate and concentrate on the distinction between *knowledge*, latent impact and symptomatic effect, as suggested by Adam (1998, Chapter 1).[10] This distinction is important for understanding the second degree of 'uncertain global risks' faced by the world risk society, because the point of impact is not obviously tied to the point of origin. At the same time the transmissions and movements of hazards are often latent and immanent, that is, invisible and untrackable to everyday perceptions. This social invisibility means that, unlike many other political issues, risks must clearly be brought to consciousness, only then can it be said that they constitute an actual threat,

and this includes cultural values and symbols ('*Le Waldsterben*') as well as scientific arguments. At the same time we know at least in principle, that the *impacts* of risks grow precisely *because* nobody knows or wants to know about them. A case in point is the environmental devastation of Eastern Europe under the communist regime.

So, once again, risks are at the same time 'real' *and* constituted by social perception and construction. Their reality springs from '*impacts*' that are rooted in the ongoing industrial and scientific production and research routines. Knowledge about the risks, in contrast, is tied to the history and symbols of one's culture (the understanding of nature, for example) and the social fabric of knowledge. This is one of the reasons why the same risk is perceived and handled politically so differently throughout Europe and other parts of the globe. Moreover, there are interesting relations between those two dimensions of risk. Thus, the enormous spatial disjuncture between knowledge and impact: perception is always and necessarily contextual and locally constituted. This local contextuality is only extendible in the imagination and with the aid of such technologies as television, computers, and the mass media. As Adam argues:

> the impact of the industrial way of life, in contrast, is spatially and temporally open and tends to extend across the globe on the one hand and to the stratosphere and the universe on the other. Radiation, synthetic chemicals and genetically engineered organisms are pertinent cases in point. (1998: 34)

Many other examples can be used to highlight the unbridgeable spatio-temporal gap between actions and their impacts. 'Contemporary environmental hazards such as ozone depletion, damage to the reproductive and immune system of species or BSE have not arisen as symptoms until years after they began their impact as invisible effects of specific actions' (Adam, 1998: 34). Thus, for example, some of the Britons who died from the new variant of CJD (Creutzfeldt-Jakob Disease) had been vegetarians for the last ten years or so, which suggests a latent impact-period of ten or more years. Other hazards externalize as symptoms only after they have combined to form a critical mass. That is to say, the impact is temporarily open-ended and becomes perceivable as symptom and thus knowable only after it materializes into a visible 'cultural' phenomenon at some time and some place. This gap between source and perceivable symptom is one of the main conflict matters of social and expert construction: pesticides in foods, radiation and chemical damage to the unborn, and global warming are just a few illustrations of this temporal disjuncture.

This in turn links back to an issue I raised before and to the recognition that *the less risks are publicly recognized, the more risks are produced* (not only because of high industrialization but because of functional differentiation too). This might be an interesting 'law' of the risk society with particular relevance to the insurance business. The neglect of risk, in the first instance, would seem to serve the interests of the insurer, not those of the potential victim. Basic to the risk society is the self-transformation of risk from technical to economic risks, market risk, health risk, political risk and so on. Important to the insurer is the *time gap* between the insurance contract and the emergence of the risk through nature and culture. So the insurer (or the insurer of the insurer) has to pay up when this time bomb explodes. The problems that befell Lloyd's of London illustrate this case well. Several elements of this case are worthy of additional attention:

- Insurers are not in the same boat as manufacturers. Instead, insurers find themselves in a 'natural coalition' with the potential victims. This means that in order to act in their business' interest, they have to trust socio-scientific risk definitions, even rumours, and they have to find out about them during early stages of technological and industrial development.
- The neglect of risk information facilitates the growth and spread of risks. Asbestos is a case in point. During the Second World War the use of this material was expanding fast because it was seen as effective, durable, and above all, cheap, while the attendant risks were ignored.
- Commercial success and freedom from litigation result in complacency. Even worse, the manufacturers turn their back on medical evidence of the link between their products and ill health. Just as the tobacco manufacturers did not—and still do not—want to know the health consequences of smoking, so the asbestos industries preferred to ignore warnings.
- This way risk industries and insurance businesses get captured in the 'time cage' between ignored impact and growing risk on the one hand and between risk knowledge and cultural sensitivity on the other. This is the very normal way the manufactured uncertainties of hazards are becoming internalized by industries and are transformed into potential *economic* disasters.

8. Finally, the notion of world risk society is pertinent to a world which can be characterized by the *loss of clear distinction between nature and culture*. When we talk about nature today, we talk about culture. Equally, when we talk about culture we talk about nature. Our persistent conception of

a separation of worlds into nature and culture/society, which is intimately bound to modernist thought, fails to recognize that we are building, acting and living in a constructed artificial world of civilization whose characteristics are beyond these distinctions. The loss of boundaries between these realms is not only brought about by the industrialization of nature and culture but also by the hazards that endanger humans, animals and plants alike. Whether we think of the ozone hole, pollution or food scares, nature is inescapably contaminated by human activity. That is to say, the common danger has a levelling effect that whittles away some of the carefully erected boundaries between classes, nations, humans and the rest of nature, between creators of culture and creatures of instinct, or to use an earlier distinction between beings with and those without a soul (Adam, 1998: 24).

> In the threat people have the experience that they breathe like the plants, and live *from* water as the fish live *in* water. The toxic threat makes them sense that they participate with their bodies in things—'a metabolic process with consciousness and morality'— and consequently, that they can be eroded like the stones and the trees in the acid rain. (Schütz (1984), quoted in Beck (1997a: 74)

That we live in a *hybrid* world which transcends our dichotomic framework of thought has convincingly been argued by Latour (1993). I totally agree with him. Both of us see that the hybrid world we live in and constantly produce is, at the same time, a matter of cultural perception, moral judgement, politics, and technology, which have been constructed in actor-networks and have been made hard facts by 'black boxing'. Yet the notion of a 'hybrid' world is necessary but insufficient to understand the new. 'Hybrid' is more of a negative than a positive concept. It somehow says what it is not—*not* nature and *not* society etc.—but it does not really say what it is. I want to suggest that we have to overcome the 'nots', 'beyonds' and 'posts' which dominate our thinking. But if you ask what begins where the ends end? my answer is: the notion of risk and risk society. Risks are *man-made hybrids*. They include and combine politics, ethics, mathematics, mass media, technologies, cultural definitions and perception; and, most important of all, you cannot separate these aspects and 'realities', if you want to understand the cultural and political dynamics of the world risk society. Hence 'risk' is not only a notion which is used in a central matter by very different disciplines, it is also the way the 'hybrid society' watches, describes, values and criticizes its own hybridity.

This complex 'and', which resists thinking in either-or categories, is what constitutes the cultural and political dynamism of global risk society and makes it so difficult to comprehend.[11] A society that perceives itself as a risk society become *reflexive*, that is to say, the foundations of its activity and its objectives become the object of public scientific and political controversies. One could say that there is a naively realistic misapprehension in the talk of risk society and this can culminate in a type of 'neo-Spenglerism'. Equally possible and rational, however, is a reflexive understanding of risks, as developed here in the eight theses above. The concept of risk and the concept of world risk society are concepts of ambivalence, meaning that they destroy distinctions and reconnect antitheses. Accordingly, as stated above, the concept of (world) risk (society) means:

1. neither destruction nor trust/security but real virtuality;
2. a threatening future, (still) contrary to fact, becomes the parameter of influence for current action;
3. both a factual and a value statement, it combines in mathematicized morality;
4. control and lack of control as expressed in manufactured uncertainty;
5. knowledge or unawareness realized in conflicts of (re)cognition;
6. simultaneously the global and local are reconstituted as the 'glocality' of risks;
7. the distinction between knowledge, latent impact and symptomatic consequences;
8. a man-made hybrid world which lost its dualism between nature and culture.

Many social theories (including those of Michel Foucault and those of the Frankfurt School of Max Horkheimer and Theodor Adorno) paint modern society as a technocratic prison of bureaucratic institutions and expert knowledge in which people are mere wheels in the giant machine of technocratic and bureaucratic rationality. The picture of modernity drawn by the theory of world risk society contrasts sharply with these images. After all, one of the most important characteristics of the theory of risk society, so far scarcely understood in science or politics, is to unfreeze—at least intellectually—the seemingly rigid circumstances and to set them in motion. Unlike most theories of modern societies, the theory of risk society develops an image that makes the circumstances of modernity contingent, ambivalent and (involuntarily) susceptible to political rearrangement (Beck, 1992b, 1994, 1995, 1996a).

Due to this often unseen and undesired self-discreditation ('reflexive modernization') which is provoked everywhere by the discourse of risk, something ultimately happens which sociologists loyal to Weber would consider impossible: *institutions begin to change*. As we know, Weber's diagnosis is that modernity transforms into an iron cage in which people must sacrifice to the altar of rationality like the fellaheen of ancient Egypt. The theory of world risk society elaborates the antithesis: *the door of the iron cage of modernity is openning up*.[12] So I disagree with Ruth Levitas (this volume): there is a utopia built into risk society and risk society theory— the utopia of a *responsible* modernity, the utopia of *another* modernity, *many* modernities to be invented and experienced in different cultures and parts of the globe (see below). Anyone who is simply focused on the risk potential of industrial society fails to understand that risks are not only a matter of unintended consequences—the 'toxin of the week'—but also of the unintended consequences of unintended consequences *in* the institutions. Using the case of BSE, one could say that it is not just cows, but also governing parties, agencies, markets for meat and consumers who are affected and thus implicated in the madness.

A Reply to Criticisms of the Risk Society Thesis

In the second part of this chapter I want to engage with some of the critiques formulated in this book and elsewhere: That there is a German, even a 'Bavariacentrism' (Alan Scott, Chapter 1 this volume) to my vision that risk society is identical with the 'Le Waldsterben-society'. If this were the case, would it mean that Great Britain, even after BSE, is *not* part of world risk society?

Maybe there is a German background to risk society theory. Being 'green' is undoubtedly part of the German national identity. Many Germans want Germany to be a greater, greener Switzerland. Testing atomic weapons may be part of the French national identity—I don't know. And the cultural significance of 'British (Sunday lunch) beef' may be an important backdrop to the BSE crisis. Yet the conflicts that arise from these national issues cannot be confined within national boundaries. People, expert groups, cultures, nations are getting involved involuntarily at every level of social organizations: a European public is born unintentionally and involuntarily from the conflict over British beef. If you, for example, visit a *Wirtshaus* (a small local restaurant) in southern Bavaria and look at the menu you will find a photograph of the local farmer with family; the intention being to build up trust in the restaurant's local 'good' beef which is to be differentiated from the 'bad' British beef.

Again the distinction between knowledge and latent impact is important as it enables us to differentiate between two phases of risk society. The first phase is dominated by identification with the 'goods' of industrial and technological progress, which simultaneously both intensifies and 'legitimates' as 'residual risks', hazards resulting from decisions ('residual risk society'). The first impacts are systematically produced but *not yet* the subject of public knowledge, scrutiny and debate and not yet at the centre of political conflict. A different situation arises when the hazards of industrial society begin to dominate public and private debates. Now the institutions of industrial society produce and legitimate hazards which they cannot control. During this transition, property and power relationships remain *constant*. Industrial society sees and criticizes itself *as* risk society. On the one hand, the society *still* makes decisions and acts on the pattern of the old industrial society; on the other, debates and conflicts which originate in the dynamic of risk society are being superimposed on interest organizations, the legal system and politics.

Throughout my work, I have sought to demonstrate that the return to the theoretical and political philosophy of industrial modernity in the age of global risk is doomed to failure. Those orthodox theories and politics remain tied to notions of progress and valorization of technological change. As such, they perpetuate the belief that the environmental hazards we face today can still be captured by nineteenth-century scientific models or risk assessment and industrial assumptions about danger and safety. Simultaneously, they maintain the illusion that the disintegrating institutions of industrial modernity—nuclear families, stable labour markets, segregated gender roles, social classes, nation state—can be shored up and buttressed against the waves of reflexive modernization sweeping across the West. This attempt to apply nineteenth-century ideas to the twenty-first century is the pervasive *category mistake* of social theory, social sciences and politics I am addressing in my writings. In risk society theory 'environmental' problems are no longer conceived as external problems. Instead they are theorized at the centre of institutions. This immanence has been recognized by the legal science in Germany (with a debate on manufactured risks and uncertainties in public law), but has not been as clearly and fully acknowledged by the sociology of risk either in Great Britain or Germany.

At this point it is pertinent to briefly outline some of the core notions of the hazards of risk society—*organized irresponsibility, relations of definition, social explosiveness of hazards*—and to summarize the arguments surrounding the *provident state*. These concepts, I want to argue, combine arguments why it is necessary not only to talk in terms of 'risk *culture*'

(Scott and Lash, Chapters 1 and 2 this volume), which lacks the institutional dimension of risk and power, but also to theorize risk society with its cultural focus on the institutional base of contemporary globalized industrial society.

The concept of 'organized irresponsibility' helps to explain how and why the institutions of modern society must unavoidably acknowledge the reality of catastrophe while simultaneously denying its existence, hiding its origins and precluding compensation or control. To put it in another way, risk societies are characterized by the paradox of more and more environmental degradation—perceived and potential—coupled with an expansion of environmental law and regulation. Yet at the same time, no individual or institution seems to be held specifically accountable for anything. How can this be? The key to explaining this state of affairs, I suggest, is the mismatch that exists in the risk society between the character of hazards or manufactured uncertainties produced by late-industrialism and the prevalent *relations of definition* whose construction and content are rooted in an earlier and qualitatively different epoch.

In risk society *relations of definition* are to be conceived analogous to Marx's *relations of production*. Risk society's relations of definition include the specific rules, institutions and capacities that structure the identification and assessment of risk in a specific cultural context. They are the legal, epistemological and cultural power-matrix in which risk politics is conducted. The relations of definition I focus on can be identified with reference to four clusters of questions (also see Beck, 1996d; Goldblatt, 1996):

1. Who is to define and determine the harmfulness of products, the danger, the risks? Where does the responsibility lie: with those who generate the risks, those who benefit from them, those who are potentially affected by them, or with public agencies?
2. What kind of knowledge or non-knowledge about the causes, dimensions, actors, etc. is involved? To whom have evidence and 'proof' to be submitted?
3. What is to count as sufficient proof in a world where knowledge about environmental risks is necessarily contested and probabilistic?
4. Who is to decide on compensation for the afflicted and on what constitutes appropriate forms of future damage-limitation control and regulation?

In relation to each of these questions, risk societies are currently trapped in a vocabulary that is singularly inappropriate not only for modern catastrophes, but also for the challenges constituted by manufactured insecurities.

Consequently, we face the paradox that at the very time when threats and hazards are seen to become more dangerous and more obvious, they become increasingly inaccessible to attempts to establish proof, attributions and compensation by scientific, legal and political means.

Of course, there is the question about the identity of the political subject of the risk society. Despite my extensive workings on this subject, however, my answer to this questions eludes critics as long as they read my texts from within the dualistic frames of Enlightenment thought: to argue that nobody and everybody is the subject. So it should not surprise us that this answer gets lost. But there is more to it, and my argument here is close to Bruno Latour's theory of quasi-objects. In my work, hazards are quasi-subjects, whose acting-active quality is produced by risk societies' institutional contradictions. Moreover, risk society is *not* about a 'dystopian warning' (Ruth Levitas, Chapter 11 this volume). I use the metaphor of the *social explosiveness of hazard* to explain the politicizing effects of risk (definition) conflicts. I explore the ways in which the virtuality, the 'becoming real' (Joost van Loon, Chapter 9 this volume) of large-scale hazards, risks and manufactured uncertainties set off a dynamic of cultural and political change that undermines state bureaucracies, challenges the dominance of science and redraws the boundaries and battle lines of contemporary politics. So hazards, understood as socially constructed and produced 'quasi-subjects', are a powerful, uncontrollable 'actor' that delegitimates and destabilizes state institutions with responsibilities for pollution control, in particular, and public safety in general.

Hazards themselves sweep away the attempts of institutional elites and experts to control them. The 'risk assessment bureaucracies', of course, have well-worn routines of denial. By utilizing the gap between latent impact and knowledge, data can be hidden, denied and distorted. Counter-arguments can be mobilized. Maximum permissible levels of acceptance can be raised. Human error rather than system risk can be cast as villain of the piece. However, these are battles where victories are temporary and defeat is probable or at least possible because they are fought with nineteenth-century pledges of security in a world risk society where such promises are hollow and have lost their purchase. No longer the preserve of scientists and experts, the nature of hazards is demonstrated everywhere and for everyone willing and interested to see.

My political description and vision is close to François Ewald's idea of *safety* and the *provident state*. Ewald's theory marks a significant shift in the interpretation of the welfare state. While the majority of social scientists have sought to explain the origins and constructions of the welfare state in terms of class interests, the maintenance of social order or the enhancement of national productivity and military power, Ewald's argument underlines the provision of services (health care), the creation of insurance schemes (pensions and unemployment insurance) as well as the regulation of the economy and the environment in terms of the *creation of security*. In relation to industries and technologies, of course, technical experts play a central role in answering the question, 'how safe is safe enough?'. We need to appreciate, however, that this model of the provident state is most closely correlated with the institutions and procedures of continental Western European and much less with those of either Anglo-American capitalism or the social democratic states of Scandinavia.

Implications for the Future of Social Theory

What follows from this for the future of a sociology of risk and risk society? In this final section of the chapter I will consider two possible implications.

First, as I said earlier, I admire the work of Bruno Latour, but with respect to the global risk society I disagree with his idea that 'we have never been modern'. Of course, the sun is rising as it has done always since ancient times. But—and this is a substantial proviso—this similarity is only a surface one. If you take the issue of risk beyond its cultural definition and explore instead the details of the management of risks in modern *institutions*, the contemporary paradoxes and dilemmas come to the fore and it becomes apparent that the global risk society and its cultural and political contradictions cannot be understood and explained in terms of pre-modern management of dangers and threats. This is not to deny, of course, that politicians as well as technical and legal experts could learn from the high priests of previous ages how to handle the demons of socially explosive hazards.

Second, risk society theory is *not* about exploding nuclear submarines, it is *not,* as Alan Scott (Chapter 1, this volume) suggests, one more expression of 'German Angst' at the millennium. On the contrary, I am working on a new and optimistic model for understanding our times. My argument interprets what others see as the development of a post-modern order in terms of a stage of *radicalized* (second phase) modernity, a stage where the dynamics of individualization, globalization and risk undermine the first phase of industrial nation-state modernity and its foundations. Modernity becomes *reflexive*, which means, concerned with its unintended consequences, risks and their implications on its foundations. Where most post-modern theorists are critical of grand narratives, general theory and humanity, I remain committed to all of these, but in a new sense. To me the enlightenment is *not* a historical notion and set of ideas but a process and dynamics where criticism, self-criticism, irony, and humanity play a central role. Where for many philosophers and sociologists 'rationality' means 'discourse' and 'cultural relativism', my notion of 'second reflexive modernity' implies that we do not have *enough* reason (*Vernunft*) to live and act in a global age of manufactured uncertainties.

Many theories and theorists do not recognize the *opportunities* of the risk society, the opportunities of the 'bads'. I argue for the opening up to democratic scrutiny of the previous depoliticized realms of decision-making and for the need to recognize the ways in which contemporary debates of this sort are constrained by the epistemological and legal systems within which they are conducted. This, then, is one of the themes I would like to see explored further, preferably on a comparative transnational, transcultural, potentially global level. It would entail that we reconstruct social definition of risks and risk management in different cultural framings, that we find out about the (negative) power of risk conflicts and definition where people who do not want to communicate with each other are forced together into a 'community' of shared (global) risks, and that we therefore combine it with the questions of *organized irresponsibility* and *relations of definition* in different cultural-political settings. This, it seems to me, would be a worthwhile new conceptual and political social science.

Notes

1. For the realism-constructivism-debate see Beck (1998a).
2. In addition to authors in this book, I owe a number of suggestions to Giddens (1990, 1995); Goldblatt (1996); Franklin (1997); Lash et al. (1996); Bomß (1991, 1995).
3. Benjamin (1973).
4. This position clearly gives us a different perspective on Alan Scott's (Chapter 1 this volume) very sophisticated distinction between Mary Douglas' and my version on 'constructed' and 'real risks'.
5. See Lindsay Prior, Chapter 5 this volume.
6. Kommission für Zukunftsfragen, Arbeitsmarktentwicklungen, Bericht Teil II, Bonn July 1997, chapter on globalization.
7. There may be one difference to the cultural theory concept of risk as advocated in the chapters by Alan Scott and Scott Lash. I sympathize very much with their (different) radical cultural approaches, but I do think 'risks' have to be understood and analysed from an inter- and trans-disciplinary perspective. Another way of operationalizing 'realism', I want to suggest, is to connect cultural, legal, and scientific approaches (besides all their differences and contradictionary background assumptions) to public perceptions of risk definitions, conflicts and politics. I am opposed to an *exclusive* view on 'risk culture' monopolized by cultural studies, but I am not sure that Scott Lash and Alan Scott would want to pursue such an exclusive status either.

8. Beck (1997) *Democracy Without Enemies*, see the chapter on 'Unawareness/non-knowledge'.
9. Maybe there is a 'Bavariacentrism' (Alan Scott, Chapter 1 this volume) and a 'taste of German security and wealth' (Hilary Rose, Chapter 3 this volume) to my risk society theory. There is no doubt, that the more Europe is becoming real, the more the differences in national cultural policies are becoming obvious. This means we have to study and concentrate on those cultural differences in risk perception and definition for example between Britain, France, Germany and Eastern European countries like Poland, Hungary or Russia in the future. But—and this BUT has to be written in big letters—is there, after the mad cow disease conflict and debate in Britain (Germany, France, etc.) any way of saying (as Hilary Rose seems to believe) that *only* Germany and *not* Britain is some kind of a risk society? Of course, we have to distinguish and develop theoretically different frameworks, *realizations* of risk societies. No doubt there is an amazing *pluralism* of risk societies—not only in Europe, but all over the world. But arguing that Britain is *not* a society trapped by the paradoxes of risk definitions and conflicts is to me like arguing that BSE in Europe is not of any (cultural) significance and (political) importance.
10. I am using Barbara Adam's (1998) arguments here.
11. For more detail on this, cf. Beck (1998b).
12. See also Beck (1996b), Beck et al. (1994).

References

Adam, B. (1998) *Timescapes of Modernity: the Environment and Invisible Hazards.* London: Routledge.

Bauman, Z. (1991) *Modernity and Ambivalence.* Cambridge: Polity.

Beck, U. (1992a) *Risk Society: Towards a New Modernity.* London: Sage.

Beck, U. (1992b) 'From Industrial to Risk Society', *Theory, Culture & Society,* 9 (1): 97–123.

Beck, U. (1994) *Ecological Enlightenment.* NJ: Humanities Press.

Beck, U. (1995) *Ecological Politics in an Age of Risk.* Cambridge: Polity.

Beck, U. (1996a) *The Reinvention of Politics.* Cambridge: Polity.

Beck, U. (1996b) 'World Risk Society as Cosmopolitan Society?' *Theory, Culture & Society,* 13 (4): 1–32.

Beck, U. (1996c) 'Risk Society and the Provident State', in S. Lash, B. Szerszynski and B. Wynne (eds), *Risk, Environment and Modernity.* London: Sage. pp. 27–43.

Beck, U. (1996d) 'The Sociology of Risk', in D. Goldblatt (ed.), *Social Theory and the Environment.* Cambridge: Polity. pp. 154–87.

Beck, U. (1997) *Democracy Without Enemies.* Cambridge: Polity.

Beck, U. (1998a) *World Risk Society.* Cambridge: Polity.

Beck, U. (1998b) *Was ist Globalisierung?* Frankfurt am Main: Suhrkamp Verlag.

Beck, U. and Beck-Gernsheim, E. (1996) 'Individualization and Precarious Freedoms: Perspectives and Controversies of a Subject-oriented Sociology', in

P. Heelas, S. Lash and P. Morris (eds), *Detraditionalisation*. Oxford: Blackwell, pp. 23–48.

Beck, U. Giddens, A., Lash, S. (1994) *Reflexive Modernization: Politics, Tradition and Aesthetics in the Modern Social Order*. Cambridge: Polity.

Beck-Gernsheim, E. (ed.) (1993) *Welche Gesundheit wollen wir?* Frankfurt am Main: Suhrkamp Verlag.

Beck-Gernsheim, E. (1995) *The Social Implications of Bioengineering*. NJ: Humanities Press.

Benjamin, W. (1973) *Illuminations*. Trans. H. Zohn. London: Fontana.

Bonß, W. (1991) 'Unsicherheit and Gesellschaft—Argumente für eine soziologische Risikoforschung', *Soziale Welt*, (42): 258–77.

Bonß. W. (1995) *Vom Risiko: Unsicherheit und Ungewißheit in der Moderne*. Hamburg: Bund.

Ewald, F. (1987) *L'Etat Providence*. Paris: Editions Grasser and Fasquell.

Franklin, J. (1997) *Politics of Risk Society*. Cambridge: Polity.

Giddens, A. (1990) *The Consequences of Modernity*. Cambridge: Polity.

Giddens, A. (1995) *Beyond Left and Right*. Cambridge: Polity.

Goldblatt, D. (ed.) (1996) *Social Theory and the Environment*. Cambridge: Polity.

Hajer, M. (1996) *The Politics of Environmental Discourse: Ecological Modernization and the Policy Process*. Oxford: Clarendon Press.

Harvey, D. (1989) *The Conditions of Postmodernity*. Oxford: Basil Blackwell.

Lash, S., Szerszynski, B. and Wynne, B. (eds) (1996) *Risk, Environment and Modernity*. London: Sage.

Latour, B. (1993) *We have never been Modern*. Trans. C. Porter, Hemel Hempstead: Harvester Wheatsheaf.

Latour, B. (1996) *Aramis or the Love of Technology*. Cambridge, MA: Harvard University Press.

Lau, C. (1989) 'Risikodiskurse', *Soziale Welt*, 3: 271–92.

Luhmann, N. (1995) *Die Soziologie des Risikos*. Berlin: De Gruyter.

Robertson, R. (1992) *Globalization: Social Theory and Global Culture*. London: Sage.

Schütz, R. (1984) *Ökologische Aspekte einer Naturphilosophischen Ethik*. Bamberg: Unpublished manuscript.

Weber, M. (1956) *Wirtschaft und Gesellschaft*. Tübingen: Mohr.

Weber, M. (1991) 'Objektive Möglichkeit und Adäquate Verursachung in der Historischen Kausalbetrachtung', in M. Weber, *Schriften zur Wissenschaftslehre*. Stuttgart: Reclam, pp. 102–31.

Wyune, B. (1996) 'May the Sheep Safely Graze?' in S. Lash, B. Szerszynski and B. Wynne (eds), *Risk, Environment and Modernity*. London: Sage. pp. 44–83.

CHAPTER 3

Risk and Governmentality

DEBORAH LUPTON

... Those who have taken up a perspective on risk drawing on the writings of Michel Foucault are also interested in the ways in which risk operates in late modernity, particularly in relation to the political ethos of neo-liberalism, which currently dominates in Anglophone countries. They similarly see the intensification of discussions of risk and risk practices as an outcome of the social changes occurring in the wake of modernization.

One major difference between the two perspectives is that while the 'risk society' approach tends to take a weak social constructionist approach to risk in concert with a critical structuralist perspective, advocates of Foucauldian approaches mostly adopt a 'strong' version of social constructionism and a poststructuralist approach to power relations. The concept of discourse ... is integral to Foucauldian theorizing. An important insight offered by Foucauldian perspectives on risk is the ways in which the discourses, strategies, practices and institutions around a phenomenon such as risk serve to bring it into being, to construct it as a phenomenon. It is argued that it is only through these discourses, strategies, practices and institutions that we come to know 'risk'. They produce 'truths' on risk that are then the basis for action. For Foucauldian writers, therefore, the nature of risk itself is not the important question for analysis. Risk is seen as a 'calculative rationality' rather than as a thing in itself (Dean 1999).

This chapter looks at the ways in which the discourses, knowledges, strategies, practices and institutions that have developed around risk both reflect and construct a distinct approach to self-hood, society and the government of populations. It begins with a discussion of the relationship between governmentality and risk, and goes on to explore the movement from the concept of 'dangerousness' to that of 'risk' in medical, legal and social welfare discourses. Then follows a discussion of three types of contemporary risk rationalities: insurantial risk, epidemiological risk and case-management or clinical risk.

Governmentality

Michel Foucault himself did not dwell specifically on the topic of risk in his writings at any great length. However, much of what he had to say on governmentality and modernity has been considered relevant by a number of scholars who have applied some of his ideas to the analysis of risk as a sociocultural phenomenon. Governmentality is the approach to social regulation and control that according to Foucault (1991) began to emerge in the sixteenth century in Europe, associated with such social changes as the breakdown in the feudal system and the development of administrative states in its place, based on the principles of legitimate rule. By the eighteenth century, the early modern European states began to think of their citizens in terms of populations, or 'society', a social body requiring intervention, management and protection so as to maximize wealth, welfare and productivity. Such features of populations as demographic estimates, marriage and fertility statistics, life expectation tables and mortality rates became central to the project of a technology of population. The body of both the individual and that of populations became the bearer of new variables. These variables included not only those between the healthy and the sick, the strong and the weak, the rich and the poor, and so on, but between the more or less utilizable, more or less amenable to profitable investment, those with greater or lesser prospects of illness or death and with more or less capacity for being usefully trained (Foucault 1984: 278–9).

Governmentality as a strategy and rationale, Foucault claims, has dominated political power in western countries since the eighteenth century. In its contemporary form it is characterized by an approach to political rule, neo-liberalism, which champions individual freedom and rights against the excessive intervention of the state. The domain of government is extensive, focusing on the complex of human's interactions with a diversity of phenomena:

The things with which in this sense government is to be concerned are in fact men [sic], but men in their relations, their links, their imbrication with those other things which are wealth, resources, means of subsistence, the territory with its specific qualities, climate, irrigation, fertility, etc; men in their relation to that other kind of things, customs, habits, ways of acting and thinking, etc; lastly, men in their relation to that other kind of things, accidents and misfortunes such as famine, epidemics, death, etc. (Foucault 1991: 93)

Foucault, like Beck and Giddens, emphasizes the role of expert knowledges in the constitution of late modern subjectivity. Expert knowledges, he argues, are integral to the reflexive techniques and practices of subjectification, or the formation of certain types of subject. For Foucault, however, expert knowledges are not transparently a means to engage in reflexivity. Rather, they are seen as pivotal to governmentality, providing the guidelines and advice by which populations are surveyed, compared against norms, trained to conform with these norms and rendered productive. Central to these technologies is normalization, or the method by which norms of behaviour or health status are identified in populations and sub-groups of populations. Through normalization, the late modern individual is fabricated within a network of instruments and techniques of power. The technologies of mass surveillance, monitoring, observation and measurement are central to this disciplinary power, helping to construct understandings of bodies in space and time and to use these understandings to regulate them.

From this perspective, risk may be understood as a governmental strategy of regulatory power by which populations and individuals are monitored and managed through the goals of neo-liberalism. Risk is governed via a heterogeneous network of interactive actors, institutions, knowledges and practices. Information about diverse risks is collected and analysed by medical researchers, statisticians, sociologists, demographers, environmental scientists, legal practitioners, statisticians, bankers and accountants, to name but a few. Through these never-ceasing efforts, risk is problematized, rendered calculable and governable. So too, through these efforts, particular social groups or populations are identified as 'at risk' or 'high risk', requiring particular forms of knowledges and interventions. Risk, from the Foucauldian perspective, is 'a moral technology. To calculate a risk is to master time, to discipline the future' (Ewald 1991: 207).

The strategies of governmentality, expressed in the neo-liberal states that emerged in the west in late modernity, include both direct, coercive strategies to regulate populations, but also, and most importantly, less direct strategies that rely on individuals' voluntary compliance with the interests and needs of the state. These strategies are diverse and multi-centred, emerging not only from the state but also other agencies and institutions, such as the mass media. A crucial aspect of governmentality as it is expressed in neo-liberal states is that the regulation and disciplining of citizens is directed at the autonomous, self-regulated individual. Citizens are positioned in governmental discourses, therefore, as active rather than passive subjects of governance. Rather than mainly being externally policed by agents of the state, individuals police themselves, they exercise power upon themselves as normalized subjects who are in pursuit of their own best interests and freedom, who are interested in self-improvement, seeking happiness and healthiness (Gordon 1991).

As will be explained in greater detail below, the concept of risk, as it is developed through normalization, initially deflects attention away from individuals and their behaviours towards aggregates or populations. The information gathered about risk from population data, however, is then often employed in advice to individuals about how they should conduct their lives. Discourses on risk are directed at the regulation of the body: how it moves in space, how it interacts with other bodies and things. These discourses also contribute to the constitution of selfhood, or subjectivity, and thus are part of the panoply of 'practices' or 'technologies of the self' (Foucault 1988). Through the technologies of the self, the individual becomes the 'entrepreneur of himself or herself' in terms of attempting to maximize her or his 'human capital' (Gordon 1991: 44). People attempt to 'transform themselves in order to attain a certain state of happiness, purity, wisdom, perfection, or immorality' (Foucault 1988: 18). In doing so, they seek out and adopt advice from institutional governmental agencies, from experts who have problematized areas of life as pervaded by risk. As expert knowledge about risk has proliferated in late modernity, the various strategies which individuals are required to practise upon themselves to avoid risk have equally proliferated.

Consider the example of the pregnant woman in the contemporary era. More so than in previous eras because of the growth of risk-related knowledges and technologies surrounding pregnancy, this woman is surrounded by, and constructed through, a plethora of expert and lay advice. This advice is directed at how she should regulate her body with its precious cargo, the foetus, which is portrayed as being highly fragile and susceptible to risk at every stage of its development. Even from the time a woman may be considering the idea of child-bearing, she is exhorted to engage in certain practices to ensure that fertilization will take place successfully and that her body is at its peak state of health. She is encouraged to read as much as possible about pregnancy and childbirth, so that she knows what to expect and what risks to avoid. She is told to avoid smoking, drinking alcohol and coffee and taking other drugs, to eat a nutritious diet and engage in regular exercise.

Once pregnant, these strategies and more must be adhered to by the woman. The pregnant woman must be highly careful of any food she eats, avoiding a range of foods that may contain listeria bacteria or toxoplasmosis protozoa, both of which may cause miscarriage or birth defects. She is advised to closely monitor her body for signs of an ectopic pregnancy or miscarriage, such as abdominal cramps or vaginal bleeding. She should not take any medicines, unless she has first checked their safety for the foetus with her doctor. She is encouraged to regularly see a doctor for antenatal checks, including a series of blood tests and such tests as ultrasound and, in some cases, amniocentesis (testing of the genetic makeup of the foetus) to monitor the health and normality of the foetus. She is encouraged to attend antenatal classes to prepare for childbirth.

Many of the discourses of risk that surround the pregnant woman suggest that it is her responsibility to ensure the health of her foetus, and that if she were to ignore expert advice, she is culpable should her baby miscarry or be born with a defect. The pregnant woman, therefore, is positioned in a web of surveillance, monitoring, measurement and expert advice that requires constant work on her part: seeking out knowledge about risks to her foetus, acting according to that knowledge. Yet the discourses of risk that surround her are generally embraced willingly, because the woman herself wants to maximize the health of her foetus, to achieve the 'perfect child'. Although some women in some countries such as the United States have been prosecuted and imprisoned for 'foetal endangerment' by refusing to take medical advice or give up using certain drugs (Handwerker 1994), most women are not coerced through overt disciplinary means to accede to expert advice. No-one forces them to buy books on pregnancy, to watch their diet, give up alcohol, attend antenatal checks and classes. Because pregnant women have been discursively positioned within a context in which the general consensus is that foetuses are fragile and that it is up to the pregnant woman to protect them, and that infants are very important individuals who deserve the best start in life, most women voluntarily engage in such risk-avoidance strategies, accepting the responsibility implied.

To resist these strategies is difficult, for it is tantamount to declaring that the woman does not care about her own health and welfare, and more importantly, that of the foetus she is carrying and is expected to protect and nourish in the proper maternal manner. Indeed, she may actively demand greater access to medical surveillance, such as numerous ultrasounds, in the attempt to alleviate her anxieties and concerns about her foetus and the risks to which it is exposed. The technologies of selfhood and embodiment in relation to pregnancy demonstrate the intersection and alignment of institutional and experts' objectives in advising and regulating the pregnant woman principally through directives intended for her to police herself, and the woman's own concerns to take such advice.

In late modern societies, not to engage in risk avoiding behaviour is considered 'a failure of the self to take care of itself—a form of irrationality, or simply a lack of skilfulness' (Greco 1993: 361). Risk-avoiding behaviour, therefore, becomes viewed as a moral enterprise relating to issues of self-control, self-knowledge and self-improvement. It is a form of self-government, involving the acceptance and internalization of the objectives of institutional government. Because the project of selfhood is never complete, but rather is continuing throughout the lifespan, so too the project of risk avoidance as a technology of the self is never-ending, requiring eternal vigilance.

From Dangerousness to Risk

Several commentators adopting the governmentality approach have observed that the concept of 'dangerousness' has been replaced by that of 'risk' in institutions' dealings with marginalized social groups and individuals. In nineteenth-century governmental discourses, as part of the emergent new ways of thinking about the citizen, the concept of 'dangerousness' tended to be used in relation to the problems of health and crime. 'Dangerous classes' and the 'dangerous individual' were identified as possessing the inherent qualities to present a danger to themselves or to others, and therefore as prime targets for governmental intervention and treatment. The notion of 'dangerousness' was derived from expert judgements on such features as the state of living conditions and moral climate in which social groups dwelt. Members of the working class and the poor were typically constituted as dangerous. Against these dangerous classes were juxtaposed their antithesis: those (generally more socially and economically privileged) classes who were seen to be 'at risk' from the depravations or contamination of members of the dangerous classes (Kendall and Wickham 1992: 11–12).

Castel (1991) links the concept of risk with that of governmentality by focusing on contemporary preventive strategies of social administration in the United States and France. He argues that these strategies are innovative in that they 'dissolve the notion of a *subject* or a concrete individual, and put in its place a combination of *factors*, the factors of risk' (ibid.: 281, original emphases). As a result, he argues there have been changes in the ways in which intervention is carried out. No longer is the essential component of intervention 'the direct face-to-face relationship between the carer and the cared, the helper and the helped, the professional and the client. It comes instead to reside in the establishing of flows of population based on the collation of a range of abstract factors deemed liable to produce risk in general' (ibid.: 281). As a result, specialist professionals are cast in a more subordinate role, while managerial policy formations take over.

In psychiatric medicine, for example, there has been a shift over the past century from the use of the notion of 'dangerousness' used in relation to people with psychiatric disorders to that of 'risk'. In classical psychiatry, '"risk" meant essentially the danger embodied in the mentally ill person capable of violent and unpredictable action' (ibid.: 283). Dangerousness itself connoted an immanent quality of the subject, a potentiality that dwelt within and may or may not have been manifested. Therefore there could only ever be imputations of dangerousness, based on observation of a patient's present symptoms and speculations about what these might mean for future behaviour. All insane people were deemed as carrying this potentiality for dangerousness within them, despite their otherwise benign exteriors, and were subsequently treated with such preventive strategies as confinement from the rest of society (ibid. 1991).

In contrast, the notion of risk, although also acknowledging potentiality, is calculated through systematic statistical correlations and probabilities based on populations rather than the close observation of individuals. Risk is therefore more selective and precise, but at the same time applies to a larger group of people than the notion of dangerousness: 'A risk does not arise from the presence of particular precise danger embodied in a concrete individual or group. It is the effect of a combination of abstract *factors* which render more or less probable the occurrence of undesirable modes of behaviour' (ibid.: 287, original emphasis). To be designated 'at risk' is to be located within a network of factors drawn from the observation of others, to be designated as part of a 'risk population'. A risk, therefore, is one step further from dangerousness in its potentiality.

Identifying and monitoring risks in populations constitutes 'a new mode of surveillance: that of systematic predetection' (ibid.: 288). This new form of surveillance may not necessarily require the actual presence of the 'risky' individual, but may be based on the monitoring of records:

> To intervene no longer means, or at least not to begin with, taking as one's target a given individual, in order to correct, punish or care for him or her.... There is, in fact, no longer a relation

of immediacy with a subject *because there is no longer a subject*. What the new preventive policies primarily address is no longer individuals but factors, statistical correlations of heterogeneous elements. They deconstruct the concrete subject of intervention, and reconstruct a combination of factors liable to produce risk. Their primary aim is not to confront a concrete dangerous situation, but to anticipate all the possible forms of irruption of danger. (Castel 1991: 288, original emphasis)

Under this new approach to surveillance, for a person to be identified as posing a risk no longer means that she or he has to be individually observed for signs of dangerousness. It is enough that she or he is identified as a member of a 'risky population', based on a 'risk profile' developed from calculations using demographic and other characteristics. Castel notes that this shift from dangerousness to risk results in the production of 'a potentially infinite multiplication of the possibilities for intervention. For what situation is there of which one can be certain that it harbours no risk, no uncontrollable or unpredictable chance factor?' (ibid.: 289).

Whereas in the early modern era members of the 'dangerous classes' were disciplined and managed via coercive, exclusionary and correctional strategies (such as incarceration), risk-based tactics and strategies may focus very little on the individual characteristics of those identified as being 'at risk', but rather direct attention at changing the environment in which such individuals operate. O'Malley (1992: 262) gives as an example situational crime prevention. As a risk management strategy, situational crime prevention deals hardly at all with individual offenders. It is not interested in the causes of crime and does not support correctional strategies for managing crime. The philosophy of this approach, as articulated in an American National Crime Prevention Institute document, is that: 'Criminal behaviour can be controlled primarily through the direct alteration of the environment of potential victims.... As criminal opportunity is reduced, so too with be the number of criminals' (quoted in O'Malley 1992: 262). The focus of this approach is upon prevention of crime rather than rehabilitation of offenders.

The shift in focus in expert knowledges and practices from the concept of 'dangerousness' to 'risk' has a number of consequences. The future behaviour of a marginalized individual deemed subject to external intervention and regulation is no longer linked exclusively to that individual's own behaviour, based on close observation of her or him. Because the concept of risk has emerged, which is predicated on techniques of the surveillance and measurement of populations and statistical calculations based on data derived from these techniques, marginalized individuals are now dealt with differently. Under the discourse of risk, these people are typically categorized as a member of a specific 'risk group' and their future behaviour is gauged and the interventions that are judged to be required are based on the characteristics of this group. These calculations rest upon a notion of management that highlights the importance of rationalized and standardized assessment and prediction and a notion of the individual actor that represents her or him as behaving predictably, in alliance with patterns identified in wider populations.

Contemporary Risk Strategies

The above discussion on the change from 'dangerousness' to 'risk' as a discourse and strategy of regulation and intervention tends to imply a homogeneous approach to risk in contemporary western societies. This is not quite the case. Dean (1997, 1999) has identified three types of risk rationality in neo-liberal societies. These include insurantial risk, epidemiological risk and case-management or clinical risk. There are certain differences between these risk rationalities, based on the types of risk calculations that are manifested and the specific risks to which they are directed.

Ewald (1991) has discussed three characteristics of insurantial risk, or that operating in the discourses and strategies of insurance. The first is that risk is distinguished from a bet in that it is seen to be calculable, governed by identifiable laws. For an event to be a risk in insurance discourses, it must be possible to evaluate the probability of it happening. The second characteristic is that risk is collective, affecting a population rather than an individual: 'Strictly speaking there is no such thing as an individual risk, otherwise insurance would be no more than a wager' (Ewald 1991: 203). Rather, risk is seen as something that only becomes calculable when it is spread over a population. Each individual in a specified population is understood to be a factor of risk or exposed to a risk, but not each individual is equally likely to fall prey to a risk or cause the same degree of risk (ibid.: 203). The third characteristic of insurantial risk is that it is a capital. What is insured against is not the injury or loss but rather a capital against whose loss the insurer offers a guarantee. The injury or loss is not prevented or repaired, but is given a price for financial compensation.

Insurance, therefore, is a means for dealing with the vagaries of fate, a technology through which risk is constructed as a schema of rationality, of ordering elements of reality, allowing for a certain way of objectifying things, people and the relationships between them. Insurers 'produce risk' by rendering a range of phenomena into a risk—death, bankruptcy, litigation, an accident, a disease, a storm—through the specialized actuarial calculations available to them, and then offer guarantees against them. These phenomena would once have been accepted with fatalistic resignation: now they have become objects of risk, given value via the compensation that has been calculated for them (Ewald 1991). It is in this sense that anything can be a risk, if it is amenable to being turned into a risk through insurantial discourse, or any other kind of discourse directed at identifying and managing risk (ibid.: 200). Participation in insurance is about conducting one's life as an enterprise, to ensure that even when misfortune occurs, it has been planned for. It is, however, a socialized rather than wholly individualized approach, for insurance distributes the burden of risk among a large population and is underpinned by a notion of social rights in which members of an association agree to accept responsibility for each other's burdens (Dean 1999).

The second type of risk rationality is epidemiological risk, in which the calculus of risk is undertaken by bringing together assessment of a range of abstract factors with the incidence of health outcomes in targeted populations. Epidemiological risk adopts a similar approach to insurantial risk, but has a different target—illness and disease rather than loss of capital. Epidemiological techniques involve the tracing of illness and disease in specified populations using statistical and screening techniques, linking illness and disease with their causal variables in the attempt to predict health outcomes at the population level and thus to better control them and reduce health risks (Dean 1997: 218).

In the past, epidemiological risk strategies tended to be directed not at individual's behaviours, but rather at altering environmental conditions in the attempt to improve health at the population level. Thus, for example, nineteenth-century public health endeavours sought to tackle hygiene and sanitary conditions in the city, such as air and water quality and sewerage arrangements, to reduce the incidence of epidemic diseases. While this focus on environmental health continues to some extent at the end of the twentieth century, there has developed a far greater emphasis on individuals' 'lifestyle' choices in relation to health status (Lupton 1995). Epidemiological risk factors are now often used to exhort individuals to engage in self regulation. Thus, for example, if a certain population group is identified through statistical calculations as being at 'high risk' of developing heart disease, based on such attributes as gender, age and diet, then members of that group are then encouraged to deal with the risk factors themselves. This process does not necessarily involve consultations and examination of individuals by health professionals, but rather often takes place through mass-targeted media campaigns which rely on individuals identifying themselves as being 'at risk' and taking steps voluntarily to reduce their exposure to risk (Lupton 1995). This is an example of 'government at a distance', for it relies upon voluntary participation in technologies of self-surveillance and a sense of self-responsibility rather than direct intervention.

The third type of risk rationality, case-management risk, is linked to clinical practice with individuals deemed to be threatening or disruptive in some way to the social order (the mad, the unemployed, the criminal, the dysfunctional, the poor, the long-term unemployed). Risk calculation in this type involves the qualitative assessment of risk for individuals and groups who are deemed to be 'at risk' (Dean 1997: 17). In contrast to the other two types of risk rationalities, the case-management approach uses more individualistic sources of date derived from interaction with and observation of specific clients, such as interviews, case-notes and files. Once risk is assessed, techniques for managing it on the part of the relevant experts (for example, social workers, health workers, police officers) are brought into play. These include therapeutic practices directed at self-help through expert assistance, pedagogic practices designed to train dangerous others and more coercive measures such as detainment and imprisonment, removing the 'risky' individuals from society (Dean ibid.: 217–18).

Population-based risk strategies, however, also now enter the clinical arena. When patients visit their doctors, for example, their symptoms are not only treated as specific to them as individuals, but as manifestations of the patient's location in a wider sociodemographic context. In this way, epidemiological calculations about the likelihood of the occurrence of a condition in a given population are implemented upon the bodies of individuals, by applying risk categories derived from large-scale data sets. The case-management approach that is central to clinical strategies, with its emphasis on individual pathology and therapeutic intervention, is brought together with epidemiological risk, with its emphasis on indirect intervention via populations (Dean 1997).

Dean argues that the case-management type of risk rationality has proliferated in neo-liberal societies, moving from the spheres of social work and clinical medicine to address such problems as unemployment and 'welfare dependency'. The language of risk is taking over from that of need or welfare in the literature on personal social services, such as probation, mental health and childcare services, with risk assessment, risk management, the monitoring of risk and risk-taking itself having become the raison d'être and organizing principle of agencies providing such services. Risk-related discourses and strategies have taken on a key role in decision-making about service delivery, including the rationing of services and decisions about need.

For all three types of risk rationality, individuals and groups are increasingly expected to engage in practices identified as ways of avoiding or minimizing the impact of risks to themselves. This approach has been called by critics the 'new prudentialism', a neo-conservative approach which progressively removes the responsibility for risk protection from state agencies—as embodied in social insurance for such misfortunes as unemployment and ill health—and places it in the hands of the individual or community-based groups (O'Malley 1992; Dean 1997, 1999). As a result, the concept of risk has become more privatized and linked ever more closely to the concept of the entrepreneurial subject, calling into question the very notion of social rights: 'Here, we witness the "multiple responsibilization" of individuals, families, households and communities, for their own risks—of physical and mental ill health, of unemployment, of poverty in old age, of poor educational performance, of becoming victims of crime' (Dean 1997: 218).

For example, as Dean notes, in several neo-liberal societies there has been an increasing focus on the importance of individuals managing their own risks by taking out private insurance rather than participating in the social insurance schemes offered by the state. The latter served to offer security through the spreading of the costs of unfortunate events among the general population, so that risk was socialized. In doing so it deflected attention away from those designated as being 'at risk', providing them with a security net rather than exhorting them to change their behaviour. In contrast, private insurance arrangements place the onus on individuals to take responsibility for insuring themselves against misfortune. It is accompanied by a range of other risk strategies that remove the responsibility for managing and dealing with risk from the state.

Under the 'new prudentialism', the acceptance of personal responsibility is presented as a practice of freedom, relief from state intervention, an opportunity for the entrepreneurial subject to make choices about the conduct of her or his life. More and more domains of life are identified as amenable to and requiring of these choices. In the context of neo-liberal democracies, which value self-autonomy over direct state intervention, these strategies are seen both to work to minimize risks and to protect individuals' rights. In this context, the role of government is to provide advice and assistance for the self-management of risks, encouraging the active, free citizen who voluntarily engages in risk avoidance, rather than providing large-scale financial support.

Contemporary technologies of risk calculation and control, therefore, comprise one aspect of a change in ways of viewing the role of society. What 'the social' is understood to be was changed from notions of a mass collectivity to dynamic smaller groupings. We are progressively understanding and acting upon ourselves not as members of a specific society or through the ethos of the welfare state, but as self-actualizing individuals who move between loose and fluid social aggregations, taking up different roles in each. Small community or affiliation-based groupings are set in place to deal with such phenomena as risk, which have limited and dynamic constituencies and interests (Dean, 1997, 1999). This is taking place in a sociocultural and historical context in which dominant notions of selfhood privilege the self who is able to exert strong control over her or his mind and body, constantly engages in self-examination, is able to engage in self-denial for the greater good and readily takes up the injunctions of experts in making 'lifestyle' choices. Those individuals who are deemed to be at 'high risk' either of being a victim of risk or of perpetrating risk are expected to take control to prevent risk through their own actions rather than rely on social insurance apparatuses as a safety-net.

This representation of the individual is that of *homo economicus*, a subject who is invested with additional moral and political characteristics and conforms to the self-interested and responsible actor found in neo-conservative discourses. Situational crime discourse, for example, represents the potential offender as a universal 'abiographical individual', a 'rational choice' actor who weighs up the pros and cons before committing an offence. So too, victims are understood as rational choice actors, with the responsibility to protect themselves, and it is therefore regarded as their fault if they become vulnerable to crime (O'Malley 1992; 264 66).

As the welfare state is wound back, there is less incentive for the state to provide social insurance schemes such as unemployment benefits or socialized health insurance: 'in the present era, the success of programs inspired by economic rationalists and neo-conservatism has been stripping away socialized risk management, and replacing it with a programmatic combination of privatized prudentialism and punitive sovereignty' (ibid.: 261). The lack of interest in the biography or motivation of the 'at risk' individual deflects attention away from the socioeconomic underpinnings of risk, and divorces misfortune from questions of social justice. This leads back to the early modern risk strategies of coercion and punishment and the construction of new 'dangerous classes' requiring active surveillance and disciplining. It appears that societies dominated by neo-liberal politics in the late modern era are returning to previous forms of discipline in relation to individuals and social groups that are identified as being 'at risk' or imposing a risk upon others. In relation to crime prevention, for example, the broader social structural underpinnings of crime, such as socioeconomic disadvantage, is ignored in favour of strategies that are punitive for those who are seen to lack self-control (ibid.: 265).

Concluding Comments

This chapter has highlighted the ways in which the concept of risk, employed to address governmental concerns, has contributed to the production of certain kinds of rationalities, strategies and subjectivities. It has been argued that according to the Foucauldian perspective, risk strategies and discourses are means of ordering the social and material worlds through methods of rationalization and calculation, attempts to render disorder and uncertainty more controllable. It is these strategies and discourses that bring risk into being, that select certain phenomena as being 'risky' and therefore requiring management, either by institutions or individuals.

The accounts provided by Foucauldian scholars of risk have shown that it is not simply a matter of risk becoming less calculable, or shifting from local to global contexts, as the 'risk society' thesis would have it (Dean 1999). Rather, changes in risk rationalities have occurred which have resulted in risk being conceptualized and dealt with in diverse ways that have strong links to ideas about how individuals should deport themselves in relation to the state. Some of those taking up a Foucauldian perspective have remarked upon recent changes in the governance of risk, in which there is far less reliance upon social insurance and far more upon individual self-management and self-protection from risk. This is an outcome of the political ethos of neo-liberalism, which emphasizes minimal intervention on the part of the state and emphasizes 'self-help' and individual autonomy for citizens.

Foucault himself and those taking up his perspectives on the regulation of subjects via the discourses of governmentality may be criticized for devoting too much attention to these discourses and strategies and not enough to how people actually respond to them as part of their everyday lives. The question of how risk-related discourses and strategies operate, how they may be taken up, negotiated or resisted by those who are the subject of them, remains under-examined. Further, the Foucauldian view of the self tends to represent it as universal, without recognizing differences between the ways in which people of different gender, age, ethnicity and so on may be treated by and respond to these discourses and strategies differently....

References

Castel, R. (1991) From dangerousness to risk. In Burchell, G., Gordon, C. and Miller, P. (eds), *The Foucault Effect: Studies in Governmentality*. London: Harvester/Wheatsheaf, pp. 281–98.

Dean, M. (1997) Sociology after society. In Owen, D. (ed.), *Sociology after Postmodernism*. London: Sage, pp. 205–28.

_____ (1999) Risk, calculable and incalculable. In Lupton, D. (ed.), *Risk and Sociocultural Theory: New Directions and Perspectives*. Cambridge: Cambridge University Press.

Ewald, F. (1991) Insurance and risks. In Burchell, G., Gordon, C. and Miller, P. (eds), *The Foucault Effect: Studies in Governmentality*. London: Harvester/Wheatsheaf, pp. 197–210.

Foucault, M. (1984) The politics of health in the eighteenth century. In Rabinow, P. (ed.), *The Foucault Reader*. New York, Pantheon Books, pp. 273–89.

_____ (1988) Technologies of the self. In Martin, L., Gutman, H. and Hutton, P. (eds), *Technologies of the Self: A Seminar with Michel Foucault*. London: Tavistock, pp. 16–49.

_____ (1991) Governmentality. In Burchell, G., Gordon, C. and Miller, P. (eds), *The Foucault Effect: Studies in Governmentality*. Hemel Hempstead: Harvester/Wheatsheaf, pp. 87–104.

Gordon, C. (1991) Governmental rationality: an introduction. In Burchell, G., Gordon, C. and Miller, P. (eds), *The Foucault Effect: Studies in Governmentality*. Hemel Hempstead: Harvester/Wheatsheaf, pp. 1–52.

Greco, M. (1993) Psychosomatic subjects and the 'duty to be well': personal agency within medical rationality. *Economy and Society*, 22(3), 357–72.

Handwerker, L. (1994) Medical risk: implicating poor pregnant women. *Social Science and Medicine*, 38(5), 665–75.

Kendall, G. and Wickham, G. (1992) Health and the social body. In Scott, S., Williams, G., Platt, S. and Thomas, H. (eds), *Private Risks and Public Dangers*. Aldershot: Avebury, pp. 8–18.

Lupton, D. (1995) *The Imperative of Health: Public Health and the Regulated Body*. London: Sage.

O'Malley, P. (1992) Risk, power and crime prevention. *Economy and Society*, 21(3), 252–75.

CHAPTER 4

Gambling as a Sociological Problem

DAVID DOWNES, B.P. DAVIES, M.E. DAVID, AND P. STONE

There have been remarkably few sociological attempts to account for gambling—and this applies whether 'accounting' is taken in the sense of explanation, in the sense of understanding, or as covering both simultaneously. Whatever the reasons for this strange gap in sociological accounting—and the sheer absence of reasonably comprehensive empirical evidence may be among them—it should soon be filled by the re-emergence in fashion of carefully conducted small-scale ethnographic inquiries, and the growing availability of officially designed statistics and opinion polls. As things stand, the theoretical perspectives against which such data can be weighed may turn out to have been false starts, or of severely limited use. Nevertheless, they are all we have, and for their authors to have constructed them at all is a high contribution in a field otherwise bereft of all but polemic.

Gambling as Play

In the most consummate attempt yet to give play its due in the creation of culture, Huizinga's *Homo Ludens*,[1] gambling is given short shrift as a parasitic, materialistic and entirely negative activity: the dark side of play. Huizinga was concerned to define play as exhaustively as possible and to link the 'play instinct' with institutions and activities hitherto conceived as embodying the antithesis of play: law, war and philosophy (as well as those conveniently viewed as closer to play: literature, art and music). By sheer force of protean example Huizinga seeks to convince us that 'civilization does not come *from* play like a babe detaching itself from the womb: it arises *in* and *as* play and never leaves it.' The less scope for play to flourish, the more its spirit is suppressed or eliminated in institutional life, the less scope also for civilization to survive. Huizinga could see regimented leisure as far more inimical to civilization than overwork in which the spirit of play was nevertheless alive.

It is on this basis that Caillois[2] seeks to build a sociology not merely *of* games but derived *from* games. He repudiates the view that games can be reduced to mere residues of former tradition, or childish imitations or substitutes for 'real' life. He defines play as (a) *free*, not compulsory or forced; (b) *separate*, circumscribed within limits of time and space, carved out from 'ordinary life'; (c) *uncertain*, as to its outcome; (d) *unproductive*; (e) *governed by rules*; and (f) *'make-believe'*—'accompanied by a special awareness of a second reality, or of a free unreality, as against real life' (p. 10). He then distinguishes four characteristics as underlying the myriad forms assumed by play: *competition* (agon); *chance* (alea); *simulation* (mimicry); and *vertigo* (ilinx)—the names in brackets are the closest terms in classical or modern language to the ideal types Caillois wishes to distinguish.

The main contrast in which we are interested is that between agon and alea. Agon stresses the ability of contestants to surmount obstacles and opponents to achieve victory. Alea renders the outcome quite independent of the players. Both stress the equality of the contestants under the rules, but seek to bring this about in different ways: agon by handicapping or equalizing *skills* as far as possible: alea by compensating with profit as closely as possible to the risk involved. In agon the contestants rely upon their own abilities and seek to minimize the role played by chance; in alea 'it is the very capriciousness of chance that constitutes the unique appeal.' The player is active in the one, passive in the other.

> In agon, his only reliance is upon himself; in alea ... he depends upon everything *except* himself. Agon is a vindication of personal responsibility; alea is a negation of the will, a surrender to destiny... Both, however, obey the same law—the creation for the players of conditions of pure equality denied them in real life (pp. 17–19).

Hence their natures are both oppositional yet complementary, a compatibility heightened by the battening of alea onto the uncertainty of outcome contrived in agon by the equalization of chances. In simulation, the escape from oneself to play the role of another, and in vertigo, 'the attempt to momentarily destroy stability of perception and inflict a kind of voluptuous panic upon an otherwise lucid mind' (p. 23), as in the whirling games of children and ecstatic dances, no such implication of equality occurs. The germ of Caillois's evolutionism emerges.

Each type contains the seeds of its own corruption: *agon* through professionalization, cheating, the ritualization of the means of victory over and above the point of the game; *alea* through the degeneration of the appreciation of impersonal chance into the belief in luck, destiny, superstitions, etc.; *simulation* through the *loss* of self in role-play, or (in modern societies) over-identification with fantasized hero-figures, as in fan-worship; and *vertigo* through the synthesizing or alteration of consciousness by resort to drugs.

Of the possible combinations of competition, chance, mimicry and vertigo, only two are truly compatible: competition-chance, and mimicry-vertigo. The latter are seen as typical of 'Dionysian' societies, ruled by masks, possession, shamanism and magic—Amerindian, Australasian, and African tribal societies exemplify this combination. The former are seen as typical of comparatively 'rational' societies—Chinese, Assyrian, Roman and Inca—in which order and merit are the basis for social cohesion. The latter are rooted in primeval fears of the unknown which they palliate by recourse to pantheism and ecstasy; the former have at least *some* notion of a *cosmos*, of a universe which can be ordered and perceived as stable in crucial respects. To Caillois, civilization can exist only in so far as the former displaces the latter as a principle of social organization.

Whatever one makes of Caillois's evolutionism, especially in the wake of Lévi-Strauss and the destruction of tribal cultures in large parts of both the American continent and Africa by civilizations which then consign their victims to the shanty town and the pursuit of alea, his central distinction seems valid, and leads him to pose the issue of the consequences for agonistically oriented societies of the stubborn persistence of the aleatory principle. Wealth/poverty, glory/obscurity, power/servitude are relatively constant polarities even in the most egalitarian societies. Despite reforms and even revolutions, most people are 'unable radically to change their station in life. From this arises the nostalgia for crossroads, for immediate solutions offering the possibility of unexpected success, even if only relative. Chance is courted because hard work and personal qualifications are powerless to bring such success about' (p. 114). Alea therefore seems, under these conditions, a necessary complement to and compensation for agon. Hence, while modern democratic societies may deplore alea and seek to eliminate it along with mimicry and vertigo, it remains tenacious and paradoxically compensates (as indeed do mimicry and vertigo) for the cruelties of merit.

Caillois cites one powerful instance of the importance of games of chance in the modern world, choosing—ironically in view of his evolutionary ideas—the Jogo de Bicho in Brazil. This lottery is played[3] by 60–70 per cent of the population, each spending *on average* 1 per cent of his monthly income *daily* on the game. All manner of corruptions are involved in its machinery and disposal of winnings, but for Caillois its main drawback is *economic*. 'The game practically immobilizes an appreciable part of disposable income by causing it to circulate too quickly. It is thus unavailable for the nation's economic development or for improving the standard of living of the inhabitants.' Once committed to gambling, capital is virtually immobilized, since winnings are usually reinvested. The Jogo de Bicho symbolizes the waste and unproductiveness of gambling.

In criticism of Caillois, two further points should be made:

1. His assessment of the aleatory factor in egalitarian societies does not cover the well-documented link between aristocratic life and gambling. If alea survives and even flourishes chiefly for compensatory reasons, why should the class most beneficently endowed with wealth and status be so clearly committed to upholding the 'Sport of Kings' and the green baize? Happily, the answer can easily be given from within Caillois's own model: those whose status is based on the aleatory principle of heredity will cultivate it at play.

2. A more serious criticism is that Caillois does not really convey the *meanings*, as distinct from the formal *essences* of different forms of games, and especially of gambling. He generally treats games as self-evidently attractive since victory or profit accrue from them, or as attractive in terms of distinctive attributes, e.g. they are free, spontaneous, etc., unlike the workaday world of everyday life. But this comes close to the very reductionism he sought to avoid at the outset. He analyses games in terms of their formal properties with great assurance; but we are left wondering why people really play them.

For illumination on that score, we turn to the work of Erving Goffman.

Gambling as Action

Goffman's essay on games and gambling[4] is so beautifully structured that the argument is best put by condensation rather than by rearrangement of its parts. Analysing outwards from the archetype of two boys tossing a coin *for* the coin, he ends by rendering gambling intelligible in the context of a total culture. The culture in question is naturally that of the USA: but the range of application is universal.

In all games of chance or skill, the outcome is problematical, the odds ideally equal. The span of play covers four quite separate phases: 'squaring off'—in which the boys decide to toss for the coin; determination—in which it describes its parabola and lands; disclosure—in which the outcome is revealed; and settlement—the winner takes the coin, or the play is renewed. These phases inhere in any game, and also in most events in everyday life. But in marriage, for example, while the span can cover anything from a few weeks to a lifetime, it usually approximates to the latter rather than the former. 'The distinctive property of games and contests is that once the bet has been made, the outcome is determined and payoff awarded *all in the same breath of experience*' (p. 156). Everyday life is usually quite otherwise; it is the *uninterrupted* nature of the sequence which gives most forms of gambling their intensity, though the lengths of each phase and the pause between them are variables which differ from game to game.

It is in his discussion of the *consequentiality* of gambling that Goffman lays the foundations for an understanding of its career structures, the termini of which are occupied by the hardened or 'compulsive' gambler on the one hand, and by the professional gambler on the other. In general, the consequentiality of gambling—'What winning allows and losing disallows the player later on to do'—is far more manageable than that of real life chance-taking. But what makes gambling consequential *at all* is the staking of money on the outcome of the bet, a practice conventionally held to originate in the human desire for gain. In a related essay,[5] however, Goffman allows a different view: that the purpose of the stake is to induce a correct seriousness in the attitude of players towards the game.[6] In common with Huizinga and Caillois, Goffman stresses that play and seriousness, far from being antithetical, eventually contrive to promote the most appropriate attitude-set towards games, which can only be enjoyed *to the full* if the players not only abide by the rules but do so with conviction. If players drift off the field halfway through a game, or play inattentively or absent-mindedly, the game is to a large extent spoilt for the rest of the players. As Huizinga first observed, it is the spoilsport, not the cheat, who is most inimical to the spirit of play. Moreover, play is not simply different from everyday life: the occasion, and often the setting for it, have to be *set apart from* everyday life, and this circumscription is not simply to facilitate the action—it is to maintain the boundaries between play and everyday life, boundaries which are fragile and have to be carefully contrived and sustained.

The stake is the player's commitment to *serious* play: it is also the prime determinant of its consequentiality. For play can become *too* serious and, as a result, increasingly consequential for the player. The greater the consequentiality, the more *fateful* the enterprise becomes. Over time, he may plunge too deeply, and what began as serious play becomes fateful action—as to why he might be drawn into such a spiral at all, we can only follow the path set out by Goffman.

The human condition is primordially fateful. The life of even the best actuarial risk is fraught with danger, both physical and psychic. Men have accordingly arranged their lives to minimize risk, and to reassure themselves. Even so, certain occupations persist which amount to 'practical gambles', shot through with problematic consequentiality and abnormally vulnerable to contingency: financially risky commercial roles; physically dangerous jobs; jobs whose holders operate against a tight margin of success and failure; performing jobs subject to switches of fashion; roles whose occupants man the boundaries of civil order—the police; the armed forces; criminal roles and professional sportsmen. Yet even in these roles, procedures and norms are developed which minimize risk and contingency as far as possible. By 'copings' (taking physical care, being provident) and by 'defences' (taking physical care to anticipate eventfulness), men seek to ward off uncertainty and contingency.

Fatefulness cannot be entirely eliminated. But even if it could, ambivalence would persist about such 'safe and momentless living'. For, in Western society at any rate, and American society in particular, we still believe that the truest record of an individual's make-up is revealed in his reaction to fateful activities sought out *without obligation*. It is these activities which constitute *action*, a term which had its slang beginning in the gambling world, for 'gambling is the prototype of action'. The term has been diffused and commercialized far beyond these boundaries, perhaps because 'we have become alive to action at a time when—compared to other societies—we have sharply curtailed in civilian life the occurrence of fatefulness of the serious, heroic and dutiful kind' (p. 193).

Action of the former kind is now to be found in commercialized sports; non-spectator risky sports; commercialized settings for action—casinos, race-tracks, fairs, amusement centres, etc.; and arenas for 'fancy milling', resort to large, tightly packed gatherings which offer the promise of excitement, contingency and proximity to 'real action' performers. Brief penetrations into high living are increasingly commercially provided by casinos, restaurants, airlines, even pubs and filling stations with an overlay of glamorous service. Action is routinely available—at a price—for those who need it only transiently, irrespective of their social and psychological state (though it is much more appealing to men than to women).

Action celebrates self-determination via the revelation of *character* under stress. Certain properties of character (as distinct from those of skill, training and technical accomplishment) can emerge only during fateful events. The performer is judged, 'essentialized', against the showing he makes at such times, is accorded a 'strong' or a 'weak' character in terms of moral extremes. The principal attributes of character to which his performance can attain are courage; gameness; integrity; gallantry; composure; and presence of mind. 'Character' can be dramatically acquired or lost—hence the particular appeal of action. '*Character is gambled* ... the self can be voluntarily subjected to re-creation' (p. 238). Even if material loss ensues, a real gain of character can occur.

Action, then, is not mere impulsiveness or irrationality, nor is the chief motivation to gamble the desire for gain. 'The possibility of effecting reputation is the spur.' Those who never risk never avail themselves of the opportunity to gain or lose 'character' in this way: they thereby lose direct connection with some of the values of society, though they may vicariously experience them via the mass media. Soap operas, thrillers, Westerns, what the French term 'histoires héroiques', re-establish and confirm our connection with values concerning character. Yet it is via gambling that men commonly struggle to achieve character in a society which has all but arranged action out of everyday life.

The force of Goffman's essay on gambling is that he lifts gambling out of the moral abyss into which successive generations of commentators and reformers have consigned it and renders possible a consideration of its meaning which is freed from *a priori* associations of a negative kind. It may well be that there is a hint of bathos in his insistence on seeing the rather drab routines of, say, fruit-machine players as even an attenuated pursuit of the heroic. But, without his analysis, we are reduced to a behaviourist model of a mindless automaton seeking profit from a machine which has been skilfully designed to minimize that eventuality. His analysis also makes sense of features of 'this sporting life' which would otherwise be inexplicable. In his social mapping of the world of the race-track, Marvin Scott[7] echoes Goffman in his characterizations of the jockey as the 'last in the line of "men of honour"', displaying attributes of coolness, gallantry and integrity most crucially when *under pressure*: 'risk-taking is an essential pre-requisite for a jockey to "emerge"'.

Such doubts as arise from his essay relate not to his analysis of gambling, action and character but to the relations he draws between these phenomena and the encircling culture and social structure. Goffman depicts a culture composed of two diverse value patterns: prudential and incremental coping (the Calvinist way) and action (what in another context have been termed the 'subterranean' values of toughness, excitement and disdain for routine work).[8] These systems can, as far as individuals are concerned, be treated in everyday life as straight preferences or as uneasy choices, which co-exist as alternative guidelines for behaviour.

Goffman does not allow himself to be drawn as to the likely distribution of such choices throughout the social system. 'Certain segments of each community seem more responsive than others to the attraction of this kind of action' (p. 200). 'Fatefulness, which many persons avoid, others for some reason approve, and there are those who even construct an environment in which they can indulge it' (p. 214). These are statements which give little help in assessing *for whom* action as he describes it is likely to be most attractive. He does suggest that lower-class street gangs—'well organized for disorganization'—are most open to fateful activities of a physical danger kind because—in a circular vein—such action is relatively 'least disruptive' and 'most tolerable' for their members. The cult of 'masculinity' ascribed by Miller[9] to lower-class culture in general is also seen by Goffman as fatefully inclined, though he prefers to subsume 'masculinity' under the rubric of 'character', rather than the reverse.

Do we then ascribe the probability of choosing prudence or action to a straight class-based matrix of cause and effect? This is exactly the kind of prediction which Goffman wishes to avoid. How do we account for the co-existence of such apparently incompatible value systems? The answer is that society needs both. 'The individual allows others to build him into their own plans in an orderly and effective way. The less uncertain his life, *the more society can make use of him*' (p. 174). However, 'although societies differ widely in the kinds of character they approve, no society *could long persist* if its members did not approve and foster this quality [i.e. integrity]' (p. 219, italics supplied). Society can afford to license integrity-generating action because 'the price of putting on these shows is likely to provide an automatic check against those who might be over-inclined to stage them' (p. 238). Finally, Goffman slides away into an ambiguous quasi-functionalism:

> Social organization everywhere has the problem of morale and continuity. Individuals must come to all these little situations with some enthusiasm and concern, for it is largely through such moments that social life occurs, and if a fresh effort were not put into each of them, society would surely suffer. The possibility of effecting reputation is the spur. We are allowed to think there is

something to be won in the moments that we face so that society can face moments and defeats them (pp. 238–9).

The chief issues that remain to be explored within Goffman's own terms of reference might be set out as follows:

1. How do the puritanical manage to survive psychologically in an action-packed culture? While Goffman's analysis was of the exact opposite question, it inevitably raises its mirror image.
2. How did it come about that the spheres in which action is now centred, gambling and mass spectator sports, etc., have displaced spheres in which fatefulness of the 'serious, heroic and dutiful' kind gained fuller expression? There is precious little reference to what has happened to political and religious definitions of character in Goffman's work.
3. Do those who undertake the 'practical gamble' of everyday life—men in physically dangerous jobs, etc.—find themselves more, or less, drawn to the pursuit of action in the sphere of sport and gambling, or is there no necessary connection between the two? This remains a central ambiguity of Goffman's analysis. Some of these issues are, however, clarified further by the third perspective, to which we now turn.

Gambling as Strain

In a monumental, but unfortunately unpublished, work completed in 1949 Devereux[10] provides what is still the most rounded and comprehensive attempt to account for the nature of gambling in relation to the social structure of the USA, or indeed of any society, urban-industrial or otherwise. To an astonishing extent, he anticipated the themes later developed rather differently by Caillois and Goffman. A then graduate student of Talcott Parsons, he approached his theme within a rigorous structural-functional framework, and rarely has the strength of that method been better exemplified. Indeed, the charges commonly made against structural-functionalism as a doctrine seem rather irrelevant when, as here, its utility as an organizing conceptual framework paid such rich dividends. There is, of course, the customary due paid to equilibrium-maintenance—but the doctrinal trappings are fortunately detachable from the substantive argument, a separability pointed to elsewhere by Homans[11] and Gellner.[12]

It would be futile in the space available to attempt an adequate summary of the full range and complexity of Devereux's argument. Rather, we shall focus initially on his characterization of gambling as predominantly characterized by *strain*, and then on his attempts to answer the following questions:

1. What are the bases for the social disapproval of gambling; and why, in the face of that disapproval, does it persist?
2. What are the social determinants of gambling?

To Devereux, while gamblers *affect* the cognitive detachment of rational, economic man, as in the attention paid to odds and probabilities, and in the cold-blooded reaction to success or failure, the façade hides the fact that each stake placed at hazard subjects the gambler to a

> veritable emotional shower bath ... to the flesh and blood gambler, the situation is full of promise, but it is also full of mystery, and danger, and meaning ... it is also fraught with strain: the conflicting valences and ambivalences of hope versus fear, risk versus security, power versus helplessness, and faith versus doubt are playing complicated melodies within his consciousness. The result is an intolerable, but not necessarily wholly unpleasant, state of tension (p. 695).

Paradoxically, this tension is often deliberately heightened by gamblers, who clearly find it pleasurable as *strain*. But it remains intolerable, and the gambler seeks ways to resolve it. Real pleasure may also lie in tension-*resolution*, which is all the more heightened the greater the strain involved. Gambling is an ordeal which produces tensions which *ought* to be intolerable but are effectively managed by self-discipline:

> it seems obvious that whereas the gambler may 'enjoy' these tensions, he is still fundamentally ambivalent about them. Having once exposed himself to the situation, he takes extraordinary pains to make himself comfortable within it.... Although most of the mechanisms function as accommodation devices, permitting gamblers to make the most of a bad situation ... many of them also figure positively among the basic motivational elements in gambling (p. 743).

Clearly Devereux is here near to formulating the view of gambling as the prototype of action, and what to him are techniques of accommodation are to Goffman 'copings' and 'defences'—the belief in luck, the resort to animism, the investiture of luck as an attribute of people and of particular objects; the mental 'writing-off' of a stake to reduce eventual disappointment; the equation of stakes with business investments or with recreational expenditures; the focus on *odds* (the stake: jackpot ratio) rather than *probabilities* (the number of prizes: number of players ratio) in lotteries; and the belief in 'systems' as distinct from rational calculation of probabilities. Devereux's insistence on the strain and ambivalence inherent in gambling, whilst very close in meaning to Goffman's emphasis on the revelation of character *under pressure*, matches his analysis of strains and ambivalences inherent in the dominant culture. To Devereux, the answer to the conundrum of why gambling elicits such powerful disapproval (to the point of remaining almost wholly illegal in the USA, except in the State of Nevada) and yet persists and even flourishes despite such disapproval, is best sought by analysis of 'fundamental cleavages and ambivalences' within a common culture rather than as the product of friction between conflicting groups and codes. Any adequate theory of gambling should provide *homologous* accounts of the dynamics of gambling as a phenomenon, the dynamic of the social reaction to gambling, both as expressed by different groups and as institutionally based, and of the relationship between the two phenomena. The account which Devereux provides takes him back to Weber's theory of the spirit of capitalism and its relationship to the Protestant ethic.

The structural features of capitalism: an 'open' market; a generalized money system; political order; some *'laissez-faire'*; the institution of contract; and the system of private property, cannot be sustained and operated without certain kinds of motivation on the part of the individual. A capitalist society will seek to standardize as far as possible certain ideal-typical characteristics in its citizens:

1. *Economic self-interest of a 'rational' kind* 'Money', 'profits' etc. are the clear goals of the economic system and should govern economic behaviour. But since men need 'non-logical rules to live by', the economic world must be institutionally separated from the larger social framework, and outside it, its values should not apply, e.g. wives are not to be treated as means to economic ends, judged impersonally, etc.

2. *Competition* For maximal efficiency, the economic system needs high levels of aspirations, effective channels for vertical mobility, ideological stress on equality of opportunity, and a visible correlation between effort and reward. At different stages of capitalistic growth, however, different motivations assume functional priority and are stressed accordingly:

in the early stages of capitalistic growth, the stress on *thrift* ensures
accumulation, and the build-up of wealth needed for capital
formation;

in later stages, the stress on *consumption* ensures expansion;

in all stages, the stress on work-discipline ensures stability of
interaction.

3. *Institutional mechanisms* to bolster the economic system but *at the
same time* to protect the broader systems from its potentially disruptive consequences. Devereux is here presumably referring to such
institutions as the banking and credit systems, which service both
producers and consumers with capital for expansion and consumption yet which operate on the basis of certain criteria whereby capital
flow is processed in more rather than less 'functional' directions.

4. *Cultural definitions* to create and maintain appropriate motivations.
These motivations find their origins in, and help regenerate, the
Protestant ethic:

(a)   as it derived from Calvin, it signalled the decline of the retreat
from the world of monasticism, and the apotheosis of the King-
dom of God on earth;

(b)   it prompted the study of science (cf. Merton's analysis of the seventeenth-century will to know God by his works);

(c)   it stressed reason as God's gift to man;

(d)   and of the individual conscience as productive of economic
freedom;

(e)   its stress on predestination incurred distrust of fellow men not
visibly blessed by membership of the Elect;

(f)   it prompted religious sanctification of work: the 'calling';

(g)   it led to the sanctification of private property, as held in trust and
'stewardship' for God.

*Not all of these elements were new: but Protestantism gave them coherence
and divine sanction.* (d), (f) and (g) in particular have become *residual
values* central to American (to some extent, Western) culture. Sources
of strain, however, are not difficult to pinpoint in this holistic system. It
is not simply that strain originates from sources of conflict *extrinsic* to
the system, as, for example, in the stubborn refusal of merit and reward
to correlate, and in the ironical consequence that virtue has too often
to be its own reward since few others are forthcoming, a state of affairs
which would be more acceptable if the un-virtuous were not so visibly and
numerously blessed instead; or in the strain exercised by the puritan ethic
on the foundations of personality, where rationality vies with illogicality,

and asceticism with hedonism. These strains could *ideally* be accommodated were the Protestant value system sufficiently institutionalized and intensively absorbed, though the cost in guilt, shame and anxiety over a wide area of human behaviour would probably be increased. It is, rather, in the sources of strain *intrinsic* to the role of the Protestant ethic in the rise of capitalism that conflicts more difficult to accommodate arise:

1. The system is inherently frustrating: it generates dissatisfaction in order to expand.

2. Some value-conflict is endemic in capitalism: thrift *v.* consumption; prudence *v.* risk-taking. This value-conflict is particularly acute as the transition is made from early capital-formation to full-blown consumer capitalism, in which the protestant 'vocabulary of motives' loses some of its functionality with regard to the economic system. Wealth as an end-in-itself is stressed far more, and the loss of the 'stewardship' motif leaves conspicuous consumption and status competition as *the* suitable criteria against which 'success' is to be judged. However, the core values of puritanism, whose decline has been prophesied since the 1660s, retain great power: even the irreligious or amoral feel impelled to 'get ahead' as a worth-while goal, irrespective of straight cash rewards; the fruits of success are increasingly suspect as the rise in GNP fails to provide any automatic 'pay-off' in terms of spiritual fulfilment—the hollowness of a purely materialistic success remains one of the great themes of our culture.

3. Some value-conflict is endemic between *capitalism and parent Christianity*: the affective neutrality of the economic order, with its stress on impersonality, self-interest, ambition and competitiveness, clashes with Christianity's central injunctions as to love, humility and self-sacrifice. This conflict is acted out in the dualism between work and the family, as for example in the conflict which arises when the values of the work-place are carried into the home, and vice versa.[13]

4. The development of capitalism towards 'rationality'—via machine technology, systematic economic analysis, scientific market information, bureaucratic business organization, etc.—and away from chance, bold, risk-taking entrepreneurship narrows the scope for initiative to activities defined as disruptive of established business norms and conventions. '*Risk has become a disutility, to be avoided, minimized, or insured against.*' Speculators, when successful, tend to be regarded as immoral, unworthy and *lucky*. However, ambivalence

towards speculation rarely becomes hostility, since to attack it is very close to attacking the entire rationale of the economic system.

'Society' handles these conflicts by structural and symbolic differentiation and segregation. It is broken up into several differentiated sub-systems, each governed by norms appropriate to its own functional requirements. Segregation is comprised of the spatial and temporal separation of these sub-systems, and the symbolic definition of appropriate contexts. Barriers to communication and role segmentation keep these contexts separate. Finally, the over-riding ethical conflict is resolved by ranking different sets of values in terms of some major scheme of allocation. Under this scheme, the major organizing imperatives of capitalism are officially defined as work, routine, thrift, prudence, conservatism, rationality and discipline. Such values as boldness, initiative, risk-taking and the pursuit of chance (shrewd or otherwise) are rated much more dubiously as necessary evils, which cannot be repudiated, but should only fleetingly be identified with, and are generally assigned to 'deviants', or specialists. Competing or threatening values are segregated contextually, 'ideal' values are confined to 'sacred' contexts. Dubious values may generate *sub rosa* contexts—in Devereux's view, this is most appropriate where the structural needs to be met are derived from and created in functional inadequacies and strain *within* the dominant system.

The disapproval of gambling centres around a basic theme: gambling rests on *chance*, and chance is a non-ethical (even *anti-ethical*) basis for the distribution of reward. Hence, its existence is a threat to the rationale in which work, merit and reward are supposed to go hand in hand, and even helps emphasize the extent to which they do not do so. Gambling is thus a threat to a properly ethical orientation, helps break down 'rationality', and fosters superstition and fatalism. In sum, gambling appears to be an *in principle* violation of capitalism. The nub of Devereux's thesis is that, in fact, the values deplored in gambling are by no means peculiar to it or foreign to the broader culture. They may in fact functionally relate to the legitimate economic system. Since these values cannot be attacked in their relation to the latter, it is only with regard to gambling, where the same values crop up in segregated contexts, where they *can* safely be attacked, thus safely 'grounding' the tensions and ambivalences they produce, and simultaneously reinforcing and bolstering the dominant system.

That gambling survives and even flourishes testifies to its meeting of needs, both social and personal, which are not, perhaps cannot be, fulfilled in other ways, at least in capitalist societies.

1. *The protest against budgetary constraints*   Few gamblers realistically suppose that gambling will truly be for them a shortcut to wealth, though it is a convenient pretext for fantasy along these lines. Their gambles are on the whole far too petty and far too limited to be more than a minor break with their budgetary discipline. Yet this break is all-important—for what irks in everyday life are the constant reminders of the needs for budgetary control, of income limitations and the gap between even modest aspirations and reality. In this closed-circuit world, where no dramatic increases in wealth are possible, the gambler can at least protest against the tyranny of the 'budget'. Winnings are usually 'blown' or perhaps rebet, though large prizes may be consumed via more solid purchases generally out of reach except to high income groups. Even if loss ensues, the pleasures of *anticipating* a win can be seen as worth the effort. A chance element is brought into the serious and orderly realm of earned income. But the break is usually carefully controlled, and the stakes kept small *relative* to income.

2. *The protest against rationality*   Many gamblers ignore or choose to suppress even that element of rationality which does obtain in gambling. In such cases, a blow is struck against a rationality which is viewed with resentment as governing too many of life's pleasures, while leaving its central mysteries unsolved

3. *The protest against ethics*   Chance is non ethical: its pursuit therefore entails *some* protest and escape from ethical constraints, especially puritanical ones. The guilt thus engendered, however, frequently involves the gambler in a great deal of self-mystification as to his motives, which he sustains by resort to symbolic refutation and disguise: 'All in fun', etc.

4. *Thrill-seeking*   Gambling involves a cycle of tension accumulation and resolution. The respectable can experience the 'safe deviance' involved in acting out the counter *mores* of daring and risk-taking in a segregated setting, which renders its insecurities 'less real' than those of everyday life. It can thus alleviate anxiety and boredom.

5. *Competitiveness and aggression*   In many forms of gambling, these motivations can be stepped up and indulged behind a 'playful' façade. In such games, rules and settings are provided in which what Goffman terms 'character contests' can be acted without any overlap into 'real life'.

6. *Problem-solving*   Gambling, like crossword puzzles and chess (though with the additional contingency of the stake), provides artificial, short-term, miniature 'capsule' problems—and their

resolution—for those who enjoy them, and who are either starved of them or who perhaps cannot face or solve them in real life. This particular motivation was amplified by Herman[14] in his analysis of horse-track betters as exemplars of displaced decision-making, compensating in gambling for work situations in which they lacked the scope for creative decision-making.

7. *Teleological motivations*   Man imposes moral order on causal order, and generates legitimate expectations thereby. Chance events often run counter to legitimate expectations, dramatizing man's ultimate ignorance and helplessness, and raising anew the problem of meaning. Men are more imbued with legitimate expectations than women due to their far more intensive involvement in the rationalistic rhetoric of the work sphere. Women are thus more 'philosophical', 'intuitive', etc., *not* because inherently so, but because they are more cut off from the moral order of the economic sphere. Chance events, which can only be incorporated in science as symptoms of inadequate knowledge, nevertheless pose problems of meaning which men resolve by resort to transcendental schemes, as in religion, magic and superstition. In our heavily rationalistic culture, gambling is the *only* area in which permissive attitudes towards such notions as luck and superstition prevail. Gambling thus encapsulates the area of mystery diffused throughout life in general but culturally 'silenced' in most institutional areas. It becomes, therefore, a laboratory for probing the meaning and grounds of the self's relationship to things and nature. Since religion imposes a different teleology, based upon an inscrutable deity, gambling is not simply non-religious but *counter-religious*.[15] Gambling signifies a break in the moral closure of the dominant system. 'Am I lucky?' has a *cosmic* significance, but no final answer is possible: hence the gambler is forever 'testing' his luck.

8. *Extrinsic or contextual motivations*
   (a)   The wager always concerns an *event* with its own event—specific interests, e.g. football, horse-racing, etc. Intrinsic interest in the event may precede the desire to stake a bet on its outcome, and may be drawn upon to assuage any guilt feelings that would otherwise stem from gambling.
   (b)   All gambling takes place in some concrete *social setting*, which may attract in other betters for social reasons, a desire to be 'one of the boys', 'not spoil the fun', etc.; 'social gambling' may thus be compared with 'social drinking'. 'Charity' bets are also structured to drag in motivationally neutral players.

(c) *Associations* of a symbolic kind, e.g. racing as the 'sport of kings', and the link between cards and gaming and spas and 'high society' may appeal to players who would otherwise be neutral towards gambling. As Goffman has stressed, commercial entrepreneurs are well aware of the status passage thus provided.

In sum, 'most motivational themes woven into gambling do *not* stem from … "human nature", but are (mainly) derived in a process of interaction with a particular social and cultural environment' (p. 986). To Devereux, the prime sociological determinant of gambling resides in where people stand in relation to this environment. In his view, the 'core culture' of American society remains the economic/religious/ethical synthesis of puritanism. And it is the challenge presented to that culture by secularization, the acquisitive materialism of the full-blown consumer capitalism to which it has given birth and the counter-mores it has thrown up, which accounts for the tremendous inconsistencies and conflicts of American culture.

The old puritan hegemony remains strongest in rural and small-town areas; among the lower middle class; and among protestants. It weakens the more one moves away, in *any* direction, from this centre of gravity. It has tremendous *staying-power*: it has been 'breaking down' since the mid-seventeenth century yet still constitutes the 'official' and approved set of values for modern America (and, for that matter, modern Britain) Its persistence can be attributed to its functional relationship to crucial imperatives of the social and economic structure. It will be more intensively 'carried' by those playing roles most salient for the *transmission* of that culture: not only churchmen, but magistrates, headmasters, and local government officials

The clear implication is that gambling varies *inversely* with the sway exerted by this culture. Among the Protestant middle class, it is likely to be predictable, of very small scope, and within the permissible limits of recreational expenditure. It operates principally as a 'safety valve' which frees the individual temporarily from budgetary constraints. This pattern of occasional and petty gambling is also the norm for the majority, whose dominant patterns of life organization lie outside gambling, though its incidence will grow the more one moves away from the small-town middle-class Protestant matrix.

By contrast, 'heavy' gamblers—those who play with sufficient frequency and for sufficient stakes so that gambling becomes a major focal centre of individual life organization—have no sense of a 'budget'. The role is incompatible with middle-class norms and membership—it is hence a safe target for moralists to condemn 'excessive' rather than 'petty' gambling as 'demoralizing'. Gambling is more habitual the greater the absence of the traditional constraints of middle-class life: i.e. ties to job, family, neighbourhood, church, regular work and incremental income, satisfactory career lines, and *some* visible relationship between effort and reward. Since many of these constraints apply also to the 'respectable' working class, habitual gambling is a *slum* rather than *stable* working-class activity. Gambling of a habitual kind is also more likely in the criminal 'demi-monde', the upper class and the 'beau monde': in the first, 'windfall' spending has status-conferring power; in the second, it represents a ritualized affirmation of superiority; and in the third, where it often *is* excessive, it stems partly from the insecurities about the stability of one's *nouveau riche* status, and partly from the reassurance provided by reassertions of 'character' in fashionable contexts. In all except perhaps the upper-class case, it remains, however, fraught with strain and ambivalence, for 'the problem is not a simple matter of opposing groups and philosophies, and their relative positions of dominance within the community. Much more fundamentally, it is a problem of basic inconsistencies and ambivalences within a common culture, and of basic cleavages within the individual conscience' (p. 769).

Conclusion

There is a certain logical continuity in the three perspectives dealt with above. Caillois provides us with the notion that modern urban industrial societies, among others, have opted for the cultural matrix based on a combination of agonistic and aleatory principles and have largely shed or suppressed the principles of mimicry and vertigo. Goffman suggests that forms of action archetypically embodied in gambling have attained a salience they formerly lacked. And Devereux suggests a socio-historical model within which Goffman's analysis can to some extent be placed: a cultural dynamic in which puritanism vies with alternative world views in a society whose central imperatives are increasingly threatened by the force of their inner contradictions.

The work of Goffman and Devereux is explicitly based upon the relationship between gambling and the American social structure. However, British society shares perhaps the most crucial characteristic germane to Devereux's theorization: a rough similarity in the relationship between the Protestant ethic and the rise, and subsequent development, of capitalism. That immense dissimilarities also obtain between the two societies, and that these make comparative theorization very difficult indeed, should never be forgotten in the application of American-based theories to British society. But that should not serve as a blind to their relevance.

Notes

1. John Huizinga, *Homo Ludens: A Study of the Play Element in Culture*, Routledge & Kegan Paul, 1949; Paladin, 1970.
2. Roger Caillois, *Man, Play and Games*, Thames & Hudson, 1962.
3. Caillois refers to the situation in Brazil in 1958.
4. Erving Goffman, 'Where the action is', in *Interaction Ritual*, Allen Lane, 1972. First published 1967.
5. E. Goffman, 'Fun in games', in *Encounters*, Bobbs-Merrill, 1961.
6. For this and other crucial connections I am grateful to Richard Daventry.
7. Marvin Scott, *The Racing Game*, Aldine, 1968.
8. See D. Matza and G. Sykes, 'Delinquency and subterranean values', *American Sociological Review*, September 1962.
9. W. B. Miller, 'Lower class culture as a generating milieu of gang delinquency', *Journal of Social Issues*, 14 (3), 1958, pp. 5–19.
10. Edward C. Devereux, Jr, 'Gambling and the social structure: a sociological study of lotteries and horse racing in contemporary America', 2 vols, unpublished Ph.D. thesis, Harvard University, 1949.
11. George Homans, 'Bringing men back in', *American Sociological Review*, 1962.
12. Ernest Gellner, 'Concepts and society', in *Transactions of the Fifth World Congress of Sociology*, Washington, 1962, vol. I, pp. 153–84.
13. See, for example, R. M. Titmuss, 'Authoritarianism and the family', in *Essays on the Welfare State*, Allen & Unwin, 1958.
14. Robert K. Herman, 'Gambling as work: a sociological study of the rack track', in *Gambling*, Harper & Row, 1967.
15. But see Jon Halliday and Peter Fuller (eds), *The Psychology of Gambling*, Allen Lane, 1974, for Fuller's introductory analysis of the different reactions to gambling of the Roman Catholic as distinct from the Protestant Church.

Gambling Histories/(Sub)cultures

Introduction

This section provides accounts of gambling history and subcultures. Gerda Reith's "The Pursuit of Chance" provides a historical overview of the commercialization of gambling in the nineteenth century, which has given rise to the popular forms of gambling that we find today. In her "Postscript," she provides a brief history of the ways in which gambling has been represented as "vice," specifically in the European context.

German critical cultural theorist Walter Benjamin wrote on gambling as a particular form of modern, and metropolitan, experience and included many of his observations in his work on the Paris Arcades (Benjamin 1999). In the excerpt from "On Some Motifs in Baudelaire" (from *Illuminations*, 1969), Benjamin provides a discussion of the likeness of forms of gambling with mechanical forms of labor—an observation no less true today when one observes the mechanical, repetitive bodily motions of slot machine players or laboring blackjack dealers in casinos. For Benjamin, (modern) gambling as a cultural form could be said to express aspects of the culture of industrial capitalism, where experience is denigrated; mass production

121

and gambling are expressive of the "atrophy of experience" in commodity capitalism (Benjamin 1973). The "shock of the new" is a feature of life in modernity, but this is experienced against the standardizing forces of industrial production where "the drudgery of the labourer is ... a counterpart to the drudgery of the gambler." While commercialized casino gambling is often marketed as providing "excitement," this representation must be considered against the disparaging reference to large North American casinos as "slot warehouses." Some of the cultural and ideological linkages between gambling and capitalism are taken up, in more contemporary contexts, in the pieces by Nibert and Neary and Taylor in Section Four.

While there are many and diverse gambling subcultures, three articles are provided here that seek to understand the social organization of particular gambling groups. Irving Zola's classic piece provides a functionalist account of "lower class" horse bettors, outlining the sociological significance of the setting for the participants, and the ways in which the gambling activities perform particular functions for the participants. According to Rosencrance (1988, 59), Zola's "research represented a sociological landmark, since the findings were generated from firsthand observations on an ongoing gambling group. He was one of the first researchers to investigate the practices of regular gambling participants in an actual gaming situation. Although impressed with the rational betting practices of horse race gamblers, Zola considered gambling a 'lower-class behaviour pattern and implicitly a deviant activity.'" While Zola's piece emphasizes the class basis of the activities, he also touches on aspects of gender as they pertain to this particular male gambling subculture, but leaves them undeveloped.

The predominantly female world of bingo provides interesting points of comparison for understanding the relationship of gambling and gender, as settings—whether the horse betting bar or the bingo hall—are constructed as gendered domains, where men and women construct interpretations of, and identities around, their gambling activities. The settings, as sites of sociability, can be thought of as play worlds that provide a respite from the demands and expectations of everyday life. The spatial decontainment of gambling occurring in many countries, and furthered by the development of varieties of Internet gambling, could be considered in terms of its effects on the gendered segregation of various types of gambling activities.

In her ethnographic investigation of on- and off-track horse race betting, Joan Allen draws upon the work of sociologist Pierre Bourdieu to consider the habitus of racetrack bettors and their orientations to economic action. Allen also provides insights into the shifting stratification of the activity. While one subcultural feature of this form of gambling is its exclusivity, based on "a cultural stock of knowledge," another feature is that "gambling losses are the cost of membership." For Allen, bettors in these environments are resisters, but not rebels, within the existing socio-economic structure of flexible and insecure employment. (For a Bourdieu-influenced analysis of the social structural aspects of poker play, see Potter 2003.) References for other gambling histories and subcultural analyses (poker, female lottery players, and so on) are listed in the Suggestions for Further Reading section.

References

Benjamin, Walter (1969) *Illuminations*, ed. Hannah Arendt, trans. Harry Zohn. New York: Schocken Books.

_____ (1973) *Charles Baudelaire: A Lyric Poet in the Era of High Capitalism*, trans. Harry Zohn. London: New Left Books.

_____ (1999) *The Arcades Project*, ed. Rolf Tiedemann, trans. Howard Eiland and Kevin Mclaughlin. Cambridge, MA: Harvard University Press.

Potter, Gary (2003) "*Sui Generis* Micro Social Structures: The Heuristic Example of Poker," *Canadian Journal of Sociology* 28(2): 171–202.

Rosencrance, John (1988) *Gambling Without Guilt: The Legitimation of an American Pastime*. Pacific Grove: Brooks/Cole.

CHAPTER 5

The Pursuit of Chance

GERDA REITH

The Nineteenth Century: Playing with Numbers

In the nineteenth century, various changes occurred which dramatically changed the face of gambling. The commercialisation of games of chance during the Industrial Revolution converged with the commercialisation of economic life and with the denouement of probability theory—the science that had 'tamed' chance. As the calculation of odds became more fully understood, the nature of the games played changed so that they became more amenable to commercial organisation, more homogeneous and, ultimately, more 'sellable'. It is in this period that the recognisably modern forms of the casino, the public racetrack and the mechanised slot-machine first appeared. In place of the huge sums wagered by the individuals of the seventeenth-century aristocracy came more democratic games for many players organised around modest stakes which allowed for prolonged rather than excessive play. These conventions are still visible in the gambling behaviour of today....

The Casino

In the industrial discipline of the nineteenth century, the separation of the spheres of leisure and work, which had been ongoing for the previous two hundred years, was finally consolidated. Such a development was particularly evident in the gambling arena which at this time was disengaged from its surrounding social life and organised into distinct, highly commercial spheres. The casino was perhaps most representative of the trend; it emerged in the second half of the century as a collection of public rooms devoted exclusively to gambling, away from its earlier formulation as a dancing saloon and summer-house (McMillen 1996).

In this period, the fashionable watering places of the aristocracy continued to be popular gaming centres and were supplemented by the development of a series of resorts throughout Europe, in which gaming houses—now casinos—were the central attraction. This development of what Turner and Ash (1975) describe as a decadent and extravagant 'Pleasure Periphery' in the French Riviera included Nice, Cannes and Monte Carlo, or, as the French called them, 'the World, the Flesh and the Devil'. Baden Baden, Bad Homberg and Wiesbaden were small localities whose deliberate expansion turned them from health spas into gambling resorts (a process which would be perfected in the twentieth century in the creation of Las Vegas).[1] Although generally exclusive, the commercialism of at least some of these resorts bore witness to some degree of democratisation. In Bad Homberg and Wiesbaden the great mass of visitors were of the middle and lower-middle classes, causing Steinmetz to note with disapproval that 'the general run of guests is by no means remarkable for birth, wealth or respectability' (Steinmetz 1870, p. 213).

By the end of the nineteenth century then, dramatic changes had transformed the nature of commercial games of chance, overseeing the formulation and codification of what we now recognise as modern casino games. Just as the economic imperatives of emergent capitalism were reflected in the growth of commercial gaming houses, so the games themselves came to reflect the social logic of a capitalist system. It is these changes we shall turn to next.

Cards

In cards, traditional games that revolved around various kinds of patterns and sequences, such as the gaining of suits, trumps and tricks or the making of combinations like flushes and marriages in melds, were being supplanted by a new form of game. This new style of play was based on the arithmetical values of the cards in their properties as individual numerals, and forms the basis of all modern casino card games.

Such a shift was made possible by an experiment of the Woolley Card Company. In 1884, in keeping with the statistical spirit of the times, they printed a numerical value at diagonally opposite corners of each card in what was known as an *indice* (Hargrave 1966, p. 189). As numbers 'poured into' the nineteenth century, so they poured on to packs of cards. With this seemingly trivial development, the face of cards was literally changed forever. The value of these new cards was depicted by a bold unequivocal number, no longer represented by an image, which was necessarily more ambiguous. The authority of the number was not open to interpretation; it was a fact. Not only was it instantly more striking, in the new style of games, but the number on these cards was also more *important* than all the other information they contained. In games based on the speedy calculation of number, it was vital that each card be immediately recognisable to the player. A simple digit in each corner met this requirement in a way that a more vague pictorial depiction never could. Given the commercial environment of the new games, it was not only important that players should quickly recognise their cards, but equally, that other players should *not*. Until now, the backs of cards had been either plain or decorated with a single one-way design. This meant that they could easily be marked, or, in the case of decorated cards, arranged with some backs upside-down, for example, to distinguish high cards from low ones, face cards or suits (Sifakis 1990, p. 57). The possibilities for cheating with such packs were unlimited; even a player with a poor memory could not fail to recognise specific cards from their backs after a while. In the nineteenth century this golden age of cheating was ended when companies began experimenting with uniform back designs so that, by the end of the century, simple two-way designs had rendered cards indistinguishable. These twin developments made cards at once both unique *and* standardised. As instances of 'the same kind of thing' they were indistinguishable, yet within this general category each one was recognisably the bearer of a specific value. Similarly, in the wider society, *l'homme moyen* was characterised by his representativeness of all others of his kind. At the same time, these characteristics came out in individual properties which displayed as much statistical variation in their particular sample as, say, the individual cards in their particular pack. In the nineteenth century then, both *l'homme moyen* and the new-style cards came to be represented as individual variations on a single, standard theme. By streamlining them, the numbering and standardisation of cards was integral to the development of new styles of play, loosely termed banking games, which evolved into casino games.

In the game of *vingt-et-un* (which later grew into pontoon, and then the casino game of blackjack), and *chemin de fer* (baccarat), suits and court cards were irrelevant, numerical values paramount. From their regal status as the most important cards in the pack (many bearing the image of their owner), in baccarat, picture cards were dethroned and given no value at all. A similar fate befell court cards in blackjack which were also democratised and given a single numerical value—ten. Consonant with the statistical spirit of the times, cards in these games, like all the others in the pack, were only important through their representation of number. Both games were basically arithmetical exercises whose principle was to assemble cards whose value did not exceed a specified number: twenty-one in blackjack, nine in baccarat.

With their emphasis on calculation and the irrelevance of any distinctions other than numerical ones, we can see in these games the mirror of the commercial, statistical interests of an increasingly capitalist society.

It was not only in card games that the dynamic relation between games and society was apparent. The early probabilists used games of chance to develop their theorems, and their discoveries in turn affected the games they experimented with. As probability became more fully understood, the games it was applied to became more complex, so that games and theory developed by feeding off each other in an ever more complex dialectic of theoretical and practical application.

Roulette

The game of E–O (even–odd) was popular during the eighteenth century in fashionable resorts like Bath and consisted of a wheel with forty cups alternately marked E for even and O for odd. A ball was released as the wheel rotated and players wagered whether it would fall into an E or O pocket. Pascal experimented with a similar ball and wheel device, but did not, as is sometimes claimed, 'invent' roulette. The game as we know it today was actually developed in the nineteenth century when the French addition of thirty-six numbers and colours to the wheel revolutionised the simplicity of the original game (Sifakis 1990, p. 256). The impact of the addition was enormous, greatly increasing the variety of betting available from one to ten, with different odds on each. Players could still bet odd or even, but now any single number or combination of numbers as well. The addition of numbers made roulette a far more exciting and complex game that its rather staid predecessor, and, with the inclusion of a zero (two in America), also made it a very commercial one, for when the ball landed in this pocket all bets were won by the house.

Dice

Advances in the study of probability, aided by commercial developments, also transformed the ancient game of hazard into a faster, more streamlined version known as craps. Hazard had been played in the same way for centuries, with players betting that they would eventually throw a certain number with two dice, throwing until they did and then continuing to throw until the original number or 'point' came up again. However, since the odds of certain numbers coming up before others varies, a competent player would require a basic understanding of probability to play well. Such an understanding of averages and odds in relation to dice simply did not exist until the seventeenth century, with the result that most bettors did not comprehend all the ways various combinations could be achieved with two dice. For hundreds of years 'A hustler could indeed have made a fortune' (Sifakis 1990, p. 147)!

In France, hazard was known as krabs (after the English word for a throw of two or three), later corrupted to creps or craps. When introduced into America by French colonists, a modified version grew in popularity among black slaves in New Orleans and took its name from French craps (Scarne 1974, p. 39). In the nineteenth century, the incorporation of ever-increasing knowledge about odds and percentages reformulated the rules of hazard into what we now know as the modern game of craps. Dozens of types of bets now became available to the player, with many more variations of each type.

With its multitude of betting strategies and combinations of odds, the appeal of craps as a lucrative commercial game was obvious. To entice it into the casino, further modifications were made, which changed its structure yet again. A small charge was made by the house whenever the thrower made two or more passes. This was known as a take-off game. Next, the house took the opposition against the thrower, so that *all* players now had to bet the dice to win against the house. A simple table layout bearing the six and eight, the field, win and come bets, was drawn up to play on, exactly half of the table layout today. The house now took its cut 'not as a direct charge, but indirectly and less noticeably by offering short odds so that it gained a percentage' (Scarne 1974, p. 41). A further development offered players the opportunity to bet the dice to *lose*, as well as to win. In effect, every bet could now be either for or against the dice or the house. Betting opportunities were doubled, and the craps table reflected the change, changing its shape from a semi-circle to a full oval, with one half a mirror image of the other. The game of craps at times appeared as the archetypal game of probability theory, with its complex permutations of odds, pay-offs and house percentages, a working (or rather *playing*) example of theoretical construction.

Gaming Machines

One of the most significant developments of the nineteenth century was the introduction of gaming machines. The Industrial Revolution had laid the foundations for automatic gambling when a London bookseller created a vending machine in order to sell proscribed literature, although the introduction and proliferation of coin-operated machines did not appear on a mass scale until the last quarter of the nineteenth century. During this period of technological innovation, the automation of the leisure sphere was complemented by that of the workplace, so that the development of what Costa (1988) called 'automatic pleasures' was symptomatic of the automation of the wider world of the late nineteenth century.

Being born into a secular, industrial age, the ancient image of divinatory drama which ran as a leitmotif through most older, established types of gambling would not be expected to feature in this young form. However, slot-machines did manage to maintain the link of all gambling with the sacred, for the automated machines from which the early gaming machines drew their inspiration were originally used for fortune-telling. In the white heat of the technological revolution, the art of divination was not made redundant, it was simply mechanised.

The earliest gaming machines invited individuals to discover their future by means of a spinning pointer, a card dispenser or some kind of animated figure (Costa 1988, p. 21). Their patents stated that they could be used either as divinatory devices or as games of chance, although in an attempt to limit their appeal, both forms of amusement were only allowed to return tokens such as cigarettes and chewing-gum and not cash, as prizes. The design of many of these first machines was simply an automatic adaptation of already existing games—hence the popularity of images of cards and horses, as well as of pieces of fruit, from which the term 'fruit machine' is derived.

The first automatic three-reel machine, or 'one-arm bandit'—the prototype of our modern gambling machines—appeared in San Francisco in 1905 when Charles Fey developed a device in which a handle was pulled to spin three wheels and, if a winning combination was made, a stream of nickels poured out into a tray below (Sifakis 1990). The one-armed bandit (which Fey patriotically named the Liberty Bell) was developed in a rush of pioneering individualism typical of the Gold Rush state of that time. Throughout the nineteenth century risk-hungry Californians, whom Findlay (1986) called 'people of chance', were possessed of a dynamic, innovative spirit which culminated in their westward advance across Nevada and the subsequent creation of Las Vegas. It is no wonder then that in an era of technological advance, it was these 'people of chance' who gave slot-machines their final configuration and so created the most modern form of gambling device.

Horses

The numerical preoccupation of the nineteenth century, along with technological innovation, was to dramatically change the face of horse-race betting. The role of newspapers became steadily more important in this process, along with newly established journals such as *Sporting Life* (1863) and *Sporting Chronicle* (1871), disseminating tips, news and forecasts to a hungry audience. For the second time in history,[2] print encouraged—and was encouraged by—gambling. This plethora of sporting journals fed the voracious public appetite for information, and was crammed full of facts and statistics about horses, races, jockeys and odds. Aided by the electronic telegraph system, which meant the press could quickly publish results and starting odds, and the establishment of a credit network, the 1880s saw the development of large-scale organised betting (McKibbon 1979; Chin 1991; Clapson 1992; Munting 1996). In a move which the aristocracy would have fought bitterly against, railways helped to make horse-racing a national spectator sport by sponsoring races and linking towns (and therefore fee-paying punters) to courses.

These nineteenth-century developments revolutionised racing. Now thoroughly democratised, its status was reversed from being the prerogative of the rich elite to being a massive working-class entertainment. Under the sway of commercial developments, spectacular, individual upper class bets disappeared and popular betting between a mass of punters—both on and off the track—took over. Such bets were subject to strict odds: the chances of a horse winning a race were calculated by taking many variables into account, and expressed in a numerical equation. Pay-offs were equally subject to strict calculation, based on the amount of the original stake and the odds on the particular horse. No longer a simple 'gentlemen's agreement' for a set amount, betting became a complex contract between bettors and central race organisers, relayed through a number of betting shops. The physiognomy of betting also changed: from being private and limited it became public and widespread. Its role in providing a source of excitement as well as hope of financial gain at a time when poverty made alternative forms of economic advance, such as saving, unrealistic, meant the popularity of betting was assured (Chinn 1991; Clapson 1992). This broad place in working-class culture was reflected in an increasing dissemination of bookmakers, runners and their agents on street corners, in the backs of shops and throughout private homes. The first betting house opened in Britain in 1847: three years later over 400 existed, and almost immediately, an 'epidemic of gambling was declared to have attacked even the poorest class' (Neville 1909, p. 99). Needless to say, a wave of legislation—the Street Betting Acts of 1853, 1874 and 1892—swiftly appeared, designed to eradicate all forms of popular, working-class betting.[3] Again, it was too late. The popular tide of betting simply went underground, largely unaffected by the 'suppression', until betting shops were reinstated in 1961.

The New Style of Play

The highly numerical nature of all these forms of gambling was consonant with the statistical milieu of the nineteenth century, and was particularly suited to the imperatives of commercial organisation. These developments were to change the experience of play forever. In gaming halls and public houses, people played all day and all night at games like craps and roulette, which had been refined and organised in such a way as to include a 'space' for a 'player' who always won—the house, or dealer. Commercialisation encouraged dealers to rely increasingly 'upon the more predictable and more secure profits provided by odds fixed inflexibly in their favour' (Findlay 1986, p. 91). Realising the impossibility of winning the games they operated, these commercial interests—'the house'—made a brilliant move whereupon winning was assured. Rather than participate in a game, they removed themselves from it altogether and allied themselves with the very law that told them they had to lose. By placing themselves actually *within* the probability equation, they could simply sit back and await the profits which would inevitably result from favourable odds once the law of large numbers was given enough time to come into effect. Backed by the indomitable authority of probability, the house could not possibly lose. On the other hand, the alliance of both odds *and* house edge meant that individual gamblers could not possibly win. They found themselves competing against an invisible opponent with a permanent place at every table and unlimited resources. What is more, they were forced to play against the house, for this element of competition had been built into commercial games and was now inherent in their structure. Gamblers no longer played against each other but against the house, whose invisible impersonal force mirrored the imperatives of economic behaviour, the 'invisible hand' of market forces.

Commercialisation also changed the social composition of play by encouraging less wealthy players. As wagers became smaller, participation dramatically increased. Hiding behind the iron laws of probability, gambling entrepreneurs made profits, not by increasing the stakes of games, but by increasing the volume of players. They might not make 'leviathan' wagers, but these more modest players could be relied on to place a regular flow of smaller bets, so guaranteeing the profits of the house.

As its nature was transformed through commercialisation, the experience of gambling itself underwent a change. Participation, not winning *per se*, became paramount and, as Findlay points out, this changed the meaning of gambling itself: 'Players still hoped to win ... but they looked upon betting more as a commodity of sale ... as an experience worth purchasing with losing wagers' (Findlay 1986, p. 92). In a capitalist economy, gambling had finally succumbed to commodification. But this was no ordinary commodity, for it had a unique experiential component. Players continued to gamble, but as much for the thrills and excitement of the game itself as for financial rewards. Fast games and moderate stakes became valued for prolonging participation and therefore maximising excitement. Now that their main motivation was participation, gamblers played simply to *play*, for: 'Next to the pleasure of winning is the pleasure of losing, only stagnation is unendurable' (Bankcroft, in Findlay 1986, p. 94).

Out of this process of commercialisation emerged a distinctive type of gambling which, despite distinct differences, also shared common elements with the gambling of the seventeenth-century aristocrat. Crucially, for both, money served only as a measure of play, unimportant in itself. The high stakes of the aristocracy showed their indifference to money and as such, the aristocrat played to *participate*, never to win. The low stakes of the nineteenth-century gambler at first seem far removed from the leviathan bets of the aristocrat, but they served a similar purpose: to lengthen participation. Again, money was only a *means* of play, and the indifference of these latter gamblers to it stemmed from their participation in play itself. These orientations are also to be found in modern gamblers...

The commercialisation of gambling was to gather speed over the following hundred years, overseeing its gradual development into a widespread, popular and—just as importantly—legal form of consumption. In this process centuries of condemnation which had persistently attempted to eliminate games of chance from social life—and especially the social life of the poor—were finally overturned. Before going on to look at the victory of commercialism ... we shall first briefly review the nature of the criticisms it vanquished.

Postscript: The Vortex of Vice

Various forms of suppression and condemnation ran alongside the long history of gambling, a persistent and largely ineffectual distraction to the serious frivolity of play. From the Roman prohibition of gaming during the Saturnalia to the medieval bans for the 'protection of archery', the practice of gambling was accompanied by a succession of specific legislative prohibitions and enforced by individual rulers. The criticism was generally constructed in terms of the threat that the chaos of chance, deliberately courted in gambling, posed to the order of society, with various eras expressing this fear in different terms. In the Reformation it was regarded as the embodiment of sin, in the Enlightenment it epitomised irrationality; the Industrial Revolution of the nineteenth century legislated against its disruptive nature, so defining it as a crime, while today its negative effects have been medicalised, and excessive gambling viewed as 'pathological' or a sign of illness.

In the sixteenth century, just as gambling reached unprecedented popularity, attempts to forbid it suddenly became more draconian, and previously disparate criticisms were focused into a coherent and intensely vitriolic assault. The fulminations of a new Protestant bourgeoisie against the 'Satanic vice' of gambling made the relatively perfunctory criticisms of feudal monarchs appear quite lenient. What had been tolerated by the Catholic Church was not by the Reformed one.

By the seventeenth century, the condemnation of gambling was virtually a shibboleth of the Protestant bourgeoisie. A stream of invective poured from the pulpits of the Reformed Church, damning gamblers for their idleness, greed, blasphemy and superstition. Games of chance displayed a blatant disregard for the values of the Protestant by divorcing the creation of wealth from the efforts of labour, and reducing it instead to the vicissitudes of chance. Hard work in a calling, glorification of God through earthly activity and an ascetic disregard for material gain were shamelessly flouted by the actions of the gambler and thus existed as a blasphemous assault on the divine order. Although Christianity had always recognised the virtues of work, with the Protestant emphasis on worldly activity, its value was 'mightily increased' (Weber 1990, p. 83). Especially for Calvinists, diligent labour in a calling became defined as a virtuous activity, which would result in gradual, predictable, and, more importantly, *virtuous* rewards, whereas idleness and the squandering of precious time were regarded as the epitome of vice. The activities of gamblers represented the antithesis of these virtuous pursuits. Their reaction to wealth was one of *immediacy* and *extremity*. Instead of the slow accumulation of money, appropriated for the future through saving and investment, gamblers' financial transactions were located firmly in the present, where their economic standing could soar to immense riches or plummet to penury, out of all proportion to physical effort. Such fluctuations were seen to disrupt the ideal of a meritocratic social balance, and, in the new moral-economic climate, gambling represented unearned, therefore immoral and illegitimate wealth. It was this orientation that prompted the Puritan John Northbrooke's outburst in his *Treatise against Dicing, Dancing, Plays and Interludes* (1577) against 'turpe lucrum, filthie gaine' which, because it was 'gotten in a trice over the thumbe, without any trafficke or loan' was simply regarded as theft,[4] and would be counted against its winners 'at the last daye of judgment if they repent it not' (Northebrooke 1843, p. 125).

It was the waste of time and money inherent in gambling that preoccupied the Protestant bourgeoisie during the period when, for the bourgeois, the systematic use of both were necessary for capitalist expansion, and for the Protestant, both were appropriated by God. The rational management of time and money was a prerequisite of the labour discipline which, in the early years of capitalist development, was pursued mainly by the bourgeoisie. Thus the aristocracy were attacked primarily for their profligacy; their gambling for its wastage of *money*, while the poor were attacked for their laziness; their gambling for its wastage of *time*. Both committed a further sin by deliberately invoking the hand of God for the resolution of a trivial matter, to 'decide the lot': a blasphemous profanation of the Divine Will. Robert Burns' (1786) later description of playing cards as 'the devil's picture beuks' indicates the continued association of the former with supernatural, and specifically diabolical, forces.[5] In this climate, gambling was the apotheosis of sin, and the gambler was defined primarily as a sinner.

In the Enlightenment climate of moderation and reason, the idea of the sinful nature of play was replaced by an emphasis on its embodiment of irrationality. The loss of reason which the Enlightenment saw inherent in gambling was anathema to its ideal of rational progress, and was a particularly abhorrent form of madness. Gamblers made a decision which no reasonable human was supposed to be able to make—they *intentionally* gave up their most precious faculty, their mark of humanity, for nothing more tangible than the vicissitudes of chance. Such a rejection of reason was contrary to the very nature of civilisation itself which was based, if anything, on the minimisation of chance and uncertainty. Writing in this Enlightenment tradition. Montesquieu stated that God forbade anything which disturbed reason, and, since they produced 'anxiety and frenzy', he especially denounced games of chance (Montesquieu 1977, p. 120).

It was not that the Enlightenment condemned gambling *per se*, but rather that it feared the disequilibrium that could be brought about by *excessive* gambling, an attitude which should be seen in the context of broader eighteenth-century ideas about rational recreation. The valuation of productive work, associated with the Protestant ethic, was also an important Enlightenment ideology, condoned by moralists and enshrined in the legislation of the period. However, the need for 'reasonable' rest and recreation was also recognised, and the balance between this and productive work admired as rational and godly (Dunkley 1985, p. 64). As legitimate recreation, games were not bad in themselves, but the danger lay in their being pursued to excess. When this happened, the reason of the individual was overcome by extremes of emotion and, worse, the social order was disrupted. In removing the principles of moderation and balance on which the individual and society rested, the entire edifice of ordered society was threatened by chaos. Thus gamblers tended to be criticised for their possession of extreme characteristics—of idleness or excess, profligacy or greed, caprice or persistence—traits which always stood to one side of the balanced, moderate bourgeois ideal. As such, the figure of the gambler was generally perceived as a member of the aristocratic or labouring classes. Jean Dusaulux in *De la passion du jeu* (1779) described the physiognomy of the gambler who succumbed to passion in this way, existing as 'an empty space within the triumphant discourse of reason' (Dusaulux, in Kavanagh 1993, p. 36). In this state, the gambler was the incarnation of that primordial chaos, *Xaos*, which, as 'an abyss or empty space', characterised 'the first state of the universe'....

... The horror of the gambler's rejection of reason continued to run as a leitmotif through the nineteenth century. However, by this time the essential irrationality of gamblers had become less important than their ability to work. The industrialising west needed labour power; time became a commodity only slightly less precious than money, and gambling squandered them both. The problems of the organisation of labour were encapsulated in the figure of the (working-class) gambler—an individual who refused to acknowledge the importance of time,[6] money or disciplined labour.[7] This figure also represented the forces of urban disruption: the perceived menace of 'the masses' out of control, roaming the cities and indulging in various immoral and illegal activities, threatening the orderly balance established by the bourgeoisie. At a time of economic and political upheaval, when British productivity was being overtaken by Germany and the USA and British soldiers were being defeated in the Boer War, gambling became a convenient scapegoat. It was blamed for declining industrial production, military failure, and general social unrest: in short, for no less than the decline of the Empire (Dixon 1991). It was in this climate that various philanthropists and moral reformers launched an ideological attack on all forms of working-class gambling. In 1890, a coalition of Nonconformist Protestant Churches formed the National Anti-Gambling League (NAGL), whose stated aim was:

> Nothing less than the reformation of England as regards the particular vice against which our efforts are aimed.... There is humiliation in the thought that the chosen Anglo Saxon race, foremost in the civilisation and government of the world, is first also in the great sin of Gambling. (Bulletin of NAGL 1893, vol. 1, no. 7, p. 1)

It was an apocalyptic vision, conceived virtually as a crusade which would halt economic decline and defend civilisation. Now, the imperative of the Protestant ethic became institutionalised in laws forbidding games of chance along with other 'vices' such as alcoholism, drug use and prostitution. Caught up in a tide of patrician legislation, the gambler, and anyone else who promoted the activity, became a criminal. The Gaming Act of 1845 removed gamblers from the protection of the law by making gambling transactions unenforceable, while the Street Betting Acts of 1853, 1874 and 1906, and the Betting and Loans (Infants) Act of 1892 actively penalised them and all those associated with them. These laws attempted to prohibit working-class gambling by outlawing betting in public places—broadly defined as anywhere individuals might congregate to play at games of chance. Advertising or promotion of such games was also prohibited, and gamblers, agents and bookmakers fined for participating. Later, the definition of 'place' was made even wider to include any equipment (such as desks and even the boxes which bookmakers stood on) necessary for gambling transactions. None of these prohibitions applied to the betting of the upper classes: members of clubs were excluded from its strictures, as were any individuals who were able to gamble without 'resorting' to public premises (Dixon 1991, p. 39).

In these statutes, we can see the bourgeoisie struggling with the problem of labour discipline and the wider fear of irrational disorder. To this end, attempts were made to sweep examples of roaming irrationality out of sight and (at least until a decision in 1892 reversed it), gamblers were frequently convicted under the terms of the Vagrancy Act. If found gambling in the street, individuals were to be 'committed to gaol as rogues and vagabonds' and sentenced to corporal punishment and hard labour. Such confinement was the remedy for the 'common and intolerable nuisance' of young boys and men 'sprawling about the pavement ... and playing ... at games of chance' (Steinmetz 1870, p. 427). Imprisonment confined gamblers to a secure space where, out of public sight, they could no longer exist as an affront to the rational industrial society around them, and where they would learn the value of hard work and self-discipline.

The nineteenth century also laid the groundwork for the twentieth century's medicalisation of the 'pathology' of gambling. Metaphorical treatments of gambling as a 'disease', a 'virus' or a 'leprosy' which attacked the healthy individual were taken almost literally and applied to its 'contagion' of the social body—and especially the social body of the lower classes (Dixon 1991, p. 60). By the beginning of the era, it was believed by certain members of the British Medical Association that gambling was explained by the nervous tension of *fin-de-siècle* Britain and psychologists began to concern themselves with the possibility of the hereditary effects of the 'disease' (Brenner and Brenner 1990, p. 141).[8] It is in this era of social Darwinism that we can see the genesis of the medical psychology of the twentieth century, including the origin of the contemporary search for a gambling 'gene'. Such perspectives were voiced in the hysterical polemic of reformers like Anthony Comstock, who wrote that gambling was a trap set by Satan which swept morals 'with the fury of a tornado' into the 'vortex of vice'. Comstock could barely articulate his loathing, which poured out in a stream of rhetoric: 'That human beings can sink so low seems almost incomprehensible.... These are caricatures of true men. They are forms hollowed out by this cursed traffic until there is nothing but form left' (Comstock 1961, pp. 58, 83). This image of gamblers as individuals somehow 'hollowed out' and devoid of humanity should be familiar by now: we have encountered it already as the primordial abyss—*Xaos*—and again in the Enlightenment's description of the gambler as an empty space within the discourse of reason. In this, it was the articulation of the perceived threat posed to civilisation by its opposite—chaos—of which the gambler was the prime representative.

However, various forces were pressing on this critical tradition, and would gradually, over the next hundred years, erode centuries of condemnation. By the twentieth century, gambling would find itself in the peculiarly ambivalent position of being, on the one hand, condemned and regulated, and on the other, tolerated and even encouraged. As the century progressed, the latter position came increasingly to dominate the former....

Notes

1. See Russell T. Barnhart's history of these gambling centres, as well as the illustrious figures who frequented them (Barnhart 1983).
2. The first being the dissemination of cards from the printing presses of the fifteenth century.
3. Both of these Acts were hugely unpopular, and largely unworkable. In particular, the 1906 legislation represented an attempt by anti-gambling lobbies (mainly the National Anti-Gambling League) to outlaw all forms of working-class gambling. In this, it has been described as 'a monstrous sample of class legislation' (Clapson 1992, p. 31), which ensured that gambling was to remain a political issue.
4. A similar view of gambling as theft was observed by Marco Polo to be held by the ruler Kubilai Khan, who told his subjects: 'I have acquired you by force of arms and all that you possess is mine. So, if you gamble, you are gambling with my property' (Polo 1958, p. 161).
5. Although, interestingly, some Protestant sects found them unproblematic, with, for example, John Wesley's Methodists utilising scriptural playing

cards to reveal the will of God, and Zinzedorf's Pietists advocating the use of the lot for the same purpose (see Hargrave 1966, p. 324).

6. On this point, a description by Steinmetz of a congregation of the poor around a lottery drawing is instructive. His criticism (and Steinmetz writes as a dispassionate observer, not an ideologue) was excited not so much by the possibility that the crowd may have stolen money to enter the draw, but by their very *presence*, which meant that they were 'stealing from their masters' time' (Steinmetz 1870, p. 402).

7. Or the importance of leisure, for on top of all this, gambling also challenged notions of 'rational leisure': the idea that free time should be used to 'better' the individual, especially if that individual was working class and therefore, presumably, more in need of 'betterment'.

8. Similar criticisms were levelled against the opium habits of the industrial working classes; see Berridge and Edwards (1981).

References

Arnold, P. (1993) *The Book of Games*, London: Hamlyn Chancellor Press.

Ashton, J. (1898) *A History of Gambling in England*, London: Duckworth.

Barnhart, R.T. (1983) *Gamblers of Yesteryear*, Las Vegas: Gamblers Book Club Press.

Baudrillard, J. (1990) *Cool Memories 1980–1985*, London: Verso.

Brenner, R. and Brenner, G. (1990) *Gambling and Speculation: A Theory, A History and a Future of Some Human Decisions*, Cambridge: Cambridge University Press.

Cassirer, E. (1944) *An Essay on Man: An Introduction to a Philosophy of Human Culture*, New Haven, CT: Yale University Press.

Chinn, C. (1991) *Better Betting with a Decent Feller: Bookmakers, Betting and the British Working Class 1750–1990*, Hemel Hempstead, Herts: Harvester Wheatsheaf.

Clapson, M. (1992) *A Bit of a Flutter: Popular Gambling and English Society 1823–1961*, Manchester: Manchester University Press.

Comstock, A. (1961) *Traps for the Young*, Cambridge: Belknap Press.

Costa, N. (1988) *Automatic Pleasures: The History of the Coin Machine*, London: The Bath Press.

Cotton, C. (1674) *The Compleat Gamester*, London: R. Cutler.

Culin, S. (1896) *Chess and Playing Cards*, New York: Arno Press.

Cunningham, H. (1980) *Leisure in the Industrial Revolution*, London: Croom Helm.

Dixon, D. (1991) *From Prohibition to Regulation: Bookmaking, Anti-Gambling and the Law*, Oxford: Clarendon Press.

Dunkley, J. (1985) *Gambling: A Social and Moral Problem in France 1685–1792*, Oxford: The Voltaire Foundation.

Findlay, J. (1986) *People of Chance: Gambling in American Society from Jamestown to Las Vegas*, Oxford: Oxford University Press.

Hargrave, C. (1966) *A History of Playing Cards*, New York: Dover Publications, Inc.

Harris, M. (1972) *Sport in Greece and Rome*, London: Thames and Hudson.

Hibbert, C. (1987) *The English*, London: Grafton Press.

Huizinga, J. (1949) *Homo Ludens*, London: Routledge and Kegan Paul.

Kavanagh, T. M. (1993) *Enlightenment and the Shadows of Chance: The Novel and the Culture of Gambling in Eighteenth-Century France*, Baltimore and London: The Johns Hopkins University Press.

McKibbon, N. (1979) 'Working class gambling in Britain 1880–1937', *Past and Present*, 82, 147–178.

McMillen, J. (ed.) (1996) *Gambling Cultures: Studies in History and Interpretation*, London: Routledge.

The Mahabharata (1975) trans. J.A.B. von Buiten, Chicago, IL: University of Chicago Press.

Mauss, M. (1954) *The Gift: Forms and Functions of Exchange in Archaic Societies*, trans. J. Cunnison, London: Cohen and West.

Mitchell, R.J. and Leys, H.D.R. (1950) *A History of the English People*, London: Longmans Green.

Montesquieu, C. (1977) *Persian Letters*, trans. C. J. Betts, Harmondsworth: Penguin.

Munting, R. (1996) *An Economic and Social History of Gambling in Britain and the USA*, Manchester and New York: Manchester University Press.

Neville, M. (1909) *Light Come, Light Go*, London: Macmillan.

Northbrooke, J. (1843) *A Treatise Against Dicing, Dancing, Playes and Interludes*, London: The Shakespeare Society.

Parlett, D. (1979) *The Penguin Book of Card Games*, Harmondsworth: Penguin.

Pepys, S. (1976) *Diaries*, vol. 9, ed. R.C. Latham and W. Mathews, London: G. Bell and Sons.

Plato (1934) *Laws*, trans. A.E. Taylor, London: J.M. Dent and Sons.

Scarne, J. (1974) *Scarne on Dice*, Harrisburg, PA: Stackpole Books.

Seneca (1986) *The Apocolocyntosis of the Divine Claudius*, trans. J.P. Sullivan, Harmondsworth: Penguin.

Sifakis, C. (1990) *The Encyclopedia of Gambling*, New York: Facts on File.

Steinmetz, A. (1870) *The Gaming Table*, vol. 2, London: Tinsley Brothers.

Stone, L. (1967) *The Crisis of the Aristocracy 1558–1641*, London: Oxford University Press.

Strayer, J.R. (1982) *A Dictionary of the Middle Ages*, New York: Scribner.

Suetonius (1958) *The Twelve Caesars*, trans. R. Graves, Harmondsworth: Penguin.

Sullivan, G. (1972) *By Chance a Winner*, New York: Dodd, Mead.

Tacitus, C. (1982) 'The Germania', in M. Mattingly (trans. and ed.) *The Agricola and The Germania*, Harmondsworth: Penguin.

Taylor, E.S. (1865) *The History of Playing Cards, with Anecdotes of their use in Ancient and Modern Games. Conjuring, Fortune-Telling and Card Sharping*, London: John Camden Hotten, Piccadilly.

Traill, H.D. (ed.) (1893) *Social England: A Record of the Progress of the People from Earliest Times to the Present Day*, London: 1893–1897.

Turner, L. and Ash, J. (1975) *The Golden Hordes: International Tourism and the Pleasure Periphery*, London: Constable.

van Rensselaer, J.K. (1893) *The Devil's Picture Books: A History of Playing Cards*. New York: Dodd, Mead and Co.

Veblen, T. (1925) *The Theory of the Leisure Class: An Economic Study of Institutions*, London: Allen and Unwin.

von Hagen, V. (1962) The Ancient Sun Kingdoms of the Americas. London: Thames and Hudson.

Weber, M. (1990) *The Protestant Ethic and the Spirit of Capitalism*, trans. T. Parsons, London: Unwin Hyman.

CHAPTER 6

On Some Motifs in Baudelaire

WALTER BENJAMIN

... The shock experience which the passer-by has in the crowd corresponds to what the worker "experiences" at his machine. This does not entitle us to the assumption that Poe knew anything about industrial work processes. Baudelaire, at any rate, did not have the faintest notion of them. He was, however, captivated by a process whereby the reflecting mechanism which the machine sets off in the workman can be studied closely, as in a mirror, in the idler. If we say that this process is the game of chance, the statement may appear to be paradoxical. Where would one find a more evident contrast than the one between work and gambling? Alain puts it convincingly when he writes: "It is inherent in the concept of gambling ... that no game is dependent on the preceding one. Gambling cares about no assured position.... Winnings secured earlier are not taken into account, and in this it differs from work. Gambling gives short shrift to the weighty past on which work bases itself." The work which Alain has in mind here is the highly specialized kind (which, like intellectual effort, probably retains certain features of handicraft); it is not that of most factory workers, least of all the work of the unskilled. The latter, to be sure, lacks any touch of adventure, of the mirage that lures the gambler. But it certainly does not lack the futility, the emptiness, the inability to complete something which is inherent in the activity of a wage slave in a factory. Gambling even contains the workman's gesture that is produced by the automatic operation, for there can be

143

no game without the quick movement of the hand by which the stake is put down or a card is picked up. The jolt in the movement of a machine is like the so-called *coup* in a game of chance. The manipulation of the worker at the machine has no connection with the preceding operation for the very reason that it is its exact repetition. Since each operation at the machine is just as screened off from the preceding operation as a *coup* in a game of chance is from the one that preceded it, the drudgery of the laborer is, in its own way, a counterpart to the drudgery of the gambler. The work of both is equally devoid of substance.

There is a lithograph by Senefelder which represents a gambling club. Not one of those depicted is pursuing the game in the customary fashion. Each man is dominated by an emotion: one shows unrestrained joy; another, distrust of his partner; a third, dull despair; a fourth evinces belligerence; another is getting ready to depart from the world. All these modes of conduct share a concealed characteristic: the figures presented show us how the mechanism to which the participants in a game of chance entrust themselves seizes them body and soul, so that even in their private sphere, and no matter how agitated they may be, they are capable only of a reflex action. They behave like the pedestrians in Poe's story. They live their lives as automatons and resemble Bergson's fictitious characters who have completely liquidated their memories.

Baudelaire does not appear to have been a devotee of gambling, although he had words of friendly understanding, even homage, for those addicted to it. The motif which he treated in his night piece "Le Jeu" was part of his view of modern times, and he considered it as part of his mission to write this poem. The image of the gambler became in Baudelaire the characteristically modern complement to the archaic image of the fencer; both are heroic figures to him. Ludwig Börne looked at things through Baudelaire's eyes when he wrote: "If all the energy and passion ... that are expended every year at Europe's gambling tables ... were saved, they would suffice to fashion a Roman people and a Roman history from them. But that is just it. Because every man is born a Roman, bourgeois society seeks to de-Romanize him, and that is why there are games of chance and parlor games, novels, Italian operas, and fashionable newspapers." Gambling became a stock diversion of the bourgeoisie only in the nineteenth century; in the eighteenth, only the aristocracy gambled. Games of chance were disseminated by the Napoleonic armies, and they now became part of "fashionable living and the thousands of unsettled lives that are lived in the basements of a large city," part of the spectacle in which Baudelaire claimed he saw the heroic—"as it is characteristic of our epoch."

If one wants to examine gambling from the psychological as well as the technical point of view, Baudelaire's conception of it appears even more significant. It is obvious that the gambler is out to win. Yet one will not want to call his desire to win and make money a wish in the strict sense of the word. He may be inwardly motivated by greed or by some sinister determination. At any rate, his frame of mind is such that he cannot make much use of experience.[1] A wish, however, is a kind of experience. "What one wishes for in one's youth, one has in abundance in old age," said Goethe. The earlier in life one makes a wish, the greater one's chances that it will be fulfilled. The further a wish reaches out in time, the greater the hopes for its fulfillment. But it is experience that accompanies one to the far reaches of time, that fills and divides time. Thus a wish fulfilled is the crowning of experience. In folk symbolism, distance in space can take the place of distance in time; that is why the shooting star, which plunges into the infinite distance of space, has become the symbol of a fulfilled wish. The ivory ball which rolls into the *next* compartment, the *next* card which lies on top are the very antithesis of a falling star. The period of time encompassed by the instant in which the light of a shooting star flashes for a man is of the kind that Joubert has described with his customary assurance. "Time," he says, "is found even in eternity; but it is not earthly, worldly time.... That time does not destroy; it merely completes." It is the antithesis of time in hell, the province of those who are not allowed to complete anything they have started. The disrepute of games of chance is actually based on the fact that the player himself has a hand in it. (An incorrigible patron of a lottery will not be proscribed in the same way as the gambler in a stricter sense.)

This starting all over again is the regulative idea of the game, as it is of work for wages. Thus it is highly meaningful if in Baudelaire the second-hand—"la Seconde"—appears as partner of the gambler:

> *Souviens-toi* que le Temps est un joueur avide
> Qui gagne sans tricher, à tout coup! c'est la loi![2]

In another place, Satan himself takes the place of this second. The taciturn corner of the cave to which the poem "Le Jeu" relegates those who are addicted to gambling undoubtedly is part of his realm.

> Voilà le noir tableau qu'en un rêve nocturne
> Je vis se dérouler sous mon oeil clairvoyant,
> Moi-même, dans un coin de l'antre taciturne,
> Je me vis accoudé, froid, muet, enviant,
> Enviant de ces gens la passion tenace.[3]

The poet does not participate in the game. He stands in his corner, no happier than those who are playing. He too has been cheated out of his experience—a modern man. The only difference is that he rejects the narcotics with which the gamblers seek to submerge the consciousness that has delivered them to the march of the second-hand.[4]

> Et mon coeur s'effraya d'envier maint pauvre homme
> Courant avec ferveur à l'abîme béant,
> Et qui, soûl de son sang, préférerait en somme
> La douleur à la mort et l'enfer au néant![5]

In this last stanza Baudelaire presents impatience as the substratum of the passion for gambling. He found it in himself in its purest form. His violent temper had the expressiveness of Giottc's *Iracundia* at Padua.

Notes

1. Gambling invalidates the standards of experience. It may be due to an obscure sense of this that the "vulgar appeal to experience" (Kant) has particular currency among gamblers. A gambler says "my number" in the same way as a man about town says "my type." Toward the end of the Second Empire this attitude prevailed. "On the boulevards it was customary to attribute everything to chance." This disposition is promoted by betting, which is a device for giving events the character of a shock, detaching them from the context of experience. For the bourgeoisie, even political events were apt to assume the form of occurrences at the gambling table.
2. Keep in mind that Time's a rabid gambler / Who wins always without cheating—it's the law!
3. Here you see the hellish picture that one night in a dream / I saw unfolding before my clairvoyant eyes; / And, over in a corner of this silent cave, / Myself I saw, hunched up, cold, mute, and envying, / Envying these people their tenacious passion.
4. The narcotic effect that is involved here is specified as to time, like the malady that it is supposed to alleviate. Time is the material into which the phantasmagoria of gambling has been woven. In his *Faucheurs de nuits* Gourdon de Genouillac writes: "I claim that the mania for gambling is the noblest of all passions, for it includes all the others. A series of lucky *coups* gives me more pleasure than a non-gambler can have in years.... If you think that I see only profit in the gold that falls to my share, you are mistaken. I see in it the pleasures that it gets me, and I enjoy them fully. They come too quickly to make me weary, and there are too many of them for me to get bored. I live a hundred lives in one. When I travel, it is the way that an electric spark travels.... If I am stingy and reserve my bank notes for gambling, it is because I know the value of time too well to invest them as other people do. A certain

enjoyment that I might permit myself would cost me a thousand other enjoyments.... I have intellectual pleasures and want no others." In the fine notes on gambling in his *Jardin d'Épicure*, Anatole France presents a similar view.

5. And my heart took fright—to envy some poor man / Who ran in frenzy to the sheer abyss, / Who, drunk with the pulsing of his blood, preferred / Grief to death, and hell to nothingness.

CHAPTER 7

Observations on Gambling in a Lower-Class Setting[1]

IRVING KENNETH ZOLA

Introduction

Studies in gambling have often focused on matters of individual pathology[2] and yet, on a number of psychological dimensions, no significant differences have been found between gamblers and non-gamblers.[3] Part of the explanation for this lack of difference is the fact that so widespread an activity as gambling can be "many things to many people."[4] Another reason is that while recognized as one of our major social problems, gambling also constitutes a major American paradox, fluctuating as it does between tolerance and condemnation, with a very thin line drawn between legal and illegal forms.[5] It seems obvious that to exist in this state of limbo, gambling must serve important social and psychological functions. This [chapter] is an attempt to delineate some functions of one form of gambling as it occurs in a small lower-class residential community.

The Setting

East Side was a small working-class area within a large New England city. Successive waves of immigrants once flooded the streets, but in recent years the population had become more stable, predominantly Italian with smaller segments of Eastern European Jews and Poles. As part of an anthropological field team, the observer spent several months in East Side, becoming an habitué of meeting places, bars, and taverns and participating actively with several sub-groups. His identity and role were, however, unknown to the community. Most of the observations on gambling were made at Hoff's Place, one of many taverns along the main street of East Side. It was a bar and grill frequented mostly by Italians and Poles who were either present or former residents of the immediate neighborhood. At Hoff's one type of gambling predominated: off-track betting where wagers are made with a "bookie" or "bookmaker." Though the men spent much of the day here, virtually all over thirty were married and relatively few were unemployed. Some were on vacation or on their day off. Some worked nearby, drove delivery trucks or taxis and dropped in and out while ostensibly working. Others worked on split shifts and visited between them. Still others had jobs which ended early in the day or started very late.

One of the first observations made at Hoff's was the dissociation of the bar from other spheres of the men's social life. Violent reactions often greeted any invasion or intrusion.

> One wife became concerned when her husband did not return for supper and so she called and asked the bartender about his whereabouts. Although he knew, he gruffly denied any knowledge. Whereupon she burst into tears, pleading with him, "Please don't tell him I called, 'cause he would beat the shit out of me if he knew."

> "One day my mother sent me after my father. It was gettin' late. When he came home was he mad! He kicked her all the way down Lawrence Street and back and said to her, 'Don't you never send anyone after me here. No buts, anything can wait till I get here.' And she never did it again."

A further distinction was made between gambling and other spheres of economic activity. A man was not expected to share his profits with his family and was thought a "damn fool" if he even told them of his winnings. The fact that most gambling activities take place in a context institutionally defined as "recreation" helps to emphasize this dissociation from ordinary utilitarian activities.[6]

A Group in Process

The men at Hoff's, however, did not constitute a group in the formal sense. Regardless of when in the day one entered, the men in the bar seemed only to be whiling away their time drinking, barely taking notice of one another. On any day the pattern would be quite similar.

> In the first booth, Hal reads the *Morning Telegraph* while Sammy naps in a corner. Behind them Smiley studies the Star Racing Section and Silvio looks at Phil's Armstrong. Phil, the bookie, sits at the bar going over his slips. Beside him Nick stares blankly at the wall and not two stools away Johnnie and Joe sip beer without speaking. Further down the bar sits an unidentified man and next to him stands Al, the bartender, gazing aimlessly out the window as he washes glasses.

Ten minutes before the start of each race, however, this changed. Men who were outside came in and those previously silent began to talk.

> "Do you think he's got a chance?"
> "I don't like the jockey."
> "He likes muddy tracks."
> "He's long overdue."
> "They've been keeping him for this one."

Some of the remarks were addressed to one's neighbor, some to no one in particular. The bookie began to take bets. Gradually, the conversation became more agitated.

> "Get your bets in while you can," kids Phil. Silvio turns and hands him five dollars while Smiley shakes his head, "He'll never win." Sal laughs, "Here Phil, a bean on the nose, number seven, a 'sure thing.'" "I'm the one who's got that," roars Al, reaching into his pocket and taking out a twenty-dollar bill. "Twenty thousand on number one. C'mon Irv, stick with me." "Uh, uh," I answer, "You're bad news, I like Principio." Meanwhile Phil proceeds gingerly down the bar as others turn and bet, rise from their booths or motion him toward them.

Some last-minute bets or changes were made and then the race began. If the race was broadcast, a group formed near the radio. The cheering was restrained and muffled.

"See, look what's happening."
"Why is the jockey holding him back?"
"Just watch him finish with a spurt."

Regardless of whether the race was broadcast, the announcement of the winner always led to the same discussion. All attention focused on the winners.

"How did you figure it?"
"How come you picked her?"
"How did you know?"

And their answers....

"I've noticed that jockey...."
"Did you see the weight shift? Well,..."
"I figure they've been saving him...."
"His last time out, he...."

If no one picked the winning horse, the discussion was still the same, but more philosophical and not as prolonged. Within five minutes, however, it was quiet again.

> Al is back washing glasses. Silvio and Smiley return each to a separate booth. Hal goes outside and Sammy goes back to sleep. Joe and Johnnie leave but Paul and Charlie replace them at the bar sipping beer without speaking. Nick studies the chart for the next race. Sal stands at the door looking at the sky and Phil, slips of paper in his hand, walks slowly toward the phone.

Once more they appeared to be strangers ... until the next race.

Yet gambling is more than a mode of communication. It creates a bond between the men—a bond which defines insiders and outsiders. This function of gambling first became apparent when a newcomer arrived at Hoff's.

> Joe did not live in East Side, though he was distantly related to one of the bookies. He worked on a nearby construction gang and gradually began to patronize Hoff's. At every opportunity, he would come in, order a drink, and sit at the bar or in one of the empty booths. Although he was through work at 4:00 p.m., he often remained until 5:00 or 6:00. When he offered to buy someone a drink, he was gently, but firmly, refused. All he gained was an occasional nod, until, in an off-hand manner, he asked

questions about the races, horses, odds, and ways to bet. At first he bet the choices of others and then finally his own. Only when he started betting did others begin to interact with him, respond more than monosyllabically, and "allow" him to join them as they sat at the bar or in the booths.

For the younger residents of East Side, gambling seemed a way of preparing them for later adulthood. A number of teenagers always hung around Hoff's, and, although they were not allowed in the bar to drink, they were welcome to place bets. It was during such times that they first initiated conversation with the younger men (19–21)—a preliminary step in "anticipatory socialization."

Thus, even though someone might appear at the same time every day, or the same day every week, this was insufficient to designate one a "member," a "regular," or an "insider." At Hoff's, this was accomplished only by off-track betting—an activity which served as the entrance fee, defining membership and initiating newcomers.

The Preservation of Group Attachment

Three observations made by Devereux in his analysis of gambling and the social structure are relevant here: (1) Although the making of a wager polarizes the field and artificially creates the gambler's bond of interest in the event, it does not follow that winning money is the dominant motivational force; (2) many gamblers go to great lengths to deny their emotional involvement in specific events; (3) the importance and relevance of competition to gambling varies with the social context in which it occurs.[7] Each of these observations was found to hold true for Hoff's, but here in East Side they have yet a secondary function. In de-emphasizing emotionality, monetary gain, and competition, not only were several basic sources of hostility often emanating from gambling eliminated but, at the same time, attachment to the "group at Hoff's" was thereby reaffirmed.

While the excitement accompanying any sporting event was present, it was restrained. The extremes of overexcitement and depression were both negatively sanctioned. On more than one occasion, a person who went "over the line" when he won was called "nuts" or told to stop "acting like a jerk," or if one persisted in bemoaning his "hard luck," he too was reprimanded. Even overconcern during a race or contest was regarded with skepticism.

Donnie was disturbed about the ball game—he had bet $10 on the outcome. He would get up, pace back and forth, sit down again. Each time he asked questions about the ability of the players or the manager. "Do you think he knows what he's doing?" As he returned to his seat once more, Mario shook his head indicating Donnie. He commented on his nervousness, adding, "After all, it's only money."

While these men cared when they lost, such depression was remarkably short-lived, perhaps until post-time of the next race. Little systematic effort was made to retain one's winnings. These men never stopped while ahead, nor reduced or even maintained the size of their bets after having won. If a person was ahead at the end of the day, it was more likely because there were no more races than through any conscious effort to accumulate profits. At Hoff's, there was no prototype of the conservative gambler who quit while ahead. People who did were disliked, and not only by the bookies. Instead of admiring them, the regulars shook their heads and called them "cheap bastards." One would have to increase the bet continually in order to gain any substantial amount of money, and yet there is still the problem of a stopping or cutting-off point. The following legend is illustrative of this:

> Bob was relating the experiences of an old East Sider. "I know a guy who won a $100,000. First here and then he wanted to gamble so badly he flew to New York and then back here and kept losing till he had nothing." "Yeah," added Spike, "it could happen. You lost twenty G's and figure you've still got eighty, so you take another shot, and finally you've got nothing."

Thus, if no limit, no matter how theoretical, exists then monetary gain *per se* becomes an indefinite goal and one impossible of attainment. Finally, individual competition was almost non-existent. Within the group itself, members were not explicitly compared with one another as being better or worse players. In part to salve the wounds of defeat, and to share the fruits of victory, there was the common practice of mutual treats where the winner paid for the drinks of his closer acquaintances.

Particularly striking was the shift of competition from within the group to "the system." There was continual talk of "beating the system," "cracking the system," "not letting the system beat you." While this ostensibly referred to the scheme or principle governing the results of races, the actual hostility was more often expressed against the agent of that system—the bookie. The group complained that "he can't be hit" or dubbed him "the undertaker," and alluded to how they would "like to bury him ... in an avalanche of losses."

Joe told of one bookie. "Why, you know why that son-of-a-bitch makes more money than anyone else? It's because all the bettors hate his guts, so they make all bets with him, even 'hot tips' just in the hope they'll break him."

"Remember the time that 'Happy' bet 20-20-0 on a long shot and won. Do you remember Sam's face? I thought he would bust a gut."

"Well, I took care of that bookie. I bet $5 on the fifth and kept betting it all on each race. By the eighth, he had to close up shop."

In this situation, the bookie served a dual function. As the personification of the system they were trying to beat, he facilitated the shifting of competition from within the group to outside the group; and by serving as the target for their hostility, he also became an integrating force of the group—their scape-goat.

Thus the de-emphasis on thrill, money, and competition not only prevented the individual member from becoming too involved with his own personal success and failure; it also made him more dependent on the group and reinforced his attachment to it and the rewards which it alone can bestow—prestige and group recognition. To understand these rewards, it is necessary to examine their dispensation.

Systems of Betting and the Prestige Hierarchy

As depicted in the opening illustration, at Hoff's all available attention and admiration was focused on those men who had chosen winners. Everyone clustered about them, prodded them to reveal the basis of their choice, praised them on their good judgment, and regarded their subsequent opinions highly. Rewarding someone in this manner assumes that he has *done* something to merit such an action. Not all types of gambling warrant such behavior. In the "numbers" or "policy game" where full rein is given to hunches, omens, dreams, and where a person may have his own special number and play it day after day, year after year, no one is congratulated on his ability if he wins, nor asked to explain the rational basis for his choice; he is rather congratulated on his good fortune or luck. In short, methods of selection and the social rewards for winning reflect a conception of the numbers as a game of chance, whose outcome is beyond human control and comprehension, explainable only in terms of luck, fortune, or fate.[8]

The methods and social rewards of off-track betting reflect a different assumption, i.e., the existence of an underlying order, a principle which can be figured out and mastered by a skilled observer.[9] While segments of the larger society deny this in their educational and legal attempts to eliminate gambling, there is hardly a single major newspaper which does not publish the opinions of at least one professional racing expert. As a rule, the latter not only names his choices but gives his reasoning. This was similar to the behavior of the bettors at Hoff's, who consulted with the winners or joined in a general discussion to explain the results, to figure out why it happened or what factors had not been sufficiently considered.

Not all criteria for making decisions were equally regarded. Basically, there were two positively valued modes, one subtype of these, and one devalued mode. Generally, an individual was characterized by his reliance on a particular mode, though it was possible that he might use more than one method on any given day. The four systems were differentiated not only by their basis of selection but also by the degree, amount, and quality of attention and recognition the group bestowed on the successful user of such methods.

Handicapping, the method which elicited the highest respect, was based on some pragmatic system of integration of available information such as past performances of horses and jockeys, weight shifts, post positions, track conditions, etc. Using any available factual data, there was an attempt to *figure out* one's choice. Calling an individual a "handicapper" was the highest compliment that could be paid. When someone wanted information about a particular horse or race, the "handicappers" were the ones to whom questions were directed. Moreover, their opinions were solicited even though their total losses might actually outweigh their gains.

> At one time, I hit upon a system of betting a number of horses in combination. For three straight days, I won the daily double and in the next five days, at least one of my choices won while the other finished second or third. Each of these bets, however, was only for fifty cents and thus the net profit on each day was between five and ten dollars and after the first three days I lost. For this eight-day period I was operating at a loss, and yet for the next few weeks I was consulted by other bettors and kidded by the bookies as being "too good." One even joked about barring me.

Thus, it seems apparent that the "handicapper" gains and retains prestige not because of monetary profits or a preponderance of winners, but because he has demonstrated some technique or skill enabling him to select winners or at least come close.

The "hot tip" was the second positively valued mode. It was based on the use of "inside information," facts about the horses not published or known to the general public. Though the knowledge was supposedly secret, "hot tipsters" usually revealed its possession. For only in so doing could they be acknowledged by the group. While the method of selection is a rational one, the distinguishing feature is *access* to information and not the exercise of any particular skill. This fact was recognized by the men at Hoff's and though they would ask tipsters, "Got anything hot?" "Any inside dope?" their seeking of advice would not usually go beyond this. Nor were the personal choices of such men given undue weight or consideration unless they had also achieved some recognition as handicappers.

The "hedge" is more complex and seems to be a subtype of the above two methods. One or more of the following statements usually introduced the "hedge."

> "You saw me give that to Spike and Angelo and the others and I told them it would win and then I go and bet on another. Whatta dope!"

> "I couldn't decide which one of these would win so I didn't bet any."

> "I had him [the winning horse] but I had to do an errand before I got here so I arrived too late to bet."

> "Remember how I figured it out at home and picked number three to win but then I came here and saw the Armstrong so I bet the six. If only I hadn't seen 'the Arm.'"

The groundwork was usually laid before the race and the sequence was often as follows:

> Before: "I like Ocean Rock but Principio is long overdue and that blasted Pilot's Express is always a threat with Hobbes aboard."

> After: The fact that he bet Ocean Rock is ignored. "See, what did I tell you, that son-of-a-bitch Hobbes brought him in. I told you that would happen."

These remarks not only covered the bettor if his choice did not win, but also communicated to the group, "See, I also picked the winner, even though I didn't play it." For the most part, it succeeded. The group listened to the "hedgers," included them in the discussion of the results, and so allowed them to share to some extent the rewards of picking a winner. Considering their verbalization, it also seems likely that acceptance hinged on the presumption that the basis of their "unbet" choice was really handicapping or a "hot tip."

At the bottom of this prestige ladder was the hunch or random choice bet—lowest because it embodied a denial of the rationality which underlies the concept of "system" and hence "figuring out" of race results. Although "hunch betting" was chided as a "woman's bet" it was difficult to ignore if it produced a winner. Congratulations might be offered, but the reasoning behind the choice was never seriously solicited nor was future advice sought. The underlying attitude toward this technique was best shown when it produced a loser.

> Jack bet on a dog called Cerullo because it was the name of a local hockey player. When it finished second, he was furious. "Damn it, that's what happens when you only have a bean [a dollar]—if I'd had more, I'd have bet him for a second too." He barely uttered this when his friends began to tease him. "Say Mickey Mantle is running in the third and Williams in the ninth." They harped on the "why" of his bet. Jack fought back, shouting, "You wouldn't act that way if the shoe was on the other foot." But this only encouraged them. They continued berating him till he began to sulk and finally walked out.

Only in "hunch" betting and only when it lost did such hostility occur in the group.

The Functional Aspects and Satisfactions of Betting

A rational-cognitive dimension seems to pervade these methods of selection. Since the races were considered capable of human understanding, this emphasis on rationality reflected and manifested the idea of understanding. By using these methods, the players were "beating the system." The "system," which they frequently mentioned, referred to more than a principle underlying the races but rather to life or fate. Miller claims that many lower-class individuals feel that their lives are subject to a set of forces over which they have relatively little control and that furthermore this world view is associated with a conception of the ultimate futility of direct effort towards a goal.[10] Gambling can help deny this futility, as illustrated by the response of one "regular."

> Joe continually talked about "hitting it big." Today was no exception as he spoke of just missing a $1000 double. I looked at him quizzically, "You know you always talk about your ship coming in. Do you ever think it will?" Startled, he raised his head and without looking at me, muttered, "No ... but what else have I got besides this?" [betting on the races].

By "beating the system," outsmarting it by rational means, these men demonstrated they *can* exercise control and that for a brief moment they *can* control their fate. Off-track betting is thus a kind of escape. It denies the vagaries of life and gives these men a chance to regulate it. At Hoff's, there was an emphasis on rewards rather than punishments, on how much can be gained rather than lost. One was rewarded by increased attention and recognition when he won but never punished or ignored when he lost except when the very structure of the group was threatened. "Hunch" betting was just such a threat because it not only denied the concept of an underlying order but also was a way of admitting defeat, of granting that everything *was* beyond one's control.

Recognition was the supreme reward of the winner. By competing against the system rather than against themselves, however, recognition was no longer a scarce commodity, for theoretically there was no limit to the number of winners. Thus, wherever possible success and recognition were shared, whether by extending the definition of winners in the acceptance of "hedgers" or sharing the fruits of victory by "mutual treats." One regular revealed the meaning of being a winner when amid the talk and praise of his selection, he yelled, "What do you think I am, a nobody?" It was a statement so appealing that it was taken up as a byword and used over and over again by the group. In some ways, it was an insightful joke, for in picking the winner and becoming the center of attention, the winner leaves the realm of the nobody for the realm of the somebody.

Conclusion

Although betting doubtless serves many idiosyncratic needs, much of its structure, function, and persistence can be understood only by an examination of the social context in which it occurs. Gambling offers these men more than a means of recreation, just as Hoff's offers them more than just a place to drink. Though such betting may produce neither recreation nor monetary gain, this does not necessarily mean that it is a sterile, non-productive, or even dysfunctional activity. As many observers have pointed out, these men are aware of the major goals and values of middle-class society but are either unwilling[11] or incapable of achieving them by the use of the ordinary methods.[12] However, as recent empirical[13] and theoretical[14] literature has demonstrated, deviance may be more than a symptom of dysfunctional structures. For these men, gambling may be a way of harnessing or channeling their otherwise destructive frustrations. Instead of lashing out at society, they lash out at "the system." In this sense, gambling may be an activity which helps reinforce and preserve some of the major values of the larger social system. At Hoff's they *can* "achieve" and *can* gain recognition for their accomplishments—by exercising skill or knowledge in the selection of horses.

Moreover, these goals of achievement and recognition can be aspired to with few of the conventional risks. In the society at large, one's success or failure alters and affects one's whole way of life while here it is completely incidental to it—a reflection of the isolation of gambling from other spheres of life. Here there is an emphasis on rewards rather than punishments, on gains rather than losses, on being a "somebody" and not a "nobody." For these men, gambling, or at least off-track betting, is not simply the flight, the withdrawal, or the escape as so often claimed. By making success and recognition possible, it allows the players to function in the larger society without suffering the consequences of the realization that they indeed have little else.

This [chapter] is necessarily limited by the way the observations were made and thus depicts only one small but significant slice of the social context of gambling—the relation of bettors to one another. Unfortunately little was known of the lives of these men outside this particular setting, so no explanation is possible of how or why the groups at such places as Hoff's originated nor of the origins of gambling in general. As with so many other phenomena, the sources or causes have long faded into the background and may even be unimportant. This [chapter] is but a single case study—an attempt to delineate some of the possible reasons for the persistence of gambling and some of the functions it may presently serve. Whether similar observations hold for different settings[15] and for different types of gambling will have to be settled by further empirical and more systematic investigations.

Notes

1. This report is part of a study entitled "Relocation and Mental Health: Adaptation Under Stress," conducted by the Center For Community Studies in the Department of Psychiatry of the Massachusetts General Hospital and the Harvard Medical School. The research is supported by the NIMH, Grant #3M 9137-C3. The author wishes to acknowledge Edward Ryan and Leonora K. Zola for their repeated readings and criticisms, and Frances Morrill, Stanton Wheeler, and George H. Wolkon for their valuable suggestions.
2. Edmund Bergler, *The Psychology of Gambling*, New York: Hill and Wang, 1957; and "The Gambler—A Misunderstood Neurotic," *Journal of Criminal Psychopathology*, 4 (1943), 379–393.
3. James Hunter and Arthur Bruner, "Emotional Outlets of Gamblers," *Journal of Abnormal and Social Psychology*, 23 (1928), 38–39; and Robert P. Morris, "An Exploratory Study of Some Personality Characteristics of Gamblers," *Journal of Clinical Psychology*, 13 (1957), 191–193.

4. Edward C. Devereux, Jr., "Gambling and the Social Structure—A Sociological Study of Lotteries and Horse Racing in Contemporary America," unpublished doctoral dissertation, Harvard University, 1949.
5. Herbert A. Bloch, "The Sociology of Gambling," *American Journal of Sociology*, 57 (1951), 215–222; and "The Gambling Business: An American Paradox," *Crime and Delinquency*, 8 (1962), 355–364.
6. Devereux, *op. cit.*
7. Devereux, *op. cit.*
8. Gustav G. Carlson, "Number Gambling—A Study of a Culture Complex," unpublished doctoral dissertation, University of Michigan, 1939; and Devereux, *op. cit.*
9. Devereux, *op. cit.*
10. Walter B. Miller, "Lower Class Cultures as a Generating Milieu of Gang Delinquency," *Journal of Social Issues*, 14 (1958), 5–19.
11. *Ibid.*
12. Albert K. Cohen, *Delinquent Boys*, New York: The Free Press of Glencoe, 1955; and Robert K. Merton, *Social Theory and Social Structure*, Rev. and Enl. Ed., New York: The Free Press of Glencoe, 1957, Chaps. IV and V.
13. Robert A. Dentler and Kai T. Erikson, "The Functions of Deviance in Groups," *Social Problems*, 7 (1959), 98–107.
14. Lewis A. Coser, "Some Functions of Deviant Behavior and Normative Flexibility," *American Journal of Sociology*, 68 (1962), 172–181; and Kai T. Erikson, "Notes on the Sociology of Deviance," *Social Problems*, 9 (1962) 307–314.
15. Robert D. Herman, "Gambling Institutions: The Race Track," unpublished manuscript presented at the 1963 Meeting of the Pacific Sociological Association.

CHAPTER 8

Entertainment or Imprudence?

An Ethnography of Female Bingo Players*

R. MACLURE, J. D. SMITH, S. L. WOOD,
R. LEBLANC, J. LI, AND A. M. CUFFARO

Introduction: Women and Gambling

Legal gambling venues have proliferated across North America over the last two decades. Evidence indicates that with substantially increased opportunities to gamble, more and more people are availing themselves of these opportunities. In Ontario, for example, between 1992 and 1998 the average annual spending of individual gamblers rose more than 300 percent (Marshall 2000). Concurrent with this increase in gambling activity has been an increase in the incidence of problem gambling over the last twenty years (Shaffer et al. 1999). While research into the factors underlying problem gambling remains relatively limited, and tends to focus on the psychology of individual problem gamblers within the framework of a medical model, there are indications that problem gambling is also a function of social context and peer-related behavior. As different groups are attracted to different types of gambling, so too it seems that problem

---

* The research project reported on in this chapter was funded by the Ontario Problem Gambling Research Center.

gambling varies from one group to another. One dimension on which such differences have been observed is gender.

The socialization processes that are unique to women have been widely documented in feminist literature of the last three decades, and it is now widely accepted that the life experiences of women are differentially shaped by their socially defined gender roles (e.g., Lips 1989; Matlin 1993). Issues of power and dependency are integral to gender socialization. Regardless of divisions of culture, region, and class, women have generally retained a status that is subordinate to that of men. In all societies, women have assumed ascribed roles to which they have been ingrained since childhood. Inevitably such socialization has determined the ways in which women perceive and respond to their immediate social surroundings. Consequently, to understand women's actions, the choices they make, and the directions they pursue, it is now generally acknowledged that due regard must be paid to the unique socialization processes of women and to the discrete perspectives that women have of their own situations.

Until recently, however, research into gambling failed to account for a gender perspective. No doubt this has been due in large part to the popular assumption that gambling is essentially a male pastime, and that problem gambling is an affliction that is detrimental mostly to men (Ettore 1989; Lesieur and Blume 1991). Within the last fifteen years, however, a number of published studies have examined gambling practices of women as a distinct population and attempted to explain how their socially defined gender roles and lived experiences affect those practices. These accumulated studies have all generally indicated that women's involvement in gambling is distinct from that of men in several significant ways. On average women tend to start gambling at a later age than men and follow different developmental trajectories to gambling. In general, too, women gamblers choose games that reflect their positions of minimal power in what are basically patriarchal societies. Studies by Grant and Kim (2002) and by Hing and Breen (2001) have demonstrated that women tend to be drawn to games that are determined by chance alone, particularly bingo and slot machines. In contrast, men are more often involved in games that require greater background knowledge and increased skill levels, such as blackjack, horseracing, and sports betting. According to these researchers, this gender difference in the appeal and selection of gambling venues is due to a pronounced fatalism that is characteristic of many women gamblers. This is reflected in the tendency among female gamblers to believe that they possess limited ability and almost no possibility of controlling and otherwise altering the forces that determine and constrain their life experiences (Ibid.).

In a similar vein, Lester's (1980) study of college students who gamble revealed that women tended to engage regularly in games of sheer chance such as lotteries and slot machines, while men were drawn more to games of skill such as poker. A key factor in women's selection of games appeared to be an orientation toward external loci of control—i.e., reliance on factors above and beyond one's own self to generate particular desired outcomes (Lester 1980). Yet another critical factor in drawing women to particular forms of gambling is a desire to escape loneliness and to engage in a recreational activity with peers. As Hing and Breen (2001) have argued, integration into the relatively secure social world of gambling venues often serves as an antidote to boredom. Hong and Chiu (1988) arrived at similar findings in their study of female gambling. In their view, gambling preferences can be partially predicted on the basis of gender differences that reflect "the different culturally approved images of men and women" (667).

Among the most popular forms of female gambling is bingo. While research on bingo is as yet relatively scarce, a number of notable studies (Brown and Coventry 1998; Chapple and Nofziger 2000; Dixey 1987, 1996; King 1985) have demonstrated similar gender-based social patterns related to the game. Dixey's analyses of bingo in Britain, in a broad national survey and through a series of interviews, have shown that a primary function of bingo is to provide a safe place for working-class women to gather and socialize with their peers. Since mid-century the bingo hall in Britain has become one of the few socially acceptable venues that women can frequent alone without husbands or other male escorts (Ibid.). In addition, as Dixey (1996) observes, while bingo offers women an opportunity for social interaction, it also allows each participant to manage the level of interaction by controlling the selection of seats and the occupation of table space. Bingo is thus a forum for "non-intimate companionship" (Dixey 1996, 139). Similarly, through their ethnographic research, Chapple and Nofziger (2000) have identified bingo as a means to enable women to escape from loneliness and from the thankless domestic routines of family life. Brown and Coventry (1998) have likewise shown that bingo in Australia acts as a form of compensation for many women who are dissatisfied with their daily lives and who seek solace in companionship and in the excitement of a possible financial windfall. As these studies show, it is not the prospect of large winnings that draws women to bingo, but rather it is the camaraderie and entertainment of a "night on the town."

Nevertheless, bingo remains a form of gambling and therefore involves different degrees and dimensions of risk. As some studies have also indicated, a proportion of regular bingo players may be regarded as problem gamblers. Chapple and Nofziger (2000) have referred to "hints of deviance" in describing the actions of women whose obsessive bingo play is detrimental to responsibilities and relationships in other areas of their lives. Brown and Coventry (1998) have likewise observed that while women are generally attracted to the social conviviality of games such as bingo, frequent and prolonged bingo playing may foster an addiction to the game that compromises work and family, and invariably provokes stress, depression, and shame among the players themselves. This is particularly evident when players focus on the prospect of bingo winnings as a source of needed income (Walker 1995).

When considering the notion of problem gambling as applied to bingo it is nonetheless important to recognize that just as women's experience with gambling tends to differ from that of men, so too do their developmental trajectories to gambling addiction. While women are no less prone to problem gambling, it seems that they are rarely attracted to illegal gambling activities and to indebtedness to loan sharks and bookies (Potenza et al. 2001). On the other hand, although women generally appear to become involved in gambling activities later in life than men, there is evidence that they progress more quickly from recreational to problematic forms of gaming (Tavares et al. 2001). As Potenza et al. (2001) suggest, one reason for this may lie in the predilection of many women for games of chance, e.g., video lottery terminals (VLTs), that require little skill and encourage a fatalistic dependence on good luck. Other reasons for problem gambling appear to relate to the social situations of women. Several studies, for example, have found that women who suffer gambling addiction generally report significantly higher levels of loneliness than women identified as occasional recreational gamblers (Grant and Kim 2002; Ohtsuka et al. 1995; Trevorrow and Moore 1998).

Despite growing understanding of women gamblers, to date there is very little published research on this topic in Canada, and no qualitative studies on women's involvement in bingo in this country. Given the extensive popularity of bingo across Canada, this is surprising. In addition, as Wedgeworth (1998) has argued, despite growing social science interest in gambling, researchers have typically spent relatively little time with gamblers who are engaged in the practice of gambling. Consequently, while knowledge of the complexity of gambling practices has been expanding, there is little research that privileges the voices of those who are immersed in gambling cultures, particularly the voices of women. In our view, if appropriate strategies for assisting women problem gamblers are to be developed and successfully implemented, it is important for researchers to undertake in-depth qualitative analyses of these women and their gambling practices. Naturalistic research that centers on women's gambling must likewise be attuned to the gender-specific socialization processes of their gambling behaviors.

With this purpose in mind, in 2002 the authors undertook an ethnographic study designed to examine the subjective experiences of female bingo players and to elicit their perceptions about the factors that have influenced their gambling. This case study was conducted in several bingo venues in a major urban center, and was part of a larger research project examining problem gambling among women in Ontario. In examining women's experiences of bingo, our intention was to delve into the culture of bingo and to gain insights into what it is that draws women to this form of gambling and what meanings it has for them. In addition, we aimed to assess, from the perspective of the women themselves, whether bingo was an entirely innocuous pastime, or whether it fosters what Chapple and Nofziger (2000) have suggested are "hints of deviance."

As we show in this chapter, women's involvement in bingo can be characterized as a form of entertainment that is not only harmless, but to some extent has a therapeutic value. At the same time, however, we also discerned actions among some players that can be characterized as imprudent in terms of the time and money they devote to bingo, and the anxiety that this causes them. Consequently, we argue that bingo is inherently paradoxical. It serves as a useful form of egress and recreation for many women who seek temporary relief from the mundane obligations of their daily lives and who tend to have limited power and opportunity. At the same time, however, the appeal of bingo lies in its illusive promise that good fortune is a function of pure chance—a turn of the numbers—rather than in personal agency and in individual skills and knowledge. As such, bingo harbors risks that can seriously jeopardize female players and their families, and thus has the potential to exacerbate women's powerlessness.

Methodology

This ethnographic study of female bingo players was conducted by a research team using methods of participant observation and informal interviewing. In so doing, we were able to elicit narratives of women's bingo playing experiences. As Cresswell (1998) has observed, ethnographic studies aim to describe the meanings that various individuals attribute to a concept or a phenomenon on the basis of their lived experiences (35). From a sociological perspective, ethnography is a way of examining how members of particular groups constitute aspects of their everyday lives, and how they consciously develop meaning from their interactions with others. In order to capture the essence of a phenomenon that is central to the experiences of a group of people, researchers must ideally observe subjects of research in natural settings, and collate and analyze the narratives of these natural-istic experiences. As an exploratory method of inquiry, the ethnographic approach greatly facilitates in-depth knowledge of specific social interac-tions that commonly occur in the field setting (Fetterman 1998).

As noted, this ethnography was part of a large study examining female problem gamblers. Members of the research team thus took on varying responsibilities for different components of the overall study. For our case study of women's involvement in bingo, one research team member, whom we refer to in this chapter as "the ethnographer," assumed the lead in field-work. Over a three-month period, she played bingo two or three times a week for approximately three hours each session. She divided her time more or less evenly at three different bingo sites in a large city in eastern Ontario. Over the course of her fieldwork she befriended several players, and thus came to know them well. Throughout this period she maintained a daily journal in which she recorded extensive field notes. In this way, through her accumulation of experiences and personal interactions with other players, she was able to document women's motivations to play, their relationships with key persons in their lives and with other players, their beliefs and "superstitions," and their discourse on various issues relating to bingo. Other members of the research team also attended bingo halls, sometimes with the ethnographer, on other occasions either alone or in pairs. On these occasions, the team members played bingo, spoke to other players intermittently, and maintained observational field notes.

Data analysis was conducted through a series of iterative stages. The authors read through all the ethnographic field notes, initially to obtain familiarity with basic content, and later in order to highlight and extract significant statements and to ascertain the context-based meanings con-veyed by these statements. Drawing upon our review of existing scholarly literature on bingo and other gaming practices, along with our respective understandings of the bingo site contexts, we identified key themes that emerged from our collective observations and from narratives of women who were interviewed by the ethnographer. We then further narrowed the range of selected statements that underscored these themes. In this way, through a reductive process involving further perusal of the ethno-graphic field notes, individual analysis, and collaborative interpretations, we elicited a number of key thematic domains related to the female players' bingo-playing experiences that we now examine.

Behavioral Patterns of Bingo Players

In common with other studies of bingo (Brown and Coventry 1998; Dixey 1996; Chapple and Nofziger 2000), our naturalistic inquiry revealed two facets of the bingo culture that explain its particular appeal to women. Most discernible to anyone entering a bingo hall for the first time is the atmosphere of female sociability and companionship. In the halls we visited, while there were always some players sitting alone, for the most part women sat in clusters and generally interacted with one another between games. The other notable feature of bingo is the game itself and the way it is played. In contrast to the relaxed and often garrulous atmosphere between games, a quieter and more intensive mood settles in when games are in play. In depicting the social environment of bingo, we therefore find it useful to delineate these different, yet recurrent, behavioral dynamics.

Social Interactions

The bingo hall is a rich forum of dialogue and relationships among female players. They gossip, complain, laugh, swear and shout sarcastically, and give and share generously. They converse easily and frequently about their bingo practices. Prior to a game they often wish each other good luck, and if someone at a neighboring table wins, it is common to say, "good for you." Between games players indulge in gossip and complain about family, their jobs and their bosses, other players, and sundry daily problems. Husbands are a frequent topic of conversation, often disparaging ("you got to cater to them, cook their meals, do your housework"). Frequently, too, players will complain about their bad luck ("the little player never gets a break, they [the owners] don't care about us").

There is ample evidence of generosity in bingo halls. Often this is manifested through sharing of food and eagerness to offer advice to novice players. Birthdays are celebrated. On one occasion the bingo caller announced a regular player's birthday to the assembled hall, upon which all the players applauded. Later in the evening her friends gathered about her to offer gifts and share a birthday cake. Kind gestures are likewise manifested when a player who is known to others wins a sizable pot. In such instances, players at the surrounding tables will congratulate the winner and she in turn is likely to buy her neighbors beverages or snacks.

On other occasions, however, as exemplified by the following utterances, exchanges are blunt and acerbic. When a cell phone rings during a game, a player yells, "Would you turn the god-damn phone off." When someone loudly blows her nose, another cries, "Holy jumping hell, go leak somewhere else." *Sotto voce* comments on the size and appearance of other players are frequent. A player snidely remarks to a companion about a woman who has suggested that she has gained weight, "Isn't she a looker ... I feel like saying, 'Look at you porker,' but I'm too polite." Caustic exchanges are likewise engendered by the inevitable tensions and irritation that stem from the competition of the game itself. On one occasion a player who is demonstrably jubilant is sharply rebuked ("Keep the noise down"). Similarly, in response to a player who is complaining about her failure to win, another turns and grumbles to her companion, "She is so full of shit, always saying she doesn't win anything, but she does. She just doesn't want people to know about it."

Comments about men are often more sarcastic, particularly when they are singled out as scapegoats for women's poor showings at bingo. As the ethnographer frequently observed, when men won games female players tended to be resentful ("Go home where you belong." ... "You should be home doing something." ... "He's got a horseshoe up his ass"). In one session, after three different men had won games, a female player muttered to the ethnographer that "they should stay home." On another occasion, a woman confided to her, "See, all the men are winning tonight—again!" Such comments reinforced the strong aura of the bingo hall as essentially a woman's world where men are tolerated but ideally should not be seen to prevail in an essentially female game.

Interaction between players and bingo hall staff ranges from shows of cordiality and affection to displays of anger and frustration. Generally the bingo caller—most often a male—is regarded as "good" by players who are winning, and "bad" if players are on a losing streak. If callers speak too quickly, or are too slow or hesitant, complaints can usually be heard throughout the hall ("He's half asleep." ... "Come on stupid, get with it"). When numbers that players need to win are not being called out, player frustration is often audibly directed at the callers themselves ("idiot," ... "turkey," ... "stupid"). Relations between players and runners (those who sell bingo cards from table to table) are commonly good-natured and trusting. Runners often cheer for "their" players who win. On occasion, while games are still in play, runners fill in the cards of players who have gone to the washroom or who are purchasing food. In turn, players often buy coffee or offer tips to "their" runners. In one session the ethnographer observed a player helping a runner to write a letter to an insurance company. On another occasion she overheard a player speaking with the hall manager in defense of a runner who risked being dismissed for being late.

Yet underlying the generally easy-going association between players and runners is an implicit employee/client relationship. The task of runners is to cater to the players and to foster a sociable atmosphere that is essential to the business of bingo. Consequently runners tend to ingratiate themselves to players through jocularity and flattery as exemplified by this exchange:

Player: I need some cards.
Male Caller: Sure. You know, you ladies control me.
Player [laughs]: You bet we do.
Caller: If you need me again just grab the strings of my apron.

In turn, players are quick to criticize runners for perceived inefficiency or if runners are seen as somehow responsible for potential or actual losses (e.g., "No, these cards, these aren't used, geez I have to train all these guys.".... "They never do it right, he could have cost me my bingo"). As one runner confided to the ethnographer: "I am used to being called bad things." Relations between players and other bingo hall personnel—notably concession stand workers—are generally impersonal. Yet here, too, player stress is sometimes reflected in outbursts of annoyance directed at employees.

In sum, the bingo halls offer a venue for women to mix freely and informally, to speak openly with companions on a wide range of topics, and to express a gamut of emotions. Our observations of bingo halls in southern Ontario thus reinforce other studies that have identified bingo as one of the few legitimate and locally accessible forums allowing women of all ages and backgrounds to share fun and conversation. At the same time, however, in light of the transactional nature of the game of bingo, it is a form of sociability that occurs within the context of a business/consumer environment. As we were constantly aware, the women we observed and spoke with in our study were at once clients and gamblers.

The Elements of Play

In many respects, bingo is a two-sided form of recreation that alternates between the open-ended sociability before and between games as outlined above and the more intensive, single-minded focus among everyone in the hall when games are in play. Over the course of our observations and informal exchanges, we identified two notable behavioral characteristics common among women who are regular players: 1) their efforts to control physical space and influence the laws of chance; and 2) their singularity of concentration during each game of bingo.

The Compulsion for Control and Influence   Bingo is entirely a game of chance. Paradoxically, however, our observations revealed that in spite of—indeed, often *because* of—the overwhelming element of luck that is integral to winning at bingo, female players demonstrated profound material and psychological efforts to control and predict bingo outcomes. When playing bingo, much of what women say and do touches in some way on the notion of control. Based on our observations, endeavors for control are manifested in two essential ways.

1. **Control of Space**   Regular players typically arrive well in advance of the beginning of each bingo session. Usually their first task is to claim their space in the bingo hall by placing bingo daubers and other personal effects on the playing tables. When players arrive together, usually one will join the line-up for cards while her companion(s) will search out the seats. Recounting one such incident, the ethnographer recorded in her field notes, "As we were waiting [for cards], Jill told me to take the daubers and get that spot (pointing) before we lost it. I followed her instruction and placed daubers in front of two seats." Choosing a seat is rarely done haphazardly; it is one way by which many women strive to influence bingo results. Generally they try to sit at the same tables each time they come to the hall. Selection of tables and chairs is integrally connected to good luck—a function of where they last won a bingo game, or where a high jackpot was previously won in the hall. Likewise, a decision to change seats is often undertaken on the basis of either premonitions of good fortune or because of previous bouts of bad luck. As the ethnographer noted on another occasion: "When I arrived today … I found Kelly in a different place than we usually sit on Wednesday nights. She told me that she changed seats because we've not been lucky on previous Wednesday nights." Regular players usually take considerable care in placing and organizing their cards and their bingo accoutrements on and around their tables. They arrive at the bingo hall with bingo bags that contain all the equipment they need to accomplish this. Many such bags are handmade and often elaborately decorated. Having claimed their space and obtained their cards, players generally tape their cards onto their tables in the order that they will be played and then daub out the spots on the cards that are "out of play" for particular games. There is a practical reason for this: seasoned players often play a large number of cards at one time—sometimes more than thirty cards in high-stakes games. This requires considerable concentration, especially since the numbers are usually called in rapid succession and transitions between games are swift. Given the need for space and mental focus during games, it is customary for many regular players to avoid sitting in adjacent chairs so as to leave space between themselves. Such actions correspond with Dixey's (1996) observations about the territoriality of bingo players, for "If one purpose of bingo playing is to interact with specific others, or to interact minimally, such control is important" (143). The ethnographer became familiar with this protocol in the early days of her immersion in bingo halls. Writing about a player with whom she had developed a close

attachment in the bingo hall, she noted in her field journal, "I went to sit next to Veronica. I noticed she placed her purse in the chair next to her. Most players do this so they have enough space to play their cards. I sat two chairs away from Veronica."

2. Efforts to Influence Game Outcomes The theme of luck permeates much of the discourse of women in the bingo halls, and banter among them often revolves around the various ways of trying to predict and control the outcome of games. Many of the players whom the ethnographer came to know had strong intuitions about what their cards would and would not yield. While games are being played, women frequently mutter comments about their cards. Players who are unable to mark many numbers in the early stages of a game sometimes declare their cards to be "bad"; some will even stop playing the round if they feel sure that the cards provide no hope of a win. To counter the low odds inherent in randomly distributed cards, regular players tend to enact rituals designed to influence game outcomes. Most visible are the lucky charms that bingo players bring with them and that are ubiquitous in the bingo halls. Primarily figurines and stuffed animals are laid out with care on the tables in front of the players. On one occasion, the ethnographer observed a woman who had close to a dozen brass elephants lined up in front of her, arranged from smallest to largest. Many women wear "lucky" items of clothing. Others retain what they consider as lucky numbers (previous winning numbers, birth dates, and so forth) that are often displayed on their bingo-accessories bags. Such credence in the vitality of numbers is reflected in this exchange recorded by the ethnographer in her log book:

> On one bingo, I need one number.... I say to the two women next to me, "I'm waiting!" One asks me, "What number do you need?" I answer, "B52." She says, "You won't get that number. It isn't lucky here. It never gets called here, but at Sussex Club [*another bingo hall*] it does. It's funny when that happens, why some numbers are called more at some halls than others."

Players likewise engage in a range of behaviors to enhance their game outcomes. Chanting lucky numbers, rubbing and waving good luck charms, and placing artifacts in certain ways on their tables are all performed in order to improve the odds of winning. When intuitions and predictions do not manifest themselves in desired outcomes, particularly in high stakes games, reactions are sometimes boisterous. As the ethnographer noted: "When they get 'bad' cards, they are annoyed. Some say things like, 'Stupid cards! I'm going to shoot these cards!'" On other occasions, as the following recorded incident reveals, frustrations are directed vociferously at particular callers who are believed to embody differential degrees of luck:

> Martha is becoming angrier because she has not won anything. She tells me that it is because of the caller—she never wins with him. She likes the caller, Jennifer, because she always wins games with her. She says that before coming to bingo she usually calls and asks who the caller is and the amount of the jackpot. She comes when Jennifer is here.

As these observations indicate, an important aspect of the appeal of bingo is the legitimacy that it lends to ritualistic and superstitious actions. This accords with other studies that have indicated that for many players luck is almost tangible (Dixey 1996; Volberg et al. 1997; Walker 1995). Wooing good luck thus requires scrupulous attention to specific rituals and routines. Through the manipulation of space and artifacts, bingo players demonstrate a common reliance on an external locus of control that many implicitly believe will steer the course of good fortune in their direction (Lester 1980; Volberg et al. 1997). While this discourse of luck and superstition clearly offers only an illusion of predicting and influencing the outcomes of games, it is nonetheless an integral, and indeed comforting, feature of regular bingo play.

The Gravity and Emotion of Play   During each bingo game, conversation among regular players almost always ceases. This is the time to concentrate. As one player remarked to the ethnographer who at the time was a fresh novice to the game: "Okay, now I can't talk. I have to concentrate. This is an important game, and I have a lot of cards." As the stakes of each game rise, so too do levels of emotion and anxiety. Since high-stakes jackpots are invariably held at the end of each bingo session, these are the times when indications of tension are most visible. During the last and usually lucrative high-stakes game, the bingo hall is suffused with a palpable mix of anticipation and fear among the players until the abrupt moment someone cries out, "Bingo!" signaling the sudden-death finish of the game.

What is striking, however, is that regardless of who wins or loses a jackpot game, there appears to be relatively little difference in the train of emotions that players experience. Among all those who do not win the jackpot, anxiety steadily rises as the game proceeds, only to end with a sudden sharp sense of disappointment when the game suddenly ends. Unless the jackpot winner is a close friend, "losing" players tend to briefly register their frustration, after which they move quickly *en masse* out of the bingo hall. Those with cars waste little time in driving out of the parking lot. Yet the pang of "losing" bingo quickly subsides and is replaced by a resurgence of hope for a win "next time." Among those who *do* win a high-stakes jackpot, the progression of emotions differs only at the moment of winning. Mounting anxiety during the jackpot game is followed by the inevitable surge of excitement when the jackpot is won. Yet after the initial rush of euphoria, a gradual "let down" sets in, and this is followed by the return of hope for another win "next time." Thus, whether one wins or loses, the end of bingo is almost always accompanied by an emotional "rush" and the conviction that good luck will either repeat itself, or is bound to occur next time round.

The Contradictions of Bingo

Having examined the behavioral patterns of women who habitually frequent bingo halls, we now turn to an examination of what it is that regular bingo players gain from this activity. What is it that draws them repeatedly to what is clearly a game renowned for its repetitiveness and lack of skill? In accordance with the findings of others researchers (Brown and Coventry 1998; Chapple and Nofziger 2000; Dixey 1996) we have discerned that many women view bingo as a genuine recreational activity. It is a form of entertainment that comprises elements of both escape and fulfillment. Yet whereas some authors have argued that bingo is an innocuous activity that enables women to get out of the house for some harmless betting and socializing with their peers (Dixey 1987; King 1985), our observations suggest that for many players regular attendance at bingo involves elements of serious financial, emotional, and social risk. In this we are closer to the perspective of Chapple and Nofziger (2000) who refer to "hints of deviance" among many bingo players. In our view, however, in reference to the women we observed in bingo halls, the notion of deviance is unfairly pejorative and is suggestive of a departure from a norm that is neither defined nor understood. Instead, our analysis led us to consider the notion of "imprudence" as a more apt description of the actions of some players who appeared to be risking their own precarious finances, or who admitted to jeopardizing their relations with close family members. As we now discuss, for regular players bingo is both a benign form of entertainment and a catalyst of potentially damaging risk.

Bingo as Entertainment

Regular players are drawn to the game of bingo for a host of idiosyncratic reasons. Yet after weeks of participant observation in bingo halls, it became apparent to us that bingo is a genuine form of entertainment that serves two inter-related functions: escape and fulfillment.

Escape   As expressed to the ethnographer on numerous occasions, bingo is an activity that enables many women to escape from what they regard as the boredom and uneventfulness of much of their daily lives. Among those without jobs, bingo appears to offer solace from sedentary home life.

> I have nothing else to do…. I come to get out of the house or I would go crazy, get depressed.

> If I stay in the house it gets me down. I get depressed so I go out shopping or play bingo.

For many players, however, home life entails responsibilities that have become tedious. For these women bingo offers relief from a continual round of domestic chores and demands of family (e.g., "I'm glad I have these [*bingo*] mornings to myself"). As a venue for female companionship, the bingo hall also provides an opportunity for players to vent their frustrations about the foibles of husbands and the constraints of marriage and parenthood.

> … no matter how much I clean, it's always messy. I left this morning, the beds weren't made, the dishes were in the sink, and the kids had taken pots out of the cupboard and were playing with them. I just picked up my bingo stuff and walked out. Let Jim have a turn with them for once. I just want to relax.

> [*Kelly*] says she needed to come to bingo today to get away from the stress and the heat. She tells me this weather makes her "cranky" and that her husband is telling her she is "too cranky," so she says she got fed up, picked up her stuff, and came to bingo.

> [*Marriage*] is not cut out to be all it's worth, let me tell you…. The only time I can come to bingo … [is] after I put the kids to sleep.

As this last comment suggests, for many women bingo is a form of recreation that needs to be slotted in during periods of family care. As the ethnographer observed, several of the women she came to know often phoned home between evening games, to speak either with their children or with their husbands who were looking after the children. Thus, while bingo allows these women some diversional "time-out" from their ascribed roles as wives and mothers, family responsibilities nonetheless remain a preoccupation for them even in the bingo hall.

As other studies have revealed (Brown and Coventry 1998; Chapple and Nofziger 2000; Dixey 1986), bingo tends to attract women who long for safe and predictable environments that contrast with the vagaries of their daily lives. It also offers a modicum of excitement that, for many women, serves as an antidote to prolonged boredom and solitude. In addition, bingo entails a minimal need for personal skill that otherwise might foster undesirable peer competition and introspective pressures. It is a form of recreation that offers an intriguing mix of safety, predictability, and excitement. As Dixey (1996) has argued, bingo is a communally consolidating ritual that provides many women with a quick and easy respite from the burdens of daily life.

Fulfillment   While undoubtedly an activity that enables many women to put aside the pressures of daily life, bingo is more than just a respite from ennui and stress. As noted earlier, the social atmosphere of the bingo hall is highly appealing. Here women can meet and socialize with their peers while engaging in a game that requires little skill and is therefore minimally competitive. Bingo fulfills a fundamental need for female companionship and fun. Based on our observations, the fulfillment regular players gain from bingo is commonly experienced in three different ways by three diverse types of women. First, many women who range in age from about twenty to fifty years old tend to congregate in groups of two to five players and, between games, often share their anxieties and frustrations. Such conversations frequently center around current relationships. As the ethnographer observed in her field journal:

> [*The women*] talk about what they are going to do for the rest of the week. They talk about their husbands (usually complaining about them, e.g., won't take them to movies), what they are cooking tomorrow night....

Co-workers that know each other congregate and talk about their bad bosses and jobs. Another woman talks about her ex-boyfriends and her new girlfriend, how she is not pretty.

Grumbling is often the tenor of these exchanges. As one player wryly retorted when asked what she and her companions talk about at bingo, "[We] bitch and complain. What else?"

A second group of women consists essentially of seniors and widows for whom bingo provides an occasion to get out of the house or apartment, to meet and talk with friends, and to share food and reading material. For this group, bingo is not so much a forum to ventilate the frustrations and annoyances that arise from daily events as it is a solace from loneliness.

A third cohort of women comprises those who are accompanied by family members. Often such family groups consist of different generations of women, i.e., mothers and daughters, and grandmothers and grand-daughters. The research team also observed male-female couples (assumed to be husband and wife), and on two occasions the ethnographer clearly observed mother/son pairs. As these observations suggest, the culture of bingo appears to be transmitted and adopted within the family context. By providing an opportunity for members of families to engage in a common activity, bingo helps to reinforce inter-generational ties.

Overall, as other studies have found, the most significant feature of bingo is that it allows women to combine the modest excitement of a game of chance with an opportunity to socialize with their peers, or with other women who are closely attached to them. Even for players who are less than avid, or who come to play alone, bingo is firmly anchored in the tradition of "a night out" among like-minded peers. In urban communities that have experienced profound socioeconomic changes and have left many women feeling marginalized and helpless (Volberg et al. 1997), bingo offers an atmosphere of companionship and social solidarity that is clearly valued by regular participants.

Bingo as an Act of Imprudence

Bingo is, of course, a game of chance, and for regular players it entails a continual financial outlay. Because it is a form of gambling, players frequently articulate their thoughts about money and the financial expenses they incur at bingo games. In general there seem to be two attitudes toward the costs of playing bingo. For women who are relatively well off or who have no dependents—usually senior citizens—bingo is a legitimate entertainment expense. Referring to her independence from her husband, one player stated:

> Anyway, it's my money I spend, not his.... What am I going to do with my money—bring it to the grave?

Another jokingly exclaimed:

> If I am going to die I might as well enjoy my money.

Yet for other women, money is a source of worry, especially among those in low-income brackets and those with family responsibilities. The constraints of limited income and restricted household budgets often generate palpable anxiety. Players with limited budgets know that the more they spend on bingo, the greater the likelihood of shortfalls for other needed expenses. This in turn will result in outspoken barbs from family members who perceive bingo playing as a "waste." Indeed, anxiety about the effect of regular bingo playing on family relationships underlies the unease of mounting bingo "losses." Players often expressed twinges of guilt and shame about the extent of their involvement in bingo. In expressing their distress, some players admitted that they conceal the amount of time and money they spend on bingo from family members.

> I have to hide how much I spend at bingo. If he knew, he would criticize and get mad, but I take from my tip money [*at work*].

> He doesn't know how much I spend. If he did, he would go crazy.

> I don't want my husband seeing me here. He will kill me if he knew how much money I spent.

Another example of concealment is outlined in the ethnographer's field journal:

> Her husband is going to the rotary, and she will say as she often does, "I am having a bad hair day; you go, I am staying in." And then she goes gambling. I know she hides a lot of her gambling from her husband.

On another occasion, the ethnographer writes about Nelly who has told her husband that she spends approximately $35 per bingo game, when in fact the figure more accurately approaches $80 per session. Nelly then confides to the ethnographer, "Sometimes they don't have to know everything." This issue of guilt and concealment from one's husband appears to be part-and-parcel of the bingo culture, for it is prominently displayed on a bingo hall poster as one of bingo's "ten commandments": *You shall not tell your husband how much you spend at bingo.*

With regard to children, worry and guilt likewise are the dominant emotions, and stem largely from women's sense of their responsibility as homemakers and caregivers. This coincides with the observation of Chapple and Nofziger (2000) that some women are anxious about absconding from family and home in order to play bingo. In part, as we discerned, a sense of guilt relates to the issue of money that could otherwise be spent on children. Perversely, this sometimes fosters a powerful urge to "win big" in bingo so as to cover children's required expenses. On one occasion the ethnographer noted:

> ... she hopes she wins a bingo today [because] she needs the money. Buying "back-to-school" stuff for her children is expensive ... she is playing sixty or more dollars worth of bingo cards.

Yet for other women, the mere fact of playing bingo on a regular basis is a cause of worry about their relations with their children.

> Now I'm nervous. that's why my kids hate it when I come [*to play bingo*].... Now I have to wait a week before I go back.

That same evening, however, this same woman contradicted herself by saying to the ethnographer, "I will call you tomorrow or Tuesday [*so*] we can go to another bingo hall." In this instance the appeal of bingo outweighed the concern for children.

Another characteristic of many of the players is their apparent lack of regard for money as a form of saving or investment. While most regular players appear to willingly acknowledge the cost of bingo as the price of entertainment, some players do occasionally lapse into a perception that the game can result in a prospective windfall—the big jackpot that will enable them to cover unpaid debts as well as future expenses. Yet for the most part, when jackpots are won, there seems to be a propensity for players to spend their winnings rapidly on attractive consumer goods. As the ethnographer noted about one of her companions:

> In the past week Veronica has won two jackpots and tells me she is on a lucky streak. She won $3,000 in a week and told me she blew it on shopping. Now she says she is anxious to win again because she needs the money. She is almost broke.

When linked to the compulsion to play bingo in a low-income situation, for some players this proclivity to view money as essentially a means to short-term spending can contribute to a cycle of welfare dependency. This was exemplified by a bingo player's comment to the ethnographer:

> You should come when it's welfare cheque day or when people get their baby bonus ... you should come when the cheque get cashed. This place is full to the maximum. People use their money and then rely on food stamps and soup kitchens and churches to eat.

In sum, while bingo is clearly a form of legitimate entertainment for most regular players, it appears also to be a source of angst for many of these same women, especially those who have family responsibilities. By devoting time and money to the game, many simultaneously worry about not satisfactorily fulfilling their ascribed roles as wives and mothers. Bingo, therefore, is a pastime that, like other pleasures of the modern industrial world (smoking, drinking, and fast-food consumption), has become a paradox—a form of pleasure and amusement that also harbors the potential for acts of imprudence that can undermine personal well-being and family relations. Yet despite the various tensions that arise from this paradox, bingo is not an activity that regular players are willing or able to give up easily.

Conclusion

Bingo is a straightforward game that requires little time to learn and virtually no skill to play. Players highlight numbers that are called out, with a prize awarded to the person who first fills in all the required numbers. In the minds of some critics bingo is a mind-numbing misuse of time, a "cretinous pastime" (*The Times*, September 14, 1961, cited in Dixey 1996, 137). Yet in many parts of the world it is a highly popular form of gambling, one that has a particular appeal to women. In line with the few other studies that have examined the world of bingo, in this ethnography we have attempted to describe the social environment of bingo from the perspective of female players. In so doing, our starting assumption has been that the obvious satisfaction of bingo does not derive from its skeletal rules of play, but rather emanates from the social environment that women themselves create around the game, and the various rituals and beliefs that their participation in the game has engendered or reinforced among them. By drawing on our observations and informal conversations with female players, we therefore conclude this chapter by commenting on the women whom we came to know in bingo halls, and on the sociological nature of the game that has become an important means of recreation and social expression for these women.

As Downes et al. (1976) and Dixey (1996) have indicated, women who regularly frequent bingo halls usually are well entrenched in their current socioeconomic positions. Although we did not inquire directly into the private lives of the women we observed and spoke with, it is safe to say that there were no signs of upward social mobility among them. By and large the patterns of life for these women had been clearly delineated. Their sense of identity was strongly tied to home, family, friends, and (if they were employed) work. Yet generally it was an identity that suggested elements of dissatisfaction and powerlessness. Many of these women seemed to be overwhelmed or fatigued by pressures that arose from these sources of identity. While we often overheard them complain about such pressures, there was never any indication that they would deliberately attempt to fundamentally change their circumstances. Instead, their way of dealing with the travails of their everyday lives was to seek solace in the familiar routines and easy rituals of bingo, and to ventilate about these same difficulties with their peers in a safe and legitimate female environment. In effect, bingo is a parody of their socioeconomic situation, which is characterized by lack of economic and job-related power and by a tendency to rely on the fortunes of fate. Surreptitiously, therefore, bingo may actually exacerbate the lack of control they have over these aspects of their lives. Yet ethnographically this is very much an "etic" perspective.

An alternative "emic" perspective, one that more aptly reflects the thinking and motives of most of the women whom we observed and interviewed, is that bingo serves as a form of rejuvenation, a way in which they can assert themselves freely. From their own perspectives, by regularly engaging in what many conventional critics have argued is a waste of time and money, these women are asserting their independence of choice and action within a broader structural context that imposes pervasive sociocultural constraints on their daily lives. While it may do little to alter their day-to-day circumstances, bingo enables these women to establish palatable and often enjoyable social spaces for themselves.

But what of the effects of the game itself on the livelihoods of female players? If it is not as pernicious or as "cretinous" as critics would suggest, is it therefore a relatively harmless, indeed therapeutic, pastime for women who have time and money for leisure activity? To a large extent, we concur with other authors (Dixey 1987, 1996; King 1985) who have indicated that bingo is an innocuous form of entertainment that enables women to congregate, socialize, and spend money on a socially acceptable diversion. Yet as our ethnographic study has also revealed, there are aspects of bingo that are troubling. Through our ethnography it became clear that bingo for some women is a compulsion that can have painful personal consequences. This is particularly so among those upon whom others—usually family members—are dependent. In such circumstances, the allure of escape and psychic thrill, combined with fancies of influencing the course of chance, tend to exacerbate women's lack of control in others areas of their lives. Instead of being a forum that allows them to manifest their autonomy, for some women bingo becomes an obsession that undermines their financial, social, and psychological well-being. If, as Caillois (1961) has suggested, games of chance offer a "second reality" to real life by providing disadvantaged people a temporary refuge from real-life problems and an illusory sense that everyone is on an even playing field, the line between frivolous entertainment and detrimental obsession is a fine one. When the realm of illusion assumes pre-eminence in a player's daily actions and worldview, and when games such as bingo become obsessions, then control is further diminished and the capacity to cope with the strains of everyday urban life is likely to be undermined. Thus, as a predominantly female pastime, bingo is inherently paradoxical: a desirable distraction that responds to a fundamental need for social interaction and contained excitement, but one that also harbors deep-seated risk for those who are prone to subsume their destiny to the vagaries of chance.

References

Brown, D., and L. Coventry (1998) *Queen of Hearts: The Needs of Women With Gambling Problems.* Melbourne: Victorian Women's Trust.

Caillois, R. (1961) *Man, Play, and Games.* New York: Free Press.

Chapple, C., and S. Nofziger (2000) "Hints of Deviance in the Account of Sociability and Profit of Bingo Players," *Deviant Behaviour* 21, no. 6: 489–517.

Cresswell, J. W. (1998) *Qualitative Inquiry and Research Design: Choosing Among Five Traditions.* Thousand Oaks, CA: Sage.

Dixey, R. (1987) "It's a Great Feeling When You Win: Women and Bingo," *Leisure Studies* 6: 199–214.

Dixey, R. (1996) "Bingo in Britain: An Analysis of Gender and Class." In *Gambling Cultures: Studies in History and Interpretation,* ed. J. McMillen, 136–47. New York: Routledge.

Downes, D., B. P. Davies, M. E. David, and P. Stone (1976) *Gambling, Work and Leisure: A Study across Three Areas.* London: Routledge and Kegan Paul.

Ettore, B. (1989) "Women and Substance Use/Abuse: Towards a Feminist Perspective—or How to Make Dust Fly," *Women's Studies International Forum* 12 (6): 593–602.

Fetterman, D. M. (1998) *Ethnography,* 2nd ed. Thousand Oaks, CA: Sage.

Grant, J. E., and S. W. Kim (2002) "Gender Differences in Pathological Gamblers Seeking Medication Treatment," *Comprehensive Psychiatry* 43, no. 1: 56–62.

Hing, N., and H. Breen (2001) "Profiling Lady Luck: An Empirical Study of Gambling and Problem Gambling Amongst Female Club Members," *Journal of Gambling Studies* 17, no. 1: 47–69.

Hong, Y., and C. Chu (1988) "Sex, Locus of Control, and Illusion of Control in Hong Kong as Correlates of Gambling Involvement," *Journal of Social Psychology* 128, no. 5: 667–73.

King, K. M. (1985) "Gambling: Three Forms and Three Explanations," *Sociological Focus* 18, no. 3: 235–48.

Lesieur, H., and S. B. Blume (1991) "When Lady Luck Loses: Women and Compulsive Gambling." In *Feminist Perspectives on Addictions,* ed. N. van Den Bergh, 181–97. New York: Springer.

Lester, D. (1980) "Choice of Gambling Activities and Belief in Locus of Control," *Psychological Reports* 47, no. 22.

Lips, H. M. (1989) "Gender-Role Socialization: Lessons in Femininity." In *Women: A Feminist Perspective,* ed. J. Freedman, 197–216. New York: Springer.

Marshall, K. (2000) "Update on Gambling," *Perspectives on Labour and Income* 12, no. 1: 29–35.

Matlin, M. W. (1993) *The Psychology of Women,* 2nd ed. Orlando, FL: Harcourt Brace Jovanovich.

Miller, J. B. (1986) *Toward a New Psychology of Women,* 2nd ed. Boston: Beacon Press.

Ohtsuka, K., E. Brutton, V. Borg, and L. Deluca (1997) "Sex Differences in Pathological Gambling Using Gaming Machines," *Psychological Reports* 80, no. 3: 1051–57.

Potenza, M. N., M. A. Steinberg, S.D. McLaughlin, R. Wu, B. J. Rounsaville, and S. S. O'Malley (2001) "Gender-Related Differences in the Characteristics of Problem Gamblers Using a Gambling Helpline," *American Journal of Psychiatry* 158, no. 9: 1500–1505.

Shaffer, H. J., M. N. Hall, and J. Vander Bilt (1999) "Estimating the Prevalence of Disordered Gambling Behavior in the United States and Canada: A Research Synthesis," *American Journal of Public Health* 89, no. 9: 1369–76.

Tavares, H., M. L. Zilberman, F. J. Beites, and V. Gentil (2001) "Gender Differences in Gambling Progression," *Journal of Gambling Studies* 17, no. 2: 151–59.

Trevorrow, K., and S. Moore (1998) "The Association Between Loneliness, Social Isolation and Women's Electronic Machine Gambling," *Journal of Gambling Studies* 14, no. 3: 263–84.

Volberg, R. A., D. C. Reitzes, and J. Boles (1997) "Exploring the Links Between Gambling, Problem Gambling, and Self-Esteem," *Deviant Behavior* 18: 321–42.

Walker, M. (1995) *The Psychology of Gambling.* London: Butterworth–Heinemann.

Wedgeworth, R. B. (1998) "The Reification of the 'Pathological' Gambler: An Analysis of Gambling Treatment and the Application of the Medical Model to Problem Gambling," *Perspectives in Psychiatric Care* 34, no. 2: 5–13.

CHAPTER 9

Playing with Hope and Despair

*Bourdieu and the Habitus of Horse Betting**

JOAN ALLEN

"The spin of a roulette wheel ... can enable a person to move in an instant from the lowest to the highest rung of the social ladder." (Dostoevsky, quoted in Bourdieu 2000, 214)

The late Pierre Bourdieu leaves for us a corpus of work that emphasizes the significance of social and philosophical inquiry for an understanding of the politics of the everyday. His work is luxurious in its diversity of topics and themes, from the plight of French foreigners (Bourdieu 1979) to the impact of television upon global culture (Bourdieu 1999). This chapter seeks to use the influence of Bourdieu in its analysis of the sociopolitical context of the horse bettor as one whose risks symbolize an act of resistance to the expected patterns of expenditure and consumption. Bourdieu not only acknowledged the political roots of his own work, but also consistently stressed that the trajectories of all actors are influenced by preexisting political structures. However, Bourdieu did not see these as unmodifiable imprints, and devoted his scholarly activism to the creation of artful platforms for the disenfranchised, which he exemplified in his

---

support of a comedian for president as an ironic commentary on "all those who will never count as politicians" (Johnson 2002).

Central to Bourdieu's commitment is the need for the theorist to acknowledge her dominant position and accompanying social responsibility. "Why have we moved from the committed intellectual to the 'uncommitted intellectual'?" (Bourdieu 1998, 44). Bourdieu suggests a model of the theorist who is committed to the possibility and necessity of the integration of philosophy and fieldwork. Like his latter-day stances against globalization and his ongoing investigations of everyday political activism (such as the French farmers' protests against McDonald's restaurants), the particular gambling community analyzed in this chapter responds to power by refusing to interpret life chances according to the logic of economic cost/benefit rationality. The North American horse track bettors who are topicalized here in these initial explorations of risk and gambling attempt to cheat not only the market, but also conventional economic structures of work and time. This chapter suggests that gambling offers an example of differing access to cultural/economic/social capital in which seemingly non-rational choices make sense as acts of resistance. This interpretation differs radically from the "problem gambling" literature that dominates much of the research, and is specifically related to Bourdieu's insights. This research seeks to describe and analyze some of the particularities of horse betting, and to place this within the context of gambling as an economic and social enterprise. The premise underlying this research is that it is necessary to gain insight into typical gambling behavior and accompanying thought processes before we can begin to develop an understanding of aberrant or addictive gamblers' actions.

Part of Bourdieu's mandate in his later years was to fight against the ills of creeping globalization and the erosion of locality (1999). An uneasy connection between global politics and horseracing was vividly illustrated when the 2000 International, a high-stakes race held at Toronto's Woodbine track, removed all signs of its connections to the United Arab Emirates. The expensive sport of racing and its relations to nationalism and international politics became uneasy economic associates in the post-9/11 marketplace. Horseracing has conventionally been formalized as an elite, upper-class form of speculation and entertainment, and we need to query what the implications of a shift away from this stratification of it as an activity are.

Gambling revenues represent an ever-increasing means by which governments can produce cash in this economic era of the "unprecedented mobility of capital" (Bourdieu 1998). The structural violence caused by the constant precariousness of job and financial security at all social class levels of the workforce is an essential part of this global marketplace, and influences the "habitus" of the gambler. Corporate globalization puts power in the hands of distant, nearly invisible, unaccountable, elites.

What does Bourdieu's insight offer for the subject of this research, the intense but slightly jaded regular at horseracing tracks and off-track sites? Canadian Frank Stronach, of Magna Entertainment Corporation, has purchased New York state off-track venues as well as numerous other horse tracks around North America, and has built a television network that will allow bettors to cast their luck from home "every few minutes, 24/7" (*Toronto Star*, September 3, 2002, E8). Woodbine Entertainment Group is explicitly targeting Asian populations as a market at the horse track in an effort to retrieve potential gambling revenues that are escaping to lotteries, casinos, and the Internet (interview with David Gorman, Vice-President Corporate Affairs, Woodbine Entertainment Group, September 28, 2000). Woodbine's recently built vast entertainment complex, centered around slot machines, is another attempt to bolster the track as a destination. Santa Anita Track's Magna Entertainment has brought in family entertainment and even boutique shopping in an attempt to normalize and neutralize the social space of the horse track. The corporate drive is on to garner market shares of what is sometimes called the luck business (Goodman 1995) with 68 percent of the nations of the world collecting revenues from gambling (Thompson 1998), and this figure does not include the vast and indeterminate underground betting economy.

This trend is in keeping with the trend toward normalizing gambling as an activity and subsuming its particular economic character into just another facet of capitalist risk and consumption with its attendant rewards and losses, and emphasizes the current promotion of horse betting as a non-deviant practice akin to shopping or seeking entertainment. "Gambling … while still retaining some moral ambiguity, has shed its pariah status and become fully incorporated into Western capitalist economic as just another type of communal enterprise" (Reith 2002, 91). This notion is exemplified by the recent discussions of incorporating wedding reception space into the Santa Anita track (*Pasadena Star News*, A1).

Horseracing, at and off-track, must seek the means to maintain and increase its particular hook on the gambling population. Tensions exist within track culture as to whether racing should maintain its cultural niche within the gambling world as a conventionally upper-class milieu or whether to increase the trend of popularizing the sport. Tracks such as Woodbine in Toronto and Gulfstream in Florida have looked to slots as a means of increasing revenues and attendance. Florida's Governor Jeb Bush has opposed this trend, "saying that gambling expansion would have a negative impact on the state, estimating that 90% of the money funneled into slot machines is lost by the gamblers" (Christine 2005).

In my interviews, horse bettors spoke of themselves as an elite within gambling culture and are traditionally contemptuous of such sheerly deterministic forms of betting, as they lack any real "play" in the strongest sense. Nonetheless, the track gamblers I interviewed universally ended financially down in the long run. What of these risk-takers, are they merely "cultural dopes" (Garfinkel 1967) subject to the manipulations of corporate capitalism? As bettors experience losses over gains, do they continue merely due to a form of self-deception, or worse, self-sabotage? Are they the "psychic masochists" (Bergler, in Herman 1967, 121) willingly subject to victimization by the business element of the track enterprise? Are they "private rebels" (Bergler, in Herman 1967, 130) who expose bourgeois values and conventional economic structures? Disciplined in their unmediated ambitions, horse bettors persist in their quest, undeterred by an awareness of the realities of the odds.

Social Space of the Horse Track

What is particular about the social space of the racetrack or its off-track affiliates? This research involves exploratory observations of and theorizing about the place of risk in horserace betting. Ethnographic work on horse track racing and betting is relatively scarce. In the North American context, a 1968 dissertation at Berkeley by Marvin Scott, *The Racing Game*, analyzed differing formulations of track bettors as they reacted to winning and losing streaks. Herman's 1967 edition of papers discussing gambling includes pieces by Herman, Zola, and McDonald as they observed the particularities of betting the ponies (Herman 1967).

Kate Fox's (1999) British work notes that the track is a space marked by its own conventions. Fox's five years of work on British punters noted that the British track is a self-contained society with its own rituals, language, and rules. It was seen as displaying a "controlled disinhibition," a conventionalized relaxation of typical social constraint. This, Fox determined, was due to the "bonding" effect of risk-taking. Her findings can be used to identify the social space of the track as a liminal environment.

Zola, quoting Devereux (a classic as one of the first to investigate the track bettor in his 1941 piece), notes that the track is historically distinguished by its "dissociation from ordinary utilitarian activities" (Zola 1967). Zola's functionalist analysis seeks to identify ways insiders are defined in opposition to outsiders. This chapter, on the other hand, seeks to understand the play of the track and its relation to external economic and communal activities, and thereby to understand its implications for everyday membership in a wage labor economy.

The four particular sites of this study are North American, with populations of varying class and ethnic backgrounds. Fieldwork to date has included observation studies, participant-observation, and interviews with bettors at four sites for horse betting. Interviews were also conducted with riders, ticket clerks, concession workers, and racecourse management.

Most gambling research in North America focuses on "problem" gambling (Shaffer 1999; Blaszczynski 2000). In contrast, this initial research on gambling attempts to avoid a discussion of the deviant or addictive aspects of the phenomenon; I rather seek to inquire into the construction of risk and loss in the practice of track betting, and to analyze the pleasure found through the fantasy the risk embodies. This analysis asks: Does the habituated gambler represent Bourdieu's "inept," the "self-drop-outs"? Are they de Certeau's actors who "remain in complicity with the system that tends to perpetuate the existing relations of force" and further enrich "those who dominate economic relationships" (de Certeau 1997, 86)? This chapter suggests that gambling offers an example of differing access to cultural/economic/social capital in which seemingly non-rational choices make sense as acts of resistance, if not of rebellion. This interpretation differs from the "problem gambling" literature and is specifically influenced by Bourdieu's insights. This research seeks to analyze the motive and sociopolitical statement made by the practice of gambling. I thus seek to avoid pathologizing gambling in the mode of earlier functionalist research on gambling, such as the interpretation by Zola (1967). Track bettors, while knowing a true economic or social transformation is unlikely, persist in their expression of the absurdities of economic and social stratification: "his rebellions take place, not within a political party, but in splendid isolation. This *private* rebel fights with neither guns nor ballots; cards, stocks, dice, chips are his weapons and his invisible colors" (Bergler, in Herman 1967, 130).

My observations have corroborated the increased sociability at track betting sites observed by Fox (1999), but I have also noted that in the contexts I observed the talk is restricted to lives inside the betting site. I also noted the intense discipline and commitment of the habitual bettor. Regulars have a look of focused fanaticism, not seekers of hedonistic pleasure. Food and alcohol are secondary to the serious gambler. At one off-site location, five minutes before the Belmont was to begin, with the tension in the room steadily increasing, I observed an elderly man who crashed to the floor from his chair with a loud thud. All of the potential bettors present instinctively threw a quick glance toward the source of the noise and then immediately re-fixed their gaze on the simulcast of global races or on the latest tally of odds for the upcoming Belmont, and the man lay on the floor unheeded.

Both off-site and track betting on ponies represents an elevated segment of gambling society in which the emphasis on superstition, fate, and luck is eschewed among regulars in relation to the valued activities of performance evaluations of horse, jockey, and track conditions. But the two kinds of loci for horserace betting differ in key ways. Spatial organization alters the atmosphere and nature of the practice. Horse tracks represent "concentrated sites" of "intense, localized activity" and "expeditionary character" (Reith 2002, 96) whose location outside of urban cores leads to a committed immersion in the raison d'être of the site. There is an awareness of the full round of players in the game: the animals, the owners, the trainers, the exercisers, the jockeys, and the spectator/bettors. All are visually available to each other (and auditorially to some degree). Between periods of high drama, aimless, bored roaming, socializing, and observing between races are activities common to all and add to the theater of the site, as these periods emphasize the cyclical drama of the day.

But at off-site simulcast betting, the degree of interaction may range from excruciatingly intense concentration to seeming indifference. At some sites betting is merely a secondary activity to dining or enjoying pub sociability. "Technology expands the 'reach' of gamblers so that they can expand and project their 'gambling body' into a thing of huge proportions over vast distances in such a way that their *actual* bodies need not be present in any single specific space" (Reith 2002, 96). Evidence of the power of this extended reach of gambling is the 255 percent rise in e-gaming stocks in fifteen months (*National Post*, April 14, 2005, 11).

Thus, the exclusivity of the horses as a form of betting, its class associations, and the aura of its space are altered. Off-site milieux range from the cliché of tawdry, all-male, intensely focused bar sites to sanitized middle-class bistro environments in which the betting seems incidental to the sale of white wine, pasta, and Caesar salad. Gambling corporations have sought to normalize and infuse gambling into the everyday life of the culture such that it can be present as a seeming afterthought to the activity at hand. In these environments, Reith's descriptive warning comes to mind: "The previous stratification of the gambling economy, with horses and high-stakes casino play the prerogative of the aristocracy and lotteries patronized mainly by the poor, is gradually breaking down. The middle classes, traditionally opposed to all forms of gambling, become incorporated into the map" (Reith 2002, 92).

The rhythm of the day at the track for on-site betting implies a day of leisure, leading to its association as a place for both the upper classes and "ne'er-do-wells." "The race track is a concentrated site within which the concentration of action waxes and wanes in a series of stages, It peaks during the two to ten minutes of the race and declines during periods of waiting in between" (Reith 2002, 110). In the lull between races, bettors roam the stands, drink, go for a smoke, eat hot dogs, socialize, or view other tracks on screen. In contrast to this total immersion environment, the simulcast of off-site horse tracks means a constant barrage of incoming race results with little time to recover between climaxes. Some bettors report that this tempts them to become over-stimulated, lose their focus, and bet on races that they have not handicapped well. Thus they express a self-contempt for allowing themselves to be distracted into a lottery-like consumption orientation to betting with little intellectual orientation where the "players are not regarded as gamblers at all, even by themselves" (Reith 2002, 103). In such a frenzy the pseudo-democracy of the gaming degrades gambling into an indiscriminate enterprise that fails to reflect work, discipline, or intelligence.

Risk

> Capital in its various forms is a set of pre-emptive rights over the future; it guarantees some people the monopoly of some possibilities... Power over objective chances governs aspirations, and therefore relation to the future. (Bourdieu 2000, p.226)

Is the gambler's action simply to be read as harboring delusional thought constructions, or does a Bourdieuian analysis offer a way of theorizing this hopeful financial planning as an intentional risk, a pleasurable flaunting of prediction and calculation? Gambling defies the system of rational accumulation of capital. Much recent work on risk offers insights that parallel those of Bourdieu by emphasizing the new uncertainty of the global economy, marked by rising individualism (Beck 1992). Beck calls ours the age of the "risk society" as we move from an industrial age. Mary Douglas and Aron Wildavsky (1982) discuss the particular and subjective nature of what counts as "risk." Adams (1988) focuses on individual perceptions of and responses to risk. What kind of play and flirtation with risk does the horse bettor exemplify?

This analysis interprets the motivation of the gambler's actions to be not only to attempt to cheat the exigencies of capitalism or of divine fate, but to enact a spirited reaction to the symbolic violence of the marketplace. Motive cannot be explained by attempting to deconstruct a simple logic. If gambling were sheerly a rational cost–benefit enterprise, the pleasure of all tension would be lost. Unlike Zola's (1967) functionalist interpretation, my analysis does not assume that attempts to influence luck through educated rather than "hunch" betting represent a true belief that the "system" can be beaten. Rather, I formulate horse gambling, even if conducted with meticulous handicapping and such, as an act of resistance that is not necessarily accompanied by expectations to win. Unlike the stock market, where a speculator might hold a stock, the track's rewards and losses are instantaneous and short-lived, defying the notion of investment that is basic to capitalism. Even controlled, or intellectualized efforts at betting do not reflect the "rational cognitive" structure that Zola attributes to the internal state of the gambler (Zola 1967).

Bourdieu's assessments of various actors in capitalism consistently emphasized that a part of its *modus operandi* in maintaining the subjective domination of the worker is the undermining of their psycho-social security due the pervasiveness of the constant threat of unemployment. The "working" gamblers in this study represent those who, in Bourdieu's terms, have attempted to choose their own employer (Bourdieu 1988, 44) and who, while working assiduously at studying racing forms, handicapping, assessing jockeys and odds, are escaping "working for the man" for a time, regardless of the particularities of their class or economic position. In gambling, the symbolic violence of the market is acted out with the "free-willed" compliance of the subject. Assumptions about "luck," desert, fate, past and future possibilities are unmasked.

Bourdieu's work offers an interpretive framework to understand this strange economic mutation of social structure, through his insistence on the revelation of the "habitus," the "'can-be' which tends to produce practices objectively adjusted to the possibilities, in particular by orienting the perception and evaluation of the possibilities inscribed in the present situation" (Bourdieu 2000, 217). For Bourdieu, the actor's internalization of objective social structure is crucial in any analysis of motive. His early critiques of the "arrogance and distance" between anthropology and its subject matter (Jenkins 1992, 13) recommend that we cannot understand the social construction of the gambler without direct engagement with the life-world that gambling represents. This analysis suggests that underlying the appearance of recklessness and absence of realistic calculation on the part of the gambler is an everyday theorizing that pedestrian routes to economic fortune are themselves essentially more like the spin of a roulette wheel. The élan of gamblers is a reflection of their place as resisters of conventional economic structure; however, they are not true rebels who question the grounds of this structure because the basic ambition to accrue, if not accumulate, capital and its concomitant status are ultimately reinforced by their betting.

All but the most naïve gambler operates with full cognizance that the house always holds the advantage. Are they thus to be read as engaging in a form of self-sabotage, or worse, self-exploitation? In my interviews at a Toronto off-track site, some of the more regular attendees experienced great wins (as much as ten thousand dollars in a day), only to "re-invest" the same in the next few days' losses. There was no expression of an attempt to correct such patterns in the future, or regret that such decisions were misguided. Rather, there is a sense that this is part of the discipline, perhaps even a strange part of the pleasure, which a commitment to the life of chance requires. For even the skills of an expert handicapper cannot consistently overwhelm the democratizing effects of chance. Reith has noted that where there is more skilled betting such as that of experienced track betters, there is less of a belief in the need to rely on superstition or luck. But "[n]o amount of skill can ever eliminate uncertainty and confer absolute control, for chance is an ontological feature of the work; its influence is pervasive and the outcome of a gamble is always a contingent event" (Reith 2002, 94). The element of play is crucial to analyzing the gambler; the attempt to control the world by risking more than one would in a technically calculated formula of expenditure and gain. "In games ... we have a chance to enact our most basic relationship to the world—our desire to prevail over adversity, to survive our inevitable defeats, to master complexity, and to make our lives fit together like the pieces of a jigsaw puzzle" (Murray 2001, 380), hence the traditional track bettors' contempt for passive betting games like slots.

Rational Action

Definition of Gambling: *The act of risking money, property, or something of value on an activity with an uncertain outcome.* (Canadian Foundation On Compulsive Gambling 2002)

Note the similarity of this definition of gambling to many types of financial endeavors that rely on speculation. The players at one Toronto off-site track I observed, mostly from the "working poor" (according to cues given in conversation), do not tend to drink excessively or socialize beyond the discussion of bets. The atmosphere is that of a lively workplace filled with intensely motivated workers. How do we account for what could be read as excessive and misguided commitment in a rational risk–reward ratio, especially given the near inevitability of re-investing (and re-risking) the rewards?

Benjamin notes in his *Arcades Project* the similarity between gambling and the stock market, and relates the everyday actor's experience of both as that of a submission to a kind of magic.

> It is useless to expect that a bourgeois could ever succeed in comprehending the phenomena of the distribution of wealth.... [T]he buying and selling of stocks is actually known as "playing" the market. Modern economic development as a whole tends more and more to transform capitalist society into a giant international gambling house, where the bourgeois wins and loses capital in consequence of events which remain unknown to him... Successes and failures, thus arising from causes that are unanticipated, generally unintelligible, and seemingly dependent on chance, predispose the bourgeois to the gambler's frame of mind.... The capitalist whose fortune is tied up in stocks and bonds, which are subject to variations in market value and yield for which he does not understand the causes, is a professional gambler. (Benjamin 1999, O4, 1)

As a result of his early fieldwork in Algiers, Bourdieu came to conclude that the production of behaviors that count as rationally grounded economic practices are the product of quite particular and class-based economic histories.

> In short, there are economic and cultural conditions for access to what is regarded as rational economic behaviour ... like access to opinion, access to enlightened economic choice, in the act of purchasing, borrowing or saving, has economic conditions of possibility, and that equality in freedom and in "rationality" is equally fictitious in either case. I was able to establish empirically that, below a certain level of economic security, provided by stable employment and a basic level of economic security and a regular income, allowing some grip on the present, economic agents can neither conceive nor perform most of the behaviours which presuppose an effort to take a grip on the future, such as the management of resources over time, saving, measured recourse to credit or the control of fertility. In short, there are economic and social conditions for access to what is regarded as rational economic behaviour. (Bourdieu 2000, 72)

Thus, Bourdieu frames his discussion of economic situatedness to offer an alternative account of "rational" behavior, as that which need not include an expectation of reward. In relation to gambling behavior, this means that the expectation is not necessarily to beat the house and increase profits. Bourdieu notes that the conventional formulation of rational risk only includes acts that might predictably influence the future.

> Individual finalism, which conceives action as determined by the conscious aiming at explicitly posed goals, is a well-founded illusion; the sense of the game which implies an anticipated adjustment of habitués to the necessities and to the probabilities inscribed in the field, does present itself under the appearance of a successful "aiming at" a future. (Bourdieu and Wacquant 1992, 43)

Bourdieu concurs with Max Weber that much of social life is organized around predictability and calculability. Gambling can be seen as such a practice, in which the actors do not actually expect to win, although the gambler does expect to *flirt* with reversals of fortune. (Note how even recreational gamblers will decide in advance how much they can afford to "spend" in a night out at the casino.) Fisher (1993) has noted that particularly among slot players, "none of these individuals gambled to win money" (Reith 2002, 109). As an example of this phenomenon from horse bettors, my fieldwork encountered Alex, a slaughterhouse butcher in his late fifties. He puts in several hours every day at one off-track site, claims that he has won more money in betting than he has earned in a lifetime of butchering, and has consistently put winnings back into bets immediately until they evaporated once again. He reports winning twenty thousand in one day only to "re-invest" the next day. We might formulate this sort of resigned decision to continue to fund one's losses as a concession that the win is the exception that proves the rule.

Since the house always has the advantage, how do we explain the dedication of resources of money and time to the enterprise of attempting to beat it? Note that a possible reversal of fortune of the sort described by Dostoevsky is nearly impossible by other means. Bourdieu laments what he sees as the failures of Rational Action Theory, because "practices depend not on the average chances of profit, an abstract and unreal notion, but on the specific chances that a singular agent or class of agents possesses by virtue of its capital, this being understood, in this respect, as a means of appropriation of the chances theoretically available to all" (Bourdieu 1977, 63). The disjuncture between the subjective fantasies of the gambler and the objective possibilities could make gambling seem to be an irrational act, but it is a situational rather than procedural rationality.

Time

Gambling has in common with other types of speculation the attempt to circumvent the seemingly inevitable linkage of time to money. The dedication of the habitual player, who typically loses (re-invests) whatever wins are made as quickly as they appear, alters the conventional sense of time, labor, investment and painfully slow accumulation of capital that is fundamental to the system of employment. As noted above, gambling is more an act of resistance than of rebellion, and it expresses contempt for wage labor. As expressed a century ago by Veblen,

> Labour comes to be associated in men's habits of thought with weakness and subjection to a master. It is therefore a mark of inferiority, and therefore comes to be accounted unworthy of man in his best estate. (Veblen, 1994 [1899], 24)

In the essay "Social Being, Time, and the Sense of Existence" (2000), Bourdieu takes up the issue of temporality in relation to economic conditions. Bettering one's opportunities in life amounts not just to an empirical relation to finance, but also to circumventing the proscribed relation of time, labor, remuneration, age, and appropriate expectations. The usual economy of time, in which it is saved or squandered, is altered through the strange habits of putting in endless hours of disciplined focus at ticket windows or at casino tables, time "spent" only superficially in the ever illusive search for an instantaneous change of status. An alternative account is that the exuberance (the gain) is contained in the very moment of risk. In gambling, the future is contained in the moment. Rosten notes that "the rich have generally given gambling wide license in their ranks. For the rich are familiar with wealth which is not derived from skill, thrift, and virtue—the cardinal middle class virtues—but via sheer luck, inheritance, 'contacts,' nepotism or lucky investments" (Rosten 1967, 48). He thus correlates Hollywood's fascination with horse racing in the forties, often expensively holding up production on films, with its comprehension of the sudden creation of wealth that defies the principles of the meritocracy.

If the wealthy, particularly that sector of the upper class created by celebrity and mass-market entertainment, are cynical about the traditional wage labor structure of financial advancement, so are the precariously employed. Bourdieu articulates the effect of global job insecurity: "Casualization profoundly effects the person who suffers it by making the whole future uncertain, it prevents all rational anticipation and, in particular, the basic belief and hope in the future that one needs in order to rebel, especially collectively, against present conditions, even the most intolerable"

(Bourdieu 1998, 82). Is such a population not ripe for the growing gaming industry which governments now rely on for revenue? He goes on to identify this "flexploitation" as "part of a mode of domination of a new kind kind, based on the creation of a generalized and permanent state of insecurity aimed at forcing workers into submission, into acceptance of exploitation" (Bourdieu 1998, 85). The horse track bettor, like bettors in some other forms of casino and sports gambling, does not abandon all hope of rational control over outcomes but walks the line between fate, chance, and self-determination.

Bourdieu's critique of education as an institution (Bourdieu and Passeron 1977) repeatedly points out that the formula of investment in education and career development most often works against those who lack the informally absorbed cultural capital. At the track window, such hope for betterment through what is conventionally construed as "work" is parodied as the bettor taunts fate, lacking a literal relation to self-betterment. The talk is only of wins, not losses. "How are you doing?" "I'm up," "I'm even." Or "It's okay." It is a contravention of track etiquette to query other bettors except in a very cursory manner about the success of their venture. Unconcern is the dominant attitude. Winnings are congratulated but there is no display of despair or sympathy over loss. This phenomenon has also been noted by Zola (1967, 31) who notes, "In the society at large, one's success or failure alters and affects one's whole way of life while here it is completely incidental to it," thus reinforcing the liminality of this social space. In my observations bettors displayed a persistent denial of emotional involvement, much like a technical analyst in the stock market surveys charts with a flat affect. A barely shakable indifference to outcome is de rigeur. It is the *play* with economic structure that is the motivation.

To understand the rationality of decisions, Bourdieu reminds us, the "unconscious" processes of decision-making must be unmasked in order to unravel the actor's strategies for organizing action. In a sense the bettor creates an alternative world; games, while having no pretense of fairness, offer more pleasurable routes of access to success.

> Those who talk of equality of opportunity forget that social games—the economic game, but also the cultural games (the religious field, the juridical field, the philosophical field, etc.) are not 'fair games'. (Bourdieu 2000, 214–15).

Bourdieu's early work on the Algerian peasant notes that the Algerian agricultural workers' sense of time was controlled by the influences of nature on the cycle of production (Pitt-Rivers 1963). In corporate capitalism, by contrast, the production schedule is controlled by management dictates, collective agreements, and arbitrary time calculation devices such as punch clocks. By contrast, the gambler's orientation to time is influenced by a fantasy of upsetting all natural or conventional expectations about the conventional social world's structures of time, energy output, and reward. It is an alternative universe. "The social world is not a game of chance, a discontinuous series of perfectly independent events, like the spin of a roulette wheel" (Bourdieu 2000, 214). (Or, we might add, at least it is founded on the illusion that it has a more solid and rational foundation.) Casinos play on this ruptured narrative of the gambler, by hiding all habitual markers of time, such as the color of the sky, the type of meal served, and separation of work and play through the hyper real space of its fantasy environment. But the horse track, by contrast, has its own rhythm, when the players are on-site or observing races through the mediation of a televised simulcast. Tension builds in anticipation of a race as last bets are placed, but it quickly dissipates as the race is called. This leisurely or repetitive nature of the activity when it is experienced on site, one race at a time, may be a part of its reputation as the "sport of kings."

Walter Benjamin noted this social gesture of the dilettantish nature of gambling, with its repetitive cycles that are akin to those of the wage laborer in the factory. "Since each operation at the machine is just as screened off from the preceding operation as a *coup* in a game of chance is from the one that preceded it, the drudgery of the labourer is, in its own way, a counterpart to the drudgery of the gambler" (Benjamin 1988, 177). At the horse track, each race is a distinct moment, offering absolution from losses in the previous runs of the day. "Gambling strenuously denies all acquired conditions, all antecedents … pointing to previous actions; and that is what distinguishes it from work. Gambling rejects … this weighty past which is the mainstay of work" (Alain, cited by Benjamin 1999, O12, 3).

The gamblers' play can be seen as a commentary on the irrationality of one's ascribed position, and of the irrationality of responding to the desire for mobility through the prolonged commitment and practices of the Protestant work ethic. Gambling parodies the holy trinity of hard work, time, and self-constraint in favor of chance and risk. Players do work with a fanatical intensity; most converse only about their bets as they follow simulcasts of five tracks at once. But the expectation of reward is not based on a direct exchange of labor for profit. Gambling, whether it results in wins or losses, works to invert the servitude to wage labor of which Veblen spoke.

Cost–Benefit Ratios

What then about the degree of risk taken within the practice of gambling?

An interview with the head of promotions for the Santa Anita Racetrack in California reveals that the most profitable opportunity wager placed is the bet-little-tremendous-gain bet. The more "rational" bet, he acknowledges, in the sense of maximizing the certainty of some profit, would be to place a wager on a favorite to place, but such gain offers less drama and thrill, though it is more easily attainable (interview with Stuart Zarnett, Director of Promotions, Santa Anita Racetrack, February 18, 2002). Those who bet large amounts on the favorite to show (come in first, second, or third) are known as "roof jumpers," because the chance of winning payout that makes transformative difference in their lives is small, but the risk is great.

One type of sophisticated gambler goes for a high rate of return through exotic bets, which include the Win 4 (one must pick the winner of four races in a row), the Win 6-Win 4, the Superfecta (top four finishes in a race, in order), Trifecta (top three finishes in a race), or Wheel—a Favorite and exactor bets. All of these are perpetuated on the hope that the punt, or player, can overcome the odds and beat the track at its own game. All decrease the likelihood of winning, but increase the percent gain on a bet. For instance, in the 2002 Preakness at Pimlico in Baltimore, Maryland, a twenty dollar bet on the favorite coming first with any other horse coming in second would have had a payout of two hundred thirty-five dollars. A more statistically probable win bet would be twenty on the favorite to win, but the payout would be only about a few dollars. In the 2002 Belmont Race, long-shot Smarty Jones going for the Triple Crown paid fifty to one, but betting the favorite to win, had it been successful, would have paid only ten cents on a two-dollar bet. The 2005 Kentucky Derby long-shot winner Giacomo paid fifty to one with George Steinbrenner's favored Bellamy Road paying out nothing.

A more everyday manifestation of this social construction of desire to gain greatly with little risk is government lottery frenzies. In a recent Canadian Super 7 draw, a two-dollar bet had the potential to net its maker more than thirty-four million. The irony is that if the regular prize is five million, the uncommitted gambler won't "invest" two dollars to win it, but will "invest" two dollars if the prize is thirty-four million. Underlying the practice of the risk-little-win-big bet's "rationale" is that one does not actually expect to win, but would rather engage in the multi-million dollar fantasy. Thus, as Bourdieu stresses, we must take into account the "conditions of the agent's existence" (Bourdieu 2000, 217). Gambling is chasing a dream, and the big bet reflects the notion expressed by rookie baseball hopefuls that "you don't get off the island by walking." Thus Rosten (1967) notes the understandable link between the growth of horseracing in Los Angeles and the burgeoning development of the movie industry in the forties, as the movies represented "a highly organized attempt to guess what the public will want and when. 'Making movies is like shooting dice all day'" (Rosten 1941, 40).

Tracks know that a typical player won't leave the premises until at least the ninth race is over (the tenth and last being hopelessly unpredictable). Such perseverance shows that the enjoyment is in the act, not the winnings, as the majority is far down in revenues by this time. Thus the track's drive is to get bodies into the stands through various enticements. The fact that most do not leave even if they are consistently losing reinforces the idea that the commitment is to the task at hand, which is gambling, and the tempting of the sudden reversal of fortune it offers, and only coincidentally the actual accumulation of capital.

Santa Anita Track in California recently used the Year of the Horse as a natural promotion to bring in the population of Chinese gamblers, who had been conspicuously absent from the track. The track's mistake was in directing advertising to the Cantonese, who responded only with a slight increase in recreational betting, because as a group in that area of Los Angeles they have relatively secure capital. The track later learned that the Mandarin community was far easier to lure into serious horse gambling, likely because they lack the capital to reverse their financial and social status by more conventional means. For the latter group, it thus looks like a more "rational" option.

> What is attempted, therefore is by and large, what is possible. The greater the number of things which become or are possible, the more options which one is offered or confronted by, the closer the fit between aspiration and reality. (Jenkins 1992, 28)

The Will to Lose

> One is always surprised to see how much people's wills adjust to their possibilities, to the capacity to satisfy them; and to discover that, contrary to all received ideas, pleonexia, the desire always to have more, as Plato called it, is the exception. (Bourdieu 2000, 216)

Why are gamblers so tolerant of their repetitive losses? One interpretation of the reasoning of the player is that gambling is an act that carries the intention to lose, thus parodying, whether consciously or unconsciously, the notion of investment and conservation of time, money, and energy, which is so fundamental to the Protestant ethic. "It becomes very clear in gambling: by constantly raising the stakes, in hopes of getting back what is lost, the gambler steers toward absolute ruin" (Benjamin 1999, O14, 4).

As well, gambling offers the social tonic of ritualistic practice of membership in a social community, in which one's gambling losses are the cost of membership. The particular lure of the track is partially its exclusivity; based on the requirements of a cultural stock of knowledge. In track culture, one obstacle to betting is inadequate cultural capital; potential bettors are insecure about appearing ignorant when placing a bet, especially if they do not understand the jargon of the track. Thus gambling entrepreneurs face seemingly conflicting demands; they must educate neophytes while preserving the caché of an insider's economy. Both Santa Anita Track and Champions in Canada now add glossaries of terms to racing programs. They also offer classes that transmit the knowledge necessary to becoming a participant rather than spectator (this has been identified as a barrier especially in attracting women to track betting, except in Japan where women under thirty are the fastest growing market at the track). However, in demystifying the culture of gambling, there is also the risk of detracting from its caché and particularity as a fantasy world.

There is a concerted effort at most tracks to mirror internally the manifestations of the class system in the world outside the track. "The architecture of the race-track itself is a monument to social stratification" (Reith 2002, 109). Class cultures are kept distinctly separate. Like opera, horseracing sports the double-edged sword of needing to increase bodies in attendance while preserving the exotics of the enterprise. Segregated parking, washrooms, bars, and restricted areas are maintained by differential fee structures. But at the same time the track flirts with the upheaval of these statuses.

At Santa Anita track in California, facing the Sierra Madre Mountains, dedicated groups of lower-status, largely ethnic, gamblers practice their trade from a vast windowless basement room. Thermoses and plastic containers of homemade food are the only visible signs of corporal pleasure. Upper-class gamblers work on higher floors in dark bars and mahogany paneled rooms (some of which cost as much as $70,000 U.S. to use), on tables littered with Scotch glasses and shrimp cocktail plates, but with an intensity of concentration that parallels that of those in the basement halls below. The social stratification of their typical socioeconomic milieu is reproduced in the track architecture. But neither set of gamblers often emerges from either of these socially stratified spaces to soak up the California sun or to gaze at the aristocratic thoroughbreds in the light of day. The intensity of the fantasy absorbs the focus of both groups. A tension for the track as a business of the track is whether to preserve the old-guard, moneyed aspect of the horseracing game or to continue along the path of new innovations and inclusion of more new economic and ethnic groups (Zarnett 2002).

And thus ironically gambling "helps to reproduce the conditions of oppression." In an economic sense, even as it offers the fantasy of instant escape from the constraints of the dictates of capitalism, gamblers could be said to be complicit in their own exploitation. Both types of gamblers at the Santa Anita track seek a life-transforming reward, but from radically different conditions. To place one's bets allows for a simulated display of frustration without an actual realistic expectation of a shift in circumstances. It is not revolutionary activity.

> "Thus power (that is, capital, social energy) governs the potentialities objectively offered to each player, her possibilities and impossibilities, her degrees of empowerment, of power-to-be, and at the same time her desire for power which, being fundamentally realistic is roughly adjusted to the agent's actual empowerment.... Various institutions conspire to direct the subject favour the adjustment of aspirations to objective chances, needs to possibilities, the anticipation and acceptance of the limits, both visible and invisible, explicit and tacit." ... Aspirations must be trained to realistically recognize "chances inscribed in the position occupied." (Bourdieu 2000, 217)

Bourdieu's work offers potential theoretical direction in order to assess actors' decision-making processes in various contexts involving risk–loss–gain assessments. A commitment to gambling does not operate according to a mere formulation of risk–loss ratios; it is a chance to alter one's life chances with the gods, but only through a determined and committed effort to access one's luck. It bears noting that governments' almost addictive relation to gambling revenues means they hold an interest in keeping much of the population flirting with the possibilities of altering their social and economic situatededness, while assuring that radical transformation of economic circumstance happens only for the few.

This conspiratorial aspect of the state's influence on the gambling citizen was noted by Benjamin through the material collected for his *Arcades Project*, when he quotes from the *Gambler's Banquet*: "Concerning the heroic element in gambling ... 'What if one were to store up all the energy and passion ... which every year is squandered ... at the gaming tables of Europe—would one have enough to make a Roman people out of it, and a Roman history?... Because each man is born a Roman, bourgeois society aims to de-Romanize him, and thus there are games of chance ... casinos, tea parties and lotteries …—all these have been introduced so that the overabundant energy evaporates unnoticed!" (Borne, quoted by Benjamin 1999, O13a, 5).

Finally we can ask, are attitudes expressed in gambling representative of other kinds of risk-taking? This latter question has ramifications for life management decisions such as the acquisition of insurance and investments, as well as for risks in sexual practices and sports behaviors. The ideation of risk embedded in (non-problem) gambling behavior should provide valuable insight for policy makers who must address the preferences made by citizens making other fundamental economic and life choices.

Bourdieu emphasizes: "Power can be exerted on the objective tendencies of the social worlds, those which are measured by objective probabilities, and consequently, on subjective experiences of aspirations or expectation.… A world founded on stable principles of redistribution is a predictable world that one can count on, even in its risks" (Bourdieu 2000, 228). It is such distributive principles that gambling defies; no player's system guarantees success for long. The commitment to gamble is a liminal activity. The players portrayed here respond to power by refusing to interpret their life chances in the logic of economic cost/benefit rationality. They also parody the system of middle-class belief in the earned rewards of the meritocracy (Rosten 1967).

To attempt to alter one's fate, to alter the balance between hope and despair, requires perseverance, discipline, and commitment, but most of all an "irrational" faith. The horse bettors described here, while not economic radicals subverting the underlying principles of capitalism, all demonstrate from their varying class positions acts of resistance to the normative institutionalized structures of investment, wage labor, and reward.

References

Bateson, Gregory (1973) "A Theory of Play and Fantasy," in *Steps to an Ecology of Mind*, 177–193. St. Albans: Paladin.

Beck, Ulrich (1992) *Risk Society: Towards a New Modernity*. London: Sage.

Benjamin, Walter (1988) "On Some Motifs in Baudelaire," in *Illuminations*, trans. Harry Zohn, 155–200. New York: Schocken Books.

———— (1999) *The Arcades Project*, trans. Howard Eiland and Kevin McLaughlin. Cambridge, MA: Harvard University Press.

Bergler, Edmund (1968) "The Psychology of Gambling," in Robert D. Herman, *Gambling*, 113–130. Pomona: Harper & Row.

Bernstein, Peter L. (1996) *Against the Gods: The Remarkable Story of Risk*. New York: John Wiley & Sons.

Blaszczynski, Alex (March, 2000) "Pathways to Pathological Gambling: Identifying Typologies," *Electronic Journal of Gambling Issues* 1.

Bourdieu, Pierre (1963) "The Attitude of the Algerian Peasant Toward Time," in *Mediterranean Countrymen,* ed. J. Pitt-Rivers. Westport: Greenwood Press.

_____ (1977) *Outline of a Theory of Practice.* Cambridge: Cambridge University Press.

_____ (1990) *In Other Words: Essays Towards a Reflexive Sociology.* Cambridge: Polity Press.

_____ (1998) *On Television,* trans. Priscilla Pankhurst Ferguson. London: Pluto Press.

_____ (1999) *Acts of Resistance: Against the Tyranny of the Market,* trans. Richard Nice. New York: New Press.

_____ (2000) *Pascalian Meditations.* Stanford: Stanford University Press (first published 1997; translated in 2000).

Bourdieu, Pierre and Jean-Claude Passeron (1977) *Reproduction in Education, Society and Culture.* London: Sage.

Canadian Foundation on Compulsive Gambling (accessed June 4, 2001) http://www.cfcgambling.org/.

Casey, Emma (2003) "Gambling and Consumption: Working-Class Women and UK National Lottery Play," *Journal of Consumer Culture* 3(2): 245–63.

Certeau, Michel de (1997) *Culture in the Plural,* edited and with an introduction by Luce Girard; translated and with an afterword by Tom Conley. Minneapolis: University of Minnesota Press.

Christine, Bill (April 2, 2005) "Slot Machines Have Varying Track Records," *Los Angeles Times,* p. A21.

Douglas, Mary, and Aaron Wildavsky (1982) *Risk and Culture: An Essay on the Selection of Technical and Environmental Dangers.* Berkeley: University of California Press.

Fox, Kate (1999) *The Racing Tribe: Watching the Horsewatchers.* London: Metro.

Franklin, Jane (ed.) (1998) *The Politics of Risk Society.* Cambridge: Polity Press.

Garfinkel, Harold (1967) *Studies in Ethnomethodology.* Englewood Cliffs, NJ: Prentice-Hall.

Goodman, Robert (1995) *The Luck Business: The Devastating Consequences and Broken Promises of America's Gambling Explosion.* New York: Free Press.

Gorman, David (2000) Interview on September 28, Woodbine Racetrack, Toronto.

Herman, Robert D. (1967) *Gambling.* Pomona: Harper & Row.

Hutchinson, Brian (1999) *Betting the House: Winners, Losers and the Politics of Canada's Gambling Obsession.* Middlesex: Penguin.

Jenkins, Richard (1992) "Reading Bourdieu," in *Pierre Bourdieu,* 182–84. London: Routledge.

Johnson, Douglas (January 28, 2002) "Obituary: Pierre Bourdieu," *The Guardian,* London. http://books.guardian.co.uk/news/articles/0,,640711,00.html. Accessed Feb. 18, 2002.

McMillen, Jan (1996) *Gambling Cultures: Studies in History and Interpretation.* London: Routledge.

Murray, Janet (2001) "Agency: Hamlet on the Holodeck" (1997), in *Multimedia: From Wagner to Virtual Reality,* ed. W. W. Randall Packer and Ken Jordan. 380–402. New York: Norton.

Maddaus, Gene (May 16, 2005) "Developer Taking the Pulse of Arcadia," *Pasadena Star News*, p. A1.

National Post (April 14, 2005) "Gambling Stocks Are Hot," p. 11.

Reith, Gerda (2002) *The Age of Chance: Gambling and Western Culture*. London: Routledge.

Rosencrance, John D. (1985) *The Degenerates of Lake Tahoe: A Study of Persistence in The Social World of Horse Race Gambling*. New York: Peter Lang.

_____ (1986) "Attributions and the Origins of Problem Gambling," *Sociological Quarterly* 27(4): 464–77.

Rosten, Leo (1967) "The Adoration of the Nag," in Robert D. Herman, *Gambling*. Pomona: Harper & Row.

Schwartz, Barry (1973) "Waiting, Exchange, and Power: The Distribution of Time in Social Systems," *American Journal of Sociology* 79: 841–70.

Scott, Marvin B. (1968) *The Racing Game*. Chicago, Aldine.

Shaffer, Howard J. (1999) "Strange Bedfellows: A Critical View of Pathological Gambling and Addiction," *Addiction* 94(10): 1445–48.

Thompson, William M. (2001) *Gambling in America: An Encyclopedia of History, Issues, and Society*. Santa Barbara: ABC CLIO.

Toronto Star (September 3, 2002) "Stronach Has Bold Vision for Racing," p. E8.

Veblen, Thorstein (1994 [1899]) *The Theory of the Leisure Class*. New York. Dover.

Zarnett, Stuart (2002) Interview, Santa Anita Racetrack, Arcadia, CA, February 18.

Zola, Irving Kenneth (1967) "Observations on Gambling in a Lower-Class Setting," in Robert D. Herman. 19–32. *Gambling*. Pomona: Harper & Row.

Adventure, Action, and Play:

Gambling as Social Action

Introduction

The pieces in this section address gambling as a form of social action. Walter Benjamin's short piece, "Notes on a Theory of Gambling," provides a framework for situating the subjective orientation of the gambler, and anticipates psychological research into the motivations of gamblers and problem-gamblers. While Georg Simmel's piece, "The Adventurer," is not directly about gambling, his interpretation of this particular social type provides insights into the experience of gambling, risk-taking, and adventure. Simmel's formal analytical approach is interested in revealing the structure of the adventure experience as it is oriented to by the participant; not only does the adventure activity mark a temporal break from the routines of everyday life, it depends upon the meaningful transformation of, and orientation to, activities such that they become adventures.

Like Walter Benjamin and preceding him, Simmel was deeply interested in forms of the modern experience, particularly as they display themselves in metropolitan life, but his brief discussions of gambling were never developed into sustained sociological formulations. If we consider Simmel's formulation of adventure as an activity that falls outside the "usual continuity of life," questions arise upon reflection on the gambling experience as a (potential) form of adventure.

At one time, Las Vegas was the only place to pursue legal gambling opportunities in North America, aside from horseracing and bingo, and to go to Las Vegas could be oriented to as an adventure—a trip to "sin city." The adventurous orientation has been popularized through the saying, "what happens in Las Vegas stays in Las Vegas." However, casino expansion, "gaming" products available in convenience stores, and Internet gambling (poker in particular) have contributed to an environment in which gambling has become "spatially decontained" (Schwartz 2003).

How does this spatial decontainment shape cultural definitions and actors' understandings of gambling activities? Is gambling work, or routine or adventure? Is widespread commercial gambling to be thought as providing more opportunity for adventure or action? Or, does its ubiquity suggest its routinization and normalization? Sociologically, what is the relationship between societal processes of rationalization and forms of risk-taking, play, and adventure (Lyng 2005)?

Written before the present era of gambling legalization and expansion, Goffman's classic essay, "Where the Action Is," addresses some of these questions, elucidating the gambling experience as motivated primarily by "action." For Goffman, certain actors seek out action, and while this can take many forms through a variety of risk-taking activities, his main focus for the analysis of action is the gambling scene. As Downes et al. (1976) note in "Gambling as a Sociological Problem" (Chapter Four), one of the great merits of Goffman's piece is that it "lifts gambling out of the moral abyss into which successive generations of commentators and reformers have consigned it and renders possible a consideration of its meaning which is freed from *a priori* associations of a negative kind." Goffman is interested in getting at the particularity of gambling as an activity without the overlay of moral evaluations of its badness or goodness. The excerpted piece introduces us to core concepts for understanding risk and gambling at the level of the actor, for example, action, character, consequentiality, and fatefulness.

Goffman also offers a sociological analysis of "risk," well before the interest in and development of the topic found in the macro-oriented work of Giddens and Beck, albeit focusing his analysis at the level of the (micro) interactional order. Goffman's discussion of action and risk-taking also anticipates the work of sociologists such as Lyng (2005) who are interested in forms of voluntary risk-taking or "edgework."

Reith's discussion draws upon a wide range of sociological, philosophical, and literary sources in order to explore the gambling experience as a form of play. She utilizes a phenomenological approach to understand gamblers in terms of their subjective orientation to play and chance, and draws from the work of Simmel, Goffman, Benjamin, and others to focus on the meanings and structures of gambling activities. Gambling "worlds" are viewed as worlds set apart for particular kinds of experiences. The Barthelmes' piece provides an interesting narrative account of the authors' attempts to understand their relationship with gambling and "action." Are these individuals "problem gamblers" who are driven by psychological forces they cannot control, or is gambling an activity that they orient to as a way of expressing certain desires, and which can be looked at in terms of its subjective meaningfulness for their lives? How do we grasp the significance of expenditure and loss in the gambling experience?

References

Downes, David, B. P. Davies, M. E. David, and P. Stone (1976) "Gambling as a Sociological Problem," in *Gambling, Work and Leisure: A Study Across Three Areas,* 11–28. London: Routledge and Kegan Paul.

Lyng, Stephen, ed. (2005) *Edgework: The Sociology of Risk-Taking.* New York: Routledge.

Schwartz, David G. (2003) *Suburban Xanadu: The Casino Resort on the Las Vegas Strip and Beyond.* New York: Routledge.

CHAPTER 10

Notes on a Theory of Gambling[1]

WALTER BENJAMIN

Certain matters are clear. What is decisive is the level of motor innervation, and the more emancipated it is from optical perception, the more decisive it is. From this stems a principal commandment for gamblers: they must use their hands sparingly, in order to respond to the slightest innervations. The gambler's basic approach must, so to speak, adumbrate the subtlest network of inhibitions, which lets only the most minute and unassuming innervations pass through its meshes.—It is also an established fact that the loser tends to indulge in a certain feeling of lightness, not to say relief. Conversely, the experience of having won weighs on the gambler's mind. (This refers to his state of mind after the game, not during it.) We must say of the winner that he has to do battle with the feeling of hubris which threatens to overwhelm him. He falls, perhaps not unintentionally, into a state of depression.—Another fact: the genuine gambler places his most important bets—which are usually his most successful ones, too—at the last possible moment. He could be said to be inspired by a certain characteristic sound made by the roulette ball just before it falls on a specific number. But one could also argue that it is only at the last moment, when everything is pressing toward a conclusion, at the critical moment of danger (of missing his chance), that a gambler discovers the trick of finding his way around the table, of reading the table—if this, too, is not just an expression from the realm of optics.—The gambler may form the impression that the winning numbers are hiding from him. This happens because—we may hypothesize—he knows every winning number in advance, except for the one that he (accidentally) bet on with an optical or rational consciousness. In the case of the others, there is a twofold possibility: either he bet on them correctly, relying on his motor innervations (inspiration), or else he knew them in advance but was unable to discover (reveal, make manifest) this knowledge in terms of motor stimuli. Hence the feeling that the number was hiding.—When a winning number is clearly predicted but not bet on, the man who is not in the know will conclude that he is in excellent form and that next time he just needs to act more promptly, more boldly. Whereas anyone familiar with the game will know that a single incident of this kind is sufficient to tell him that he must break off instantly. For it is a sign that the contract between his motor stimuli and "fate" has been interrupted. Only then will "what is to come" enter his consciousness more or less clearly as what it is.—Also established is the fact that no one has so many chances of betting on a winning number as someone who has just made a significant win. This means that the correct sequence is based not on any previous knowledge of the future but on a correct physical predisposition, which is increased in immediacy, certainty, and uninhibitedness by every confirmation, such as is provided by a win.—The happiness of the winner: the winner's highly remarkable feeling of elation, of being rewarded by fate, of having seized control of destiny. Comparison with the expression of love by a woman who has been truly satisfied by a man. Money and property, normally the most massive and cumbersome things, here come directly from the hands of fate, as if they were the caressing response to a perfect embrace.—Furthermore, one should note the factor of danger, which is the most important factor in gambling, alongside pleasure (the pleasure of betting on the right number). It arises not so much from the threat of losing as from that of *not winning*. The particular danger that threatens the gambler lies in the fateful category of arriving "too late," of having "missed the opportunity." We could learn something from this about the character of the gambler as a type.—Last, the best that has thus far been written about gambling focuses on the factor of acceleration, acceleration and danger. What Anatole France has said on pages 14ff. of *Le jardin d'Epicure* [The Garden of Epicurus] must be combined with what has been noted here: gambling generates by way of experiment the lightning-quick process of stimulation at the moment of danger, the marginal case in which presence of mind becomes divination—that is to say, one of the highest, rarest moments in life.

See, on this subject, "The Path to Success, in Thirteen Theses" [*Walter Benjamin: Selected Writings*, Vol. 2]; and Alain, *Les idées et les âges* (Paris, 1927), under "Le jeu."

Note

1. Fragment written in 1929 or 1930; unpublished in Benjamin's lifetime. *Gesammelte Schriften*, VI, 188–190. Translated by Rodney Livingstone.

CHAPTER 11

The Adventurer
1911[*]

GEORG SIMMEL

Each segment of our conduct and experience bears a twofold meaning: it revolves about its own center, contains as much breadth and depth, joy and suffering, as the immediate experiencing gives it, and at the same time is a segment of a course of life—not only a circumscribed entity, but also a component of an organism. Both aspects, in various configurations, characterize everything that occurs in a life. Events which may be widely divergent in their bearing on life as a whole may nonetheless be quite similar to one another; or they may be incommensurate in their intrinsic meanings but so similar in respect to the roles they play in our total existence as to be interchangeable.

One of two experiences which are not particularly different in substance, as far as we can indicate it, may nevertheless be perceived as an "adventure" and the other not. The one receives the designation denied the other because of this difference in the relation to the whole of our life. More precisely, the most general form of adventure is its dropping out of the continuity of life. "Wholeness of life," after all, refers to the fact that a

---

[*] Reprinted from *Georg Simmel, 1858–1918: A Collection of Essays, with Translations and a Bibliography*, edited by Kurt H. Wolff. Copyright 1959 by the Ohio State University Press. All rights reserved. Translated by David Kettler. Originally published in German as "Das Abernteuer," in Georg Simmel, *Philosophische Kultur: Gesammelte Essays* (Leipzig: W. Klinkhardt, 1911).

consistent process runs through the individual components of life, however crassly and irreconcilably distinct they may be. What we call an adventure stands in contrast to that interlocking of life-links, to that feeling that those countercurrents, turnings, and knots still, after all, spin forth a continuous thread. An adventure is certainly a part of our existence, directly contiguous with other parts which precede and follow it; at the same time, however, in its deeper meaning, it occurs outside the usual continuity of this life. Nevertheless, it is distinct from all that is accidental and alien, merely touching life's outer shell. While it falls outside the context of life, it falls, with this same movement, as it were, back into that context again, as will become clear later; it is a foreign body in our existence which is yet somehow connected with the center; the outside, if only by a long and unfamiliar detour, is formally an aspect of the inside.

Because of its place in our psychic life, a remembered adventure tends to take on the quality of a dream. Everyone knows how quickly we forget dreams because they, too, are placed outside the meaningful context of life-as-a-whole. What we designate as "dreamlike" is nothing but a memory which is bound to the unified, consistent life-process by fewer threads than are ordinary experiences. We might say that we localize our inability to assimilate to this process something experienced by imagining a dream in which it took place. The more "adventurous" an adventure, that is, the more fully it realizes its idea, the more "dreamlike" it becomes in our memory. It often moves so far away from the center of the ego and the course of life which the ego guides and organizes that we may think of it as something experienced by another person. How far outside that course it lies, how alien it has become to that course, is expressed precisely by the fact that we might well feel that we could appropriately assign to the adventure a subject other than the ego.

We ascribe to an adventure a beginning and an end much sharper than those to be discovered in the other forms of our experiences. The adventure is freed of the entanglements and concatenations which are characteristic of those forms and is given a meaning in and of itself. Of our ordinary experiences, we declare that one of them is over when, or because, another starts; they reciprocally determine each other's limits, and so become a means whereby the contextual unity of life is structured or expressed. The adventure, however, according to its intrinsic meaning, is independent of the "before" and "after"; its boundaries are defined regardless of them. We speak of adventure precisely when continuity with life is thus disregarded on principle—or rather when there is not even any need to disregard it, because we know from the beginning that we have to do with something alien, untouchable, out of the ordinary. The adventure lacks that reciprocal interpenetration with adjacent parts of life which constitutes life-as-a-whole. It is like an island in life which determines its beginning and end according to its own formative powers and not—like the part of a continent—also according to those of adjacent territories. This factor of decisive boundedness, which lifts an adventure out of the regular course of a human destiny, is not mechanical but organic; just as the organism determines its spatial shape not simply by adjusting to obstacles confining it from right and left but by the propelling force of a life forming from inside out, so does an adventure not end because something else begins; instead, its temporal form, its radical being ended, is the precise expression of its inner sense.

Here, above all, is the basis of the profound affinity between the adventurer and the artist, and also, perhaps, of the artist's attraction by adventure. For the essence of a work of art is, after all, that it cuts out a piece of the endlessly continuous sequences of perceived experience, detaching it from all connections with one side or the other, giving it a self-sufficient form as though defined and held together by an inner core. A part of existence, interwoven with the uninterruptedness of that existence, yet nevertheless felt as a whole, as an integrated unit—this is the form common to both the work of art and the adventure. Indeed, it is an attribute of this form to make us feel that in both the work of art and the adventure the whole of life is somehow comprehended and consummated—and this irrespective of the particular theme either of them may have. Moreover, we feel this, not although, but because, the work of art exists entirely beyond life as a reality; the adventure, entirely beyond life as an uninterrupted course which intelligibly connects every element with its neighbors. It is because the work of art and the adventure stand over against life (even though in very different senses of the phrase) that both are analogous to the totality of life itself, even as this totality presents itself in the brief summary and crowdedness of a dream experience.

For this reason, the adventurer is also the extreme example of the ahistorical individual, of the man who lives in the present. On the one hand, he is not determined by any past (and this marks the contrast between him and the aged, of which more later); nor, on the other hand, does the future exist for him. An extraordinarily characteristic proof of this is that Casanova (as may be seen from his memoirs), in the course of his erotic-adventurous life, ever so often seriously intended to marry a woman with whom he was in love at the time. In the light of his temperament and conduct of life, we can imagine nothing more obviously impossible, internally and externally. Casanova not only had excellent knowledge of men but also rare knowledge of himself. Although he must have said to himself that he could not stand marriage even two weeks and that the most miserable consequences of such a step would be quite unavoidable, his perspective on the future was wholly obliterated in the rapture of the moment. (Saying this, I mean to put the emphasis on the moment rather than on the rapture.) Because he was entirely dominated by the feeling of the present, he wanted to enter into a future relationship which was impossible precisely because his temperament was oriented to the present.

In contrast to those aspects of life which are related only peripherally—by mere fate—the adventure is defined by its capacity, in spite of its being isolated and accidental, to have necessity and meaning. Something becomes an adventure only by virtue of two conditions: that it itself is a specific organization of some significant meaning with a beginning and an end; and that, despite its accidental nature, its extraterritoriality with respect to the continuity of life, it nevertheless connects with the character and identity of the bearer of that life—that it does so in the widest sense, transcending, by a mysterious necessity, life's more narrowly rational aspects.

At this point there emerges the relation between the adventurer and the gambler. The gambler, clearly, has abandoned himself to the meaninglessness of chance. In so far, however, as he counts on its favor and believes possible and realizes a life dependent on it, chance for him has become part of a context of meaning. The typical superstition of the gambler is nothing other than the tangible and isolated, and thus, of course, childish, form of this profound and all-encompassing scheme of his life, according to which chance makes sense and contains some necessary meaning (even though not by the criterion of rational logic). In his superstition, he wants to draw chance into his teleological system by omens and magical aids, thus removing it from its inaccessible isolation and searching in it for a lawful order, no matter how fantastic the laws of such an order may be.

The adventurer similarly lets the accident somehow be encompassed by the meaning which controls the consistent continuity of life, even though the accident lies outside that continuity. He achieves a central feeling of life which runs through the eccentricity of the adventure and produces a new, significant necessity of his life in the very width of the distance between its accidental, externally given content and the unifying core of existence from which meaning flows. There is in us an eternal process playing back and forth between chance and necessity, between the fragmentary materials given us from the outside and the consistent meaning of the life developed from within.

The great forms in which we shape the substance of life are the syntheses, antagonisms, or compromises between chance and necessity.

Adventure is such a form. When the professional adventurer makes a system of life out of his life's lack of system, when out of his inner necessity he seeks the naked, external accidents and builds them into that necessity, he only, so to speak, makes macroscopically visible that which is the essential form of every "adventure," even that of the non-adventurous person. For by adventure we always mean a third something, neither the sheer, abrupt event whose meaning—a mere given—simply remains outside us nor the consistent sequence of life in which every element supplements every other toward an inclusively integrated meaning. The adventure is no mere hodgepodge of these two, but rather that incomparable experience which can be interpreted only as a particular encompassing of the accidentally external by the internally necessary.

Occasionally, however, this whole relationship is comprehended in a still more profound inner configuration. No matter how much the adventure seems to rest on a differentiation within life, life as a whole may be perceived as an adventure. For this, one need neither be an adventurer nor undergo many adventures. To have such a remarkable attitude toward life, one must sense above its totality a higher unity, a super-life, as it were, whose relation to life parallels the relation of the immediate life totality itself to those particular experiences which we call adventures.

Perhaps we belong to a metaphysical order, perhaps our soul lives a transcendent existence, such that our earthly, conscious life is only an isolated fragment as compared to the unnamable context of an existence running its course in it. The myth of the transmigration of souls may be a halting attempt to express such a segmental character of every individual life. Whoever senses through all actual life a secret, timeless existence of the soul, which is connected with the realities of life only as from a distance, will perceive life in its given and limited wholeness as an adventure when compared to that transcendent and self-consistent fate. Certain religious moods seem to bring about such a perception. When our earthly career strikes us as a mere preliminary phase in the fulfillment of eternal destinies, when we have no home but merely a temporary asylum on earth, this obviously is only a particular variant of the general feeling that life as a whole is an adventure. It merely expresses the running together, in life, of the symptoms of adventure. It stands outside that proper meaning and steady course of existence to which it is yet tied by a fate and a secret symbolism. A fragmentary incident, it is yet, like a work of art, enclosed by a beginning and an end. Like a dream, it gathers all passions into itself and yet, like a dream, is destined to be forgotten; like gaming, it contrasts with seriousness, yet, like the *va banque* of the gambler, it involves the alternative between the highest gain and destruction.

Thus the adventure is a particular form in which fundamental categories of life are synthesized. Another such synthesis it achieves is that between the categories of activity and passivity, between what we conquer and what is given to us. To be sure, their synthesis in the form of adventure makes their contrast perceptible to an extreme degree. In the adventure, on the one hand, we forcibly pull the world into ourselves. This becomes clear when we compare the adventure with the manner in which we wrest the gifts of the world through work. Work, so to speak, has an organic relation to the world. In a conscious fashion, it develops the world's forces and materials toward their culmination in the human purpose, whereas in adventure we have a nonorganic relation to the world. Adventure has the gesture of the conqueror, the quick seizure of opportunity, regardless of whether the portion we carve out is harmonious or disharmonious with us, with the world, or with the relation between us and the world. On the other hand, however, in the adventure we abandon ourselves to the world with fewer defenses and reserves than in any other relation, for other relations are connected with the general run of our worldly life by more bridges, and thus defend us better against shocks and dangers through previously prepared avoidances and adjustments. In the adventure, the interweaving of activity and passivity which characterizes our life tightens these elements into a coexistence of conquest, which owes everything only to its own strength and presence of mind, and complete self-abandonment to the powers and accidents of the world, which can delight us, but in the same breath can also destroy us. Surely, it is among adventure's most wonderful and enticing charms that the unity toward which at every moment, by the very process of living, we bring together our activity and our passivity—the unity which even in a certain sense *is* life itself—accentuates its disparate elements most sharply, and precisely in *this* way makes itself the more deeply felt, as if they were only the two aspects of one and the same, mysteriously seamless life.

If the adventure, furthermore, strikes us as combining the elements of certainty and uncertainty in life, this is more than the view of the same fundamental relationship from a different angle. The certainty with which—justifiably or in error—we know the outcome, gives our activity one of its distinct qualities. If, on the contrary, we are uncertain whether we shall arrive at the point for which we have set out, if we know our ignorance of the outcome, then this means not only a quantitatively reduced certainty but an inwardly and outwardly unique practical conduct. The adventurer, in a word, treats the incalculable element in life in the way we ordinarily treat only what we think is by definition calculable. (For this reason, the philosopher is the adventurer of the spirit. He makes the hopeless, but not therefore meaningless, attempt to form into conceptual knowledge an attitude of the soul, its mood toward itself, the world, God. He treats this insoluble problem as if it were soluble.) When the outcome of our activity is made doubtful by the intermingling of unrecognizable elements of fate, we usually limit our commitment of force, hold open lines of retreat, and take each step only as if testing the ground.

In the adventure, we proceed in the directly opposite fashion: it is just on the hovering chance, on fate, on the more-or-less that we risk all, burn our bridges, and step into the mist, as if the road will lead us on, no matter what. This is the typical fatalism of the adventurer. The obscurities of fate are certainly no more transparent to him than to others; but he proceeds as if they were. The characteristic daring with which he continually leaves the solidities of life underpins itself, as it were, for its own justification with a feeling of security and "it-must-succeed," which normally only belongs to the transparency of calculable events. This is only a subjective aspect of the fatalist conviction that we certainly cannot escape a fate which we do not know: the adventurer nevertheless believes that, as far as he himself is concerned, he is certain of this unknown and unknowable element in his life. For this reason, to the sober person adventurous conduct often seems insanity; for, in order to make sense, it appears to presuppose that the unknowable is known. The prince of Ligne said of Casanova, "He believes in nothing except in what is least believable." Evidently, such belief is based on that perverse or at least "adventurous" relation between the certain and the uncertain, whose correlate, obviously, is the skepticism of the adventurer—that he "believes in nothing": for him to whom the unlikely is likely, the likely easily becomes unlikely. The adventurer relies to some extent on his own strength, but above all on his own luck; more properly, on a peculiarly undifferentiated unity of the two. Strength, of which he is certain, and luck, of which he is uncertain, subjectively combine into a sense of certainty.

If it is the nature of genius to possess an immediate relation to these secret unities which in experience and rational analysis fall apart into completely separate phenomena, the adventurer of genius lives, as if by mystic instinct, at the point where the course of the world and the individual fate have, so to speak, not yet been differentiated from one another. For this reason, he is said to have a "touch of genius." The "sleepwalking certainty" with which the adventurer leads his life becomes comprehensible in terms of that peculiar constellation whereby he considers that which is uncertain and incalculable to be the premises of his conduct, while others consider only the calculable. Unshakable even when it is shown to be denied by the facts of the case, this certainty proves how deeply that constellation is rooted in the life conditions of adventurous natures.

The adventure is a form of life which can be taken on by an undetermined number of experiences. Nevertheless, our definitions make it understandable that one of them, more than all others, tends to appear in this form: the erotic—so that our linguistic custom hardly lets us understand by "adventure" anything but an erotic one. The love affair, even if short-lived, is by no means always an adventure. The peculiar psychic qualities at whose meeting point the adventure is found must be added to this quantitative matter. The tendency of these qualities to enter such a conjuncture will become apparent step by step.

A love affair contains in clear association the two elements which the form of the adventure characteristically conjoins: conquering force and unextortable concession, winning by one's own abilities and dependence on the luck which something incalculable outside ourselves bestows on us. A degree of balance between these forces, gained by virtue of his sense of their sharp differentiation, can, perhaps, be found only in the man. Perhaps for this reason, it is of compelling significance that, as a rule, a love affair is an "adventure" only for men; for women it usually falls into other categories. In novels of love, the activity of woman is typically permeated by the passivity which either nature or history has imparted to her character; on the other hand, her acceptance of happiness is at the same time a concession and a gift.

The two poles of conquest and grace (which manifest themselves in many variations) stand closer together in woman than in man. In man, they are, as a matter of fact, much more decisively separated. For this reason, in man their coincidence in the erotic experience stamps this experience quite ambiguously as an adventure. Man plays the courting, attacking, often violently grasping role: this fact makes one easily overlook the element of fate, the dependence on something which cannot be predetermined or compelled, that is contained in every erotic experience. This refers not only to dependence on the concession on the part of the other, but to something deeper. To be sure, every "love returned," too, is a gift which cannot be "earned," not even by any measure of love—because to love, demand and compensation are irrelevant; it belongs, in principle, in a category altogether different from a squaring of accounts—a point which suggests one of its analogies to the more profound religious relation. But over and above that which we receive from another as a free gift, there still lies in every happiness of love—like a profound, impersonal bearer of those personal elements—a favor of fate. We receive happiness not only from the other: the fact that we do receive it from him is a blessing of destiny, which is incalculable. In the proudest, most self-assured event in this sphere lies something which we must accept with humility. When the force which owes its success to itself and gives all conquest of love some note of victory and triumph is then combined with the other note of favor by fate, the constellation of the adventure is, as it were, preformed.

The relation which connects the erotic content with the more general form of life as adventure is rooted in deeper ground. The adventure is the exclave of life, the "torn-off" whose beginning and end have no connection with the somehow unified stream of existence. And yet, as if hurdling this stream, it connects with the most recondite instincts and some ultimate intention of life as a whole—and this distinguishes it from the merely accidental episode, from that which only externally "happens" to us. Now, when a love affair is of short duration, it lives in precisely such a mixture of a merely tangential and yet central character. It may give our life only a momentary splendor, like a ray shed in an inside room by a light flitting by outside. Still, it satisfies a need, or is, in fact, only possible by virtue of a need which—whether it be considered as physical, psychic, or metaphysical—exists, as it were, timelessly in the foundation or center of our being. This need is related to the fleeting experience as our general longing for light is to that accidental and immediately disappearing brightness.

The fact that love harbors the possibility of this double relation is reflected by the twofold temporal aspect of the erotic. It displays two standards of time: the momentarily climactic, abruptly subsiding passion: and the idea of something which cannot pass, an idea in which the mystical destination of two souls for one another and for a higher unity finds a temporal expression. This duality might be compared with the double existence of intellectual contents: while they emerge only in the fleetingness of the psychic process, in the forever moving focus of consciousness, their logical meaning possesses timeless validity, an ideal significance which is completely independent of the instant of consciousness in which it becomes real for us. The phenomenon of adventure is such that its abrupt climax places its end into the perspective of its beginning. However, its connection with the center of life is such that it is to be distinguished from all merely accidental happiness. Thus "mortal danger," so to speak, lies in its very style. This phenomenon, therefore, is a form which by its time symbolism seems to be predetermined to receive the erotic content.

These analogies between love and adventure alone suggest that the adventure does not belong to the life-style of old age. The decisive point about this fact is that the adventure, in its specific nature and charm, is a *form of experiencing*. The *content* of the experience does not make the adventure. That one has faced mortal danger or conquered a woman for a short span of happiness; that unknown factors with which one has waged a gamble have brought surprising gain or loss; that physically or psychologically disguised, one has ventured into spheres of life from which one returns home as if from a strange world—none of these are necessarily adventure. They become adventure only by virtue of a certain experiential tension whereby their substance is realized. Only when a stream flowing between the minutest externalities of life and the central source of strength drags them into itself; when the peculiar color, ardor, and rhythm of the life-process become decisive and, as it were, transform its substance—only then does an event change from mere experience to adventure. Such a principle of accentuation, however, is alien to old age. In general, only youth knows this predominance of the process of life over its substance; whereas in old age, when the process begins to slow up and coagulate, substance becomes crucial; it then proceeds or perseveres in a certain timeless manner, indifferent to the tempo and passion of its being experienced. The old person usually lives either in a wholly *centralized* fashion, peripheral interests having fallen off and being unconnected with his essential life and its inner necessity; or his center atrophies, and existence runs its course only in isolated petty details, accenting mere externals and accidentals. Neither case makes possible the relation between the outer fate and the inner springs of life in which the adventure consists; clearly, neither permits the perception of contrast characteristic of adventure, viz., that an action is completely torn out of the inclusive context of life and that simultaneously the whole strength and intensity of life stream into it....

CHAPTER 12

Where the Action Is

ERVING GOFFMAN

"To be on the wire is life; the rest is waiting."[1]

A decade ago among those urban American males who were little given to gentility the term "action" was used in a non-Parsonian sense in reference to situations of a special kind, the contrast being to situations where there was "no action." Very recently this locution has been taken up by almost everyone, and the term itself flogged without mercy in commercials and advertisements.

This [chapter], then, deals with a term that points to something lively but is itself now almost dead. Action will be defined analytically. An effort will be made to uncover where it is to be found and what it implies about these places.

Chances

Wheresoever action is found, chance-taking is sure to be. Begin then with a simple illustration of chance, and work outward from there.

Two boys together find a nickel in their path and decide that one will toss and the other call to see who keeps it. They agree, then, to engage in a *play* or, as probabilists call it, a *gamble*—in this case one go at the *game* of coin-tossing.

A coin can be used as a decision machine, much as a roulette wheel or a deck of cards can. With this particular machine it is plain that a fully known set of *possible outcomes* is faced: heads or tails, obverse or reverse. Similarly with a die: in ordinary manufacture and use,[2] it presents six different faces as possible outcomes.

Given the two outcomes possible when a coin is tossed, the probability or *chance* can be assessed for each of them. Chances vary from "sure" to "impossible" or, in the language of probability, from 1 to 0.

What a player has in hand and undergoes a chance of losing is his stake or *bet*. What the play gives him a chance of winning that he doesn't already have can be called his *prize*. The *payoff* for him is the prize that he wins or the bet that he loses. Bet and prize together may be called the *pot*.[3]

In gaming, *theoretical odds* refers to the chances of a favorable outcome compared to those of an unfavorable one, the decision machine here seen as an ideal one; *true odds* are a theoretical version of theoretical ones, involving a correction for the physical biases found in any actual machine—biases never to be fully eliminated or fully known.[4] *Given odds* or *pay*, on the other hand, refers to the size of the prize compared to that of the bet.[5] Note that outcomes are defined wholly in terms of the game equipment, payoffs in terms of extrinsic and variable resources currently committed to particular outcomes. Thus, with theoretical odds and given odds, somewhat the same term is employed to cover two radically different ideas.

Weighting the pot by the chance on the average of winning it, gives what students of chance call the *expected value* of the play. Subtracting the expected value from the amount bet gives a measure of the price or the profit on the average for engaging in the play. Expressing this measure as a proportion of the bet gives the *advantage* or percentage of the play. When there is neither advantage nor disadvantage, the play is said to be *fair*. Then the theoretical odds are the reciprocal of the given odds, so that he who *gives* or *lays* the odds, gambling a large sum in the hope of winning a small one is exactly compensated by the smallness of his chance of losing to the individual who *takes* the odds.

There are plays that allow a multitude of possible outcomes to choose among, each of which pays differently and may even provide the bettor differing disadvantage. Casino craps is an example. Still other plays involve a set of favorable possible outcomes that pay differently so that the expected value of the play must be calculated as a sum of several different values: slot machines and keno provide examples.

In the degree to which a play is a means of acquiring a prize, it is an *opportunity*; in the degree to which it is a threat to one's bet, it is a *risk*. The perspective here is objective. A subjective sense of opportunity or risk is quite another matter since it may, but need not, coincide with the facts.

Each of our coin tossers can be defined as having a life course in which the finding of a nickel has not been anticipated. Without the find, life would go forward as expected. Each boy can then conceive of his situation as affording him a gain or returning him to what is only normal. A chance-taking of this kind can be called opportunity without risk. Were a bully to approach one of the boys and toss him for a nickel taken from the boy's own pocket (and this happens in city neighborhoods), we could then speak of a risk without opportunity. In daily life, risks and opportunities usually occur together, and in all combinations.

Sometimes the individual can retract his decision to pursue a line of activity upon learning of likely failure. No chances, whether risky or opportune, are taken here. For chanciness to be present, the individual must ensure he is in a position (or be forced into one) to let go of his hold and control on the situation, to make, in Schelling's sense, a commitment.[6] No commitment, no chance-taking.

A point about determination—defining this as a process, not an accomplished event. As soon as the coin is in the air, the tosser will feel that deciding forces have begun their work, and so they have. It is true, of course, that the period of determination could be pushed back to include the decision to choose heads or tails, or still further back to include the decision to toss in the first place. However, the outcome (heads or tails) is fully determined during the time the coin is in the air; a different order of fact, such as who will select heads or how much will be chanced, is determined before the toss. In brief, an essential feature of the coin tossing situation is that an outcome undetermined up to a certain point—the point of tossing the coin in the air—is clearly and fully determined during the toss. A *problematic* situation is resolved.

The term problematic is here taken in the objective sense to refer to something not yet determined but about to be. As already suggested, the subjective assessment of the actor himself brings further complication. He may be quite unaware that something at hand is being determined. Or he may feel that the situation is problematic when in fact the matter at hand has already been determined and what he is really facing is revealment or disclosure. Or, finally, he may be fully oriented to what is actually happening—alive to the probabilities involved and realistically concerned over the consequences. This latter possibility, where a full parallel is found between objective and subjective situation, will be our main concern.

The causal forces during the period of determination and prior to the final result are often defined as ones of "mere chance," or "pure luck." This does not presume some kind of ultimate indeterminism. When a coin is tossed its fall is fully determined by such factors as the prior state of the tosser's finger, the height of the toss, the air currents (including ones that occur after the coin has left the finger), and so forth. However, no human influence, intended and legitimate, can be exercised to manipulate the relevant part of the result.[7]

There *are* to be sure chancy situations where relevant orders of humanly directed determination are involved by virtue of skill, knowledge, daring, perseverance, and so forth. This, in fact, marks a crucial difference between games of "pure" chance and what are called contests: in the former, once the determination is in play, the participants can do nothing but passively await the outcome; in the latter, it is just this period that requires intensive and sustained exercising of relevant capacities. None the less, it is still the case that during contests something of value to be staked comes up for determination; in terms of the facts and often their perception as well, the intended and effective influences are insufficiently influential to render the situation unproblematic.

A crucial feature of coin-tossing is its temporal phases. The boys must decide to settle the matter by tossing; they must align themselves physically; they must decide how much of the nickel will be gambled on the toss and who will take which outcome; through stance and gesture they must commit themselves to the gamble and thereby pass the point of no return. This is the bet-making or *squaring off phase*. Next there is the in-play or *determination phase*, during which relevant causal forces actively and determinatively produce the outcome.[8] Then comes the revelatory or *disclosive phase*, the time between determination and informing of the participants. This period is likely to be very brief, to differ among sets of participants differently placed relative to the decision machinery,[9] and to possess a special suspensefulness of its own. Finally there is the *settlement phase*, beginning when the outcome has been disclosed and lasting until losses have been paid up and gains collected.

The period required by participants in a given play to move through the four phases of the play—squaring off, determination, disclosure, and settlement—may be called the *span* of the play. The periods between plays may be called *pauses*. The period of *a* play must be distinguished from the period of playing, namely, the *session*, which is the time between making the first bet and settling up the last one on any one occasion perceived as continuously devoted to play. The number of completed plays during any unit of time is the *rate* of play for that time.[10] Average duration of the plays of a game sets an upper limit to rate of play, as does average length of pauses; a coin can be tossed 5 times in half a minute; the same number of decisions at the track requires more than an hour.

Given these distinctions in the phases of play, it is easy to attend to a feature of simple games of chance that might otherwise be taken for granted. Once a play is undertaken, its determination, disclosure, and settlement usually follow quickly, often before another bet is made. A coin-tossing session consists, then, of a sequence of four-phase cycles with pauses between cycles. Typically the player maintains a continuous stretch of attention and experiencing over the whole four or five seconds course of each play, attention lapsing only during the pauses, that is, after the settlement of one play and before the making of another. Everyday life is usually quite different. Certainly the individual makes bets and takes chances in regard to daily living, as when, for example, he decides to take one job instead of another or to move from one state to another. Further, at certain junctures he may have to make numerous vital decisions at the same time and hence briefly maintain a very high rate of bet-making. But ordinarily the determination phase—the period during which the consequences of his bet are determined—will be long, sometimes extending over decades, followed by disclosure and settlement phases that are themselves lengthy. The distinctive property of games and contests is that once the bet has been made, *outcome is determined and payoff awarded all in the same breath of experience.* A single sharp focus of awareness is sustained at high pitch during the full span of the play.

Consequentiality

We can take some terms, then, from the traditional analysis of coin-tossing,[11] but this framework soon leads to difficulties.

The standard for measuring the amount of a bet or prize is set by or inputed to the community, the public at large, or the prevailing market. An embarrassment of game analysis is that different persons can have quite different feelings about the same bet or the same prize. Middle class adults may use a nickel as a decision machine, but will hardly bother tossing just to decide who keeps the machine. Small boys, however, can feel that a co-finder's claim to a nickel is a big bet indeed. When attention must be given to variations in meaning that different persons give to the same bet (or the same prize), or that the same individual gives over time or over varying conditions, one speaks of subjective value or *utility.* And just as expected value can be calculated as the average worth remaining to a nickel pot, so *expected utility* can be assessed as the utility an individual accords a nickel pot weighted by the probability of his winning it.

The expected utility of a nickel pot must be clearly distinguished from the expected utility of tossing for this pot; for individuals regularly place a subjective value—positive or negative—on the excitement and anxiety generated by tossing. Further, after the toss, the displeasure at losing and the pleasure at winning are not likely to balance each other off exactly; the difference, on whichever side, must also be reckoned on the average as part of the expected utility of the play.[12] Objective standards can be used in getting at the meaning of bets; but we must use the murky notion of utility to get at the meaning of betting.

When we move from the neat notion of the expected value of a pot to one that will be relevant for our concerns, namely, the expected utility of playing for the pot, we move into almost hopeless complexities. When an individual asserts that a given period of play involves a big gamble, or when he feels that it is chancier than another, a whole set of considerations may be involved: the scale of betting; the length of the odds (and whether he is giving them or getting them); the brevity of the span of play; the smallness of the number of plays; the rate of play; the percentage paid for playing; the variation of size regarding prizes associated with favorable outcomes. Further, the relative weight given each of these considerations will vary markedly with the absolute value of each of the others.[13]

For us this means that different individuals and groups have somewhat different personal base-lines from which to measure risk and opportunity; a way of life involving much risk may cause the individual to give little weight to a risk that someone else might find forbidding.[14] Thus, for example, attempts to account for the presence of legalized gambling in Nevada sometimes cite the mining tradition of the state, a type of venturing that can be defined as very chancy indeed. The argument is that since the economy of the state was itself founded on gambles with the ground, it is understandable that casino gambling was never viewed with much disapproval.

In simple, literal gambling, then, the basic notion of "chanciness" is shot through with a multitude of half-realized, shifting meanings. When we turn from gaming to the rest of living, matters get worse.

In coin tossing, there are *a priori* and empirical reasons for assessing the chances of either outcome in effect as fifty-fifty. The ultimate validity of this assessment need not concern those who toss coins. That's the nice thing about coins. In many ordinary situations, however, the individual may have to face an outcome matrix that cannot be fully defined. (This could arise, for example, were our two boys to pause before a deep, multi-tunneled cave, trying to decide what might befall them were they to try to explore it.) Further, even when the full set of outcome possibilities is known, the chances that must be attached to each of them may be subject to only rough assessment based on vague appeals to empirical experience.[15] Moreover, the estimator will often have little appreciation of how very rough his assessment is. In most life situations, we deal with *subjective probability* and hence at best a very loose overall measure, *subjectively expected utility.*[16]

Further, while coin tossers typically face a "fair" game, and casino gamblers a slightly disadvantageous one, wider aspects of living present the individual with much less balance in this regard; there will be situations of much opportunity with little risk and of much risk with little opportunity. Moreover, opportunity and risk may not be easily measurable on the same scale.[17]

There is an important issue in the notion of value itself—the notion that bets and prizes can be measured in amounts. A nickel has both a socially ratified value and a subjective value, in part because of what its winning allows, or losing disallows, the tosser *later on* to do. This is the gamble's *consequentiality*, namely, *the capacity of a payoff to flow beyond the bounds of the occasion in which it is delivered and to influence objectively the later life of the bettor.* The period during which this consequentiality is borne is a kind of post-play or *consequentiality phase* of the gamble.

A tricky matter must be considered here. "Objective value" and "utility" are both means of establishing instantaneous equivalents for consequences that are to be actually felt over time. This is achieved by allowing either the community or the individual himself to place an appraisal on this future, and to accept or to give a price for it now. I want to avoid this sophistication. When, for example, a man proposes matrimony, it is true that the payoff is determined as soon as the girl makes up her mind, reported as soon as she gives her answer, and settled up when the marriage is consummated or the rejected suitor withdraws to court elsewhere. But in another sense, the consequence of the payoff is felt throughout the life remaining to the participants. Just as a "payoff" is the value equivalent of an outcome, so "consequentiality" is the human equivalent of a payoff. We move then from pots and prizes, neatly definable, to protracted payoffs, which can be described only vaguely. This is a move from pots to consequentiality, and from circumscribed gambles to wider arenas of living.

In addition to all these limitations on the coin-tossing model, there is another and quite central one that we can only begin to consider now. The subjective experience enjoyed by small boys who toss a coin for keeps develops from the feel of light-heartedly exercising will. A decision to gamble or not gamble is made under conditions where no alien pressure forces the decision, and not gambling would be an easy, quite practical choice. Once this decision is made affirmatively, a second one is made as to possible outcome to bet on—here an illusory right, but fun none the less, and certainly not illusory in games involving skill. Once the result is in, this can be treated as a possibility that was foreseen and the gamble taken anyway. In consequence, the whole situation can easily come to be seen prospectively as a chance-taking occasion, an occasion generated and governed by the exercise of self-determination, an occasion for *taking* risk and *grasping* opportunity. In daily life, however, the individual may never become aware of the risk and opportunity that in fact existed, or may become alive to the gamble he was making only after the play is over. And when the situation *is* approached with its chanciness in mind, the individual may find that the cost of not gambling is so high that it must be excluded as a realistic possibility, or, where this decision is a practical one, that no choice is available as to which of the possible outcomes he will be betting on. Some freedom of choice, some self-determination is present here, but often not very much. The coin-tossing model can be applied to all of these situations, but only by overlooking some important differences between recreational chance-taking and real life gambles. Apart from the question of the amount at stake, our two boys who toss a coin are not engaged in quite the same type of chance-taking as is unenjoyed by two survivors who have mutually agreed that there is no other way than to toss to see who will lighten the raft; and they, in turn, are subject to chance differently than are two sick passengers who are forced by their well companions to submit to a toss decision to see which of the two will no longer share the life boat's supply of water.

Fatefulness

An individual ready to leave his house to keep an engagement finds he is thirty minutes early and has some "free time" to use up or put in. He could put the time to "good" use by doing now an essential task that will have to be done sometime. Instead he decides to "kill" this time. He picks up a magazine from the ones at hand, drops into a comfortable chair, and leafs through some pages until it is time to go.

What are the characteristics of this activity used to kill time with? Approach this question through another: What are the possible effects of this little piece of the individual's life on the whole of the rest of it?

Obviously, what goes on during killed time may have no bearing at all on the rest of the individual's life.[18] Many alternative lines of activity can be pursued and still his life will go on as it is going. Instead of reading one magazine, he can read another; or he can while away the time by watching TV, cat-napping, or working a puzzle. Finding he has less time to put in than he had thought, he can easily cut his dawdling short; finding he has more time, he can dawdle more. He can try to find a magazine that interests him, fail, and yet lose little by this failure, merely having to face the fact that he is temporarily at loose ends. Having nothing to kill time with, or to kill enough time with, he can "mark" it.

Killed moments, then, are inconsequential. They are bounded and insulated. They do not spill over into the rest of life and have an effect there. Differently put, the individual's life course is not subject to his killed moments; his life is organized in such a way as to be impervious to them. Activities for killing time are selected in advance as ones that cannot tie up or entangle the individual.[19]

Killing time often involves the killer in problematic activity. The decision as to magazine or TV may be a close one whose determination is not begun until the individual is about to sit down. Here then is problematic behavior that is not consequential. (Interestingly, this is exactly the case in tossing for a nickel. Our youthful gamblers may subjectively place great value on winning the toss, yet the payoff can hardly be consequential.)

In contrast to time off we have time on and its world of collectively organized serious work, which gears the individual's efforts into the needs of other persons who count on him for supplies, equipment, or services in order to fulfill their own obligations. Records are kept of his production and deliveries, and penalties given if he fails to perform. In brief, the division of labor and the organization of work-flow connect the individual's current moments to other persons' next ones in a very consequential manner.

However, the consequentiality of properly attending to one's duties on any one occasion is very little noted. Results are, to be sure, more or less pictured in advance, but the probability of their occurrence is so high that little attention seems required in the matter. Nothing need be weighed, decided, or assessed; no alternatives have to be considered. This activity is indeed consequential, but it is well managed; it is not problematic. Incidentally, any moment, whether worked or killed, will have this element. It is a matter of total consequentiality that our coin tossers continue to inhale and exhale and do not run their heads against a concrete wall; any failure in the first and any success in the second can have very far-reaching effects on all a boy's moments to come. However, continuing to breathe and not beating one's head against the wall are objectives so continuously and unthinkingly sought and so assuredly and routinely realized, that the consequentiality of lapse need never be considered.

Time-off activities, then, can be problematic but are likely to be inconsequential, and time-on activities are likely to be consequential but not problematic. Thus both types of activity can easily be uneventful: either nothing important happens or nothing important happens that is unexpected and unprepared for.

However, an activity *can* be problematic *and* consequential. Such activity I call *fateful*, although the term eventful would do as well, and it is this kind of chanciness that will concern us here.

234 • The Sociology of Risk and Gambling Reader

It must now be admitted that although free time and well-managed work time tend to be unfateful, the human condition is such that *some* degree of fatefulness will always be found. Primordial bases of fatefulness must be reckoned with.

First, there is the adventitious or literary kind of fatefulness. An event that is ordinarily well managed and unnoteworthy can sometimes cast fatefulness backwards in time, giving to certain previous moments an uncharacteristic capacity to be the first event in a fateful conjunction of two events. Should one of our youthful gamblers need a nickel to make a crucial telephone call with at the moment the nickel is found, then the chance to win the toss can become fateful. Similarly, our time-killing individual can become so caught up in a magazine story that he loses all track of time[20] and does not surface until too late—an irritation, merely, unless the appointment that is missed happens to be important. Or, leafing through the magazine, he can come upon an article on intelligence tests containing sample questions. His appointment is an examination in which one of these questions appears. A moment to fritter away is not totally cut off from the moments to come; it *can* have unexpected connections with them.

Although individuals and their activities are always subject to some adventitious fatefulness, there are some enterprises whose vulnerability in this regard is marked enough to serve as a characterization of them. Where co-ordination and concealment are vital, a whole range of minor unanticipated hitches lose their usual quality of correctability and become fateful. Stories of near-perfect crimes and nearly exposed commando raids enshrine this source of fatefulness, as do tales of strategic goofs:

> Maidstone, England: A gang of masked men wielding blackjacks and hammers ambushed a car carrying $28,000 to a bank here yesterday but they grabbed the wrong loot—a bag of sandwiches.
>
> The cash was locked in the trunk of the car and the bag containing the bank official's lunch was on the car seat.[21]
>
> Three robbers who completely botched what was supposed to be a simple little bank robbery in Rodeo were sentenced in Federal Court here yesterday....
>
> All three were nabbed by some 40 police officers Jan. 7 as they struggled to make off with $7710 stuffed into a laundry sack they had just taken out of the United California bank, the only bank in Rodeo....
>
> Pugh walked in with a sawed off shotgun and lined up the 13 employees and two customers, while Fleming, carrying a pistol,

went to the vault and started filling the laundry bag with currency and, alas, coins.

"The coins can't be traced," he said cleverly. He kept piling in coins until the bag weighed about 200 pounds. Then he dragged the bag across the floor to the door—and the frayed rope snapped.

Both men then lugged the bag through the door, but it caught and ripped a hole, letting coins trail behind them as they dragged the bag to the getaway car, with Duren at the wheel.

Duren though, had parked too close to the high curb, so the three could not open the door to get the loot inside. Finally they did, by moving the car, and raced away—around the corner. There the car stopped when the three saw the clutter of sheriff, Highway Patrol and police cars.[22]

These mistakes are everyday ones and would ordinarily be easily absorbed by the reserve for correction that characterizes most undertakings. What is special about criminal enterprise (and other military-like operations) is the narrowness of this reserve and hence the high price that must be paid for thoughtlessness and bad breaks. This is the difference between holding a job down and pulling a job off; here an act becomes a deed.[23]

Second, no matter how inconsequential and insulated an individual's moment is and how safe and well managed his place of consequential duties, he must be there in the flesh if the moment is to be his at all, and this is the selfsame flesh he must leave with and take wherever he goes, along with all the damage that has ever occurred to it. No matter how careful he may be, the integrity of his body will always be in jeopardy to some degree. While reading, he may slip in his chair, fall to the floor and injure himself. This is unlikely to be sure, but should he kill time by taking a bath or earn his living by working at a lathe, in a mine, or on construction jobs, the possibility of injuring would be considerably more likely, as actuarial data show. Physical danger is a thin red thread connecting each of the individual's moments to all his others. A body is subject to falls, hits, poisons, cuts, shots, crushing, drowning, burning, disease, suffocation, and electrocution. A body is a piece of consequential equipment, and its owner is always putting it on the line. Of course, he can bring other capital goods into many of his moments too, but his body is the only one he can never leave behind.

A third pertinent aspect of the human condition concerns co-presence. A *social situation* may be defined (in the first instance), as any environment of mutual monitoring possibilities that lasts during the time two or more individuals find themselves in one another's immediate physical presence, and extends over the entire territory within which this mutual monitoring is possible.

By definition, an individual's activities must occur either in social situations or solitarily. Does which it will be, make a difference for the fatefulness of his moments?

For the special kind of consequentiality we are concerned with, the fateful kind involving the significant problematic bearing of one moment's activity upon the next, it should not matter whether the event is socially situated or not. Our concern, after all, is with the later effects of an action, not its current condition. None the less, the difference between solitary and socially situated activities has a special relevance of its own.

Just as the individual always brings his body into every occasion of his activity and also the possibility of a fortuitous linking of an already consequential event to one that would otherwise be innocuous, so he brings himself as an upholder of conduct standards like physical adeptness, honesty, alertness, piety, and neatness. The record of an individual's maintenance of these standards provides a basis others use for imputing a personal make-up to him. Later they employ this characterization in determining how to treat him—and this is consequential. Of course, most of these standards are unthinkingly and consistently maintained by adults; they are likely to become aware of these norms only when a freak accident occurs or when, in their mature and ritually delicate years, they essay for the first time to ride a horse, skate, or engage in other sports requiring special techniques for the maintenance of physical aplomb.

In some cases solitary misconduct results in a record of damage that can later be traced to the offender. In many other cases, however, no such responsibility is found; either the effects of the misconduct are ephemeral (as in gestured acts of contempt) or they cannot be traced to their author. Only the conscience of the individual can make such activity consequential for him, and this kind of conscience is not everywhere found. However, when the conduct occurs in a social situation—when, that is, witnesses are present—then these standards become immediately relevant and introduce some risk, however low.

A similar argument can be made about opportunities to display sterling personal qualities. With no witnesses present, the individual's efforts may have little identifiable lasting effect; when others are present, some kind of record is assured.

In social situations, then, ordinary risks and opportunities are confounded by expressions of make-up. Gleanings become available, often all too much so. Social situations thus become opportunities for introducing favorable information about oneself, just as they become risky occasions when unfavorable facts may be established.

Of the various types of object the individual must handle during his presence among others, one merits special attention: the other persons themselves. The impression he creates through his dealings with them and the traits they impute to him in consequence have a special bearing on his reputation, for here the witnesses have a direct personal stake in what they witness.

Specifically, whenever the individual is in the presence of others, he is pledged to maintain a ceremonial order by means of interpersonal rituals. He is obliged to ensure that the expressive implications of all local events are compatible with the status that he and the others present possess; this involves politeness, courtesy, and retributive responses to others' slighting of self. And the maintenance of this order, whether during time off or time on is more problematic than might first appear.

A final word about social situations: The ceremonial order sustained by persons when in one another's presence does more than assure that each participant gives and gets his due. Through the exercise of proper demeanor, the individual gives credit and substance to interaction entities themselves, such as conversations, gatherings, and social occasions, and renders himself accessible and usable for communication. Certain kinds of misconduct, such as loss of self-control, gravely disrupt the actor's usability in face to face interaction and can disrupt the interaction itself. The concern the other participants have for the social occasion, and the ends they anticipate will be served through it, together ensure that some weight will be given to the propriety of the actor's behavior.

I have argued that the individual is always in jeopardy in some degree because of adventitious linkings of events, the vulnerability of his body, and the need in social situations to maintain the properties. It is, of course, when accidents occur—unplanned impersonal happenings with incidental dire results—that these sources of fatefulness become alive to us. But something besides accident must be considered here.

The physical capacities of any normal adult equip him, if he so wills it, to be immensely disruptive of the world immediately at hand. He can destroy objects, himself, and other people. He can profane himself, insult and contaminate others, and interfere with their free passage.

Infants are not trusted to forego these easy opportunities (which in any case they are insufficiently developed to exploit fully) and are physically constrained from committing mischief. Personal development is the process by which the individual learns to forego these opportunities voluntarily, even while his capacity to destroy the world immediately around him increases. And this foregoing is usually so well learned that students of social life fail to see the systematic desisting that routinely occurs in daily living, and the utter mayhem that would result were the individual to cease to be a gentleman. Appreciation comes only when we study in detail the remarkable disruption of social settings produced by hypomanic children, youthful vandals, suicidals, persons pathologically obsessed by a need for self-abasement, and skilled saboteurs. Although our coin-tossers can be relied upon not to hold their breath or run their heads up against a concrete wall, or spit on each other, or besmear themselves with their own fecal matter, inmates of mental hospitals have been known to engage in exactly these behaviors, nicely demonstrating the transformation of unproblematic consequential activity into what is fateful.

Practical Gambles

The human condition ensures that eventfulness will always be a possibility, especially in social situations. Yet the individual ordinarily manages his time and time off so as to avoid fatefulness. Further, much of the eventfulness that does occur is handled in ways that do not concern us. There are many occasions of unavoided fatefulness that are resolved in such a way as to allow the participants to remain unaware of the chances they had in fact been taking. (The occurrence of such moments, for example while driving, is itself an interesting subject for study.) And much of the fatefulness that occurs in consequence of freakish, improbable events is handled retrospectively; only after the fact does the individual redefine his situation as having been fateful all along, and only then does he appreciate in what connection the fatefulness was to occur. Retrospective fatefulness and unappreciated fatefulness abound, but will not be considered here.

And yet of course there are extraordinary niches in social life where activity is so markedly problematic and consequential that the participant is likely to orient himself to fatefulness prospectively, perceiving in these terms what it is that is taking place. It is then that fateful situations undergo a subtle transformation, cognitively reorganized by the person who must suffer them. It is then that the frame of reference employed by our two small boys is brought into serious life by serious men. Given the practical necessity of following a course of action whose success is problematic and passively awaiting the outcome thereof, one can discover an alternative, howsoever costly, and then define oneself as having freely chosen between this undesirable certainty and the uncertainty at hand. A Hobson's choice is made, but this is enough to allow the situation to be read as one in which self-determination is central. Instead of awaiting fate, you meet it at the door. Danger is recast into taken risk; favorable possibilities, into grasped opportunity. Fateful situations become chancy undertakings, and exposure to uncertainty is construed as willfully taking a practical gamble.[24]

Consider now the occupations where problematic consequentiality is faced and where it would be easy to define one's activity as a practical gamble voluntarily taken:

1. There are roles in commerce that are financially dangerous or at least unsteady, subjecting the individual to relatively large surges of success and failure over the short run; among these are market and real estate speculators, commercial fishermen,[25] prospectors.

2. There are roles in industry that are physically dangerous: mining, high construction work,[26] test piloting, well-capping.

3. There are the "hustling" jobs in business enterprise where salesmen and promoters work on a commission or contract-to-contract basis under conditions of close competition. Here income and prestige can be quickly gained and lost due to treacherous minor contingencies: a temporary let-up in effort, the weather, the passing mood of a buyer.

4. There are performing jobs filled by politicians, actors, and other live entertainers who, during each stage appearance, must work to win and hold an audience under conditions where many contingencies can spoil the show and endanger the showman's reputation. Here, again, any let-up in effort and any minor mishap can easily have serious consequences.

5. There is the soldier's calling[27] and the policeman's lot—stations in public life that fall outside the ordinary categories of work, and make the incumbent officially responsible for undergoing physical danger at the hands of persons who intend it. The fact that these callings stand outside civilian ranks seems to reinforce the notion of self-determination.

6. There is the criminal life, especially the lesser non-racketeering varieties, which yields considerable opportunity but continuously and freshly subjects the individual to gross contingencies—to physical danger, the risk of losing civil status, and wide fluctuations regarding each day's take.[28] "Making it" on the street requires constant orientation to unpredictable opportunities and a readiness to make quick decisions concerning the expected value of proposed schemes—all of which subject the individual to great uncertainties. As already seen, getting to and getting away from the scene of a crime subjects the participants to the fateful play of what would ordinarily be minor incidents.

7. A further source of fatefulness is to be found in arenas, in professional spectator sports whose performers place money, reputation, and physical safety in jeopardy all at the same time: football, boxing, and bullfighting are examples. Sterling Moss's vocation is another:

> ... motor-racing on the highest level, in the fastest, most competitive company, *grand-prix* driving is the most dangerous sport in the world. It is one of the riskiest of man's activities. Motor-racing kills men. In one recent year the mortality rate was twenty-five percent, or one out of four. These are odds to be compared with those cited for fighter pilots and paratroopers.[29]

8. Finally, there are the recreational non-spectator sports that are full of risk: mountain climbing, big game hunting, skin diving, parachuting, surfing, bob-sledding, spelunking.

Adaptations

Uneventful moments have been defined as moments that are not consequentially problematic. They tend to be dull and unexciting. (When anxiety is felt during such moments it is felt for eventful ones slated to come later.) Yet there are many good reasons to take comfort in this uneventfulness and seek it out, voluntarily foregoing practical gambles along with risk and opportunity—the opportunity if only because it is so often related to the risk. The question is one of security. In uneventful situations, courses of action can be managed reliably and goals progressively and predictably realized. By such self-management the individual allows others to build him into their own plans in an orderly and effective way. The less uncertain his life, the more society can make use of him. It is understandable then that the individual may make realistic efforts to minimize the eventfulness—the fatefulness—of his moments, and that he will be encouraged to do so. He engages in *copings*.

One basic technique is physical care. The individual handles himself so as to minimize the remote danger of accidental injury to his body. He does not tip his chair too far back or daydream while crossing a busy intersection.[30] In both the matter of exercising physical care and the need for doing so, idle pursuits make the same claims as obligated, serious ones. *Some* care must always be exerted. Taking care is a constant condition of being. Thus it is one of the central concerns that parents in all societies must impress upon their young,[31] the injunction being to "take care" and not become unnecessarily involved in avoidable fatefulness.

Another means of controlling eventfulness, and one almost as much employed as physical care, is sometimes called providence: an incremental orientation to long-range goals expressed through acts that have a very small additive long-term consequence. The work of building up a savings account is an example; the acquisition of seniority at a workplace and working one's way up by the gradual acquisition of training are two others. The raising of a large family might also qualify. The important point here is that any one day's effort, involving as it does only a small increment, can be sacrificed with little threat to the whole. Here is the Calvinistic solution to life: once the individual divides his day's activities into ones that have no effect and others having a small contributive consequence, nothing can really go wrong.

Another standard means of protecting oneself against fatefulness is insurance in whatever form, as when householders invest in candles and spare fuses, motorists in spare tires, and adults in medical plans. In this way the cost of possible trouble can be easily spread over the whole course of the individual's life, a "converting of a larger contingent loss into a smaller fixed charge."[32]

Systems of courtesy and etiquette can also be viewed as forms of insurance against undesired fatefulness, this time in connection with the personal offense that one individual can inadvertently give to another. The safe management of face to face interaction is especially dependent on this means of control.

Note that the availability and approval of risk-reducing measures creates a new contingency, a new basis for anxiety. When an untoward event occurs during a moment meant to be uneventful, and the event spills over the boundary of the moment and contaminates parts of the individual's life to come, he faces a double loss: the initial loss in question plus that of appearing to himself and others as having failed to exercise the kind of intelligent control, the kind of "care," that allows reasonable persons to minimize danger and avoid remorse.

These, then, are some of the means—largely avoidant—by which the individual realistically copes with situations of fatefulness. Another issue must now be considered, which is easy to confuse with this—defensive behavior.

Anticipated fateful activity creates anxiety and excitement. This is implied in the notion that the utility of what is bet is likely to be quite different from the utility of betting it. Also, as suggested, the individual often feels remorse when something undesirable happens, the chance of which he had failed to reduce, and disappointment when something desirable does not, the occurrence of which he had failed to assure. Any practice that manages the affective response associated with fatefulness—affects such anxiety, remorse and disappointment—may be called a *defense*.[33]

When we shift consideration from the management of fatefulness to the management of an affective state associated with it, we are required to review against the phases of a play. For in fact there are situations in which objectively inconsequential phases of play are responded to with a sense that they are fateful. Our individual, about to open the letter containing examination results, may feel excited and anxious to the point of engaging in little rituals of propitiation and control before casting his eyes on the awful news. Or, when the nurse approaches him with information about the condition of his wife and gender of his child, he may feel that the moment is fateful; as he may when the hospital staff returns with news gleaned from a biopsy performed on him to see whether a growth is malignant or benign. But it should be plain that these moments are not really fateful, merely revelatory. In each case the individual's fate has been determined before he entered the news-acquiring situation; he is simply apprised of what is already in force, of something that, at this late date, he can do nothing about. Opening a letter or analyzing a bioptic section cannot generate or determine a condition, but only reveal what has already been generated.[34]

Just as disclosures can create the excitement and concern of fate being generated, so can settlements, that is, occasions when crucial matters known to have been determined in a particular way are finally executed. Thus, in modern Europe, a condemned man's last walk has not been fateful even though each step has brought him closer to death; his execution was merely dramatic, it was his trial that was fateful. In the eighteenth century, when many death sentences were passed and most of these commuted, the trial was not as fateful as the period following it. Very recently, of course, with the agitation against capital punishment, the post-trial period has again become appreciably fateful.

Now we can return to consider defenses, if only in a passing manner, in order to bring a much discussed topic into relationship with the subject-matter of this [chapter].

The most obvious type of defense, perhaps, is the kind that has no objective effect on fate at all, as in the case of ritualistic superstitions. The behavior said to be true of boxers will serve as an example:

> Since most bouts are unpredictable, boxers usually have super-
> stitions which serve to create confidence and emotional security
> among them. Sometimes the manager or trainer uses these super-
> stitions to control the fighter. One fighter believed that, if he ate

certain foods, he was sure to win, because these foods gave him strength. Others insist on wearing the same robe in which they won their first fight; one wore an Indian blanket when he entered the ring. Many have charm pieces or attribute added importance to entering the ring after the opponent.... Some insist that, if a woman watches them train, it is bad luck. One fighter, to show he was not superstitious, would walk under a ladder before every fight, until this became a magical rite itself. Consistent with this attitude, many intensify their religious attitudes and keep Bibles in their lockers. One fighter kept a rosary in his glove. If he lost the rosary, he would spend the morning before the fight in church. Although this superstitious attitude may be imported from local or ethnic culture, it is intensified among the boxers themselves, whether they are white or Negro, preliminary fighters or champions.[35]

Gamblers exhibit similar, if less religious, superstitions.[36]

Clearly, any realistic practice aimed at avoiding or reducing risk—any coping—is likely to have the side effect of reducing anxiety and remorse, is likely, in short, to have defensive functions. A person who coolly resorts to a game theory matrix when faced with a vital decision is reducing a painful risk to a calculated one. His frame of mind brings peace of mind. Like a competent surgeon, he can feel he is doing all that anyone is capable of doing, and hence can await the result without anguish or recrimination. Similarly, a clear appreciation of the difference between the determinative phase of a play and the disclosure and settlement of the play can help the individual deal with the anxiety produced during the span of the activity; such discriminations can have defensive functions.

It is not surprising, then, that when a causal basis is not readily found for discounting the determinativeness of the current situation, it may be sought out; and where it can't be found, imagined. Thus, for example, we find that events determined locally may be interpreted as a consequence of prior determination. A version of this "defensive determinism" is found in the belief in fate, predestination, and kismet—the notion that the major outcomes regarding oneself are already writ down, and one is helpless to improve or worsen one's chances. The soldier's maxim is an illustration: "I won't get mine 'till my number's up so why worry."[37]

Just as causality can be sought outside the situation, so it can be sought in local forces that similarly serve to relieve one's sense of responsibility. A type of scapegoating is involved, pointing to the function of lodging causal efficacy within what is seen as the enduring and autonomous parts of the individual's personality, and thereby transforming a fateful event into something that is "only to be expected." Suffering an accident because of carelessness, the individual can say, "That's just like me; I do it all the time." About to take a crucial examination the individual can ease matters by telling himself that the exam will be fair, and so everything depends on how much work he has or has not long since done.

Further, belief in pure, blind luck can protect the individual from the remorse of knowing that something could have and should have been done to protect himself. Here is the opposite tack to defensive determinism—a kind of defensive indeterminism—but the consequences are much the same. "It's nobody's fault," the individual says. "It was just a question of bad luck."[38]

Obviously, then, a traditional statement of coping and defense can be applied in connection with fatefulness. But this neglects a wider fact about adaptation to chance-taking. When we look closely at the adaptation to life made by persons whose situation is constantly fateful, say that of professional gamblers or front-line soldiers, we find that aliveness to the consequences involved comes to be blunted in a special way. The world that is gambled is, after all, only a world, and the chance-taker can learn to let go of it. He can adjust himself to the ups and downs in his welfare by discounting his prior relation to the world and accepting a chancy relation to what others feel assured of having. Perspectives seem to be inherently normalizing: once conditions are fully faced, a life can be built out of them, and by reading from the bottom up, it will be the rises not the falls that are seen as temporary.

Action

Although fatefulness of all kinds can be handled both by coping and by defense, it cannot be avoided completely. More important, there are, as suggested, some activities whose fatefulness is appreciable indeed if one combines the amount chanced, the rate of chance taking, and the problematicalness of the outcome. It is here, of course, that the individual is likely to perceive the situation as his taking of a practical gamble—the willful undertaking of serious chances.

Given the claims of wider obligation that commit some individuals to what they can perceive as chancy undertakings, virtue will sometimes be made of necessity. This is another defensive adjustment to fatefulness. Those with fateful duties sometimes hold themselves to be self-respecting men who aren't afraid to put themselves on the line. At each encounter (they claim) they are ready to place their welfare and their reputation in jeopardy, transforming encounters into confrontations. They have a more or less secret contempt for those with safe and sure jobs who need never face real tests of themselves. They claim they are not only willing to remain in jobs full of opportunity and risk, but have deliberately sought out this environment, declining to accept safe alternatives, being able, willing, and even inclined to live in challenge.[39]

Talented burglars and pickpockets, whose skill must be exercised under pressure, look down, it is said, on the petty sneak thief, since the only art he need have for his calling is a certain low cunning.[40] Criminals may similarly disesteem fences as being "thieves without nerve."[41] So, too, Nevada casino dealers may come on shift knowing that it is they who must face the hard intent of players to win, and coolly stand in its way, consistently blocking skill, luck, and cheating, or lose the precarious reputation they have with management. Having to face these contingencies every day, they feel set apart from the casino employees who are not on the firing line. (In some casinos there are special dealers who are brought into a game to help nature correct the costly runs of good luck occasionally experienced by players, or to remove the uncertainty a pit boss can feel when a big bettor begins to play seriously. These dealers practice arts requiring delicacy, speed, and concentration, and the job can easily be visibly muffed. Moreover, the player at this time is likely to be heavily committed and searching openly and even belligerently in a small field for just the evidence that is there. Skilled card and dice "mechanics" understandably develop contempt not only for *non*-dealers but also for *mere* dealers.)[42] The small-scale fishermen I knew on the Shetland Islands had something of the same feeling; during each of the five or six runs of a day's fishing they subjected themselves to a serious gamble because of the extreme variability of the catch.[43] Peering into the net as the winch brought the bag and its fish into view was a thrill, known by those who experienced it to be something their fellow islanders would not be men enough to want to stomach regularly. Interestingly, Sir Edmund Hillary, who came to practice a truly chancy calling, provides us with the following view of the work he and his father lived by, namely, beekeeping:

> It was a good life—a life of open air and sun and hard physical work. And in its way it was a life of uncertainty and adventure; a constant fight against the vagaries of the weather and a mad rush when all our 1,600 hives decided to swarm at once. We never knew what our crop would be until the last pound of honey had been taken off the hives. But all through the exciting months of the honey flow the dream of a bumper crop would drive us on through long hard hours of labor. I think we were incurable optimists. And

during the winter I often tramped around our lovely bush-clad hills and learned a little about self-reliance and felt the first faint stirrings of interest in the unknown.[44]

When we meet these stands we can suspect that the best is being made of a bad thing—it is more a question of rationalizations than of realistic accountings. (It is as if the illusion of self-determinacy were a payment society gives to individuals in exchange for their willingness to perform jobs that expose them to risk.) After all, even with chancy occupational roles, choice occurs chiefly at the moment the role itself is first accepted and safer ones foregone; once the individual has committed himself to a particular niche, his having to face what occurs there is more likely to express steady constraints than daily re-decidings. Here the individual cannot choose to withdraw from chance-taking without serious consequence for his occupational status.[45]

However, there are fateful activities that *are* socially defined as ones an individual is under no obligation to continue to pursue once he has started to do so. No extraneous factors compel him to face fate in the first place; no extraneous ends provide expediential reasons for his continued participation. His activity is defined as an end itself, sought out, embraced, and utterly his own. His record during performance can be claimed as the reason for participation, hence an unqualified, direct expression of his true make-up and a just basis for reputation.

By the term *action* I mean activities that are consequential, problematic, and undertaken for what is felt to be their own sake. The degree of action—its seriousness or realness—depends on how fully these properties are accentuated and is subject to the same ambiguities regarding measurement as those already described in the case of chanciness. Action seems most pronounced when the four phases of the play—squaring off, determination, disclosure, and settlement—occur over a period of time brief enough to be contained within a continuous stretch of attention and experience. It is here that the individual releases himself to the passing moment, wagering his future estate on what transpires precariously in the seconds to come. At such moments a special affective state is likely to be aroused, emerging transformed into excitement.

Action's location can easily and quickly shift, as any floating crap game attests; indeed, should a knife fight develop next to a crap table, the action may shift in location even while it is shifting in kind, and yet participants will apply the same word, as if the action in a situation is by definition the most serious action in that situation at the moment, regardless of its content.[46]

In asking the famous question, "Where's the action?" an individual may be more concerned with the intensity of the action he finds than its kind.

Whoever participates in action does so in two quite distinct capacities: as someone who hazards or chances something valuable, and as someone who must perform whatever activities are called for. In the latter capacity the individual must ordinarily stand alone,[47] placing in hazard his reputation for competence in play.[48] But in the former he can easily share his gamble with others or even let them "take" all of it. Action, then, is usually something one can obtain "a piece" of; the performer of the action is typically a single individual, but the party he represents can contain a quickly shifting roster of jointly committed members. For analysis, however, it is convenient to focus on the case where the performer takes all his own action and none of anyone else's.

It is, of course, in the gambling world that the term action had its slang beginning, and gambling is the prototype of action. In the casinos of Nevada, the following usages can be found: "Dollar action," refers to light bettors and their effect on the day's take; and "good [or real or big] action," refers to heavier takes. Dealers who get flustered by heavy bettors are said to be unable "to deal to the action," while cool dealers are said to be "able to handle the action." Naturally, new dealers are "pulled out of the action," and when bets get heavy and multitudinous at a crap table, the better of the base men may be "put on the action side." Casinos that try to avoid high limit games are said "not to want the action," while houses that can face heavy bettors without becoming nervous are said "to be able to take the action." A "high roller" known to "drop" a lot of money may find himself warmly welcomed at a casino because "we like his action." Pit bosses, ever concerned to show that they are somehow earning their keep, will, from a tactful distance, "keep their eye on the action." Someone known to cheat, or to be able to "count cards" in 21, may be asked to leave the casino permanently with the statement, "We don't want your action." Players who are indecisive "hold up the action," and one who fails to cover all of what is considered a good bet may cause another player to ask if he can "take the rest of the action." Deserving casino managers may be rewarded by being "given a piece of the action," that is, a share of ownership ("points"). In casinos with only one cluster of tables (one "pit") there is likely to be one table that because of location or special maximum is called the "action table," just as in large casinos there will be a high minimum "action pit."[49]

Although action is independent of type and concerned with amount, amount itself cannot be taken as a simple product of the size of each bet and the number of players betting. This is most evident in craps. A table whose sole player is making hundred-dollar bets can be seen as having more action than another table whose twenty players are making five- and ten-dollar bets. A table "jam up" with players, all of whom are making many different kinds of bets, can be seen as having more action than another table where ten players are betting a higher aggregate by means of simple line and field bets. Correspondingly, to say that a dealer can "handle the action" may mean, either, that he can deal coolly to a very large bettor, or that he can deal accurately and rapidly when a large number of calculations and payoffs must be made quickly.

Another aspect of the gambler's use of the term action arises from the fact that action and the chance-taking it involves may constitute the source of the gambler's daily livelihood. Thus, when he asks where the action is he is not merely seeking situations of action, but also situations in which he can practice his trade. Something similar is found in the thief's and the prostitute's conception of where the action is—namely, where the risks to earn one's living by are currently and amply available.[50] Here, compressed pridefully into one word, is a claim to a very special relationship to the work world.

No doubt it was gamblers who first applied their term to non-gambling situations, thus initiating a diffusion of usage that non-gamblers have recently extended still further. Yet almost always the use seems apt. Underlying the apparent diversity in content is a single analytical property that can be sensed with sureness by persons who might be unable to define closely what it is they sense....

... The social world is such that any individual who is strongly oriented to action, as some gamblers are, can perceive the potentialities for chance in situations others would see as devoid of eventfulness; the situation can even be structured so that these possibilities are made manifest.[51] Chance is not merely sought out but carved out.

Notes

1. Attributed to Karl Wallenda, on going back up to the high wire after his troupe's fatal Detroit accident.
2. A die can be used like a coin if, for example, 1, 2, or 3 is called tails, and 4, 5, or 6 is called heads. Among the types of unsporting dice are misspotted ones variously called tops and bottoms, horses, tees, tats, soft rolls, California fourteens, door pops, Eastern tops, etc. These dice do not have a different number on each of the six sides, and (as with a two-headed coin) allow a player to bet on an outcome that is not among the possibilities and therefore rather unlikely to occur. Note that dice, much more frequently than coins, do land on their edges (by virtue of coming to rest against objects) and do roll out of bounds. The management of these regrettable contingencies is one of the jobs of the members of a craps crew, especially the stickman, in

the sense that their very quick verbal and physical corrections are designed to make perfect a very imperfect physical model.

3. The track has a word for it, "extension."

4. Here and elsewhere in matters of probability I am indebted to Ira Cisin. He is responsible only for the correct statements.

5. To increase the apparent attractiveness of certain bets some crap-table layouts state winnings not in terms of given odds but in terms of the pot; thus, a bet whose given odds are 1 *to* 4 will be described as 1 *for* 5.

6. T. C. Schelling, *The Strategy of Conflict* (Cambridge, Harvard University Press, 1960), esp. p. 24.

7. See the argument by D. MacKay, "The Use of Behavioral Language to Refer to Mechanical Processes," *British Journal of the Philosophy of Science*, XIII, 50 (1962), 89–103; "On the Logical Indeterminacy of a Free Choice," *Mind*, 69 (1960), 31–40.

8. In coin-tossing this phase begins when the coin goes into the air and terminates when it lands on the hand—a second or two later. In horse racing determination begins when the barrier is opened and terminates when the finish line is crossed after the last lap, a little more than a minute in all. In seven-day bicycle races, the determination phase is a week long.

9. Horse-racing con games have been based on the possibility of convincing the mark that the period between an outcome at the track and its announcement at distant places is long enough to exploit for post-finish sure betting, that is, "past-posting,"—a condition that can in fact occur and has been systematically exploited. It might be added that friendly 21 dealers in Nevada, after completing a deal, will sometimes look at their hole card and josh a player about a destiny which has been determined and read but teasingly delayed in disclosure.

10. For example, assume that the nickel-finders are engaged in a sudden-death game, one toss determining who gets the nickel. If the two boys are together on this occasion for one hour, their rate of chance-taking is once per hour. Should they change the nickel into pennies and toss these one at a time, each penny only once, then the rate of chance-taking is five times greater than it was before although the resulting swing in fortune no more and probably less.

11. A sound, if popular, treatment may be found in R. Jeffrey, *The Logic of Decision* (New York, McGraw-Hill, 1965).

12. In gambling, these factors are not independent. No doubt part of the experience obtained from the toss derives from the difference between the satisfaction at contemplating winning and the displeasure at the thought of losing.

13. Recent work, especially by experimental psychologists, has added appreciable knowledge to this area by a design which obliges individuals to show a preference among gambles involving various mixes of elements. See, for example, J. Cohen, *Behaviour in Uncertainty* (London, George Allen and Unwin, 1964), chap. 3, "Making a Choice," pp. 27–42; and W. Edwards,

"Behavior Decision Theory," *Annual Review of Psychology*, 12 (1961), 473–98.

14. For this and other suggestions, I am grateful to Kathleen Archibald.

15. Reputable firms specializing in crooked gambling devices sell variously "shaped" dice that provide the customer with a choice among five or six degrees of what is called "strength." Probably the ranking is absolutely valid. But no company has tested dice of any alleged strength over a long enough series of trials to provide confidence levels concerning the favorable percentage these unfair dice afford their users.

16. In the literature, following F. Knight (*Risk, Uncertainty and Profit* [Boston, Houghton Mifflin, 1921], esp. chaps. 7 and 8) the term "risk" is used for a decision whose possible outcomes and their probabilities are known, and the term "uncertainty" where the probabilities across the various outcomes are not known or even knowable. Here see R. Luce and H. Raiffa, *Games and Decisions* (New York, Wiley & Sons, 1958), p. 13ff. Following John Cohen, B. Fox (*Behavioral Approaches to Accident Research* [Association for the Aid to Crippled Children, New York, 1961], p. 50) suggests using the term hazard for objective dire chances, and risk for subjective estimates of hazard. Fox equates this with a slightly different distinction, that between risk as perceived to inhere in a situation and risk perceived as something intentionally taken on. See also Cohen, *op. cit.*, p. 63.

17. The concept of utility, and the experimental techniques of a forced-choice between singles and pairs probabilistically linked, can attempt to reduce these variabilities to a single scheme. However these efforts can be questioned. Many actual plays are undertaken in necessary conjunction with the player remaining unappreciative of the risk (while focusing on the opportunity), or unaware of the opportunity (while attending to the risk). To place a utility on this unappreciateness in order to balance the books seems hardly an answer.

18. Although, of course, his choice of means of killing time can be expressive of him.

19. Time off comes in all sizes, a few seconds to a few years. It comes between tasks on the job; in transit between home and work; at home after the evening meal; week-ends; annual vacations; retirement. (There is also—largely in fantasy—the time away from ordinary life that Georg Simmel calls "the Adventure.") When time off is killed, presumably this is done with freely chosen activity possessing a consummatory end-in-itself character. Whether the individual fills his time off with consequential or inconsequential activity, he usually must remain on tap at the place where serious, scheduled duties are located; or he must be within return-distance to his station. Note that time off to kill is to be distinguished from a close neighbor, the time that unemployed persons are forced to mark and cannot justify as an earned respite from past duties or imminent ones.

20. In our urban society the individual is likely to check up on the time periodically and can almost always estimate the time closely. Light sleepers may even orient themselves constantly in time. Struck on some occasion how

"time has flown," the individual may in fact mean only one or two hours. Finding that his watch has stopped, he may find in fact that it stopped only a few minutes ago, and that he must have been checking himself against it constantly.

21. *San Francisco Chronicle*, March 10, 1966.

22. *Ibid.*, May 6, 1966.

23. In fictional vicarious worlds, criminal jobs (as well as the structurally similar undercover operations of various government agents), are realized in the teeth of a long sequence of threatened and actual hitches, each of which has a high probability of ruining everything. The hero manages to survive from episode to episode, but only by grossly breaking the laws of chance. Among young aspirants for these roles, surely the probabilistically inclined must be subtly discouraged.

24. Decision theorists currently demonstrate that almost any situation can be usefully formulated as a payoff matrix enclosing all possible outcomes, each outcome designated with a value that is in turn weighted by the probability of occurrence. The result is that conduct that might be construed as unproblematical and automatic or as an obligatory response to inflexible and traditional demands, can be recast as a rational decision voluntarily taken in regard to defined alternatives. Further, since the choice is among outcomes that have only a probability of coming out, or, if certain, then only a probability of being satisfactory, the decision can be seen as a calculated risk, a practical gamble. (Characteristically, the payoff matrix equally handles a possible outcome whose probability is a product of nature, as when an invasion decision considers the probability of good or bad weather across the several possible landing points, or whose probabilistic features have been intentionally introduced by means of gambling equipment, as when one of the available alternatives involves dicing for a specified prize.) Resistance to this sort of formulation can be attributed to a disinclination to face up to all the choosing implied in one's act. Acceptance of this formulation involves a certain amount of consorting with the devil; chance taking is embraced but not fondled. Whatever the social and political consequence of this decision-theory perspective, a purely cultural result might be anticipated, namely, a tendency to perceive more and more human activity as a practical gamble. One might parenthetically add that the Bomb might have a somewhat similar effect—the transformation of thoughts about future society into thoughts about the chances of there being a future society, these chances themselves varying from month to month.

25. See F. Barth, "Models of Social Organization," *Royal Anthropological Institute Occasional Paper, No. 23* (Glasgow, The University Press, 1966), p. 6.

26. A recent description is G. Talese, *The Bridge* (New York, Harper & Row, 1965).

27. Which features, of course, an interesting dilemma: in battle a tradition of honor and risk-taking must be maintained, yet behind the lines the organization needs steady men in gray-flannel uniforms. See M. Janowitz, *The Professional Soldier* (New York, The Free Press, 1960), pp. 35–36.

28. A useful autobiographical portrait of the chance-taking continuously involved in the life of a slum hustler specializing in mugging may be found in H. Williamson, *Hustler!* (New York, Doubleday, 1965). See also C. Brown, *Manchild in the Promised Land* (New York, Macmillan Co., 1965), for the Harlem version.
29. S. Moss (with K. Purdy), *All But My Life* (New York, Bantam Books, 1964), p. 10
30. Much of this care, of course, is built into the environment by safety design. Chairs are constructed to limit the possibility of their breaking, stools of their tipping, etc. Even cars are coming to be designed to minimize possible injuries.
31. Suggested by Edward Gross.
32. Knight, *op. cit.*, p. 246.
33. The distinction between coping and defense is borrowed from D. Mechanic, *Students Under Stress* (New York, The Free Press, 1962), p. 51. A somewhat similar distinction is employed by B. Anderson in "Bereavement as a Subject of Cross-Cultural Inquiry: An American Sample," *Anthropology Quarterly*, XXXVIII (1965), 195: "Stressor-directed behavior is oriented toward removing, resolving, or alleviating the impinging circumstances themselves; strain-directed behavior, toward the assuagement of the physical or psychological discomfort that is a product of these happenings."
34. Of course, where the fate is not a matter of immediate life or death, mere apprisal of what has befallen can begin the work of adjusting to the damage, so that a *failure* to learn *now* about an eventual loss can itself be fateful. Here disclosure of fate cannot effect what is disclosed but can effect the timing of reconstitutive efforts. Similarly, if the quickness of the individual's response to the situation is of strategic significance in his competition with another party, then the *timing* of his learning about the outcome can be fateful, even though the disclosure of the outcome cannot influence that particular outcome itself.
35. K. Weinberg and H. Arond, "The Occupational Culture of the Boxer," *American Journal of Sociology*, LXVIII (1952), 463–64.
36. In modern society such practices tend to be employed only with appreciable ambivalence and are no doubt much on the decline. For the changing situation with respect to one traditionally superstitious group, commercial fishermen, see J. Tunstall, *The Fishermen* (London, Macgibbon & Kee, 1962), pp. 168–70.
37. See W. Miller's discussion of fate in "Lower Class Culture as a Generating Milieu of Gang Delinquency," *Journal of Social Issues*, XIV (1958), 11–12. The religious roots, of course, are to be found in John Calvin and ascetic Puritanism.
38. An example is cited in Cohen, *op. cit.*, p. 147: "The possibility of a falling back on 'luck' may also be a great comfort in other circumstances. In 1962, British universities rejected some 20,000 applicants for entry. Many of them reconciled this rejection with their pride by saying that the offer of a university place depends as much on luck as on merit. The rejects are described as

'submitting applications, like a gambler putting coins into a fruit-machine, sure that the jackpot must come up at last.'"

39. E. Hemingway, *Death in the Afternoon* (New York, Scribners, 1932), p. 101, suggests that men of this stamp, being disinclined to calculate too closely, have their own disease: "Syphilis was the disease of the crusaders in the middle ages. It was supposed to be brought to Europe by them, and it is a disease of all people who lead lives in which disregard of consequences dominates. It is an industrial accident, to be expected by all those who lead irregular sexual lives and from their habits of mind would rather take chances than use prophylactics, and it is a to-be-expected end, or rather phase, of the life of all fornicators who continue their careers far enough." Penicillin has undermined this route to manliness.

40. C. Shaw, "Juvenile Delinquency—A Group Tradition," *Bulletin of the State University of Iowa*, No. 23, N.S. No. 700 (1933), p. 10, cited in R. Cloward and L. Ohlin, *Delinquency and Opportunity* (New York, The Free Press, 1960), p. 170.

41. S. Black, "Burglary," Part Two, *The New Yorker*, December 14, 1963, p. 117.

42. With some reverence, dealers cite as a reference model the blackjack mechanics in New York who worked next door to the hang-out of the Murder Incorporated mob, and daily "dealt down" to customers likely to be demonstrably intolerant of dealers caught cheating them. Surely those who could survive such work must have known themselves to be men of considerable poise, a match in that department for anyone they could imagine.

43. Field Study, 1949–50.

44. E. Hillary, *High Adventure* (New York, Dutton, 1955), p. 14.

45. Dean MacCannell has suggested that there are jobs that holders gamble with, as when a night watchman takes time off to go to a movie during time on and enjoys the gamble as much as the movie. However, these jobs are characteristically "mere" ones, taken up and left rapidly by persons not specifically qualified for them and not qualified for anything better. When these jobs are subjected to only spot supervision, gambling with the job seems to occur.

46. Thus, Ned Polsky in "The Hustler," *Social Problems*, XII (1964), 5–6, suggests that a pool game between skilled players for a small bet will take second place to one between lesser players who are gaming for higher stakes.

47. The capacity to perform tends to be imputed to the individual, but there are situations, as in gang molestations, where this capacity clearly derives from the visible backing he can readily call on. Further, there are some situations whose action arises because a set of actors have committed themselves to closely coordinated acts—as in some current robberies. The sheer working out of the interdependencies in the face of various contingencies becomes a source of action.

48. It is quite possible for an individual to be more concerned about his reputation as a performer than for the objective value of the pot at stake. For example, casino dealers, especially in the "break-in" phase, can find it more difficult to manage dealing to a big bet during the shift than to manage the placing of the same bet as a customer after work.

49. Similarly Polsky, *op. cit.*, p. 5, reports that certain pool halls are nationally identified as "action rooms," and within one hall there will be one or two tables informally reserved for the action.
50. Suggested by Howard Becker, *The Dictionary of American Underworld Lingo*, ed. H. Goldin, F. O'Leary, and M. Lipsius (New York, Twayne Publishers, 1950), defines action: Criminal activity. "Shape up (be present) tonight, Joe, there's action—a Brooklyn score (robbery)."
51. Suggested by Sheldon Messinger. The garden variety, as popularized by Damon Runyon, is the small-time Broadway gambler who perceptually reconstitutes the immediate environment into a continuous series of soon-to-be-determined bettable outcomes on which propositions can be offered. The culture hero here is John W. "Bet-a-Million" Gates, the barbed-wire king, who, in 1897 on a train between Chicago and Pittsburgh, apparently won $22,000 by betting on raindrop races, a window-pane serving as a course. (See H. Asbury, *Sucker's Progress* [New York, Dodd Mead, 1938], p. 446.)

CHAPTER 13

The Experience of Play

GERDA REITH

The Experience of Play

So far we have been talking about gambling as a material phenomenon: in various ways as consumption, as leisure, as something that is bought and sold in capitalist enterprise as though it were just another type of commodity. But it is more than this. It *is* a form of consumption, but it is a special *type* of consumption, with a unique experiential component. It is the purpose of this chapter ... to provide a description of the nature of this experience. This takes us from an analysis of the formal properties of particular types of games to an examination of that which is general across all forms of gambling. Obviously, such a portrait is bound to be, to a certain extent, an ideal type—an attempt to go beyond the specific and the particular to discover something about gambling which is general and fundamental. Therefore many of the assertions made will not apply to all gamblers or to all forms of gambling, but it is hoped that they will at least say *something* about them which will reveal the common features which link their varied historical expressions.[1] In a very broad sense then, [this chapter] will focus on the experiential aspects of gambling in an attempt to provide some kind of answer to the question: What is it *like* to play at games of chance?

This question can be approached by a phenomenological analysis of what Kant called the fundamental categories of perception: those of time, space and cause. It is through these 'building blocks' of consciousness that our relationship with the world is mediated: whatever we experience affects or is affected by them so that together they can be said to comprise a Gestalt: as Ey puts it, a 'total structure of experience' (Ey 1978, p. 94).

However, despite our general dependence on these categories, they are not fixed and absolute but rather vary according to a range of factors. Certain situations and environments can affect them and so alter the nature of subjective experience—and of course, in a reciprocal relationship, the categories of time, space and cause can also affect that experience itself.[2] Conditions such as physical and psychological illness (Straus 1968; Charmaz 1992), stress-related disorders (Straus 1966; Minkowski 1970; Ey 1978), states of extreme tension or excitement (Bergson 1910, 1911), addiction (Reith 1999) or even incarceration (Cohen and Taylor 1972) can have a dramatic effect on the way individuals perceive their surroundings and even their own self-identity. In these situations, the world appears to take on subtly different nuances: for instance, when we are happy, it appears to be open and expansive, but in states of pain or fear, our attention narrows and our surroundings accordingly seem to contract. This is exemplified in the state of depression for instance, which, Straus tells us, is characterised by an alteration of the basic structures of space and time in which 'Familiar surroundings become estranged, everything shows a new, bewildering physiognomy' (Straus 1966, p. 290).

From all this we can see the fundamental relativity of consciousness— the fact that our relation to the world is not fixed and unchanging, but rather depends very much on how we feel, what we are doing, where we are. As William James put it, 'the world of our present consciousness is only one out of many worlds of consciousness that exist, and those worlds must contain experiences which have meaning for our life also' (James 1982, p. 519). It should therefore come as no great surprise to find that the perceptions and consciousness of gamblers are similarly conditioned by their situation, for the gambling arena imparts its own peculiar qualities to consciousness.

This is in part caused by the nature of the gambling environment itself, which has been extensively commented on by many writers. Although ... every gambling site forms its own separate world with dramatic variations in the nature and experience of play in each, the gambling sites are, in a broader sense, united by certain common features which have been described by Huizinga (1949), Caillois (1962), and Goffman (1961, 1963) in their delineations of the formal properties of 'playgrounds'.

For all three writers, the 'peculiar character' of games is characterised essentially by their *separateness*, both temporally and spatially, from everyday life.[3] They involve both a physical and a mental crossing of a threshold out of the ordinary world and into the world of play. For Huizinga, this involves a 'stepping out of "real life" into a temporary sphere of activity with a disposition all of its own' (Huizinga 1949, p. 8). In the same way, Goffman describes them as 'world building activities' whose events constitute 'a field for fateful, dramatic action, a plane of being, an engine of meaning, a world in itself, different from all other worlds' (Goffman 1961, p. 25). Play is also separated by strict temporal limits which 'end as inexorably as the closing of a parenthesis' (Caillois 1962, p. 43), so necessitating the constant repetition of games. Furthermore, just as the play world is animated by a different set of rules from those which govern everyday life, so players within it are animated by a different set of motivations from those of their everyday routines in which they are free to experiment with new roles and to temporarily adopt new identities.

Its essential feature of 'separateness' means that the gambling arena forms a self-contained realm of activity, set against the world of utilitarian goals, with its own rules and conventions and within which the gambler's orientation to the everyday world is altered. In fact, for Gadamer, so extreme is this feature that he argues that the play world actually constitutes a specific mode of *being*. Thus 'play does not have its being in the consciousness of the attitude of the player, but on the contrary draws the latter into its area and fills him with its spirit', meaning that ultimately, 'the player experiences the game as a reality that surpasses him' (Gadamer 1975, p. 89). In this way, the basic perceptual categories of time, space and cause become distorted, for submersion in an environment of chance creates a kind of experiential chaos in which players cease to perceive their surroundings in the ordered, logical manner of 'rational' consciousness, but as a barrage of information, or, to use Cassirer's phrase, in a 'rhapsody of perception' (Cassirer 1953, p. 21).

At this point, it will be evident that (certain) type(s) of enquiry … cannot provide us with an adequate tool for gaining insight into the nature of the gambling experience, which brings us to a methodological problem of all social investigation: how to describe something as intangible as a state of consciousness; a phenomenon which by definition we have no access to. This is a problem that has long occupied the traditions of phenomenology, existentialism and hermeneutics, and has found resonance in the disciplines of philosophy, psychology and sociology. Edmund Husserl established the phenomenological method of enquiry when he attempted to undertake the pure inspection of consciousness and the objects of that consciousness. Although Husserl was more interested in the intellectual forms of mental life, existentialist philosophers such as Heidegger, Kierkegaard and Sartre applied the phenomenological method to questions of being and existence and specifically to the understanding of mental states. Their ideas were influential in social science, where Schutz's focus on the manner in which individuals construct and interpret their everyday existence introduced them into sociology, and Minkowski's and Binswanger's analyses of the varieties of conscious experience brought them to clinical psychiatry. Hermeneutics and interpretive understanding are frequently utilised in the methodological application of these insights. Ever since Dilthey stated that we can only understand (*verstehen*) the world in terms of the meanings and intentions which individuals attribute to it, it has been recognised that the understanding of 'lived experience' requires a special method of analysis. For Weber, this *verstehnde* method involved the interpreter placing him/herself in the position of the interpreted, while other researchers emphasised the gaining of knowledge more through a process of emotional participation and empathetic understanding of their subjects' world.

It is within this broad phenomenological tradition that the nature of the gambling experience and the mental life of the gambler can best be understood. In this context then, [this chapter] … will draw on the comments and experiences of players themselves, as well as on the insights of various writers who were also gamblers and who can therefore provide an articulate window into that 'inner life' so sought after by phenomenologists. We are fortunate in that the world of play has captured the literary imagination of many great writers, including Alexander Pushkin, Honore de Balzac, Charles Baudelaire and, of course, Fyodor Dostoevsky.[4] The latter is perhaps its most eloquent spokesman, for as well as being a great analyst of human motivation, Dostoevsky was an inveterate gambler who thus wrote from the privileged position of having actually experienced firsthand that which he described. His disastrous tour of the gambling capitals of Europe was fictionalised in the novel *The Gambler*,[5] and revealed with dramatic insight the 'rhapsody of perception' experienced within the gambling arena. This position lent his description of the gambling experience an authenticity and verisimilitude that is absent from subsequent, more 'scientific' accounts.

In this section, then, the various components of the general experience of play will be examined, followed by a consideration of the perception of the specific categories of time and space, and of the medium of the gambling world, money.…

Excitement

The Adventure—Dream State   When they enter the gambling arena gamblers temporarily step out of the real world, leaving their everyday concerns and routines behind and embarking on an adventure which, as well as being exciting, is also experienced as a state of dream-like dissociation from their surroundings. Their shared feature of separateness means that both gambling games and adventures can assume the properties of dreams, a peculiarity which is caused by the occurrence of the adventure outwith the usual stream of life. Just as, for Huizinga, the world of play is a 'stepping out' of real life, so the adventure for Simmel is a 'dropping out of the continuity of life' (Simmel 1971b, p. 187). The 'otherness' of the play world lends to it the quality of an adventure, while the strangeness of the stimuli inside contributes to the dream-like nature of the experience within it.

While immersed in a game, gamblers tend to shut out the world around them, leaving everyday life behind and narrowing their field of attention to concentrate on the action immediately in front of them. Leiseur (1984) called this a 'twilight zone' or 'dream world', while Jacobs (1988) and Brown (1994) have described this feature of gambling as the experience of *dissociated states*. These can include feelings of depersonalisation and *déjà vu*, trance-like or hypnotic states, somnambulism and fugue and even the experience of mystical religious states and multiple personality. Common to all these states they found a quality of 'separateness' or 'disconnection from the normal flow of mental life' (Brown 1994, p. 3), in which players often felt disembodied or 'outside' of themselves, as though in a trance, watching themselves play.

We can regard these dissociated states as a specific form of consciousness which Ey calls 'oneiric states' and in which individuals are in a condition of 'pathological dreaming'. Neither asleep nor awake, they experience a kind of 'awake dream' in which they feel disembodied; as if a spectator, watching themselves from without (Ey 1978, p. 65). As he succumbed to this dream-like absence of mind, Dostoevsky's gambler Alesky also lost awareness of himself as subject, and could not recall what had happened. He related: 'I lost track of the amount and order of my stakes. I only remember as if in a dream' (Dostoevsky 1992, p. 241).

The Thrill of Play—Vertigo   One of the most striking aspects of the experience of gambling is the tension or 'thrill' of the game: the irresistible seduction of money and chance which Balzac called the *Spirit of Gaming*: 'a passion more fatal than disease' (Balzac 1977, pp. 22–26). This affective experience is generated by the creation and resolution of the tension in a game, and centres on the risk faced by the individual while awaiting the outcome of their stake. It begins the moment the bet is placed and ends when the outcome of the round is known. In between, the gambler waits in anticipation, and in this state of suspended animation 'the conflicting valences of fear or hope run in tingling arpeggios up and down his spine' (Devereaux 1949, p. 699). One gambler described the sense of expectation characteristic of his encounters with chance in a particularly vivid metaphor: 'Imagine going into a dark room. When the lights are turned on the room could be empty or it could be filled with the most extraordinary objects you've ever seen. A game of cards is like that' (*Observer*, 25 June 1995, p. 12). It was a similar state of tension upon which another gambler's experience of play was founded: 'My feelings when I play roulette are of tension—partly painful, partly pleasurable and expectant' (in Bergler 1970, p. 83), and which defined the exquisite agony of Tolstoy's relation with roulette, of which he wrote: 'it is a long time since anything tormented me so much' (in Barnhart 1983, p. 110).

The apex of the gambling experience is the moment when excitement peaks and gamblers are gripped by the fever of play, playing on and on, oblivious to their surroundings, to their losses, to the passage of time and even to themselves. This is the experience of what Caillois calls *ilinx*. Derived from the Greek 'whirlpool' or 'vertigo', it is a governing principle of Dionysian or pre-rational societies, and can also be found in a type of play which consists of an 'attempt to momentarily destroy the stability of perception and inflict a kind of voluptuous panic on an otherwise lucid mind' (Caillois 1962, p. 23). In it, players are unaware of what is going on around them and oblivious to fatigue. It is this state that is responsible for some of the marathon gambling sessions of popular gambling folklore, such as the forty-eight-hour game in which Lord Sandwich refused to stop playing, inventing the sandwich as a means of having food brought to him without leaving the table.

Baudrillard explains the hypnotic appeal of this vertigo in terms of the gambler's challenge to fate:

> By itself each throw produces only a moderate giddiness, but when fate raises the bid … when fate itself seems to throw a challenge to the natural order of things and enters into a frenzy or ritual vertigo, then the passions are unleashed and the spirits seized by a truly deadly fascination. (Baudrillard 1990, p. 147)

In this sensory maelstrom, perceptions of time and space are shattered. Time freezes, and gamblers become absorbed in a total orientation to the immediate Here and Now. In this state they become creatures of sensation; seeing, but not really being aware of their surroundings; perceiving, but not truly cognisant of what is going on. One punter described his thoughts, shattered into incoherence by the tension of the game: 'I thought I'd gone mad; I'd completely flipped ... I don't think I've ever come close to another experience that produced as much adrenaline ... it was a near death experience.' Utyeshitelny, in Gogol's *The Gamblers*, was similarly shaken, saying: 'The loss of money is not so important as losing one's peace of mind. The mere agitation experienced during play, people may say what they like, but it obviously shortens one's life' (Gogol 1926, p. 228).

It is during this stage that physiological changes such as increased respiration, heart rate, blood pressure and adrenaline have been found to occur in gamblers, changes which provide the strongest evidence for those who argue that gambling can be a physiological addiction. Having staked—and won—at roulette, Dostoevsky's Alesky experienced a degree of excitement so intense as to be a visceral sensation: 'I was a gambler; I felt it at that very moment. I was trembling from head to foot, my head was throbbing' (Dostoevsky 1992, p. 203). He goes on to give perhaps the definitive account of vertigo in the description of Alesky's penultimate bet at the roulette tables. Alesky stakes everything, flinging his money down at random; then there is 'one moment of waiting in which my impressions were perhaps similar to those experienced by Madame Blanchard when she plunged to the ground from a balloon in Paris' (Dostoevsky 1992, p. 241).

His choice of the plunging analogy is revealing, for it is also the one used by Caillois to describe the sensation of vertigo. Children's spinning games and whirling dervishes, he writes, create states of ecstasy, disorientation and hypnosis, as do physical activities like rapid accelerations and falling through space (Caillois 1962, p. 24). Alesky's feeling of hurtling through space is the sensation of such vertiginous disorientation; a mental sensation transposed into a physical one and caused not by physical exertion but by the sheer excitement of play. In such moments of intense physical and perceptual disorientation, gamblers' links with reality are tenuous, and loosen still further as they surrender to the immediacy of the present. For Boyd, such an individual is 'lost in a world of his own.... There is no longer an outside reality.... Even time is non-existent, and in a certain sense he is insane' (Boyd 1976, p. 372). Madness is a recurrent theme in the gambling literature. Alesky certainly wondered if he had gone mad during one particularly intense session: 'Had I taken leave of my senses at that time, and was I not sitting somewhere in a madhouse and perhaps that is where I am now' (Dostoevsky 1992, p. 225), while the narrator of *The Mahabharata* observed a similar effect on gamblers 'drunk with playing dice' who 'prattle[d] like madmen of things they had not seen asleep or awake' (*The Mahabharata* 1975, p. 136).

The Alteration of Identity—Transcendence   From among all this disorientation comes one of the most frequently discussed aspects of gambling—its ability to act as a conduit for the alteration of identity. Its separation from the routines of everyday life as a kind of fantasy world means that, while engaged in it, individuals are temporarily released from the strictures which usually govern their actions. Freed from habit in this way, they are able to imagine themselves in other identities and to explore alternative ways of being. Caillois (1962) and Goffman (1969) have pointed out that all games consist in becoming an illusory character; of temporarily adopting a new identity which endures for the duration of the game. Jacobs (1988) described such states, in which gamblers underwent a shift in persona, as part of the more general phenomenon of 'dissociated states', while Rosenthal (1986) reported that many individuals in his study often talked of becoming someone else when they played, and even went so far as to call each of their play 'selves' by a different name.

This fluid 'gambling identity' is one in which the everyday self is left behind and another persona, more pertinent to the ritualised social situation in which gamblers find themselves, is adopted. With the interruption of habit and routine and the removal of familiar surroundings, the reference points of the personality disappear. As the traditional categories of orientation loosen and shift, so the gamblers' axes of identity become less fixed and allow for the investigation and creation of new roles. As Caillois explains, when players leave the everyday world behind they also leave *themselves* behind: 'In one way or another, one escapes the real world and creates another. One can also escape oneself and become another' (Caillois 1962, p. 19). The most radical illustration of this is probably Luke Rhinehart's famous creation, *the Dice Man* (1972), an individual who lived out the ultimate existentialist fantasy by surrendering his life's decisions to the roll of a dice. Cinematically, the protean gambling identity has also been portrayed in Fritz Lang's eponymous film of *Dr. Mabuse, The Gambler*. Mabuse is depicted as an individual with no fixed character, appearing in every scene in disguise. Just as the gambler of the eighteenth century was perceived as an individual of 'no distinct physiognomy', Mabuse's constant changes reveal his chameleon-like personality, his refusal of any fixed characteristics.

Goffman (1969), Zola (1967), Herman (1967, 1976) and Newman (1972) have all focused on the gambling arena as a site in which qualities and abilities not normally utilised in the outside world can be given free rein.

Goffman describes the 'rules of irrelevance' which delimit the gambling situation, and signify the freedom from needing to act for 'real'; the licence to 'play act' or behave out of character according to the situation at hand. Zurcher (1970) described a similar feature: the 'ephemeral role' which is specially designed and created by the individual to 'fit' the gambling occasion and then discarded once it is over. In this way, gambling provides the opportunity to present an idealised identity to the self and others (Holtgraves 1988). Through the display of skill and knowledge, gamblers in games such as horse-race handicapping or poker can become experts within their social group and so win the respect and admiration of their peers. The taking of risks, or as Goffman puts it, exposing oneself to fate, that is involved in gambling contests creates a social situation in which character—or 'face', qualities such as self-discipline, courage and integrity—can be displayed and abilities and skills not otherwise used can be exercised. By virtue of the fact that they are solely responsible for their own actions, that they *make things happen* in the consequent unfolding of a game, gambling confers a degree of autonomy on players, and, according to Kusyzyn (1990), it is this that affirms gamblers' self-worth and makes gambling a site in which one's existence can be confirmed. As one player put it: 'gambling is a replacement of the fantasies [we] have as children.... For me, the fantasy in gambling is not monetary. It's a question of fulfillment: being who I really am, doing things well, being involved—just feeling good' (in Alvarez 1991, p. 138).

Boredom

Just beyond the 'kind of pain' of play hovers another kind of pain—boredom. The tension of a round is short-lived, for a sensation of such intensity can only be sustained for a few fleeting moments. In the inevitable let-down that follows, reality appears dull and colourless; the gambler is deflated, for the converse of the vertigo experienced during gambling is the torpor felt when *not* at play. Thus Shohnev, in Gogol's *The Gambler*, describes how, between games, a gambler feels 'just like a general when there is no war! It's simply a deadly interval' (Gogol 1926, p. 224).

Stepping outside of the gambling arena, players find the real world unutterably dull in comparison to the one they have just left. Pascal recognised the threat of boredom that lingered behind the excitement in games of chance, warning, 'a man enjoying a happy home-life has only to spend ... five or six pleasant days gambling, and he will be very sorry to go back to what he was doing before' (Pascal 1987, p. 51). That is why, for Pascal, gambling was such a useful, but dangerous, diversion from boredom; useful because it agitates and so diverts us, dangerous because it exacerbates the tedium of the initial condition.

For de Jong, the problem of boredom is intrinsic to modernity, and has its roots in the nineteenth century when the breakdown of a sense of metaphysical order gave birth to the distinctive feature of the modern age—the syndrome of intensity. The desire to experience intense sensation—of which gambling is typical—replaced the pursuit of meaningful activity and had as its converse the existence of apathy and boredom (de Jong 1975). Benjamin was among the first writers to realise the true horror of this contemporary malaise, declaring after Strindberg: 'Hell is not something which lies ahead of us,—but *this life, here*' (Benjamin 1985, p. 50). By secularising it and changing its temporal location from the remoteness of the afterlife to the immediacy of the present, Benjamin brought hell to earth and announced boredom as a fundamental condition of modernity.

As the chief poet of modernity, Baudelaire understood very well the existence of boredom as a kind of secular hell:

Nothing is slower than the limping days
when under the heavy weather of the years
Boredom, the fruit of glum indifference
gains the dimension of eternity.
(Baudelaire 1982, p. 75)

He also recognised the desire to banish its aching emptiness in its polar opposite—excitement, and in particular, the excitement of gambling. Baudelaire's gamblers are essentially degraded characters, and desperate to feel *anything* rather than nothing. What he calls these 'ancient whores' with their 'lipless faces' and 'toothless jaws', are possessed of a 'stubborn passion', a 'deadly gaiety':

Horrible that I should envy those
who rush so recklessly into the pit,
each in his frenzy ravenous to prefer
pain to death and hell to nothingness!
(Baudelaire 1982, p. 101)

Pushkin's portrayal of *Eugene Onegin* also draws on the association between gambling and boredom. Eugene is a 'superfluous man' who has no place in the rush of modern life and despite all his travels and distractions finds himself supremely bored:

nothing caused his heart to stir
and nothing pierced his senses blur.
(Pushkin 1983, p. 52)

Like Baudelaire's gamblers, Eugene occasionally escapes boredom through play; the one thing that can pierce his 'senses blur':

pursuits of a monstrous breed
begot by boredom out of greed.
(Pushkin 1982, p. 149)

The continued association between boredom and excitement is encapsulated in gambling. Just as gambling embodies de Jong's intensity cult, so it embodies the converse of intensity: boredom. Seeking release from monotony, gamblers plunge into the tension of a game, only to come face to face with the everyday world and all its attendant tedium when they reemerge from play.

Repetition

Their fleeting nature, and their vacillation between excitement and boredom, makes repetition an intrinsic feature of games of chance. Put simply, because a game ends so quickly, it must be repeated, and this is one of the most essential features of play. The gambler plays in order to experience the tension and expectation of a game, but because it is over almost as soon as it begins, it must be continually repeated. The gambling sites reverberate to the drum of this steady repetition. In the casino, bets are made, cards shuffled, dealt and collected over and over again; dice are shaken and rolled *ad infinitum*, just like Nietzsche's 'iron hands of necessity' shaking 'the dice box of chance for an infinite length of time' (Nietzsche 1982, p. 81). Roulette wheels spin for eternity on unchanging, regular axes, while balls tumble out of the lottery drum week after week and month after month in a ritual which, like all those of the gambling sites, is unflinching in its exact repetition of what went before.

For Gadamer, repetition is the essence of play: 'The movement which is play has no goal which brings it to an end; rather it renews itself in constant repetition' (Gadamer 1975, p. 93). By creating a formal structure which is absolute and unchanging, it confers order on the random play of chance events, and so removes the burden of initiative from the player (see Huizinga 1949, p. 10; Caillois 1962, p. 5).

Baudrillard sees, in this tendency to repeat, something which is more than simply a definitive feature of games of chance but a movement which annihilates the relation between cause and effect. 'Their true form is cyclical or recurrent. And as such they ... put a definite stop to causality ... by the potential return (the eternal return if one will) to an orderly conventional situation' (Baudrillard 1990, p. 146). This eternal return, for Baudrillard, is an important factor in the generation of vertigo, for the desire to know the result of the next round, to put one's fate to the test once more entices the gambler to play on, and so creates 'the vertigo of *seduction*' (Baudrillard 1990, p. 148).

Walter Benjamin shares with Baudrillard the image of gambling as a phenomenon whose fundamental structure denies the relation of cause and effect. However, the implications of this denial are very different for Benjamin, for while Baudrillard sees a seductive vertigo as the mode of experiencing an a-causal universe, Benjamin's universe is made of the austerity of hard work and the divorce of gamblers from the fruits of production. Such a distinction can be seen as analogous to the different responses of the Protestant-bourgeois and the gambler to chance which we saw earlier. For Benjamin, repetition is the factor which connects gambling with the production line. The former shares with the latter:

> the futility, the emptiness, the inability to complete something which is inherent in the activity of a wage slave in a factory. Gambling even contains the workman's gesture that is produced by the automatic operation, for there can be no game without the quick movement of the hand by which the stake is put down or a card picked up. (Benjamin 1977, p. 179)

The lines of slot-machine players, adeptly operating their machines, is a panorama which Benjamin could never have seen, and yet it is the visual apotheosis of his comparison. He goes on:

> The jolt in the movement of a machine is like the so-called *coup* in a game of chance. The manipulation of the worker at the machine has no connection with the preceding operation for the very reason that it is its exact repetition. Since each operation at the machine is just as screened off from the preceding operation as a *coup* in a game of chance is from the one that preceded it, the drudgery of the labourer is, in its own way, a counterpart to the drudgery of the gambler. The work of both is equally devoid of substance. (Benjamin 1977, p. 179)

Although he effectively highlights its repetitive, insubstantial nature, Benjamin is mistaken in equating the drudgery of work with the excitement of play. For him, all gambling is like the punishment inflicted on Claudius: 'useless labour ... an illusory hope of gratifying some desire' (Seneca 1986, p. 232). Benjamin's mistake stems from his implicit conflation of games of chance with those based on skill for, as we shall see, if anything it is the calculation and self-restraint involved in games of *skill* that represent such drudgery. Certainly, both unskilled labour and games of chance involve repetition, but here the similarity ends, for games of chance are animated by the affective excitation of the thrill; a sensation entirely lacking from the dull routine of factory labour. Thus the category of repetition does *not* bring gambling into the realm of work, since such work as Benjamin outlines and the structure of gambling share only their repetitive *forms*. The subjective response to each is quite different, and, as Kierkegaard (1983) has pointed out, repetition contains the qualities of self-realisation and transcendence, which make it amenable to a response of seductive vertigo rather than austere drudgery.

The Categories of Play

In the arena of play, the articulation of the gambler's field of consciousness breaks down so that perception of the fundamental categories of space— according to Kant, the form of our 'outer experience', time—the form of our 'inner experience', cause and (unique to the gambling world), money are distorted. The basic categories of the gambler's world thus assume a bewildering new physiognomy, which constitutes a perceptual Gestalt and in which the passage of time freezes into repetition, space contracts, and the value that accrues to money is obliterated.

Time

The perception of time is crucial to the experience of play, for

> time is the material into which the phantasmagoria of gambling
> has been woven. (Benjamin 1992, p. 137)

Since Bergson's distinction between two different 'types' of time—'homogenous and independent Time' and 'true duration, lived by consciousness' (Bergson 1911, p. 275)—it has become a phenomenological axiom that the experience of time is a medium for experience in general. The former absolute, Newtonian time is the time of the scientist. Broken down into quantifiable units and applied equally to everyone, this 'clock time' is exemplified in modern life in the almost ubiquitous habit of wearing wrist-watches. The lived time, the *durée*, which we experience, is quite different however, and is unique to the individual and their particular position in the world at any one moment. Bergson thus opens up a *relativistic* notion of time, the experience of which is contingent on different states of consciousness. As Proust put it: 'for certain people, the *tempo* of Time itself may be accelerated or retarded' (Proust 1983, p. 986). The gambler is one such individual.

The case studies of phenomenological psychologists such as Eugene Minkowski and Erwin Straus illustrate the non-homogeneous nature of personal, 'lived' time. It can pass quickly or slowly depending on the situation, actions and mood of the subject. For example, on a boring day time seems to drag, whereas on one filled with activity and interest it appears to pass quickly. The perception of time has an *active* and an *affective* component; how we experience it depends on what we 'fill' it with, what we are doing, and how we feel about it. In turn, experience itself 'receives its specific significance, its specific value, from its temporal position' (Straus 1966, p. 292). Experience in general, and the experience of time in particular, exist in a dynamic relation, each one containing and affecting the other. Minkowski describes a case in which a patient conflated his personal time, his *durée*, with homogeneous time, and regarding his watch as the literal embodiment of the latter, shot it with a revolver in order to 'kill' time (Minkowski 1970, p. 15)! This gesture, which we would regard as symbolic, highlights the distinction which we take for granted between the two 'types' of time separated by Bergson.

As an example of the effect of temporal position on experience, Straus cites imminent death: 'With such transitions from indefiniteness to finality, everything changes its physiognomy' (Straus 1966, p. 292). He does not elaborate, but we know from Raskolkinov's walk to give himself up in *Crime and Punishment* that the subject, seeing the world for the last time, is fully aware of its every detail, avidly drinking in the minutiae of life and engrossed in every fleeting second (Dostoevsky 1951, pp. 535–536). This example is particularly illuminating in the gambling context, for many gamblers themselves choose a similar analogy. The protagonist Raphael in *The Wild Ass's Skin* experienced a similar moment of clarity to that of the condemned man on his way to execution, in which he felt as if he had just escaped certain death. Despite the noise of the casino—'the buzz of voices', 'the chink of coins' and 'the strains of orchestra'—Raphael related that: 'thanks to a privilege accorded to the passions which gives them the power to annihilate space and time, I could distinctly hear what the players were saying' (Balzac 1977, p. 95). Dostoevsky too described these moments of lucidity during intense play, and, as someone who had experienced such moments of finality during his mock execution as a political prisoner, was well placed to relate the two experiences to each other. His description of gambling is imbued with the sense of urgency and intensity which he would have felt during what he thought were his final moments; a sensation he re-created at the gambling table.

Like any other individuals, gamblers' time is 'true duration, lived by consciousness', and its nature is dependent on what they are doing and their emotional state while they are doing it. In turn, their experience of play receives its specific value from its temporal position. In this way the nature of time in the gambling arena is twofold. On the one hand, it is a perception in the mind of individual gamblers, measured by their rate of play and dependent on factors such as the type of game they are playing, the size of their stake in relation to their total bankroll and the crowdedness of the table. As we have seen, a gambler with a limited bankroll, playing high stakes at a deserted roulette table, will have a shorter experience of play than one with a large bankroll, playing low stakes at a busy blackjack table. Since the experience of time is coloured by the situation of the subject, they will perceive it moving quickly or slowly depending on the length of their period of involvement in play. Such a perception of time is unique for each gambler, distinguished ever so slightly from all their other games and those of all other gamblers by the particular combination of many factors.

Over and above the *specific* nature of time in each game played can be discerned a *general* experience of time; a set of characteristics that come to light through the frequent playing of many games. This perception of time, common to all gamblers in all games, is of a *constant repetition of a fleeting present.*

In games of chance, the present is all-important. The field of gamblers' attention is defined by the unfolding of the event on which they have their stake. However long the rate of play, the resolution of the risk is over in an instant. It is the moment when the lottery ball bounces out of the drum; the moment when the dice fall; the moment when the roulette ball slips into the pocket. In an instant, the uncertain becomes known; the future becomes the present. It is this instant that the gambler lives in; the time of the eternal present, in which the gambler Jack Richardson felt he 'existed in a sharp, exhilarating present that refreshed itself over and over again' (Richardson 1980, p. 86). Because it has no bearing on the present, the past and the future are irrelevant to the experience of the round being played at any particular moment. In the frozen instant, in which the gambler lives only for the moment, time has lost its articulation. This is the moment Benjamin talks about, in which 'gambling converts time into a narcotic' (Benjamin 1992, p. 54). The narcotic effect is experienced as an isolated and fleeting moment which is constantly repeated in every round of play.

This state of perennial expectation, in which the future is rendered obsolete, is an instance of what Straus would call a 'pathology of becoming'. The 'normal' experience of time, Straus tells us, occurs in individuals who are in a state of *becoming*. However, when their temporal perception becomes so disoriented that 'the context and the continuity of time crumbles', a disjunction between individuals and their orientation to the world opens up, and a 'pathology of becoming' exists (Straus 1966, p. 293).

This essential transience is captured by Baudelaire in *The Clock*, where, for him, it also encapsulates the nature of modernity:

Thirty six times in every hour
The second whispers: Remember! And Now replies
In its maddening mosquito hum I am Past,
Who passing lit and sucked your life and left!
(Baudelaire 1982, p. 82)

The problem of the fleetingness of the present has occupied philosophers since Augustine, and was partially resolved by Bergson's notion of *durée*. This 'lived time' contains the past, as memory, within the future. His *durée* involves both 'past and present melting into one another and forming an organic whole' (Bergson 1910, p. 128). For Bergson then, the present is not an isolated instance, but part of an organic 'melting' of past, present and future. The role of memory is instrumental in this process, for it is the mechanism by which 'the past tends to reconquer, by actualising itself, the influence it had lost' (Bergson 1911, p. 169).

Unfortunately, Bergson's solution is completely inapplicable to the gambler. While at play, the latter's experience of time lacks the historical element of *durée*, for in games of chance, Bergson's all-important past has no place. Each round is a self-contained island in time, existing independently of what came before or what will come after. The perception of time that arises from this is made up of a succession of unrelated instants and absolutely opposed to the flowing organicism that is the lived time of the *durée*.

The past can never 'actualise' itself in gambling, for it requires the operation of memory to do so, and the abolition of time in gambling means the abolition of memory too. In a world of chance, the past has a little relevance for the future as the future does for the past. The only thing which can transcend the timelessness of this contingent world is the passage of time itself—realised in the repetition of games—whereupon the law of large numbers can take effect and some semblance of order be restored. This uncompromising law of probability is given lyrical expression by Baudelaire:

> Remember! Time, that tireless gambler, wins on every turn of the wheel. That is the law. (Baudelaire 1982, p. 82)

Gamblers, however, caught in the particular instant, are, by their simple corporeality, denied such a vantaged position. Forever bound to the outcome of a single round, of a single moment of play, they exist as individuals without memory. The nature of chance means that 'gambling invalidates the standards of experience' and betting works as 'a device for giving events the character of a shock, detaching them from the context of experience' (Benjamin 1992, p. 136).[6]

Experienced in a timeless void, the thrill of gambling is an essentially *insubstantial* sensation, and one which leaves no traces for the gambler to hold on to and recollect. Nothing is produced, nothing changes, nothing really happens—there is therefore nothing to anchor memory on to in play. It is because of this feature that Mr. Astley observes of Alesky by the end of *The Gambler*: '"You've become dull ... you've not only renounced every aim whatsoever in your life, you've even renounced your memories"' (Dostoevsky 1992, p. 269). But then this is all part of the fascination, part of the *enchantment* of gambling—the 'crystalline passion that erases memory traces and forfeits meaning' (Baudrillard 1990, p. 135).

The advertising campaign of the British lottery's scratch cards utilises the appeal of this feature in a particularly apposite slogan: 'Forget it all for an instant[s]', which encapsulates the instantaneity of the gambling experience in tones of hedonistic abandon.

The repetition of the ever-same in the mind of the gambler corresponds to the repetition of the ever-same in the economic realm of play. Nothing is ever produced in gambling, and in lieu of any such creative activity we have the endless circulation of money. It changes hands, but nothing substantial is ever produced, and the endless cycle of this money in the economic sphere is perceived as an endless cycle of the ever-same in the mind of the gambler. The constant repetition of the ever-same implies a cycle of no real change. Nothing occurs to distinguish one night in the casino, one day at the bookmakers, from any other. Nothing out of the ordinary disturbs the ebb and flow of winning and losing; no landmarks appear to signify change in the monotonous sea of repetition. With the absence of any real change, it becomes impossible to measure the passage of time, and so play goes on, suspended in a timeless void. The narcotic effect of gambling which Benjamin talks about is experienced as an escape from time.

This state of timelessness reaches its apogee in the removal of clocks from the casino. Clocks exist as markers of a shared, objective temporal consensus, imposing order on the flux of human relations and their surroundings. In this, they symbolise the victory of absolute Newtonian time over human time. However, the order of such scientific time is absent from the casino, banished since the nineteenth century as a distraction from the world outside. In a London club of this period, two gamblers playing *ecarte* were asked to leave after closing time. 'Their only answer was to stop the clock, an irritating reminder of the fleeting hours' (Neville 1909, p. 19). With the removal of the clock went the last vestige of the outside world, and the last fragment of memory tying the gamblers to it. In the twentieth century, no such removals have to be made, for clocks are never present in casinos. Their absence signifies the breakdown of temporal articulation altogether. Unchartered by measurement and with nothing to differentiate it, the experience of time is of an eternal present, recurring at various speeds, in the mind of the gambler. In giving licence to the experience of subjective temporalities, the casino exists as a physical embodiment of the dramatic action of the patient who shot his watch with a revolver in order to 'kill' time.

In the gambling arena players close off the outside world, shed their personality and forget their past, thus freezing themselves in a present which, without reference to the past and without enjoying real change, is empty. Simmel recognised, in their lack of memory and invalidation of experience, the uniquely modern nature of gamblers as an extreme example of the ahistorical individual: 'On the one hand, he is not determined by any past ... nor on the other hand, does any future exist for him' (Simmel 1971b, p. 196). This is the type of individual with whom Benjamin was concerned when he described how the conditions of modernity were distorting the experience of temporality; eroding genuine experience and replacing it with an experience of a present, 'a *Now* which is incessantly emptying, always already past' (in Spencer 1985, p. 61).

The insubstantial time of the gambler is thus an extreme instance of the empty time of modernity: cut adrift from past and present, it is perceived more as a succession of fleeting, fortuitous moments than as the organic wholeness of Bergson's *durée*.

Space

Spatial perception is a fundamental mode of existence which, according to Merleau-Ponty, resides at the core of the subject's being and provides 'a communication with the world more ancient than thought' (Merleau-Ponty 1981, p. 254). Contrary to the Cartesians who spoke of a 'natural geometry', spatial perception must be grasped *from within*. There are a great many ways of experiencing this kind of space, for lived space, like lived time, is not a homogeneous, geometrical construct, but is rather heterogeneous and relative to the experience of the individual. It can be conceived as a 'field of consciousness', or to use Husserl's term, an 'inner horizon': 'that zone of indeterminacy and ambiguity found in lived experience' (Ey 1978, p. 90).

In fact, the experience of space is inextricably linked with the experience of time, with the former defining our 'outer' and the latter our 'inner' experience. Thus in games of chance, the perception of space undergoes a distortion similar to that of time: the cessation of duration has its counterpart in the contraction of space in the mind of the gambler. Just as time freezes and loses its articulation, so space shrinks and loses *its* articulation.

Gamblers' experience of space is conditioned by the parameters of the game being played; their inner horizon stretches no further than the circumference of the roulette wheel. In the excitement of a game, the perception of space contracts to encompass no more than the physical dimensions of the highly charged area of play. Such spatial disorientation is inherent in the nature of intense sensations themselves, which contain, for Bergson, 'the image of a present contraction and ... of a compressed space' (Bergson 1910, p. 4). This concentration destroys the harmony of perspective to the extent that the centre of the visual field is magnified and the surrounding space of the periphery obliterated—a sensation which most of us have had when intense concentration momentarily blocks out our immediate surroundings. When tension peaks, all that is perceived is that which contains the action, and it is because the gambler's gaze is so limited in this way that the stage upon which the spectacle of gambling is played out is so correspondingly small.

Just as time needs the unfolding of events to mark its passage, so space requires points of orientation to delimit its parameters, for an empty space is also a formless space. However, with everything external to the action obliterated, gamblers are oblivious to the passage of time, to their surroundings and even to themselves. Absorbed to such an extent in the game, they are subject to a degree of indissociation with their surroundings, a phenomenon which is apparent in one individual's description of the experience of the play world in general: 'You are so involved in what you are doing, you aren't thinking of yourself as separate from the immediate activity ... you don't see yourself as separate from what you are doing' (in Csikszentmihalyi 1975, p. 46).

Since spatial perception is a primary mode of existence and guarantees the security of the body in space, when it breaks down or becomes distorted, disorder reigns and the sensation of 'plunging', so common to gambling, is experienced. Merleau-Ponty describes how the instability of perception 'produces not only the intellectual experience of disorder, but the vital experience of giddiness, and nausea, which is the awareness of our contingency and the horror with which it fills us' (Merleau-Ponty 1981, p. 254). This disorientation is experienced in gambling as the sensation of 'plunging', and was described by Dostoevsky as a feeling of actual immersion in the game. Rootless in space and time, he felt as though he was being swept along by the roulette wheel, in a 'whirlwind which caught me in its vortex ... spinning, spinning, spinning' (Dostoevsky 1992, pp. 225–226).

The primacy of *movement* in the field of spatial orientation has been emphasised by many phenomenologists, but is given perhaps its simplest expression by Ey when he stated that space 'is in movement ... is nothing but movement' (Ey 1978, p. 104). Physical mobility is a means of orientating oneself and establishing a direct spatial relation with the world, and as such 'is on the same footing as perception' (Merleau-Ponty 1981, p. 111). However, one of the most striking features of gamblers in action is their indifference to their surroundings and to their own physical comfort; an indifference manifest in immobility. Most will not tolerate interruption and ignore, with single-minded concentration, the distractions of the world around them. At one time, legend has it, Las Vegas almost became the scene of a disaster when players, oblivious to fire alarms, had to be forcibly removed from a burning downtown casino! Slot-players are frequently so stationary for long periods that when they eventually move they suffer excruciating cramps and dizziness. During one particularly tense game, one punter described how he felt immobilised in an out-of-body state, saying: 'You get what's called a "red mist". You can't leave the table; you're frozen to the table ... you can't move'. We can see from all this that gamblers' space is *not* a dynamic one conditioned by movement, but is rather characterised by a *breakdown* of such movement; by stasis. The gambler does not move and does not avert his/her gaze from the immediate spectacle of the action in front of him/her, with the result that the surrounding space loses its extensity and its articulation. This is part of the breakdown of the articulation of space in which the latter shrinks into a single point and loses its extensity and, in this sense, we can describe the experience of space in games of chance as conditioned by a 'pathology of being'.

The perception of space is related to other modes of experience, and in particular the shrinkage of space affects the perception of causation. This is apparent in the gambling arena when, in the heat of the moment, the usual relations between cause and effect become disjointed in the gambler's mind. The particular form of this disjunction will be considered in the following section; for now it is sufficient to entertain it, after Merleau-Ponty, as a possible mode of perception:

The shrinkage of lived space ... leaves no room for chance. Like space, causality, before being a relation between objects, is based on my relation to things. The 'short circuits' of delirious causality, no less than the long causal chains of methodical thought, express ways of existing. (Merleau-Ponty 1981, p. 286)

Money

Although Benjamin thought that 'it is obvious that the gambler is out to win' (Benjamin 1992, p. 136), most gamblers do *not* in fact usually play to win.[7] Nor, as psychoanalytic theory would have it, do they play out of a masochistic desire to lose. The intentions of gamblers are not to be found between these two extremes, for they are generally indifferent to the possibility of winning or losing *per se*. The aim of gamblers is simply to experience the excitement of the game, and so the main goal is thus the indefinite continuation of play. As Spanier expresses it, 'win or lose, everyone feels the thrill' (Spanier 1992, p. 13).

Although ... the motives for gambling can be almost as heterogeneous as the variety of games themselves, with sociability (for example, with women in bingo and young people with slot-machines), financial gain (for example, in lottery play) and the exercise of skill (for example, in horse-race handicapping) cited as important elements of different gambling experiences, underlying all this variation is a common element—the quest for excitement, or the thrill of the game, as an end in itself. This is present, to a greater or lesser extent, in *all* forms of gambling, and fundamental to it is the devaluation of money and the indifference to winning or losing. Even lottery players, who, it could be argued, are the group of gamblers most interested in financial gain, are not immune to this common feature. As evidence, we can cite the existence of players who continue to play even after winning enormous jackpots. In a study of Ohio State lottery winners, Kaplan (1988) found that no one actually stopped playing after winning, and that, on the contrary, most players had actually gone on to *increase* their expenditure on tickets. In other forms of gambling, such as horse-race betting, winning is important not so much for the sake of money itself, but rather for what a successful outcome shows about a gambler's skill and ability. Money here is associated with social rather than financial rewards; with factors such as recognition, status and peer approval being paramount.

Despite the fact that gamblers do not play primarily to win it, the *presence* of money in play is nevertheless important: it is vital for the game to be meaningful, as it is the medium through which participants register involvement in a game. In modern gambling, money is both a means of communication and a tangible symbol of the player's presence. The ritual of risk, penalty and reward is couched in the language of money so that in games like poker it eloquently expresses 'every subtle nuance of meaning' (Alvarez 1991, p. 174). In this sense, its presence is vital for the unfolding of a game, for it is the universal equivalent, the dynamo of play. Money is necessary for the generation of the affective tension—the excitement—in games of chance, for at stake in a game is not simply the financial value of the wager, but what it represents—gamblers' opinion, their judgement, their very identity. With the placement of a bet, gamblers become vicariously involved in the game: the fate of their wagers becomes a test of character, and players who manage to control themselves and shrug off their losses in the face of adversity demonstrate strength of will or what Goffman calls 'face' (Goffman 1969).

Any game can be played with a measure other than money, but the thrill will not be the same. Playing poker for matchsticks is perceived as child's play because without the existence of an authentic measure of value, gamblers cannot enter wholeheartedly into the game. As a measure of the degree to which they are prepared to back their opinion, the wager is a measure of the gamblers' integrity, and so must be represented by something worthy of them—hence Richardson regarded his chips as the embodiment of himself, his 'tokens of specialness' (Richardson 1980, p. 121). To have themselves embodied in something as worthless as matchsticks would be demeaning, for it would be to render the player equally as worthless, an object of ridicule. Insofar as money exists as a measure of self-esteem, winning validates gamblers' self-worth. It is in this sense that Rosenthal writes: 'the more money one has, the more substance to oneself, the more one *is*' (Rosenthal 1986, p. 112).

The role of money in gambling however, is ambiguous. On the one hand, it can be seen to be vital, both as the language of play and as a constituent of the thrill. On the other, it is not a sufficient reason for play itself and, paradoxically, once *in* a game, it becomes instantly devalued. Such a contradiction led Baudrillard to state: 'The secret of gambling is that money does not exist as value' (Baudrillard 1990, p. 86). What then *does* it exist as? To answer this, we must look at the effect of money on the gambler at play.

Dostoevsky was adamant that 'The main thing is the play itself. I swear that greed for money has nothing to do with it' (Dostoevsky 1914, p. 119), while Richardson gave a more considered account of his relation to money, writing that gambling had invested it with 'the quality of a medium necessary to the conditions of life. It was not that I wanted to *do* anything with it, any more than I wanted to *do* something with oxygen or sunlight; it was simply that cash had become the element I needed for my personal evolution' (Richardson 1980, p. 75).

It would appear then that gamblers do not play to win but play *with* instead of *for* money. In fact, when they continue to win in games that offer little real challenge, they become quickly bored. Jack Richardson went through such a period of playing poker solely for gain. The result?—'I grew tired of winning every day. ... The game had become nothing but empty labour' (Richardson 1980, p. 201). Without the element of chance, the risk of losing all, the game lost its thrill and became mere monotonous work. This effect is evident in the behaviour of top poker players who, after winning large sums of money through concentrated effort and skill, frequently go out and lose it betting on things they have no control over, such as craps and roulette.[8]

Pascal was well aware of the ambiguity of money in games of chance, realising that it was not *only* the money or *only* the play itself that made gambling such an effective antidote to boredom. In the *Pensées* he imagined a hypothetical life in which boredom lurks at every corner:

> A given man lives a life free from boredom by gambling a small sum every day. Give him every morning the money he might win that day, but on condition that he does not gamble and you will make him unhappy. It might be argued that what he wants is the entertainment of gaming and not the winnings. Make him play then for nothing, his interest will not be fired and he will become bored, so it is not just entertainment he wants either. (Pascal 1987, p. 70)

Money must be present in games of chance, but it cannot be important. In fact, contrary to its status in the outside world as a desirable medium of value, in play, money is apprehended as a thing that is virtually worthless in its own right. As such, it is *devalued* in the mind of gamblers. In order to play without reserve, they must be unconcerned with money for its own sake. As they play, a gulf opens up in their minds between the value of money in the world outside and its value (or lack of) in play. As this gap widens, and the 'real' value of money recedes ever further from the game, gamblers are able to play with increasing insouciance. Chip Reese explains the mechanism of this devaluation:

> Money means nothing. If you really cared about it you wouldn't be able to sit down at a poker table and bluff off $50,000. If I thought about what that could buy me I wouldn't be a good player. Money is just the yardstick by which you measure your success. You treat

chips like play money and don't think about it 'til it's over. (In Alvarez 1991, p. 42)

This devaluation is one of the 'tricks' which gambling plays on value, and it is in this, according to Baudrillard, that its truth is to be found. Gambling, he says, is 'immoral' because it explodes the relation between money and its embodiment of value. This is the crucial relation for 'In gambling, money is *seduced* ... [it is] no longer a sign or representation once transformed into a stake. And a stake is not something one invests; but as we have seen, it is something which is presented as a challenge to chance' (Baudrillard 1990, p. 139). Removed from the realm of material necessity, money becomes a part of the means of play; a plaything devoid of economic value. Its seduction is even embodied in the language of gambling where stakes, wins and losses are always euphemistically couched in the neutral adjectives of volume and weight as 'heavy', 'large' or 'small', thus avoiding the harsh imperatives of economic reality, of financial profit and loss.

Such devaluation is instrumental in creating the sense of unreality that is a feature of the general tension of games of chance, and is exemplified in the use of 'currencies' such as DigiCash Internet gambling, and chips in the casino. In the latter, money is changed into chips at the beginning of play; and chips back into money at the end. In the interim the chip is the unit of value. A piece of plastic, with no exchange value outside the casino, inside it is nevertheless the medium of play; the currency of chance. Money—the ultimate measure of value in the world outside—is dethroned in the gambling exchange. It is worthless, its magical effects on the everyday world are redundant here and, its role thus inverted, it must be transformed into chips for play to commence. The act of changing money into chips changes the way the gambler thinks about the latter for the duration of play. As if by magic, the arena of play transforms the prosaic character of money into something fantastic and strange, a process that is described by Alvarez as 'like a conjurer's sleight of hand that turns ... a necessity of life into a plaything, reality into illusion' (Alvarez 1991, pp. 44–45). The value of the real world, measured in drab green and brown paper, becomes a toy of the play world measured in shiny bright plastic. Looking at the chips on the table in front of him, Richardson 'felt for a moment that they were radiant things. Gold, green, orange, they encased, like pearls in amber, rusty undulations of colour beneath their surface, gay fusions of light and shadow that made one's thoughts reckless and playful' (Richardson 1980, p. 254).[9]

In games, chips are regarded as things which are not quite real, and as a result gamblers tend to lose track of the value of the flow of coloured discs streaming through their hands. When money is turned into plastic in this way it is no longer perceived as an efficacious part of the real world[10] but as an inconsequential counter in a play world, and so players find it easy to let go of their usual pecuniary reserve and abandon themselves to the flow of play. The use of money is here not directed by an awareness of needs which may arise in the future, but by the imperatives of the next round of play in the immediate present.

In the moment of staking, the economic value of money is far outweighed by the excitement it creates in play. Here the gambler is like Simmel's spendthrift, for whom 'the attraction of the instant overshadows the rational evaluation of either money or commodities' (Simmel 1971a, p. 182). For Simmel, the immoderation of both the miser and the spendthrift stems from the same source, the same 'daemonic formula' whereby every pleasure attained increases the desire for more in a spiral that can never be satisfied. Such a formal identity suggests a 'capricious interplay' between the two tendencies, which explains why 'miserliness and prodigality are often found in the same person, sometimes in different areas of interest and sometimes in connection with different moods' (Simmel 1971a, p. 186). This is a tendency also found in gambling, where the inversion of its value lends a dual nature to money in the mind of the player: a 'capricious interplay' of miserliness and prodigality. Gamblers frequently refuse to 'waste' money on necessities, instead hoarding every penny to save enough for enormous bets on games of chance. This orientation was recognised by Balzac, who described the 'strange indifference to luxury' in people who came to the casino to 'perish in their quest of the fortune that can buy luxury' (Balzac 1977, p. 23). Such a blend of parsimony and extravagance is institutionalised in Las Vegas, where casinos absorb the hundreds of thousands of dollars saved for high-stakes play by gamblers living in budget motels and eating only the cheapest food.

As a measure of play, money is also a measure of time, for the two exist in an intimate relation. Low intensity play (i.e. long games with low stakes) makes money, and therefore playing time, last longer. Leaving aside the vicissitudes of luck, a player can gamble longer at a table which costs £1 a game than at one which demands £500. This relation is strikingly evident in the casinos of Las Vegas, which reward time spent at play with a sliding scale of free goods and services. At the Flamingo, breakfast is free for gamblers who have played a $5 slot-machine for an hour or a 25-cent machine for eight hours. They are presented with a complimentary hotel room after four hours on the $8 machine or twenty hours on the 25-cent one. Table awards range from a complimentary room for placing $10 bets for four hours, to free room, food, beverages and health spa for gamblers and their guests for playing for four hours at a table which takes $500 bets.

The casino draws attention to its policy; its guide inadvertently articulating the conflation of time and money in play: 'Excess playing time reduces the average bet requirement and higher average bets reduce the playing time requirement. Consideration for airfare reimbursements are based on a minimum of twelve hours playing time' (*The Flamingo Casino Guide*).

It can be seen then that money is necessary as the dynamo of gambling. As the currency of the world of play, it comes to assume magical properties, becoming an insubstantial chimera that contributes to the sense of unreality and the affective tension experienced by gamblers during play. Once in a game however, it is immediately devalued, becoming merely a means of sustaining or prolonging the action. As one player explained: 'The whole point of money is to allow you to remain in the action. Once you have no money, it's axiomatic. You're out of action' (in Martinez 1983, p. 361). The repetition of play is evidence of this goal for, even when winning vast amounts, gamblers tend to continue playing anyway. As we have seen, repetition is an intrinsic element of both the form and the content of play, and one that prevails whether the outcome of a round is loss or gain. A common sight in slot-machine arcades and the casinos of Las Vegas is slot-machine players emptying their winnings from a previous round back into the machine, thrusting handfuls of coins in as fast as they pour out, in the pursuit of further play. Even multi-million-dollar lottery winners play on, one remarking wistfully: 'It'd be nice to get one more win.'

The Varieties of Gambling Experience

Unproductive Expenditures

This devaluation highlights one of the most striking characteristics of play: its essentially *unproductive* and non-utilitarian nature. No wealth or goods are ever created in its endless circulation of money, and in this sense 'Play is an occasion of pure waste, waste of time, energy, skill and often money' (Caillois 1962, p. 5). Despite the tone of residual Puritanism in many statements about its unproductive nature, it is undeniably true that with its flamboyant squandering of money, gambling *is* such an occasion of pure waste, or what Bataille calls 'unproductive expenditures': activities which are pursued for their own sake and whose principle is pure consumption. Contrary to bourgeois rationality which recognises 'the right to acquire, to conserve and to consume rationally' (Bataille 1985, p. 117) exists the notion of non-productive expenditure—the waste, destruction or conspicuous consumption of wealth in activities which have no end beyond themselves. This expenditure exists as the converse of wealth creation and production and represents the fundamental human need to 'use up' wealth (Bataille 1985, p. 121). Bataille cites sacrifice, potlatch and gambling as examples of this broadly non-utilitarian, anti-bourgeois approach to wealth, and it is an approach which we saw earlier in the gambling orgies of the seventeenth-century aristocracy. The obligation to expend accompanies the possession of wealth, and, he says, the two have always existed harmoniously until the 'fairly recent' ascendancy of the bourgeoisie in economic life, when such obligations broke down as the principle of 'restrained expenditure' began to dominate. Now 'everything that was generous, orgiastic and excessive' has disappeared, overtaken by a bourgeoisie who 'having obtained mediocre or minute fortunes, have managed to debase and subdivide ostentatious expenditure, of which nothing remains but vain efforts tied to tiresome rancour' (Bataille 1985, p. 124).

By 'restrained expenditure', Bataille means the rationalist orientation developed by the bourgeoisie in the seventeenth century, coming to power out of the humiliating shadow of a more powerful, noble class. This orientation defined the nature of the bourgeoisie; 'This rationalism meant nothing other than the strictly economic representation of the world', with the result that their hatred of expenditure became 'the *raison d'être* and the justification for the bourgeoisie' (Bataille 1985, p. 124). Their narrow economic rationality opposed the excesses of aristocratic display, making the existence of the bourgeoisie 'a sinister cancellation' of all that had gone before: 'the shame of man' (Bataille 1985, p. 125).

Bataille's notion of expenditure is the economic counterpart to the excitement generated by gambling. It represents the desire to 'plunge', realised in primitive and feudal social groups, and negated in the economic utilitarianism of bourgeois society. Gambling can be seen as an arena in which a non-capitalist disregard for money prevails and where bourgeois rationality, dominant since the seventeenth century, is inverted. While playing, gamblers' orientation to wealth is contained in the notion of this type of 'unproductive expenditure'. Without concern for the rational accumulation of wealth, they play rather for the sheer sake of play itself; for self-realisation, status and pure enjoyment. The nobility of the seventeenth century demonstrated honour in their wholehearted pursuit of play, and in their disinterest in its base, pecuniary potential. In the same vein, modern gamblers demonstrate character and realise their selves in their pursuit of play: an unproductive expenditure; an activity in and for itself.

Gambling, Chance and Status

Plunging into a game is not the automatic response of *all* gamblers however: we only have to remember Dangeau and his 'bourgeois' play at the court of Louis XIV to be aware that different styles of play exist, each with its own rationale and social affiliation.

The polarisation between 'bourgeois' and 'aristocratic' play which emerged in the seventeenth century produced a form of gambling based on a patrician disdain for money and display of honour, as well as a 'bourgeois' mode of play whose aim was pecuniary gain. In the nineteenth-century wave of commercial and democratic expansion, another style of play emerged whose dynamic was based neither on winning nor on the ostentatious display of wealth, but simply on participating in the game. As we have seen, aspects of both types are also present in contemporary gambling: in the latter, in games which are pursued for their own sake, simply for the pleasure of participating; and in the former, in games where status and character can be demonstrated in facing up to the challenge posed by risk itself.

Dostoevsky is illustrative of the opposition between what can be termed bourgeois or utilitarian play for financial gain, and the type of gambling that is pursued purely for its own sake, for although he was involved in the latter camp, he remained unaware of the existence of such an opposition. At first he appears to demonstrate a remarkable lack of awareness of the laws of probability, and even of the rules of gambling themselves, for he is convinced that with prudence and calculation he can win and that it is only when he becomes excited that he gets 'carried away' and loses. This may be useful advice for those playing games of skill, but Dostoevsky was playing roulette, where such tactics would have made absolutely no impression on the outcome of a game. This gambler's (mis)application of the betting ethos to games of chance which can only be *played* is interesting, less for what it tells us about his knowledge of probability than for what it reveals about his notion of the nature of play itself. In the catalogue of disaster that is the content of his published letters, Dostoevsky explains the infallibility of his system:

> I have observed as I approached the gaming table that if one plays coolly, calmly and with calculation *it is quite impossible to lose!* I swear—it is an absolute impossibility! It is blind chance pitted against my calculation; hence I have an advantage over it. ... If you gamble in small doses every day, it is impossible not to win. (Dostoevsky 1987, pp. 345, 346)

Dostoevsky is convinced of the efficacy of his system: to win, one must simply remain calm and rational; his problem is that he quickly loses his reason when he plays: instead of holding back he plunges into the game—and into disaster. Having won a small amount by staking one or two gulden at a time and sensibly allowing his profits to accumulate, he reflects that that was the time to have stopped, but he could not restrain himself: 'I lost my composure, became tense, started to take chances, became exasperated, laid my bets haphazardly because my system had broken down—and lost' (Dostoevsky 1987, p. 246).

Dostoevsky aspired to the success of Dangeau—'the scientific man, the average man, the economic man'—and thought he knew how he could achieve it. By maintaining the bourgeois imperative of reason in the face of disorder and passion, he believed everything would fall into place and the world and, more importantly, the *game*, would become as ordered as he was. The problem for Dostoevsky however was that he could *never* play in this way, for he despised such 'bourgeois mentality', and was repeatedly overcome by his disregard for winning and desire for excitement, for risk. This orientation meant that he would always 'plunge', always lose control and experience the excitement of gambling instead of remaining aloof, holding back and coolly calculating his gains. He chose (as does any gambler who experiences the thrill) the excitement of play itself over pecuniary gain, abandon over restraint, the 'aristocratic' over the 'bourgeois' ethic. Lamenting his losses to Anna Suslova, he wrote: 'What could I possibly have done to deserve this? Is it my disorderly ways? I agree I have led quite a disorderly life, but what is all this *bourgeois morality*!' (Dostoevsky 1987, p. 219). The true gambler, he believed, played 'simply for the sake of the game itself, only for amusement ... not out of a plebeian desire to win' (Dostoevsky 1992, p. 138).

In this style of play, we see a disregard for money, a deliberate seeking out of risk and chance, and a realisation of the self: values which are encapsulated in Nietzsche's allegorical 'dice throw'. In a philosophy which rejects as slavish the values of bourgeois morality and which uploads the masterful ones of aristocratic excess, the dice are thrown on to the earth and fall into the sky; 'for the earth is a table ... trembling with ... the dice-throws of the gods' (Nietzsche 1969, p. 245). The good player must be as anti-rational as Zarathustra, repudiating reason and logic and actively *courting* chance. Rules and systems must be abolished and chance affirmed in one, single, all-or-nothing throw. In terms of the master–slave dialectic, the gambler who risks all and 'plunges', or affirms chance, is the stronger, while the one who holds back and whose object is pecuniary gain is subject to the slave mentality. For Nietzsche, to play successfully is to affirm chance, an approach which will necessarily produce the winning number. Players lose because they do not affirm strongly enough, counting on a great number of sensible, cautious throws to win:

Timid, ashamed, awkward like a tiger whose leap has failed: this is how I have often seen you slink aside.... A *throw* you made had failed. But what of that, you dice throwers! You have not learned to play and mock as a man ought to play and mock. (Nietzsche 1969, p. 303)

Gambling in twentieth-century Las Vegas, Richardson displayed an almost intuitive understanding of his role as a modern dice thrower. While ostensibly aware of probabilities and odds, in a more profound sense he felt that *real* winning, as opposed to the various rational calculations which ultimately only ever amount to loss minimisation, could only be achieved by a single, brave gamble. In keeping hold of himself, he wrote: 'I thought I was displaying admirable self-control but I was really afraid to face the risk of a large gamble, to submit to the full force of chance and feel my entire being at stake in the encounter' (Richardson 1980, p. 153). He could not find the strength to affirm chance strongly enough: 'I kept demanding to win, but still could not find the courage to make winning possible' (Richardson 1980, p. 168). Thus he lost, over a period of days, his entire bankroll.

In a sense, Nietzsche is right: given finite funds in commercial games of chance, one all-or-nothing bet at least contains the possibility of a big win. Otherwise, the longer gamblers play with small stakes, the longer the house edge has to eat into their bankroll, gradually taking its cut and reducing them to penury. One large bet at least has the chance of winning a sum untouched by this steady, relentless erosion.

The affirmation of chance provides an opportunity to demonstrate character, to display courage and honour in the face of risk. In this way the affirmation of chance is also an affirmation of the *self*. It is here that the relationship between gambling and status, risk and ennoblement, is most obvious. Alesky found redemption through his gambling, for Dostoevsky writes of him that 'deep down he feels that he is despicable although the need to take *risks* ennobles him in his own eyes' (Dostoevsky 1987, p. 186). He set an arbitrary test for himself, betting his last money on the turn of the roulette wheel, to decide whether he was 'a man or a nothing.' The risk paid off: 'I had achieved this at the risk of more than my life, I had dared to take the risk and now I was *once again among the ranks of men*!' (Dostoevsky 1992, p. 267; my italics). A similar sentiment was expressed by Gogol's Utyeshitelny, who declared: 'the chief zest lies in the risk. Where there is no risk, anyone is brave; if the result is certain, any paltry scribbler is bold' (Gogol 1926, p. 236).

It is not only the plunging into chance that has this effect; games of skill also provide a stage for self-realisation. Although ... the orientation involved in the two is different (with games of skill utilising calculation and planning), crucially, the element of risk is still paramount. The similarity derives from the fact that it is mainly social rewards, not financial ones, that derive from the taking of such risks. Exposure to risky or uncertain situations provides individuals with the opportunity to display courage and integrity, and so to earn the respect of their peers. As top poker player Jack Strauss explains, it is not mathematical ability but 'heart'—'the courage to bet *all* their money'—when the odds are in their favour which is the criteria by which a player is judged (in Alvarez 1991, p. 31).

Despite their manifold differences, games of chance and those of skill are united in their common disregard of financial gain. In neither one is money the primary motive for gambling, rather it is the aspiration to be a 'dice thrower': the demonstration of character and courage and the consequent affirmation of the self that makes the play meaningful. Despite the victory of the bourgeois ethos, represented by the winnings of Dangeau, subsequent generations of gamblers like Dostoevsky and Richardson have *not* played to win, but rather for the continued experience of the game itself. The orientation of the modern gambler can be seen to be inspired not by the 'rational' goal of financial gain, but rather by ever-renewed play, and it is here that the relationship between gambling, self-realisation and, as Goffman puts it, 'face', is most striking. Thus the abandonment of reason embodied in Dostoevsky's plunging parodied the bourgeois style of play; a style eternally constrained by the discipline of self-consciousness over oblivion and restraint over excess. By not risking all, such gamblers will never lose all, but nor will they ever gain anything of value. Their greatest reward will be a few pennies, carefully won in an eternity of sensible, cautious play.

Play-in-Itself

The rationale of the repetition of play, and the fundamental aim of gamblers, is the ever-continued pursuit of play. They attempt to sustain the fleeting sensation of the thrill by repeating their actions, striving for a state that cannot be—the *continual* sensation of the thrill. For Gadamer, the essence of all play is that it is divorced from the realm of utilitarian ends and pursued entirely for its own sake. Thus 'the being of all play is always realisation, sheer fulfillment, energia which has its telos within itself' (Gadamer 1975, p. 101). Win or lose, play is all; it is an end in itself and so the goal of the gambler is simply to remain in play. The outcome of a game is not so important as the possibility of its being brought to a conclusion, for this means that that particular round is over. So, having won or lost, gamblers are frustrated by having brought the game to an end and to re-create the sensation of play must repeat their actions again and again. The repetition of such activity so engrosses players that their very *being* becomes absorbed in it; as Steinmetz puts it: 'the gamester lives only for the sensation of gaming.... All the rays of [his] existence terminate in play; it is on this centre that his very existence depends' (Steinmetz 1870, p. 49).

In trying to hold on to this elusive sensation, gamblers are caught in the eternal repetition of the ever-same. Time freezes, space contracts, and players hang, it could be said, in a state of suspended animation. They possess no past, and are unable to consider the future beyond the next round. Forever pursuing the fleeting sensation of play—a sensation which vanishes almost as soon as it is reached—they are caught in a state akin to what Schopenhauer describes as a state of becoming and never being. For Schopenhauer, it is not the end but the sensation of striving for a goal that satisfies us. Any pleasure we experience ceases as soon as we reach it and so the more distant it is the better, for its very distance gives us the illusion that its eventual attainment would satisfy us. He writes that 'we take no pleasure in existence except when we are striving after something in which case distance and difficulties make our goal look as if it would satisfy us (an illusion which fades when we reach it)' (Schopenhauer 1970, p. 54). Thus by the time a game has been won or lost, it is over, the thrill is dissipated and the gambler must begin again to re-create it. Such a frustrating predicament underlies all gambling, and was well understood by Balzac when he described the typical player as a 'modern tantalus, one of those men who live just out of reach of the enjoyments of their times ... a kind of reasoning madman who consoles himself by nursing a chimera' (Balzac 1977, p. 25).

Notes

1. Nor should it be taken to imply that gambling has some kind of 'essential' nature: the heterogeneity of the topology ... should have demonstrated that this is not the case.
2. See the work of phenomenologists and existentialists on this: e.g. Merleau-Ponty 1981; Straus 1966; Minkowski 1970; May *et al.* 1958; Ey 1978.
3. Exemplified, for example, in the radical sequestration of Herman Hesse's ultimate game of chance, *The Glass Bead Game* (1975).
4. Similar literary accounts of the alteration of consciousness under extreme conditions have been given by other writers. For example, Thomas Mann's *The Magic Mountain* (1962) describes the effects of long-term illness, while Jean Cocteau's *Opium* (1930), Thomas De Quincey's *Confessions of an English Opium Eater* (1821) and William Burrough's *Junky* (1977) describe the experience of drug addiction.

5. Described by his translator as 'a wrenching of biography into fiction' (Wasiolek 1972, p. xxxviii).
6. See also e.g. Bjorgvinsson and Wilde (1996) on the effect of risk taking on the perception of the future.
7. Cheating is an exception. This is the pursuit of pure profit, a form of work which attempts to impose a rational order on chance. Its calculative attitude removes it from the sphere of play, and so cheating can be disregarded as gambling proper. Caillois (1962) discounted it as a 'perversion' of the spirit of chance, as did Baudrillard (1990), for whom it was a 'refusal of the vertigo of seduction'.
8. Such actions contradict Benjamin's assertion that games of chance exist as the counterpart to the drudgery of the machine labourer. If anything, as we have already stated, it is the calculation and self-restraint involved in games of *skill* that represent such drudgery.
9. The manufacture of these magical discs from plastic is a particularly suitable combination, for plastic itself is 'the stuff of alchemy' (Barthes 1976, p. 97). In his essay on its metaphysical properties, Barthes wrote that plastic is a miraculous substance' which, like the chip as a temporary representative of value, has no real character of its own. It is a uniquely modern substance for it has no origins and is thus, according to Barthes, a 'universal equivalent' just as the chip is the universal equivalent of value in the casino.
10. A similar psychological effect can be found with the use of credit cards.

References

Alvarez, A. (1991) *The Biggest Game in Town*, Herts: Oldcastle Books.
Balzac, H. (1977) *The Wild Ass's Skin*, trans. H.J. Hunt, Harmondsworth: Penguin Classics.
Barnhart, R.T. (1983) *Gamblers of Yesteryear*, Las Vegas: Gamblers Book Club Press.
Bataille, G. (1985) *Visions of Excess*, trans. A Stoekl, C.R. Lovitt and D.M. Leslie, Manchester: Manchester University Press.
Baudelaire, C. (1982) *Les Fleurs du Mal*, trans. R. Howard, Brighton: John Spiers/The Harvester Press.
Baudrillard, J. (1990) *Cool Memories 1980–1985*, London: Verso.
Benjamin, W. (1977) *Illuminations*, trans. M. Zohn, Glasgow: Fontana/Collins.
_____ (1985) 'Central Park', *New German Critique*, 34, winter, 32–58.
_____ (1992) *Charles Baudelaire: A Lyric Poet in the Era of High Capitalism*, trans. H. Zohn, London: Verso.
Bergler, E. (1970) *The Psychology of Gambling*, New York: International Universities Press.
Bergson, H. (1910) *Time and Free Will*, trans. F.L. Pogson, New York and London: Macmillan.
_____ (1911) *Matter and Memory*, trans. N.M. Paul and W.S. Palmer, New York and London: Macmillan.

Brown, R.I.F. (1994) 'Dissociation phenomena among addicted gamblers', *Paper presented at the Ninth International Conference on Gambling and Risk-Taking Behaviour*, Las Vegas, June.

Caillois, R. (1962) *Man, Play and Games*, trans. M. Barash, London: Thames and Hudson.

Cassirer, E. (1944) *An Essay on Man: An Introduction to a Philosophy of Human Culture*, New Haven, CT: Yale University Press.

Charmaz, K. (1992) *Good Days, Bad Days: The Self in Chronic Illness and Time*, New Brunswick, NJ: Rutgers University Press.

Cohen, S. and Taylor, L. (1972) *Psychological Survival: The Experience of Long-Term Imprisonment*, Harmondsworth: Penguin.

Csikszentmihalyi, M. (1975) 'Play and intrinsic rewards', *Journal of Humanistic Psychology*, 15, 3, 41–63.

de Jong, A. (1975) *Dostoevsky and the Age of Intensity*, London: Secker and Warburg.

Devereaux, E. (1949) *Gambling and the Social Structure*, unpublished Ph.D. thesis, Harvard University.

Dostoevsky, F. (1914) *Letters*, trans. E.C. Mayne, London: Chatto and Windus.

_____ (1951) *Crime and Punishment*, trans. D. Magarshack, Harmondsworth: Penguin.

_____ (1987) *Selected Letters of Fyodor Dostoevsky*, trans. A.R. MacAndrew, ed. J. Frank and D. Goldstein, New Brunswick and London: Rutgers University Press.

_____ (1992) *The Gambler*, trans. J. Kentish, Oxford: Oxford University Press.

Ey, H. (1978) *Consciousness*, trans. J.F. Floodstrom, Bloomington: Indiana University Press.

Gadamer, H. (1975) *Truth and Method*, trans. G. Barden and J. Cumming, London: Sheed and Ward.

Goffman, E. (1961) *Encounters: Two Studies in the Sociology of Interaction*, Indianapolis: Bobbs-Merrill.

_____ (1963) *Behaviour in Public Places: Notes on the Social Organisation of Gatherings*, Free Press of Glencoe: Collier Macmillan.

_____ (1969) *Where the Action Is: Three Essays*, London: Allen Lane.

Gogol, N. (1926) 'The gamblers', in *The Government Inspector and Other Plays*, trans. C. Garnett, London: Chatto and Windus.

Herman, R. (ed.) (1967) *Gambling*, London: Harper and Row.

_____ (1976) *Gamblers and Gambling*, Lexington: Lexington Books.

Holtgraves, T.M. (1988) 'Gambling as self-presentation', *Journal of Gambling Behaviour*, 4, 2, 78–91.

Huizinga, J. (1949) *Homo Ludens*, London: Routledge and Kegan Paul.

Jacobs, D. (1988) 'Evidence for a common dissociative-like reaction among addicts', *Journal of Gambling Behaviour*, 1, 4, 27–37.

James, W. (1982) *The Varieties of Religious Experience: A Study in Human Nature*, Harmondsworth: Penguin.

Kaplan, R. (1988) 'Gambling among lottery players: before and after the big win', *Journal of Gambling Behaviour*, 3, 4, 171–182.

Kierkegaard, S. (1983) *Repetition*, trans. H.V. Hong and E.H. Hong, Princeton, NJ: Princeton University Press.

Kusyszyn, I. (1990) 'Existence, effectance, esteem: from gambling to a new theory of human motivation', *International Journal of the Addictions*, 25, 2, 159-177.

Leiseur, H. (1984) *The Chase: Career of the Compulsive Gambler*, Cambridge: MA: Schenkman Books.

The Mahabharata (1975) trans. J.A.B. von Buiten, Chicago, IL: University of Chicago Press.

Martinez, T. (1983) *The Gambling Scene*, Springfield, IL: Charles C. Thomas.

Merleau-Ponty, M. (1981) *The Phenomenology of Perception*, trans. C. Smith, London: Routledge and Kegan Paul.

Minkowski, E. (1970) *Lived Time: Phenomenological and Psychopathological Studies*, Evanston: Northwestern University Press.

Neville, M. (1909) *Light Come, Light Go*, London: Macmillan.

Newman, O. (1972) *Gambling: Hazard and Reward*, London: Athlone Press.

Nietzsche, F. (1969) *Thus Spoke Zarathustra*, trans. R.J. Hollingdale, Harmondsworth: Penguin.

_____ (1982) *Daybreak*, trans. R.J. Hollingdale, Cambridge: Cambridge University Press.

Pascal, B. (1987) *Pensées*, trans. A.J. Krailsheimer, Harmondsworth: Penguin.

Proust, M. (1983) *Remembrance of Things Past*, vol. 3, trans. C.K. Scot-Moncrieff, T. Kilmartin and A. Mayor, Harmondsworth: Penguin.

Pushkin, A. (1962) *The Queen of Spades and Other Stories*, trans. R. Edmonds, Harmondsworth: Penguin.

_____ (1983) *Eugene Onegin*, trans. C. Johnston, Harmondsworth: Penguin.

Reith, G. (1999) 'In search of lost time: recall, projection and the phenomenology of addiction', *Time and Society*, 8, 1, 101–118.

Rhinehart, L. (1972) *The Dice Man*, London: Collins, Grafton Press.

Richardson, J. (1980) *Memoir of a Gambler*, London: Jonathan Cape.

Rosenthal, R. (1986) 'The pathological gambler's system for self-deception', *Journal of Gambling Behaviour*, 2, 2, 108–120.

Schopenhauer, A. (1970) *Essays and Aphorisms*, trans. R.J. Hollingdale, Harmondsworth: Penguin.

Seneca (1986) *The Apocolocyntosis of the Divine Claudius*, trans. J.P. Sullivan, Harmondsworth: Penguin.

Simmel, G. (1971a) 'The miser and the spendthrift', in D.N. Levine (ed.) *On Individuality and Social Forms*, Chicago, IL: University of Chicago Press.

_____ (1971b) 'The adventurer', in D.N. Levine (ed.) *On Individuality and Social Forms*, Chicago, IL: University of Chicago Press.

Spanier, D. (1992) *All Right, O.K., You Win: Inside Las Vegas*, London: Mandarin.

Spencer, L. (1985) 'Allegory in the world in the commodity', *The New German Critique*, 34, winter, 59–77.

Steinmetz, A. (1870) *The Gaming Table*, vol. 2, London: Tinsley Brothers.
Straus, E. (1966) *Phenomenological Psychology*, trans. E. Eng, London: Tavistock.
Zola, I. (1967) 'Observations on gambling in a lower class setting', in R. Herman (ed.) *Gambling*, London: Harper and Row.
Zurcher, L.A. (1970) 'The friendly poker player: a study of an ephemeral role', *Social Forces*, 49, 173–185.

CHAPTER 14

Good Losers

FREDERICK AND STEVEN BARTHELME

Rick telephones Steve at midnight Wednesday. Rick has finished classes for the week. Steve has a class Thursday, but it's a night class. Rick says, "So, let's roll. I want to be back by six in the morning."

"No chance of that," Steve says. "You driving?"

"Yeah. Let me call Mary."

Steve hangs up the phone, asks his wife, Melanie, if she wants to go. She doesn't. It's a routine. Rick phones Steve at midnight; Steve asks Melanie if she wants to go; she never does.

Rick and Steve are brothers, college professors and writers, who since 1995 have been doing all-night blackjack sessions at the Mississippi-coast casinos. At first, they played on paychecks, tiny savings accounts, credit-card advances; later, they used money from their parents' estate. They've been gambling at a frenetic pace at "the boats," as the locals call them, and, without knowing it, they're heading for a fall.

Steve changes into a heavy shirt with flaps over the pockets—it's cold in the casino, and the pocket flaps hide the hundred-dollar bills he always ends up carrying. He puts his credit cards in a neat stack on the table in the kitchen. "Call me when you get down there," his wife says.

Across town, Rick imagines how his girlfriend, Rie, will react to another midnight trip to the coast. If he wins, he's discovered, she tends to hate it less.

Rie lives in another house, with her daughter and their two dogs. She doesn't like the gambling and she doesn't want Rick gambling. But after months of argument she has given up. "It's your money," she says. "Throw it away if you want to." He can't call her now, because she's asleep.

He picks up the phone and calls his friend Mary Robison, a gambling buddy and a colleague at the university.

"We're thinking of going to the coast," he says.

"We shouldn't," she says.

"Yeah, I know," he says. "But we are. I'm calling Steve back. We're leaving right away. You going?"

"I'll take my car," she says. "I like to drive."

Rick and Steve and Mary stop at an Exxon station for gas and Cokes and then head out onto Highway 49 and into the darkness. They make a short parade—Rick's car, Mary's car.

The night is clear, and once they're out of town they can see stars in between rows of pines, the north-south lanes of the highway separated by trees that are a hundred years old. On either side, more pines. At first, the conversation in Rick's car is sparse. There are remarks about students, an M.A. thesis, a person in a workshop. Rick mentions a particularly fine story by one of the graduate students.

They sit in silence for a few minutes, enjoying the sound of the car.

Darkness. The pines. Then Steve says, "What did you lose last week?"

"Twenty-four hundred," Rick says.

"After everything?"

"Yeah, twenty-four. I was up a thousand, lost it on a couple of hands. If I could just keep from chucking all my money out onto the table."

"That'd be good," Steve says. "On the other hand, sometimes you win."

"True," Rick says.

"When I hit one of the slots for a grand or two right away, I'm usually good for the whole night," Steve says.

"How often has that happened?"

"Frequently. It's a regular event."

"Oh, really?" Rick says. He's watching the rearview, keeping an eye on Mary. "How frequently?"

"About twice," Steve says. "Two times," he adds, for clarification.

There are a lot of trucks on the highway. They all seem to be new trucks, white and clean, tall, and they roar when they go by. Rick says, "I'm keeping it to twenty-five hundred. If I get down twenty-five hundred, I'm leaving. Mary can take me home."

They drive in silence. A good moment. Alone and yet together, and the night seems very big. It goes on for miles. The land is low rolling country, and all they see is the trees alongside the highway and an occasional road-side stand. They pass through Wiggins, about thirty miles south of Hat-tiesburg. They pass Perkinston, a junior college. They pass a pine-milling operation, acres of it right by the highway, where the trunks of pine trees, forty feet in length, are turned into two-by-fours.

They pass a Bible store—"Thousands of Bibles in Stock!"—and cruise through the little all-night town by the bend in the highway—one build-ing, a small white store with two restaurants, and a state trooper's car. Steve's got his eyes shut. Rick sets the cruise control at seventy-two, seven miles over the limit.

When they reach the highway sign that says twelve miles to I-10 and fourteen to Gulfport, Steve calls his wife. "We're at the twelve-fourteen sign. We'll be there shortly." This is more of the routine.

At the casino, they pull into the garage, tuck the car in for the night. The walk from the garage to the casino is all nerves—like the walk from locker room to football field. They swagger, they lope. It's jokes and jitters. They imagine stacks of chips. Everything is still possible.

"Start slow," Steve says, cautioning Rick against his tendency to jump the bet early.

"Yeah, yeah. I know," Rick says.

Mary says, "I can't afford to lose a penny. I've got forty dollars here and I can't afford to lose a penny." She's tough, tall, good-looking but deadly thin. In her black clothes, she looks like scaffolding.

"You've only got forty dollars?" Rick says.

"That's all I've got in my pocket," she says, pretending this is an impor-tant distinction. "I've got my cards. But I can't afford to lose a penny."

Mary often says things because she loves the way they sound. She loves the word "penny."

The casino appears to float atop, sloppy green water you wouldn't want to fall into. Huge concrete piers anchor the "boat." The idea is that the casinos can't be on Mississippi land, so the owners have dug out pits on the beachfront, flooded them, and floated these barge-casinos there, literally feet off the beach. They cross the carpet-covered metal gangplank, nod at the white-shirted security guy there with his chrome clicker. Three clicks and they're counted. Then it's only the doors between them and the air-conditioning and the noise and the screeching players and the ingratiating dealers and the thick wine-red swirled carpet and the floating scent of a thousand people smoking. It's at this point things change.

Steve swears it's the air-conditioning. As soon as it hits you, he says, you're gone. They open the doors, and they're washed with treated air, the din, the scent of money, liquor, smoke. Adrenaline and aftershave. They're keyed up now, giddy, hopeful. They walk with a sure step. Something is suddenly clear, precise, desired.

Almost as soon as they're inside, they split up, lose sight of each other. It's two in the morning, and there are plenty of people gambling. People who, after a time, blur together, along with the wins and the losses, as they do in this story, in which long nights have been compressed into one and names have been changed.

Steve gets four hundred on a credit card to go with six in cash he has brought with him. He remembers when he first started gambling, how he laughed at the A.T.M. machines in the casino, how he promised himself never to use an A.T.M. there. He remembers thinking, That's death. He sits down at a one-dollar video-poker machine. Playing dollars is a sort of therapy, to get his bearings. After ten or fifteen minutes, he'll try some five- and ten-dollar slots, in the hope of hitting an early score to set up the night. Then, win or lose, he'll move on to blackjack.

Rick checks the chip racks of all the blackjack dealers—looking for a depleted one, which might mean the dealer has paid out heavy. He knows most of the dealers. He says hello, waves, smiles. They seem glad to see him.

At the casinos, chips come color-coded. White is a dollar, red five, green twenty-five, black a hundred, purple five hundred, orange a thousand. Rick drops a green chip, a "quarter," in the last betting circle on Roxie's table. Roxie's short, about forty-five. He's played with her before and won. She pats the felt in front of him and says good luck, as most dealers do when you start with them.

Rick goes through half his hundreds in no time at all, then breaks a couple of hundred down into greens and some reds. He bets two of those and continues playing.

Roxie makes a big deal out of the shuffle. She's dealing two-deck pitch, which means she's got two decks of cards mixed together, and deals out of her hand instead of a plastic "shoe."

People come and go, playing a little bit, leaving. After an hour, Rick is down seven hundred dollars. Steve walks up, raises his eyebrows to ask, "How're you doing?" Rick shakes his head, raises his eyebrows in return. Steve makes a thumbs-up sign and then a little-bit sign, using his thumb and forefinger.

He taps Rick's shoulder. "Why don't you try another table?"

"Soon as I lose the rest of this," Rick says.

Mary appears with a bucketful of dollar tokens, the fake coins from the slot machines. You have to change them at the cashier's cage in order to get real money. She sits in the chair next to Rick and asks how he's doing.

"Not so well," he says.

She rattles her cup of coins nervously and nods, lights a cigarette. Casinos are smokers' last refuge. She wants to get away but doesn't want to leave too suddenly. She fears that Rick will think she's a jinx. If you're playing blackjack, especially when it's going particularly well or badly, every blip in the environment thrives with meaning. You think Alanis Morissette on the sound system is a jinx, that the number of ice cubes in your glass brings bad luck.

Mary stubs out her cigarette, watches the end of another hand, which Rick loses, then points off in the direction of the slot machines.

"I'm going over here," she says.

A couple of pit people lean on the side of the table. Rick's known to them. They've heard that he's writing a gambling novel, and they want to know what he's going to write about them. He tells them he'll say they were kind and they dealt him winners. They laugh at that.

After another half hour, Rick's finished with the thousand and has to go back to the cage. This time, he gets fifteen hundred on a credit card. He takes the cash to the table. He sits for a minute and then says to Roxie, "I think I'll do the salon."

She smiles, "I would. Stay away from me. I'm too hot."

The salon is at the far side of the casino, behind frosted Art Deco glass. There are tables with twenty-five-dollar minimums; two have fifty-dollar minimums. Once in a while, the minimum bet can be as high as five hundred dollars. The tables in the salon have fewer seats, and players are treated with particular care.

A Chinese guy with what looks like ten thousand dollars in a chip carrier is playing at a table by himself. Rick sits down at a table with a dealer named Lollie, who has two players, one with only three hundred dollars and the other with about five thousand. Rick waits until after the next shuffle—it's etiquette—and puts out his quarter, starting slow. Lollie is very friendly with the guy who has the five thousand. It's like they're old buds. He has a powerful smell about him—he wears too much cologne—and a heavy beard and mustache. He's smoking, drinking some kind of highball. The two of them are talking about a boating party.

The cards come and go, and pretty soon Rick has won a little something. He bumps his bet up to fifty dollars and wins, increases it to a hundred and then two hundred. In no time, he's got twenty-five hundred dollars and is even for the night. The cards are right at Lollie's table. She's busting a lot, much more than usual. The guy with five thousand is cleaning up as well. The guy with the three hundred is just about gone, and when he finally leaves the table Rick thinks about taking his place and playing two spots. He waits to see if the guy with the five thousand wants it, and when he doesn't Rick starts playing a second spot. This new hand would have been the loser's, so he goes there with the short money, just in case.

A small woman with rugged skin steps up to him out of the pit, writing his name on a card, asking him how much he brought to the table.

"Fifteen hundred," he says.

"You didn't buy it here?" she says.

"The cage," he says.

After a couple of quick hands, the guy with the five thousand is up to eight thousand. He's playing first base—the first position dealt to, immediately to the dealer's left. Rick is playing third base, the dealer's extreme right. The short hand is between them. Rick bets a quarter on that hand and two hundred and fifty on third base. The cards come out. He gets two face cards on his big hand, a thirteen on his little hand. He hits the thirteen, gets a seven, for twenty, stands on both hands. The dealer flips and has seventeen. Rick continues to play this way, shorting the middle hand but winning anyway, and pretty soon he's up to four thousand.

It's now a quarter to four in the morning. Steve appears and sits at the table, between Rick and the other guy.

"I've been playing two hands. Works fine."

"O.K. if I play one?" Steve says.

"Don't care," Rick says.

Steve drops a quarter where Rick was playing his short hand. The cards come out—he wins. Rick wins. The next hand is dealt. They both win again. And again. They play on like this until Lollie's replaced by a gangly kid who says he's a graduate student in chemistry. The big-money guy leaves. By four-thirty Rick has fifty-five hundred dollars. Steve has won about fifteen hundred dollars, but he's still down for the night.

Rick colors up his chips, getting ready to leave the table.

Steve continues playing fifty to a hundred a hand, occasionally two hundred. Separately, two Vietnamese women join the table, one small and sharply dressed, the other big and square-shouldered. The small one doesn't like the way the other one plays her cards. She does a running critique, out loud. The bigger woman's play is slightly irregular, she splits fours against a four, a bad play by the book, and she hears about it. She's getting angrier and angrier, muttering about all the advice. Now the opinionated one, who looks like a fashion model, turns to Steve and says, "What do you think?"

What Steve thinks is that their argument is distracting. He'd rather she hadn't invited him into it. He says, watching the dealer's hand, without looking at either woman, "Maybe we should play our own cards?"

He's within sight of even. He has got close three times, and each time lost again. Losing everything trying to get the last hundred is familiar, but he's still four down and can't quit. At the next shuffle, he says, "Could you hold two spots?" The dealer puts out two clear plastic circles—"lammers"—reserving his places.

Steve wanders over to the high-ticket slots and runs into Roylynn, a waitress he knows—a little worn out but nice-looking, lots of dark hair, about thirty, has a kid. "How you doing tonight? Diet Coke?" she says. She hands him a Coke. He takes the glass, checks his pocket for chips, hands her a red.

"Thanks," she says.

Roylynn looks at the slot machines.

"You doing any good? That ten-dollar Double Diamond on the end," she says, pointing, "it's been hitting all night. Last night, too." She pats the machine as she walks away.

Steve sits down and feeds it a hundred-dollar bill. First pull: double diamonds in two windows, but the third turns up empty. Nothing. Still, the heart stops. He plays the machine for a while, winning some, losing some, working it up to three hundred before it tanks. When he's down to four credits, he decides to go two at a time. On the second pull, the last of his original hundred, he hits two double diamonds and a single bar—eight hundred dollars.

"Was that so hard?" he says to the machine.

He collects the coins, carefully wedging them into plastic racks the casino provides, then cashes in and heads for the blackjack table.

Rick is standing there watching the game. "Where are you?" he says as Steve sits down.

"Close," Steve says. "You?"

"Up three," he says. "I'm going to find Mary and take a break." He wanders out into the main casino and sees Mary in front of a Wild Cherry machine. She's surrounded by buckets of tokens. There are six buckets, each full of dollar tokens.

"Jesus Christ," Rick says. "What are you doing here?"

"I don't know," Mary says. "I just keep pulling and they keep coming."

He watches her hit two more jackpots, then asks if she's hungry.

"Food's bad," she says. "Besides, what do you think, I'm nuts? I'm playing here." She knuckles the machine.

He goes upstairs and gets a hamburger, eats it staring at his reflection in the black window that's supposed to overlook the Mississippi Sound. The restaurant is bright and smells of soaps and cleaning solvents. No people.

When he's done, Rick returns to the salon, to another table. He plays there until six, buying in twice more, and losing eight thousand dollars. Just like that. The last three thousand goes on a single bet.

"Always the big ones," Rick says as the dealer sweeps his chips.

"Seems that way, doesn't it?" she says.

He's now five thousand down. He goes back to Lollie's table. There's a replacement dealer, Lou Ann, a young, plain woman in her late twenties, brown hair, glasses, a schoolmarmish look. No one else at the table. He buys two thousand and starts by betting hundreds. She's good, fast, efficient, sure. The cards seem to come to him, and soon he's betting two hands at once, and winning. In another few minutes, he's got sixty-five hundred in black chips stacked up, ten to a stack, six and a half stacks. They stretch out along the cushion of the table.

He's only five hundred dollars shy of his nut, so he begins to play cautiously, reducing his bets. Looking the length of the casino, he can see light outside. It's six-thirty in the morning. For some reason, the caution hurts his game, and he starts losing again.

He ups the bet, loses. Ups again, loses more. By seven, he's out of chips.

He goes back to the cage for another two thousand, returns to find Lollie back from her break. He kills some time going to the men's room, waiting for the replacement dealer.

Lou Ann's wearing a bracelet of black web cloth with the letters "WWJD" embroidered in it. When she's back, he plays a few hands on his new chips—small hands, quarters and fifty-dollar bets.

He asks her what "WWJD" stands for.

"What would Jesus do," she says.

"Right," he says. "Why didn't I know that?"

He starts winning. In a few minutes, he's back to forty-five hundred. At ten after eight, he bets two thousand dollars, the table maximum, and gets an eleven, a hand you always double down on. Lou Ann has a six showing. Things couldn't be better. The six means she'll have to hit, and her chances of busting are good. With eleven, Rick can't bust. Any face will work.

He puts out another two thousand. He's now got four thousand bet and only five hundred left in front of him. He tells the dealer to wait a minute.

Steve has appeared and is standing nearby. "Monkey," he says. "Big monkey. Joe Young." Monkey means face card. Rick nods and smiles, and then slides behind the empty adjacent table until he's a full table away. Ethel, the pit person, is watching him with curiosity.

"Go ahead. Deal it," Rick says. "Deal it face down, please."

Shenanigans of this kind are allowed when they don't disturb anybody and when you're betting four thousand dollars. Lou Ann looks to Ethel, who nods. Lou Ann slides Rick's hit card face down under the seven and the four. Hitting a double down, you get only one card.

Then the dealer turns her down card over; it's a two, so she's got eight total. She deals herself another card, a three. Now she's got eleven. She pauses.

Rick's heart sinks. He shakes his head. He's lost confidence in his hand. He knows he's lost everything. She's got eleven and she's bound to turn up a face card, a ten, for twenty-one. He's hasn't looked at his card, but he'll probably have a crappy six to go with his eleven.

Rick is now hiding behind Ethel, who is chubby, five and a half feet tall. He has his hands on her shoulders. The dealer turns over her next card. It's a five; she now has sixteen. She must hit it again. She looks at Rick, then at Ethel, then slowly rolls the card.

Ethel, a good twelve feet away from the table, says quietly, "Too much. She's gone."

Rick looks. He can't imagine how Ethel can read the card from that distance. But she's said it, so he believes it. He pecks Ethel on the back of her head and then does a little jump before returning to the table to watch the dealer count out his four thousand dollars' worth of winnings. Two new stacks, twenty chips tall, two thousand dollars each.

He's now five hundred dollars short of his nine. He counts out five hundred, slides it into the circle, wins a quick hand with a twenty to the dealer's eighteen. Now he's even.

He says to Lou Ann, "Have you got one more in you?"

She says, "I don't know." She's clearly not eager for him to bet again. Not because she's afraid he'll win but because she's afraid he'll lose.

He takes five hundred dollars off his stack and puts it in the betting circle, wins another hand, and pushes the five hundred he's won across the table.

"For you guys," he says to Lou Ann.

She looks at Ethel, who nods. Lou Ann then changes the blacks into greens and drops the chips into the plastic toke box. "Dropping five hundred for the dealers," she says.

"Thank you," Rick says, his heart suddenly pounding.

"It was my pleasure," she says.

Rick colors up and says to Steve, "Are we ready? I hope we're ready. You all right?"

"Yeah," Steve says. "Mary's over by the escalator."

Steve goes to clean up and Rick goes to get Mary and soon they are on their way out of the casino and out to the cars. It's light out and hot, almost nine o'clock. Mary has won sixty dollars and Steve four hundred, and Rick has risked a little fortune and come away unbloodied. After some traffic in Gulfport, Highway 49 is quiet, nearly empty, and there's not much on the roadsides, either. It's fields and power lines and early-morning sun. It's a big farm out there.

II

Rick and Steve Barthelme arrived in Hattiesburg nine years apart. They'd both held plenty of jobs—cabdriver, construction worker, advertising copywriter, journalist, gallery worker, architectural draftsman—and had both got graduate degrees at Johns Hopkins University, in Baltimore, and now they were ready to settle down and teach.

Rick arrived in the mid-seventies, terrified because the state had a reputation—burning, hanging, rape, etc. He grew up in Houston and lived in New York City for five years, and had just finished graduate school at Hopkins; he figured that he was profoundly enlightened and that Mississippi wasn't. Indeed, his introduction to Hattiesburg was at an all-night gas station on Highway 49 where a lone half-wit teen-ager was corralling "pinching" bugs and dropping them in a five-gallon bucket of sand—a diversion he favored because, he said, he liked to watch the bugs kill one another. This was at two in the morning, and Rick and his girlfriend had been driving all day from Baltimore, where the week before they'd had brunch with the British literary critic Tony Tanner in the polished-mahogany restaurant of a hundred-year-old hotel. Now instead of talking about postmodernism they were staring at it, and it didn't seem to know their name.

In time, Rick discovered that Mississippi was as civilized as anywhere else. Things had apparently changed, the gas jockey notwithstanding, and at least in Hattiesburg and around the university there wasn't any burning and hanging. In fact, taken as a whole, the people in Mississippi seemed gentler and more humane than many he'd run into in ostensibly finer settings.

Steve arrived nine years later, having spent the previous two years teaching at a university in Monroe, a dim, depressed, trash-strewn Louisiana town where even the snakes hung their heads. To Steve, Hattiesburg was clean and bright. A decided improvement.

So there they were, college professors, fiction writers. They were born in Texas, reared in a family of fallen Catholics, with a father who was a successful and innovative architect and a mother who was an English teacher. One older brother, Donald, had been a leading literary figure. Two other older siblings made their living writing: Joan as a public-relations vice-president for Pennzoil Company, Pete as a Houston advertising executive and author of mystery novels.

Aesthetics and writing, art, music, film, narrative, character, culture—this stuff made up their lives. Books and movies in a pleasant little town handsome beyond probability, lush and green year round, forty-five thousand souls at the intersection of a few highways. Perfectly congenial, although, perhaps, short on excitement.

Enter the boats: suddenly, in 1992, there were casinos in Mississippi. The casinos appeared as paddle wheelers docked against the beaches. They were cramped, crowded, intimidating, with long lines of customers waiting to get in.

The beaches had never been much good. The sand had been sucked out of the Mississippi Sound and carefully spread alongside Highway 90 like something in the bottom of an aquarium. It looked wrong, like a bad hairpiece. The water was the color of well-done beef; locals said people loved Florida's emerald water, but fish, shrimp, and crab preferred Mississippi's brown. They were an industry. The towns strung along the coast had some of the dumpy charm of Galveston, where Rick and Steve's father was born, where they'd visited their grandparents as children, and where they'd played on the winningly disheveled Stewart Beach.

From Biloxi to Pass Christian to Bay St. Louis and Waveland, the coast towns were similarly distressed, beat up and ugly in an interesting way, but now, with the advent of "gaming," the towns were tarted up to look new and wholesome. The honorable if cheesy glitz of miniature golf and bright-pink seashell emporia gave way to paddleboat quaint: cheap tux shirts, black bow ties, red cartoon suspenders.

Gaming interests wanted casino gambling to seem like fun for the whole family, so casinos started looking like pirate ships and cowboy saloons, illumined by harmlessly cheerful neon (splashy pots of gold) instead of the furtive neon of the old beachfront strip ("Nudes! Nudes! Nudes!"). There were ten- and twenty-story hotels, parking lots, restaurants, stores.

Biloxi had a great old restaurant called Fisherman's Wharf, a shoddy woodframe thing built up on telephone-pole pilings right on the Sound. It had been serving seafood for over forty years. Family-owned, dilapidated, but the food was marvelous in the way that only coastal dives can manage—fresh fish, fried chicken, big glasses of sweet tea. Gerald Ford had eaten there, and the restaurant had pictures of him arriving in a big limousine. Gerald Ford's plate was preserved behind glass, along with the silverware he'd used, his napkin, the menu he'd looked at.

After 1992, an Oriental-motif casino called Lady Luck appeared next door—a barge decked out like a Chinese restaurant, complete with dragons and lanterns and fans. One Saturday when Rick and Rie were eating at the restaurant, they spent the meal eyeing this new casino. Afterward, they decided to give it a try.

Lady Luck was larger than the paddleboats—higher ceilings, more room. It was garish and silly inside, but charming in its way. The Oriental decoration was oddly coupled with loud pop music, waves of colored lights, and women in startlingly short skirts and tight tops. It was chilly in the casino, even in August.

They walked around, looked over the shoulders of the table-games players, tried their hand at video poker and at the slot machines. They started with quarters and won a little, then moved up to half-dollars and dollars. At a bank of dollar machines, one of them hit a small jackpot, and then the other hit one. Two sevens and a wild cherry. A minute later, Rick hit a five-hundred-dollar jackpot.

Pretty soon they were carrying around buckets of dollar tokens, and gambling didn't seem so bad. They walked out with eleven hundred dollars of the casino's money, feeling as though they'd won the lottery. Eleven hundred dollars that wasn't theirs.

Later, a similar thing would happen to Steve and Melanie.

They learned that this was typical, that it happened just this way for a lot of people who went to casinos. You won something sizable, and thereafter gambling took up residence in your imagination. You remembered the visit when you decided to return. It was a key to the business—the first time, you walked away with the casino's money.

When Rick and Steve compared notes about these first trips, they indulged a light euphoria. Casinos were garish and grotesque and maybe the people were seedy, but money was swell. They talked about buying books on slot machines, finding out which ones to play, what the odds were, how to maximize advantage and minimize risk. They were serious and excited; something new had come into their otherwise quiet lives. But they had no idea just how much those first jackpots would eventually cost.

III

In the first few years after the boats came to the coast, we gambled when we could. We played at Gulfport, Biloxi, Natchez, and Lafayette, but we didn't play for much—a couple of hundred dollars here and there.

It was entertainment. We'd go in, wander, play the slot machines, play video poker, tell jokes, come home. Once, Rick lost six hundred dollars in Natchez, and it seemed as if the sky had fallen. He and Rie walked back to the wonderful old Eola Hotel, where they had a penthouse room with a view of the Mississippi, and Rick promised that his gambling was over. This was a promise he would make often in the future.

Then, early in 1995, our mother died. On the preceding December 23rd, she'd entered the hospital, eighty-seven, malnourished, only intermittently lucid, and a week later she stopped eating.

It's possible that both our mother and our father played inordinately important roles in our lives. We had girlfriends and wives but no children, no new families to replace the one in which we had grown up, so right into middle age "the family" still meant our parents. Even nephews and nieces were a little outside the immediate circle—Mother, Father, and the five children, making up a tiny, insular, private world.

When Mother died, we were fiercely quiet. People had spoken too much when our brother Don died, in 1989. Two old friends—Roger Angell, Jack Barth—wrote brief, lovely eulogies. But Don was a minor public celebrity, as well as a major figure in the literary community, and everybody wanted a piece of him. And took it, too, one after another. People who knew him in passing, or professionally, published intimate poems and essays about him. People of the most tenuous acquaintance attached themselves ever so firmly in public after his death, distorting his memory a bit, commodifying him for their own purposes. It was a messy thing and went on for years after he died, until there was no more mileage to be wrung out of public mourning.

So Mother's death was matter-of-fact, and private, and afterward the gambling got much more intense. We were no longer playing little slots. We played only the five-, ten-, and twenty-five-dollar machines. And we stuck to salon blackjack, where the minimum bet was twenty-five dollars and the tables were dressed in glamorous purple felt. Dealers would stop what they were doing to say hello, and cashiers knew us by name and were eager to slide our credit cards through their machines. Everyone seemed to like us a lot. We became regulars at the casinos in Biloxi and, later, Gulfport.

We won sometimes, four or five trips in a row, coming home with hundreds, sometimes thousands, of dollars of the casino's money, but there always seemed to be that sixth trip, or a seventh, when we would lose ten thousand in one night, a loss that easily eliminated the winnings.

There was a new intensity to our play, something so subtle that we only vaguely noted it, putting it down to a combination of factors—a feeling that we ought to be able to figure out a way to win, coupled with the knowledge (from the books we'd been reading) that we probably weren't going to win and, added to that, the recognition that our gambling wasn't "sensible."

We might not notice the intensity of what we were doing until we were on the way home, down fifteen hundred dollars. Or it might appear in the way we cursed the slot machine that we'd just hit for a big jackpot, while we were waiting for the little ceremony with the cash payoff and the W-2G form. It might be felt when we pushed whatever money we had left—three hundred dollar bills, say, or a couple of twenties—out onto a spot at a blackjack table and said, "Money plays," a loser custom we made our own.

At the table, losing our money, we were all smiles, as if it were nothing. In fact, it felt like nothing. Money isn't money in a casino. At home you might drive across town to save a buck on a box of Tide, but at the table you tip a cocktail waitress five bucks for bringing a free drink. You do these things on the same day.

And then, on July 16th the following year, our father died. Rick was executor, and we had to leave for Houston, eight hours away, that afternoon.

We would be the "cleaners," as in a spy movie—our job to get in, take care of the mess, make it look as if our father had never been there, and get out. Father was the last of the original Barthelmes in Houston, and when we were done there wouldn't be a trace of us left, which mattered only in its echo of a time when the city was part of our sense of something that might last forever: the family.

The drive over was eerie—a little too familiar, too commonplace. We stopped for hamburgers at the Burger King in Crowley, Louisiana, just as we'd always stopped when driving to Houston for Christmas and summer visits. We spent time acquainting ourselves with Father's death, trying it on, getting the sense of it. When we got to his town-house apartment in Houston, the bed things were all clean and folded on the bare mattress in the living room. He had moved downstairs, been living there, not using the second floor, where the bedrooms were. The dining-room table was covered with papers, a big checkbook, reminder lists, worn twenty-year-old green file folders, labelled "Bills," "Investments," "Gas & Electric," carefully arranged. Everything orderly. His wallet, his keys. His financial records. That first night, sitting with nothing to do in the silent apartment, we glanced through the files, looking for wills and codicils, debts, deeds. When everything was done, it seemed the remaining four children would inherit something over half a million dollars.

We spent a week cleaning up the place, tearing down things Father had built there, tearing out built-in cabinetry, drafting tables, the stereo system, emptying the closets, throwing away everything we could bear to throw away: beds and pots and pans and half-bottles of liquor; paper, pens, and pencils. Soap, salt, houseplants, toothpaste, towels, Windex, zinc ointment, the ordinary supplies of day-to-day living.

There were some psychological leaks. On the fourth day, Steve was in the upstairs office working on the trash lumber for more than an hour, using a couple of Father's screwdrivers and a claw hammer to remove the nails and screws from the stacked pine and plywood of the already disassembled homemade filing cabinets and tables, working maybe a half hour ahead of the guy coming to haul it all away to the dump.

Rick piled clothes and junk we didn't want on our parents' bed, waiting for the Salvation Army people to come. A few things we packed in boxes, some stuff of Mother's—slippers, dresses she wore often, what jewelry there was left, a coffee cup. We did the same with Father's things, though we picked different objects. Not his clothes or shoes or leather jacket, though we did pick his hat, the comical gray leather cap he used to wear on his walks, cocked back on his head, but other things that were special to him, or seemed especially like him. We picked architectural books—Corbu and Mies, Gropius, Neutra, Wright, Aalto. His Leicas. A seventy-year old handsaw that had belonged to his father, who had owned a lumberyard in Galveston.

We spent long days packing, taking things apart, and throwing junk away. It was hard work, sweaty work, and it went on from ten o'clock in the morning until two or three the next morning, seven days solid. Our father and mother had lived in the apartment for twenty years. They were dug in. We worked like maniacs, crating and carrying and dragging stuff to a Dumpster, wrapping and packing and labelling. Non-stop. One of our nephews helped out one day, and Pete drove in a couple of times, but mostly it was just the two of us working in that apartment, erasing our parents bit by bit.

It amounted to burying them in brand-new cardboard boxes, and we stacked the boxes carefully in the apartment, numbered each one of them, detailed their contents on the outside. We planned, made lists, telephoned, decided, bought, shipped, worked together. Without realizing it, this funeral had become a weeklong affair, a ceremony that evoked for us the projects of our childhood, times when the family used to pull together for some house or landscaping chore, or even to prepare for a hurricane that the radio was sure was coming straight up Galveston Bay. In these projects, everyone would get assigned tasks, day after day, and the air was electric with the importance of the undertaking, and the family was a goddam army.

So were we when tearing down the house. And finally, after visits from Goodwill, the Blue Bird Circle, a last walk-through by the movers, we were back on Interstate 10, headed home, our parents' things relegated to the boxes, and then—a week later, when the movers made it to Hattiesburg—to Outback Storage shed 233, a place for them in perpetuity, a modern-day mausoleum. As if they were Egyptian royalty, we buried their property, their jewels, tools, and stationery, and for months afterward we went to the shed, mostly late at night—two, three, four in the morning—unlocked the padlock, lifted the rolling steel door, clicked on the light with the fifteen-minute timer, and walked among the boxes of their papers and photographs and clothes, among the chairs we'd saved, the dining table padded with packing quilts, the Laverne-covered folding screen that Father had built, the marble slab that had been a coffee table.

Now they were entirely dead, and we were alone and middle-aged and nothing really mattered all that much any way. They had seen us through to comfortable adulthood. We had seen them through to death.

Later, on drives to the casino—the two of us alone for an hour and a half, driving through the hot Mississippi nights, through an impenetrable swampy fog, so thick that tail-lights emerged suddenly in front of us like miniature U.F.O.s—our parents came to mind and the exchanges between us grew short, tight, and clean; not much needed to be said. There was a shared knowledge, a common experience, harmonies of sadness, melancholy, loss. Each of us knew how the other felt. So the exchanges were elliptical—lots of dots, just what was needed. And it was a reassuring thing, to be in that car together, driving to Biloxi or Gulfport, each knowing what the other felt, not needing to make it explicit, understanding the loss. The complexity and strangeness of it, the two of us, the last and youngest of the original Barthelmes, now alone.

IV

Before our father died, we paid for our gambling from our salaries or our savings. But after he died we had an inheritance. We drove to the coast, played all night, lost five thousand dollars, came home, taught our classes, made jokes about how horrible it had been, and waited for the next chance to go. The losses didn't bother us—after all, it wasn't really our money, it was his—and in hindsight we should have been tipped off that something wicked that way was.

Instead, we went home in the morning, called newfound brokers handling accounts to which our father's estate had been distributed, sold stocks and bonds to cover the night's losses. At first, there was plenty of money in the accounts and not so much being lost. It was easy to sell five thousand dollars' worth of bonds to cover a loss. It felt like high finance. Arriving at home at nine in the morning, we might make a few calls to Boston, tycoon style, move some money, cover debts before going to bed and trying to catch four or five hours of sleep before classes that afternoon.

We were playing in Gulfport because it was closest. We tried craps and Mini-Bac, but we concentrated on blackjack. We bought books—Edward O. Thorp's, Arnold Snyder's, Bryce Carlson's, others. We researched card counts—the Red Seven count, the Thorp count, the Zen count. We memorized "basic strategy," a system that determined how you should play based on the two cards you'd been dealt and the card the dealer had showing, simple mathematical probabilities compressed into an action table that you could print on the back of a business card. They sold these cards at the casinos, but we made our own—"The Win While You Sleep Blackjack Strategy Card."

The problem is that none of the strategies work unless you are counting cards. Counting, you can get a slight advantage—a half per cent, sometimes as much as one and a half. A blackjack table goes through sixty to a hundred hands an hour, so even if you're betting modestly you can make money counting, just as long as the standard deviation doesn't get you.

But the more we studied the less interesting counting became. You had to concentrate and be careful and watch everything with headache eyes. Card counting was about as much fun as waste management. The whole thing started looking like work, and we already had work. We didn't want more. So, in the end, although we learned "basic strategy," we played pretty much by ear. We counted cards sometimes, but ad hoc, not a way experts recommend. And we lost. At first not so much, but then a lot. And then we lost a lot more.

We played blackjack with different styles, although the result was the same for both of us. Steve played cautiously, thoughtfully, with patience, marshalling his money, inching ahead, then falling behind, and then, in the course of twelve, eighteen, or twenty-four hours, fighting his way back from terrible losses. He might play from midnight until eight in the morning and lose four thousand dollars, and then play from eight that morning until two the following morning and win three thousand of it back. On a good night, he might take home a thousand dollars.

Rick played kamikaze style, betting carefully at first, and then, abandoning caution, jacking up his bets to five hundred dollars, or suddenly putting everything he had on the table—two thousand dollars on a single deal. Why not? Or he'd bet three thousand on each of two hands, and then double both, leaving him with six thousand dollars hanging on the turn of the next card. Play like this resulted, more often than not, in punishing losses.

When one of us got far behind and started getting anxious and betting aggressively, the other tried to counsel him, slow him down. It never worked, but we tried anyway.

In fact, one of the curiosities of our co-dependency was that we were rarely both down or both up at the same time. This made for some tension. Once Rick was up sixty-five hundred at first light while Steve was still down two grand. Rick felt that he had to wait, and moseyed around the casino pushing money into slot machines. After a time, he got interested in a particular twenty-five-dollar machine and took a seat. Always a bad sign. Half an hour later, Steve came by to report that he was even, but by then Rick had dropped five grand and was seething.

It's a terrible feeling to be far ahead and then start losing in a way that you just can't stop—an ineluctable fall, like gravity. It makes for a frenzied abandon. You don't care about money anymore. You want to lose it. You stuff cash into the slots as fast as it'll go, and even as you're doing it you know it's hopeless. This is not the routine hopelessness of regular slot play; this is different, a unique despair, gambling in the recognition that you have no chance, that you will lose whatever you do. You persist in playing anyway. It happens at blackjack tables, too—you throw money on a spot, make wild, silly bets, which, were they to come in, would make you whole again. But you know they're not coming in.

How do you know? That's also a puzzle. You begin to sense that, for all the mathematics, the calculations, the odds, the multiplying strategies of working the percentages, some wholly other thing is at work, some loopy otherworldly thing. It seems built into the cards. There sometimes comes a point when you begin to think you know the cards before they're dealt. You've made a big bet, you're holding an eighteen and the dealer is show-ing an eight, and you think you've "pushed," you're safe. Then you think, Unless she has an ace. No sooner have you had the second thought than you know that she has the ace. You wish she didn't, but you know she does. And when she flips her down card there it is, the ace. And you lose again. Then you think that you caused her to have the ace by thinking of it.

One time, Steve was playing video poker, sitting in the middle of a row of machines. On one side was a Vietnamese guy and on the other a chubby middle-aged white woman. They were playing when Steve arrived and had already struck up an acquaintance. They were loudly cajoling their machines to behave and talking to each other over Steve's head. Sometimes the woman called the guy down to her machine to show him what she'd got, and sometimes it was for his advice about a draw. It was clear that they had just met.

Steve was there half an hour, winning and losing. He turned up a new hand: four hearts—ace, queen, jack, and ten—and the seven of clubs. That is, four of the five cards you need to form a royal straight flush, the best possible hand in poker.

Steve carefully pressed the "hold" button above each of the hearts and double-checked that he'd pressed the buttons correctly. He said, "King," and pressed the "draw" button. The seven of clubs fell away and the king of hearts appeared. The perfect hand.

The Vietnamese guy knew instantly. "Royal flush," he declared, in a way one might say "It's a girl!" or "He's alive!" He looked from Steve to the screen and back again. The screen itself was pretty excited, flashing the cards of the royal flush on and off in mysterious sequence.

"Let me tell her," the guy said. He pointed to the chubby woman. It wasn't "Please let me tell her." It was "Stop. Don't do a thing until I tell her." He waved for her attention, told her what had happened on a machine that she herself had probably been playing minutes earlier. The woman gave a slight smile, sighed, and returned to her machine more fiercely committed than ever.

That win was on a dollar machine, two hundred and fifty dollars, but the money wasn't the point. The point was perfection. A perfect thing had happened. This is the seduction and the appeal of gambling: the idea that perfection is possible. All the people in a casino understand the concept; they may be crude or dizzy or deluded, but they all know how to imagine life as something more than a dreary chore. They can see that something wonderful might happen, something that could change their lives—this is their fool's secret, one they share with drunks, children, and artists.

We found that we understood these gamblers better than we understood the men and women of the university where we worked, people who—full of purpose and high sentence and, often, considerable charm—seemed curiously reduced when it came to vision and possibility. They had grown up, become professional, acquired some wisdom, and accepted things as they were.

We had dear friends among these folks, but taken as a whole the milieu of the department was a bit quiet. Our gamblers were serious not like academics but in the furious way that children are serious, concentrating on play, oblivious, intense yet at ease. They came to the casino to be children, because gambling is a child's vice practiced by adults, often by the old. Every day, after eight in the morning, clouds of gray-haired folk arrived in buses from the airport or along the coast from Florida. We were often there to greet them. Many were sixty and seventy. They had come to play. Because money is involved, this play had an extra edge, but it was still play, and they were still children. That was something we understood. We were children. We had, we felt, suffered enough boredom, done enough work, assumed enough responsibility, and watched enough hypocrisy not to worry about or feel shame in being children again.

It may have had something to do with our father, whose childishness was among his most attractive features. He had a child's curiosity and a child's fascination, a capacity for focusing on things with an extraordinary present-tense intensity. He had a child's intolerance of boredom and an innocent passion: he was always doing things because they were, he felt, the things he should do; he was an optimist and an idealist. He held on to the insistent hope that things could be better, would be better if you tried hard enough, if you just kept at it. It was a gambler's optimism and a dreamer's idealism. That idealism was one of his abiding gifts to his sons, who customarily disguised their own, incomplete version of it with a flinty, defensive irony, which they were bright enough not to take seriously.

Maybe our childlike interest in play blossomed without warning because, suddenly, we no longer had our parents. Because suddenly, in middle age, we were children again, and we were lost without Mother and Father. Or it might have been the notion that this money of theirs was a poor substitute for the people themselves, who had taught us everything, told us that jokes were proper and complex, shown us the ambiguities of the everyday.

In the year after our mother's death, we lost about a hundred thousand dollars. We played less in the early part of 1996, but after our father died, in July, we started gambling with renewed determination. We lost seventy thousand dollars in the three months after his death. In 1997, we lost considerably less, but by November our combined losses amounted to well over a quarter of a million dollars.

We rationalized the losses by reminding ourselves that it was money we'd inherited, and that, as we'd never had much money, money had never really meant that much to us—so why not spend it? After all, we had been gambling before we had an inheritance: we didn't want to stop now. And, besides, with the new money, we had a chance to win back what we'd lost. Our father had worked long and hard to acquire and then save this money, and we knew it was the only large sum we would ever see. But, with money to cover our losses, gambling became a lot easier—more efficient, even comfortable. When we exceeded our lines of credit at the casino, we borrowed against our credit cards, sometimes ten or fifteen thousand dollars at a time, which we then paid back from investment money. Then we started in on Father's bonds. The money was going out and never coming back, and even though the money was ours, it was Father's, too, held in separate accounts, which we talked about and treated as if he were still around, looking over our shoulders.

But we didn't stop. We never said, "Hey, let's don't do this. Let's do something else. Let's use the money wisely." What we were doing would drive the old man crazy, and we knew it. We could imagine him hearing that Rick had lost twenty-two thousand dollars in one night. We could see him sitting in his desk chair in his home office, his elbow on the drafting table, his forehead in his hand, his eyes staring at the rug as if there, in that pile, some answer sat.

Maybe in his college days, when he was a swashbuckler, he might have been amused by what we were doing. On occasion, we remarked that it would have been good to have had him with us, since he was easily the best gambler in the family. Of course, we had seen him only at family poker games, but there he was a champ. Who knew, maybe at the casino he could do as well. But he was not with us on our sprees, or if he was with us he was there only in token form, in the hundred-dollar bills folded in half in our pockets, money that was blessed with none of his shrewdness.

V

We thought we knew what to expect. We'd seen the movies. In the next, final stage, we were supposed to get so intoxicated with our vice that we lost everything: the bank forecloses on the house and the car, we get rid of the cats and dogs, and we land in dereliction and divorce. But none of that happened. At the end of 1996, we still had a little money, we still did our work week in and week out, and our lovers, though exasperated, were still loyal.

So we were winging along, losing big, waiting for the life-destroying catastrophe that all the hand-wringing articles about gambling and vice, all the movies and stories always use as their slam-bang climax, like the scene in "Days of Wine and Roses" where Jack Lemmon tears his father-in-law's greenhouse apart, ripping plants from their pots, looking for the one in which he has hidden his last bottle of booze. And then it came, our catastrophe. But it came in a form so bizarre that no self-respecting movie would use it.

On the morning of November 11, 1996, after we'd been playing black-jack all night long, several security people came up to our table and ordered us to pick up our chips and follow them. They walked us to the cashier's cage and told us to turn over our chips, refusing to give us money for them and demanding that we pay off markers the casino was holding from a previous trip. As the cashier did the paperwork, we noticed that the shift manager was shaking. The casino's usual chummy behavior—all the sweet grease that its staff used to keep us content and gambling at the tables—had disappeared in an instant.

We followed two of the security people out of the casino, across the gangplank, and into a small concrete room in the parking garage, where they interrogated us and accused us of cheating, in a conspiracy with the dealer, even though we'd lost nearly ten thousand dollars to that dealer that night. They made a few ugly insinuations about us and the dealer. They took Polaroid photographs of us and copied the information off our driver's licenses. And then they told us to leave. If we ever came back to the casino, they said, we would be arrested.

We were amazed, then angry, then afraid. For the first time in more than two years, we stopped gambling.

A short time later, the dealer phoned Rick. She knew that he taught at the university and called him there. She had lost her dealer's license and asked us to testify for her at a gaming-commission hearing. We agreed, but friends told us to see a lawyer. They suggested Boyce Holleman, a former D.A. in Gulfport, now a defense attorney.

On January 31, 1997, we met Mr. Holleman, polite and friendly, a man in his seventies, who listened to our story, his eyes closed most of the time, except when he lurched forward to drink a root beer from a glass bottle. When he was done, he tossed the bottle over his shoulder into the wastebasket. He had bushy but thinning hair, cowboy boots, a cane, and a drawl worthy of the movies (we learned later that he had used it in film and on television, in the show "In the Heat of the Night"), and he chewed on the wettest, stubbiest unlit cigar you have ever seen in your life. The office, a well-worn wood-panelled ranch-style house just off the water, was peppered with Mr. Holleman's memorabilia—a personal note from J.F.K. and loads of pictures (Holleman chatting with Bob Hope, Holleman in front of an airplane as a Second World War pilot, Holleman with Carroll O'Connor).

He told us that he'd played some blackjack himself, and he was no fan of the gaming laws. There are only felony offenses in Mississippi gaming laws. Some kid takes a dollar token out of a slot tray, it's a goddam felony, he snorted. He told us a story he'd heard about an old man who sat down on a stool to rest, not realizing the stool was situated in front of a slot machine that had hit a jackpot some moments before. Suddenly people appeared and started giving him money—the winnings from somebody else's jackpot. "You know, he hadn't looked where he was, he's just sitting there. He's takin' a load off. These people were giving him money, and so he said, 'Sure, thank you.'" Mr. Holleman held his hand out, accepting the imaginary money, and shrugged. "They arrested him, charged him with a felony."

We told him about the dealer's gaming-commission hearing, and, for a number of reasons, he didn't want us to testify, and he said he would see to it that the hearing got postponed until after the dealer's trial, which we all hoped would never take place.

Though we'd been told that Mr. Holleman was the best defense lawyer in the region, meeting him produced in us an odd joy, such as you might feel upon finally meeting the Wizard of Oz. Because of the wonderful things he does. On our way home that day, we felt that having Mr. Holleman on our side, notwithstanding that he had seemed asleep for much of our conference, was powerfully reassuring. From then on, we always called him Mr. Holleman, out of a special respect. And, as the months passed, we worked with his son Tim, a bright, funny chip off the block, whose obvious affection for his father was utterly winning—it was part of his charm. When, by summer, nothing happened, we allowed ourselves to believe that the Hollemans' easygoing attitude had been right all along, that we'd been a touch hysterical. We allowed ourselves to believe that the whole regrettable business had faded away.

And so the inevitable occurred: we started gambling again. It had been only a matter of time. We settled on Biloxi's Casino Magic, an architectural curiosity, faux modern, a barge. It was smaller than the Grand, but the people were pleasant, and we began playing and losing there. Occasionally, we ran into dealers from the Grand —some of them were now working at the Magic—and we wondered whether our difficulties at the Grand were known. Later, we found out that the people at the Magic did know, had known all along, and didn't much care.

This attitude made us exceedingly fond of the Magic, and it became our regular stop. We went once a week, sometimes twice, and had what seemed like markedly better luck there than we had had at the Grand. But we still lost. And, gradually, in the way of these things, our gambling intensified once again. We went more often, stayed longer, played harder, lost more money. By late fall, we had made around thirty trips. We had finally lost the remainder of our inheritance, about eighty thousand dollars.

Then, in early December, 1997, more than a year after the incident at the Grand, the dealer called to tell us that she'd been indicted and that we were named in the indictment. Later, we learned that we weren't just named; we had been indicted as well. We were charged with a felony and if found guilty might be sentenced to a fine and two years in prison.

We were eventually indicted on two counts, one applying to November 3, 1996, and one applying to November 11th. The charge was the same in both instances. The indictment said that Cynthia Bernice Wojciechowski (the dealer), Steve Barthelme, and Frederick Barthelme

> did wilfully, unlawfully and feloniously acquire knowledge, not available to all players, of the outcome of blackjack games at Grand Casino-Gulfport, a Minnesota corporation, and then did use that information to place or forego bets on same by having knowledge of the dealer's cards for the purpose of placing or not placing insurance bets on the game of blackjack.

"Insurance" is the bet you can place once all the cards have been dealt and the dealer is showing an ace. At that moment, you don't know what the dealer's second card is, but there's a chance that it could be a face card and that the dealer would have blackjack. When the dealer gets blackjack, she wins; if you have insured, you don't lose anything.

The charges were the first step in our descent into a bewildering, terrifying legal mess that was far worse than Jack Lemmon's trashed greenhouse. In December, we drove to the Harrison County jail and were booked. It was the first time either of us had seen the inside of a jail. The cops were polite, as were our fellow prisoners, and we were there only an hour or so. But we got the idea.

That was fifteen months ago. Since then, we've been waking up thinking about this catastrophe and going to sleep at night thinking about it. Our lives have not been destroyed, but they aren't particularly happy. If we were younger, this might have been an adventure—good old-fashioned Strangelovian fun. But we are not younger. And it has not been fun.

For obvious reasons, and on the advice of our counsel, we are unable to discuss the charges any further. Although we believe the charges have no basis and should be dismissed, we are resigned to the prospect of a trial. That trial was recently scheduled for March 1st. It has now been postponed again.

And, of course, all through last year, we carried on playing, even though, by now, we'd lost everything we had managed to save and everything our parents left us. But the casino still had its allure. We loved the place. We liked the smiles on the dealers' faces, the greetings from the pit personnel, the snide sideways inclusive jokes people made that seemed to say, You're one of us, you guys belong here. We knew better, but sometimes the satisfactions of being taken for a ride exceed the discomfort of knowing that you have been. Or, put another way, the ride is so much fun you want to take it regardless of the cost.

The psychiatrist who works at the bus stop would have a field day with us—guilt, depression, loss, loneliness, destroying the inheritance. But that doesn't take into account the seductiveness of gambling itself. The excitement. The giddy foolish mindlessness. To go there and to lose felt strangely heroic. How crazy we were being, how bad, how stupid. It's easy to diminish this magic in hindsight, but at the time we were deeply in its thrall. It was a remarkably powerful and seductive bit of theatre, with real and bitter consequences, consequences that we wanted. We would have been willing to win, but we were content to lose.

The State, Regulation, and Politics

Introduction

The relationship of the state to gambling is the focus of the first two chapters of this section. The pieces by Nibert and Neary and Taylor view the state's role in gambling legitimation, particularly lotteries, from Marxist perspectives. Nibert is critical of the consequences of the state promotion of lotteries in the United States. He discusses some of the social consequences of large-scale lottery promotion such as the denigration of work and the fostering of superstition among lottery participants. Neary and Taylor analyze the British state's response to economic risks, in which the management of state enterprises and programs more and more resembles a lottery form. Their piece can be seen as a development and critique of formulations of risk presented by theorists such as Beck, and in particular they develop an "alternative materialist analysis of risk." For them, capitalist social relations are reproduced through this lottery form, whereby social security risks are transferred from the state to the citizens. This notion of the transference of risks toward the citizen nevertheless echoes aspects of

Beck's analysis of the changing status of work within an environment of general insecurity in risk societies (Beck 2000).

While Anthony Giddens has discussed the failure of the welfare state in relation to the manufactured risk conditions of late modernity, the involvement of the state in gambling enterprises appears to be a move in a direction counter to his notion of the "social investment state" (Giddens 1998; Loyal 2003). For Neary and Taylor, the lottery-like state form is prompted by the uncertain conditions generated by the globalizing forces of late capitalism.

Collins's piece provides a historical discussion of the rise of the category of "pathological gambler," drawing upon the governmentality perspective outlined by Lupton in Chapter Three. While Collins does not seek to provide an account of how gambling activity has come to be medicalized in the twentieth century, his piece develops the sociological concern with how categories ("pathological gambler") get generated as discursive constructs within particular socio-historical settings, and how particular social conditions give rise to the creation of such categories. Collins is interested in how "the psy sciences (psychiatry, psychology and psychoanalysis) produce new means of governing populations."

The final chapter is a journalistic account of the political machinations and social conflicts involved in the promotion of VLTs (video lottery terminals) in South Carolina in the 1990s. In Plotz's piece, first published as an article in *Harper's Magazine* in 1999, we see the politics of individualism at their meanest, as the individual's right to gamble is shown against the backdrop of a depressed economy. Compulsive VLT play is spotlighted as a sad outcome of economic opportunism and political ideology. According to Rose (2003), "At its height, South Carolina had 34,000 devices (Nevada has only 17,922 slots outside of casinos) and attracted more than $2.1 billion in wagers, for $610 million profits.... The state's 14 year experiment with video poker ended on July 1, 2000. In May 2002, the State Supreme Court held 'habitual gamblers' could recover their losses from the now nonexistent slot machine operators under unique state statutes." South Carolina is the only jurisdiction to completely ban slot machines after their introduction, but other jurisdictions continue to grapple with the negative consequences of their presence.

References

Beck, Ulrich (2000) *The Brave New World of Work*, trans. Patrick Camiller. Cambridge: Polity Press.

Giddens, Anthony (1998) *The Third Way: The Renewal of Social Democracy*. Cambridge: Polity Press.

Loyal, Steven (2003) *The Sociology of Anthony Giddens.* London: Pluto Press.

Rose, I. Nelson (2003) *Gambling and the Law©: Status of Gambling Laws,* www. gamblingandthelaw.com, August 3.

CHAPTER 15

State Lotteries and the Legitimation of Inequality

DAVID NIBERT

Economic concentration, deindustrialization, and state policies that favor the interests of the economically powerful have been detrimental for tens of millions of people in the United States. Underemployment, poverty, hunger, and homelessness have increased steadily over the past two decades. The majority teeter precariously, just a paycheck or two from bankruptcy, under enormous household debt. For example, in the early 1950s the average household debt as a percentage of after-tax income was approximately 33 percent. By 1997 it had climbed to almost 95 percent.[1] Not surprisingly, personal bankruptcies in the United States kept pace. Today, tens of thousands of U.S. households are kept afloat financially with the use of high-interest credit cards.[2] Concomitantly, in 1997, 16.1 percent of people in the United States, amounting to 43.4 million people, had no health insurance for the entire year.[3]

Why do people in the United States accept these conditions? Why is it that working and devalued people have demonstrated little discernment of what C. Wright Mills called their "long run, general, and rational interests"?[4] This chapter will go into more detail about the process of legitimation: first, a brief examination of how acceptance of inequality is generally achieved, and then a look at how state lotteries buttress widespread acceptance of the status quo.

The Process of System Legitimation

For the powerful, convincing the masses of people that individual control of great wealth is legitimate is preferable to compelling compliance with an ever-vigilant and costly threat of force. In order for a privileged few to enjoy luxury and extravagance while the many who create the wealth experience hardship, economic marginality, and insecurity, individual possession of wealth must be widely accepted as normal and appropriate. This has been true throughout history and remains true today.

The process of legitimation occurs at two levels, a micro- or social psychological level and a macro- or structural level. The relationship between these two levels is dialectical, as they are interdependent and influence one another. At the social psychological level, inequality in the United States has been supported by a general belief in the existence of equal opportunity. According to sociologists, this assumption about the existence of opportunity is at the base of a system-supporting ideology that has been referred to as the dominant stratification ideology, "dominant when it represents the views of those groups which have most of what there is to get."[5] The dominant stratification ideology, reduced to its most basic form, states: (1) there are abundant economic opportunities in the United States; (2) individuals should be industrious and competitive; (3) rewards are, and should be, the result of individual talent and effort; and (4) the distribution of inequality is generally fair and equitable.[6] The pillar of the dominant stratification ideology is belief in opportunity. To the extent that people accept this ideology, individuals are held responsible for their poverty, and substantive threats to the status quo are unlikely.

Research has demonstrated strong public adherence to the dominant ideology, which is strongest among the affluent. An analysis of the beliefs of a sample of residents of Muskegon, Michigan, in 1966 found that most respondents believed in the existence of equal opportunity, although those with higher incomes were more likely to believe than lower-income respondents. Higher-income respondents were inclined to hold individuals responsible for their poverty while lower-income people were more likely to question the availability of opportunity.[7]

Similarly, in 1969 a national survey found strong support for individual-level explanations of poverty, with a smaller number of respondents, notably lower-income people, young people, and African Americans, giving structural explanations.[8] In 1980 another national study found that, while the majority of respondents continued to adhere to the dominant stratification ideology, the percentage who agreed was declining. The authors of this study cited a 1952 national survey, which found that 88 percent of the respondents agreed with the statement "There's plenty of opportunity and anybody who works hard can go as far as he wants," and noted that the 1966 Muskegon study found that only 78 percent of respondents agreed with the statement. The 1980 study found that only 70 percent agreed with the statement "There's plenty of opportunity and anybody who works hard can get ahead."[9] Like the earlier studies, the 1980 study also found that lower-income respondents were less likely to accept the dominant ideology than higher-income respondents.[10]

This general belief in the availability of opportunity in the United States supports, and is supported by, the macro- or structural process of legitimation.... Miliband believed that citizens of twentieth-century capitalist societies are indoctrinated to accept values that support existing social arrangements. Miliband's contention is supported by sociological analyses of forces of socialization and control. For example, families, considered by many to be the most powerful agent of socialization, play a powerful role in the legitimation of inequality. Friedrich Engels wrote critically of the family in 1884, viewing it as a social arrangement that oppressed women and children and supported social inequities.[11] Despite the gains produced by the women's movement of the nineteenth and twentieth centuries, families continue to reflect and reinforce gender inequalities.[12] Moreover, many families teach children those values and behaviors considered appropriate and necessary for social adaptability. For example, there is a tendency for working-class parents to teach their children the importance of conformity, while middle-class parents are more likely to emphasize initiative and independence, different orientations that help to reproduce class structures in the next generation.[13]

Religion also plays a role in the legitimation of inequality. Marx viewed religion as the "opium of the people," a powerful narcotic that sedated people and promoted their acquiescence in hardships created by privilege and injustice. Throughout history religion has frequently legitimated social inequality, in many instances by asserting that inequities were the consequence of divine will. Religion has been used, and is still used by some, to justify discrimination and inequality based on gender, race, sexual orientation, and class. While appeals to religious ideals are occasionally used to challenge inequality and legitimate grievances, religion continues to be a significant pillar of the status quo. Charles E. Hurst writes:

> Particularly branches of Christianity ... have legitimated people's beliefs about inequality. Protestantism, in general, which focuses on the individual relationship between each individual and God, stresses the importance of hard work and equality of opportunity in attaining success.... The "American way" that is so blessed

incorporates the values of individualism, freedom, capitalism, and equality of opportunity which make up a core part of the ideology supporting inequality.[14]

The system of education in any society also serves to promote the acceptance of existing arrangements. In most societies students largely are taught to conform to rules and procedures that promote uniformity and control. In the United States they are generally taught to respect hierarchy and to be competitive. History is usually presented in ways that sanitize past injustices and establish a firm basis for the acceptance of existing social arrangements.[15] Reflecting on the educational system, Joe R. Feagin writes:

> Teachers and administrators are important socializers of children. What is taught in school communicates and reinforces basic values and conventional beliefs about United States society. Many teachers, directly or indirectly, teach the ideology of individualism, prevailing conceptions of the poor, positive views of capitalism (less often unions), or stereotypes about minorities and women. Sometimes the formal curriculum communicates beliefs and values supporting the status quo.[16]

The educational system in the United States "looms as one of the more influential purveyors of dominant values."[17]

As Miliband noted, another powerful structural source of legitimation is the mass media. It has been suggested the mass media both support government policy and present views favorable to the interests of the economically powerful.[18] Newspapers throughout the United States are increasingly coming under the control of a relatively small number of corporations,[19] and major television networks are controlled by powerful conglomerates. For example, General Electric purchased the National Broadcasting System (NBC) in 1995. Then, in 1995, the Walt Disney Company conducted one of the largest buyouts in U.S. history by purchasing Capital Cities/ABC Incorporated, which controls the ABC television network and numerous newspapers and radio stations. This transaction created a major convergence of entertainment, news, and multimedia systems. That same year, the media giant Time Warner acquired cable powerhouse Turner Broadcasting. Most recently, in the fall of 1999, Viacom—which owns such cable networks as MTV, VH1, and Nickelodeon, the Paramount film studio, and the Blockbuster video-rental chain—announced its intent to purchase the Columbia Broadcasting System (CBS), a purchase that will create the world's second largest media company, second only to Time Warner. It is predicted that such huge entertainment-communication conglomerates will continue to form and that the thousands of independent cable system operators throughout the country "will be forced out within the next 10 to 12 years, and only five or six companies will remain in business."[20]

This concentrated and centralized control of the major media in the United States exerts a tremendous control over how we see ourselves and the world. For example, it is maintained that news programs in the United States are largely slanted to protect corporate and upper-class interests because (1) much of the news media are owned by the affluent, (2) the mass media are largely dependent on advertising to stay in business and are consequently subject to pressure from corporate sponsors, (3) much news information is provided by government and business experts, and (4) an anticommunism theme is often used to justify corporate and government actions that actually reflect the interests of the privileged.[21] Under these circumstances, for example, corporate mergers, takeovers, and other events that increase economic concentration are generally presented as unrelated and benign occurrences, and their implications for the public or their relationship to systemic trends are seldom analyzed.

Such powerful societal processes—the family, religion, the educational system, the mass media, the state—are among those powerful social institutions that form an organized system of ideas and social arrangements referred to as the *superstructure*. As Marx noted in the nineteenth century, inequality is accepted in large part due to the pervasive system legitimating ideas and processes that confront people as reality. The dominant stratification ideology, promulgated by the superstructure, underlies societal acceptance of dramatic inequality in the United States and sends a disturbing message about, and to, the tens of millions of people living in or near poverty: that they are primarily responsible for their own fate. It is maintained that, through lack of initiative, lack of thrift, lack of talent, or lack of appropriate values, people who do not "make it" have only themselves to blame. This message not only reinforces existing social arrangements but also has devastating psychological consequences for people who blame themselves for their lack of economic success while failing to recognize the deterministic role frequently played by the social structure.[22] They have been taught that capitalism is good, opportunity is plentiful, and all "capable" people should be self-reliant. From this ideological vantage point, the wealthy are glorified and envied and those with few resources are devalued. Attention is diverted from systemic problems and the collective welfare, with the value of individualism elevated above all others. False consciousness is prevalent as most people accept the explanations provided by the dominant ideology for striking inequalities and personal deprivations. As a result, the system is rarely challenged in any meaningful way and the interests of the economically powerful are protected. Although disparities are increasing and belief in opportunity is slipping, state lotteries may be preserving the conservative ideology, especially among many who otherwise are least likely to believe it.

Lotteries as the New Opportunity

At a time when chances for economic security are declining for most people in society, the state lottery stands out as a *new opportunity* for individual economic advancement. The mass media has been widely used to legitimate and promote lottery play, and states send the message that a life-altering opportunity is only one dollar away. State lotteries are now largely viewed as a normal, rational, and acceptable way for people to pursue their hopes and dreams. Widely publicized stories of lottery winners, like the bankrupt, fifty-two-year-old telephone installer, David Demarest, whose "life had changed in more happy ways than even he anticipated"; or the police officer and waitress who shared lottery jackpot brought them love and happiness in the film *It Could Happen To You*; or the fictional lottery winner Claire Goddard, a woman previously of "modest means," who went on a spending spree buying luxury cars and mansions—all send dramatic messages to the public that opportunity still exists, for everyone.

A study conducted by the author provides some empirical support for the contention that state lotteries—specifically the Superlotto—are related to perceptions of economic opportunity in the United States. A 1992 survey of 450 randomly selected adult residents of a small midwestern city found that 77 percent had played the state lottery. For 63 percent of this group, the Superlotto was the game of choice. Interestingly, more than 45 percent of respondents believed the most likely way they would achieve wealth would be to win it—and 94 percent of this group believed they would most likely win it through the lottery. Those most likely to put their chances with the lottery were older than forty, did not have high-school diplomas, and had incomes less than $40,000 a year. Importantly, it was found that 77 percent of the respondents who played the Superlotto game believed that America is the "land of opportunity," compared to only 61 percent of those who reported a preference for instant games and other lottery games with more modest prizes.[23] These results provide evidence that state lotteries are now a consequential aspect of people's beliefs about opportunity and their hopes for economic advancement. This contention is further supported by the words of a lottery player in a letter to the editor of a magazine called *LottoWorld*: "Lotteries ... create a level playing field for each of us who dares to buy a ticket."[24]

Lotteries and the Acquisition of Wealth

A primary theme in state lottery advertisements is that acquisition of wealth is a wonderful, transcendent experience—and that the opportunity is available to all. For example, an Illinois lottery television commercial showed images of a huge mansion with the following voice-over:

> In America we do not have kings nor queens or even dukes. What we have is far more democratic. It is called Superlotto and it gives each individual a chance for untold wealth. So play Superlotto because, even though you can't be born a king, no one said you can't live like one.

Similarly, Charles T. Clotfelter and Philip J. Cook observed:

> A California television commercial for an instant game called *The Good Life* touts the advantages of wealth with images of an elegantly dressed couple dancing, a woman walking expensive dogs, a red carpet being unrolled, and a couple on a yacht. A Michigan ad puts it simply: "The rich. Join them."[25]

In December 1998, the U.K. National Lottery ceremoniously boasted that in the four years since its creation it had enabled 710 people to "join the rich" by making them millionaires.[26]

In their frenzy to sell lottery tickets, governments are promoting the desirability of wealth just as much as the television program *Lifestyles of the Rich and Famous* and every other program, film, book, and magazine that glamorizes and legitimates indulgence. By dangling before the public expensive cars, yachts, and even, in the case of the New York lottery, a mansion so extravagant that a fictional one had to be created, state governments are directly promoting what the turn-of-the-century sociologist Thorstein Veblen called "conspicuous consumption."[27] Veblen viewed the long-held infatuation with wealth in capitalist society as a carry-over from earlier periods in human history he characterized as "barbarian." In such societies people relegated to the positions of peasants and slaves performed work that was indispensable to the survival of the community, but they were exploited by priests, chieftains, and other members of the "leisure class." Veblen noted that excess consumption of quality goods and ostentatious displays of wealth go well beyond satisfying individual physical needs and instead become symbols of one's rank and status and "superior character." Conversely, the "low-grade character" of those who live at subsistence levels are made similarly obvious to all. As Veblen noted,

> Since the consumption of these more excellent goods is an evidence of wealth, it becomes honorific; and conversely, the failure to consume in due quantity and quality becomes a mark of inferiority and demerit.[28]

Veblen viewed conspicuous consumption as "waste" because such a pattern of consumption "does not serve human life or human well-being on the whole."[29] Veblen suggested that these anachronistic values and standards of human worth were particularly problematic in the later nineteenth century because they served to detract many from the industry and hard effort necessary to sustain industrial society.

Veblen's ideas warrant consideration, especially today. In the late twentieth century, a time when the human population is growing at a prodigious rate, natural resources are being rapidly depleted, increasing numbers of people in the United States and throughout the world are living at subsistence levels, and millions of laboring people continue to have the value of their labor expropriated, is it rational public policy for state governments to extol the virtues of private accumulation of great wealth? Whose responsibility is it to consider these questions and to integrate them into the realm of public discourse? Certainly, questions concerning the general welfare and public interest are not given much consideration by governments, lottery officials, or advertising executives, whose basic focus and goal is the continuous increase in lottery ticket sales. When such questions are considered, they are asked at the federal level—and usually produce few results, as evidenced by recent events in the U.K. and the U.S....

Lotteries as Diversion

Reflecting on the social consequences of state lotteries, H. Roy Kaplan remarked:

> This illusory dream [of great wealth from the lottery] can also be used as a method of social control—to placate people by diverting attention from their misfortunes and meaningless lives. This social control aspect of lotteries and legalized gambling assumes greater significance as they proliferate.[30]

State lotteries help to divert attention people's attention from their troubles and misgivings, while serving as a safety valve, siphoning stress and frustration into a system-enhancing activity and thus helping to avert the potential threat of a mass uprising. Furthermore, lotteries also help to divert attention from problems and social arrangements that affect people's lives. Questions about who makes major economic decisions, why certain decisions are made, why the quality of life is slipping, why working conditions are frequently tedious and unrewarding, and related questions, are seldom publicly contemplated in meaningful ways.

This diversion of focus is troubling when one considers that education and the fairness of societal arrangements are necessary for the development of social and economic justice. Marx believed that people oppressed by the social order would eventually recognize their collective interests and act to change the system. Bertell Ollman suggested that traditional Marxian theory generally views wage earners as a

> class of people whose conditions of life, whose experiences at work and elsewhere, whose common struggles and discussions will sooner or later bring them to a consciousness of their state and of what must be done to transform it.[31]

There is evidence that people with low incomes today are inclined to challenge aspects of the economic order. This traditional Marxist tenet is supported if we recall that people with lower incomes are somewhat less likely than higher-income people totally to accept conventional explanations of inequality. We saw, for example, that people with lower incomes are less accepting of the dominant stratification ideology and more inclined to believe individual problems are caused by the social structure. Moreover, the 1992 study of the small midwestern city cited earlier also compared the responses of people in different income categories on several questions regarding economic policies. People with low and moderate incomes were more likely than higher income respondents to favor (1) placing limits on income, (2) government ownership of basic industries, (3) government guarantee of jobs for everyone, (4) the democratization of corporate decision-making, and (5) socialist participation in economic decision-making—all at levels of statistical significance.[32]

State lotteries, however, are among those forces that mitigate against this inclination to challenge the economic structure. We saw that 77 percent of the respondents in the 1992 study had played the lottery, and people who prefer the Superlotto—constituting the majority of state lottery players—express strong agreement with the statement "America is the land of opportunity where anyone who works hard can get ahead." Moreover, those respondents who pinned their hopes of wealth on winning the lottery were disproportionately people with low levels of education and income. Consequently, state lotteries have joined those other powerful superstructural forces that stifle the formation of a political consciousness among people with low and moderate incomes.

People with lower incomes are not the only group whose potential inclination to push for social change is muted by state lotteries. The young frequently play an important role in the promotion of social change.[33] Young people are better able to be proponents of change if they can assess critically the conditions and ideologies that confront them. Bertell Ollman notes:

> [I]t is possible to fight against the character structure of workers by fighting against its construction, by counteracting the disorienting influence of family, school, and church, whatever in fact makes it difficult for the individual once [he/she] becomes an adult to make an objective assessment of [her/his] oppression and to act against it.
>
> The concrete aims of this radical activity ... are to get teenage and even younger members of the working class to question the existing order along with all its leaders and symbols, to loosen generalized habits of respect and obedience, to oppose whatever doesn't make sense in terms of their needs as individuals and as members of a group.[34]

There is little indication that the youth of the United States in the late twentieth century possess the historical, sociopolitical, or economic knowledge to counteract the contemporary ideology and its "disorienting influence." Socialized by educational and media systems that champion the status quo, millions of young people have come of age in a society where debates about the merits of great wealth are almost nonexistent and where state government inducements to gamble precede their birth. Not surprisingly, states have been known to target lottery games and advertisements at young people. For example, the aim of Oregon's Sports Action games was to increase participation among young men, and the Ohio lottery created television ads showing young people admiring expensive cars and yachts to the Hall and Oates pop song "You Make My Dreams Come True."

Thus the superstructure of U.S. society does little to arouse organized dissent among the nation's youth, and the lottery further undermines the development of political consciousness in young people by glorifying wealth and material acquisition through the promotion of lottery tickets. Moreover ... some experts are very concerned with the increase in gambling among young people, and one professional believes gambling problems have surpassed drug-related problems among teenagers.

Lotteries and the Denigration of Work

Another message promoted by state lotteries that is particularly effective at selling tickets is the undesirability of work. For example, several Ohio lottery winners were featured in advertisements that reflected anti-work values. One winner comments:

> Everybody talks about, "I'm not going to work tomorrow—if I don't show up, I won the Lotto." I *won* the Lotto and I *didn't* go to work today.

Another winner says:

> Eight years ago—the first thought that went through my mind was that I didn't have to go to work today—and I didn't for seven years.

Alan J. Karcher discusses an advertisement for the New Jersey lottery that

> showed a popcorn and soda vendor working at a ball game trying to deal with three customers at once. With a terribly harried look on his face, his hat askew, and his tray about to fall, the message reads, "If I win Pick 6, I won't have to do this any more." These print ads were just part of a general advertising campaign, whose principle message was this: Jobs requiring physical labor won't be necessary if you win the lottery. A series of half-completed billboards went up with a message scrawled reading: "I don't have to do this job! I just won the lottery."[35]

Lottery promoters are shrewd in their validation of worker dissatisfaction. Marx believed that meaningful work is important for human beings because it can be a creative and satisfying experience necessary for individual development and happiness. However, he maintained that under capitalism the process of work became alienating and hostile. Increasing automation and loss of worker control resulted in people becoming distanced from the finished product of their labor and isolated from other workers, with whom they were made to be competitors. Work became an alienating experience in which workers also became estranged from their own creative nature and potential.

The degradation of work has increased under capitalism in the twentieth century.[36] Many people occupy jobs that allow for little autonomy, participation in decision-making, or other characteristics that make work meaningful and rewarding. Consequently, many find work to be a tedious, dehumanizing, and sometimes dangerous experience.[37] A recent national study of employee attitudes found that millions of workers throughout the United States feel ignored by company managers. Almost two-thirds yearned to become more involved in decisions that affected their companies or places of employment; most do not protest because they fear they are expendable.[38]

The trying working conditions experienced by millions of people in the United States are compounded further by the loss of decent-paying jobs as the result of deindustrialization, mega-mergers, and the continuing process of automation. This loss of jobs has been accompanied by a significant increase in lower-paying, service-sector jobs and part-time jobs, thus expanding the numbers of the working poor.[39] Many of the "lucky" ones who have managed to survive corporate mergers and downsizing and retain their positions now quietly struggle with heavier work loads, fearful of falling victim to new rounds of employee cutbacks. Under these conditions, loaded with stress, anxiety, and hardship, it is not surprising that many people feel estranged from their work.

A logical and rational strategy for workers would be to organize themselves and promote democratic workplaces that allow for the promotion of decent wages, job security, worker participation in decision-making, and the creation of more meaningful and safer working environments. However, the possibility for such organization and action is reduced by lottery advertisements that validate worker unhappiness but which provide an individualistic and system-defending answer—*play the lottery, become rich and quit your job.*

Moreover, state lotteries deprecate people with low incomes in advertisements that portray lower-income status as inferior, to be remedied *only* by the acquisition of wealth. Lottery advertisements frequently juxtapose images of great wealth with scenes that depict people who are not wealthy as second-rate. Clotfelter and Cook noted:

> The District of Columbia ran a series of before-and-after ads.... In one such print ad the "before" picture shows a bedraggled man, face covered in stubble, hair matted down, wearing glasses and sloppy clothes. In the "after" picture he is clean shaven, well groomed, wearing a tuxedo but no glasses, conspicuously holding a copy of a theater program. The ad proclaims, "Just One Ticket ... and It Could Happen To You."[40]

Such messages from state lotteries do a great disservice to the millions of people with modest incomes whose hard work and labor continue to generate the goods and services essential for the survival of the society. However, they are not surprising. People with limited social, economic, or political power have long been devalued in the United States, and used as scapegoats for social problems since the advancement of social Darwinism.[41] Lottery ads reinforce this perception through their defamation of people with few resources and their promulgation of the view that individuals with wealth merit public adulation and envy.

State lotteries are now major practitioners of the custom of celebrating the privileged and devaluing people with few resources—what will be referred to here as the "Ratchet-Cratchit Syndrome" in honor of Ebenezer Scrooge's much-abused clerk in Charles Dickens's *A Christmas Carol*. This syndrome simultaneously exalts the privileged and subjects laboring people to grinding social and psychological denigration. It also severely restricts political mobilization because it contributes to the constant divisions and conflicts among those devalued members of society who compete with each other for jobs, housing, and other necessities. Today, as in the past, social groups whose economic interests are closely related continue to compete for crumbs and desperately try to advance their social status in relation to other, "really inferior" people—often those who are different because of their ethnic background, sexual orientation, or gender. In their efforts to distance themselves socially from other unjustly defamed groups, oppressed people unwittingly continue to reinforce those values and social arrangements that underlie their oppression. As Holly Sklar observes:

> The cycle of unequal opportunity is intensifying. Its beneficiaries often slander those most systematically undervalued, underpaid, underemployed, underfinanced, underinsured, underrated and otherwise undeserved and undermined—as undeserving and underclass, impoverished in moral values and lacking the proper "work ethic."

> The angry, shrinking middle class is misled into thinking that those lower on the economic ladder are pulling them down, when in reality those on top are rising at the expense of those below. People who should be working together to transform the economic policies that are hurting them are instead turning hatefully on each other.[42]

The Ratchet-Cratchit messages promulgated by state lotteries feed these misconceptions. Unfortunately, unlike in Dickens's tale, where Scrooge's Christmas Eve visions suddenly make him kindly and generous to Cratchit, and everyone else he sees, the lives of people in the United States will not improve so quickly. Rather, as history has demonstrated repeatedly, improvements in the quality of life for people are typically the result of years of struggle.[43] Moreover, the collective political consciousness necessary to catalyze an early twenty-first-century struggle for social justice is further hampered by yet another alienating aspect of state lotteries—superstition and magic.

State Lotteries Promote Superstition

Lottery games such as Superlotto provide a measure of buyer participation by allowing ticket buyers to select numbers instead of participating in a passive random drawing. Statistically, since every possible outcome has the same probability of winning, players cannot actually increase the probability of winning by selecting their own numbers. However, players may not know or believe this. Indeed, as one lottery critic in the U.K. observed, "[g]overnment initiative ... has done the most to undermine the public understanding of statistics: The National Lottery."[44] Allowing players to select their own numbers creates a perception of increased control that helps increase participation. Ticket buyers use various methods to select numbers, often relying on some form of superstition. Many ticket buyers seek to select "lucky" numbers, frequently based on birthdays or anniversary dates or derived from dreams.

An entire industry has emerged to help would-be lottery winners find their "lucky numbers." Players can buy an array of pamphlets and books or consult one of countless "psychics and mystics" who are available to help them get lucky—for a fee. For example, the following advertisement appeared in the magazine *LottoWorld*:

Your Direct Connection
To Your Lucky Numbers!
Lottoworld's Psychic Connection
Our Dynamic Line-up
of Psychics, Astrologers and Numerologists
give you their daily picks for Pick 3, 4, 5, 6 and Powerball
A new set of weekly predictions updated
every day by our lottery experts
$1.49 per minute[45]

The cover of another issue of *LottoWorld* featured "The Amazing Kreskin" holding a lottery form to his forehead.

In Ohio, a leaflet selling for $1.75 called *Ohio Daily Number Handbook: Lucky Numbers* gives readers suggestions on how to determine their "lucky numbers," and it lists lucky numbers selected by the "Mysterious Strategy Man." The text reads:

> This man is noted for his unerring accuracy in deciphering the numerical mysteries of the atmosphere, both within and beyond ourselves. Inspired by the incense of his lamp, his mind drifts and explores the dreams of all who pass his way, translating each thought into it's numerical significance. This amazing power to interpret dreams into numerology has astonished people for 3,000 years. The Mysterious Strategy Man is the latest in a long line of Mystics who have benefited mankind.[46]

The following story appeared in the July 1995 edition of the *Bull's Eye Lottery Book*, a thirty-page booklet selling for $1.75 that lists "lucky numbers" for specific names and zodiac signs:

> *New Orleans*—Down-and-out mom Mimi Dealah was dead broke and desperate till she won a whopping $2 million lottery jackpot—two days after praying at the grave of famed voodoo priestess Marie Laveau....
>
> "I was desperate. My husband died last year and left nothing but a pile of unpaid bills and it was a struggle just to feed my three kids.
>
> "Then my friend here in New Orleans suggested I come visit her and make a trip to Marie Laveau's grave." And two days after that fateful trip, the elated lady learned that she'd won just over $2 million in a multi-state lottery.
>
> "I don't know how she did it, but I think they should make Marie Laveau a saint," said mystified Mimi.[47]

This tendency for people to resort to superstition in their efforts to achieve economic security is not just a by-product of state government policy. As Clotfelter and Cook observed,

> Instead of providing information that would be helpful in parimutuel games, the lottery agencies appear to be interested in encouraging rather than dispelling the fallacy that numbers are important for their own sake. While most have introduced a

random selection option for on-line games, they continue to foster player loyalty to personal lucky numbers.[48]

Many states continuously exhort people to "play your lucky number." This
advice fosters alienation by reinforcing the notion that some supernatural
force can determine their economic fate.

Perhaps the modern-day reliance on superstition is to be expected.
In some respects, the ordeal experienced by people today in one of the
wealthiest and most scientifically advanced nations in the world trying
to feed, clothe, house, and otherwise sustain themselves is similar to that
faced by their early ancestors who also relied on superstition and magic.

In earlier societies where people relied heavily on climatic conditions
for life-sustaining harvests, people used various forms of magical manipulation to try to affect the weather and environment, elements over which
they really had no control. In the face of their helplessness, they used various types of incantations and rituals to appeal to supernatural and spiritual forces, creating the illusion that they could exert at least a modicum of
control over their fate. With the advent of science and technology, human-
kind has developed the potential to exert a considerable degree of control
over the forces that affect our lives. Indeed, in the face of expanding scientific knowledge, many regard magic and superstition as irrational, delusional, and anachronistic.

Still, in the late twentieth century, magic and superstition abound.
This reliance on the supernatural is not surprising, however, when millions of people experience such a precarious economic existence. They are
estranged from an economic system that can take away their jobs, homes,
and health care—if they have secured such necessities—with the apparent arbitrariness of a random act of nature. Certainly, most have no more
control over a corporate decision to merge, downsize, or relocate operations than they do over the weather. For some, like those who preceded
them centuries earlier, this feeling of dependence and uncertainty is eased
and a modicum of perceived control is achieved by resorting to magic and
superstition. Encouraged by state governments, millions today concentrate on finding those elusive "lucky numbers" that can bestow security
and respect. The need for, and state encouragement of, superstition in the
late twentieth century raises serious issues about both the rationality and
the ethics of economic and political policy in the United States.

Postscript

While the author was doing research ... he went into a convenience store to
buy copies of *LottoWorld*, the *Ohio Daily Number Handbook*, and the *Bull's*

Eye Lottery Book. The woman working behind the counter asked if he was trying to win the lottery; he replied that he was doing some research and believed the advice and information contained in the booklets were bogus. The woman said that she followed the advice offered in these publications, frequently playing the lucky numbers associated with her zodiac sign. He suggested to her that this strategy would probably not increase her chances of winning, to which she angrily replied, "I've got just as much chance of winning as anybody else." In retrospect, this exchange challenged the woman's sense of control, and she responded in a predictably defensive way. Her response, however, validates a theory about system legitimation and social control in the twentieth century offered by Herbert Marcuse. While systems of injustice in the past occasionally saw people reject unconvincing ideologies and attempt revolts and rebellions in challenge to the power and excesses of the privileged, armed soldiers stood ready to turn them back. However, in late-twentieth-century capitalist society, system-challenging actions are largely nonexistent. Writing in 1969, Marcuse pondered the following question:

> At this stage, the question is no longer: how can the individual satisfy his needs without hurting others, but rather: how can he satisfy his own needs without hurting himself, without reproducing, through his aspirations and satisfactions, his dependence on an exploitative apparatus which, in satisfying his needs, perpetuates his servitude?[49]

Marcuse's reflection in 1969 becomes even more relevant today with the proliferation of state lotteries in the United States. Like the woman working at the convenience store who apparently had invested part of her hopes and dreams in the lottery, millions like her have found a new attachment to the status quo, the chance of becoming a millionaire. While a tiny number will succeed, the vast majority do not need armed soldiers to keep them from seeking their "long run, general, and rational interests." Their conservative socialization, coupled with state-sponsored lottomania, secure their fidelity to a system that offers wealth for a few, and hardships and insecurity for the many.

Notes

1. "Squeezing Debtors," *Left Business Observer*, 84 (July 21, 1998), 1–2.
2. Ibid., 1–2.

3. Laura Meckler (Associated Press), *Surveys, Many Americans Still Lack Health Insurance*. http://cnn.com/ALLPOLITICS/stories/1998/10/19/hmo. ap/(1998).

4. C. Wright Mills, *The Marxists* (New York, 1962) 115; reprinted in *Capitalist Society: Readings for a Critical Sociology*, ed. Richard Quinney (Homewood, IL: Dorsey Press, 1979), 170.

5. Joan Huber and William H. Form, *Income and Ideology: An Analysis of the American Political Formula* (New York: Free Press, 1973), 2.

6. Robert A. Rothman, *Inequality and Stratification: Class, Color, and Gender*, Second Edition (Englewood Cliffs, NJ: Prentice Hall, 1993), 57.

7. Huber and Form, *Income and Ideology*.

8. Joe R. Feagin, "When It Comes to Poverty, It Is Still 'God Helps Those Who Help Themselves'," *Psychology Today*, 6 (1972), 101–29.

9. See James R. Kluegel and Eliot R. Smith, *Beliefs About Inequality: Americans' Views of What Is and What Ought to Be* (Hawthorne, NY: Aldine De Gruyter, 1986), 43–45.

10. Ibid.

11. Friedrich Engels, *The Origin of the Family, Private Property and the State* (New York: Penguin Books, 1972 [1884]).

12. See Randall Collins, *Sociology of Marriage and the Family: Gender, Love and Property* (Chicago: Nelson Hall, 1985); and Carol Smart, *The Ties That Bind: Law, Marriage and the Reproduction of Patriarchal Relations* (London: Routledge & Kegan Paul, 1984).

13. Melvin L. Kohn, *Class and Conformity*, Second Edition (Homewood, IL: Dorsey Press, 1977).

14. Charles E. Hurst, *Social Inequality: Forms, Causes, and Consequences* (Boston: Allyn & Bacon, 1992), 303–04.

15. See, for example, Samuel Bowles and Herbert Gintis, *Schooling in Capitalist America: Education Reforms and the Contradictions of Economic Life* (New York: Basic Books, 1976).

16. Joe R. Feagin, *Social Problems: A Critical Power-Conflict Perspective*, Second Edition (Englewood Cliffs, NJ: Prentice Hall, 1986), 199.

17. Michael Parenti, *Democracy for the Few*, Fifth Edition (New York: St. Martin's Press, 1988), 37.

18. G. William Domhoff, *The Powers That Be* (New York: Vintage, 1979); and Thomas R. Dye, *Who's Running America? The Reagan Years* (Englewood Cliffs, NJ: Prentice Hall, 1983).

19. See Michael Parenti, *Inventing Reality: The Politics of the Mass Media* (New York: St. Martin's Press, 1986); and Ben H. Bagdikian, *The Media Monopoly* (Boston: Beacon Press, 1987).

20. This prediction comes from Jim Sayer, Professor of Communications at Wright State University. He was cited in the *Dayton Daily News* on August 1, 1995, 1.

21. Edward S. Herman and Noam Chomsky, *Manufacturing Consent: The Political Economy of the Mass Media* (New York: Pantheon, 1988).

22. See William Ryan, *Blaming the Victim* (New York: Vintage, 1976); and Michael Lewis, *The Culture of Inequality* (Amherst: University of Massachusetts Press, 1978).

23. David Nibert, "State Lotteries and Perceptions of Opportunities" (Paper presented at the Annual Meeting of the American Sociological Association, Los Angeles, August 1994).

24. *LottoWorld*, July 24, 1995, 10.

25. Charles T. Clotfelter and Philip Cook, *Selling Hope: State Lotteries in America* (Cambridge, MA: Harvard University Press, 1989), 207–08.

26. *Electronic Telegraph*, "Lottery Adds 226 to List of Millionaires," December 28, 1998, 1, http://www.telegraph.co.uk.

27. Thorstein Veblen, *The Theory of the Leisure Class* (New York: Penguin Books, 1979 [1899]).

28. Ibid., 74, 84.

29. Ibid., 97.

30. H. Roy Kaplan, "The Social and Economic Impact of State Lotteries," *Annals of the American Academy of Political and Social Science*, 474 (July 1984), 104.

31. Bertell Ollman, "Toward Class Consciousness in the Working Class," *Politics and Society*, 3 (Fall 1972); reprinted in *Capitalist Society*, ed. Quinney, 170.

32. David Nibert, "An Examination of the Dominant Stratification Ideology in the Post-Reagan Era" (Paper presented at the Annual Meeting of the American Sociological Association, Washington DC, August 1995).

33. See Robert H. Lauer, *Perspectives on Social Change* (Boston: Allyn and Bacon, 1982), 262–73.

34. Ollman, "Toward Class Consciousness in the Working Class," 184.

35. Alan J. Karcher, *Lotteries* (New Brunswick, NJ: Transaction, 1992), 76–77.

36. See Harry Braverman, *Labor and Monopoly Capital: The Degradation of Work in the Twentieth Century* (New York: Monthly Review Press, 1975); and Craig Calhoun, "The Political Economy of Work," in *Political Economy: A Critique of American Society*, ed. Scott G. McNall (Glenview, IL: Scott, Foresman & Co., 1981), 272–99.

37. See, for example, Jeffrey Reiman, *The Rich Get Richer and the Poor Get Prison: Ideology, Crime and Criminal Justice* (Needham Heights, MA: Allyn and Bacon, 1995), 70–76.

38. Susan Dentzer, "Anti-Union, But Not Anti-Unity," *U.S. News and World Report*, July 1995, 17.

39. Robert J. Sheak, "U.S. Capitalism, 1972–1992: The Jobs Problem," *Critical Sociology*, 21, no. 1 (1995), 33–57.

40. Clotfelter and Cook, *Selling Hope*, 207.

41. See, for example, David Nibert, "The Political Economy of Developmental Disability," *Critical Sociology*, 21, no. 1 (1995), 59–80.

42. Holly Sklar, *Chaos or Community? Seeking Solutions, Not Scapegoats, for Bad Economics* (Boston: South End Press, 1995), 2–3.

43. See, for example, Frances Fox Piven and Richard Cloward, *Poor People's Movements: Why They Succeed, How They Fail* (New York: Pantheon, 1977).

44. Roger Highfield, "Editors of the Paranormal in a Flutter Over Angels and the Lottery," *Electronic Telegraph*, January 22, 1997, 2, http://www.telegraph.co.uk.

45. *LottoWorld*, July 10, 1995, 70.

46. *Ohio Daily Number Handbook: Lucky Numbers*, 179 (July 1995).

47. *Bull's Eye Lottery Book*, July 1995, 22–23.

48. Clotfelter and Cook, *Selling Hope*, 89.

49. Herbert Marcuse, *An Essay on Liberation* (Boston: Beacon Press, 1969), 4.

CHAPTER 16

From the Law of Insurance to the Law of Lottery

An Exploration of the Changing Composition of the British State

MIKE NEARY AND GRAHAM TAYLOR

Recent years have seen important changes in both the social form of the capitalist state and the theorisation and analysis of capitalist state forms from within the Marxist intellectual tradition. The crisis and decomposition of Keynesian and social democratic state structures is, of course, intimately related to the crisis of the rigid and closed world of Althusserian structuralism. Recent years have seen a proliferation of 'open' and dialectic analyses which have made a significant contribution to our understanding of the historical and logical development of capitalist state forms (Clarke, 1991b; Bonefeld and Holloway, 1991; Bonefeld et al., 1992a, 1992b, 1995). These advances include a recognition that the state is a social form of the capital relation determined in and through class struggle and a recognition that the separation between political, ideological and economic aspects of the capital relation are both a precondition for and a focus of struggle in the domination of the working class by capital. These accounts have highlighted the serious theoretical limitations and the disastrous political implications of both essentialist analyses of the state and structuralism in both its Althusserian and regulationist forms. Also, these dialectic and

339

'open' accounts have opened up an exciting opportunity to develop a non-essentialist analysis of the state as a social form of the capital relation.

There can be little doubt that the work around 'open Marxism' does mark a major theoretical advance in overcoming the essentialism and formalism of the many variants of structuralist Marxism. Our intention [here] is to push 'open Marxism' further in the direction of its own radical conclusions. We present an exploration of the recent recomposition of the state through an exploration of the historically specific contradictions through which institutional state forms are composed and decomposed. The institutional and 'middle-range' conjunctural analysis provided by Marx in *Capital* attests to the importance of this type of analysis and its absence in contemporary theorising on state forms would seem to constitute an important obstacle to further theoretical advances being made. This is particularly evident in respect of the impact of the global recomposition of capital on the nation-state. While there have been attempts to explore the relationship between global capital and the international state system (Burnham, 1996) there have been few attempts to explore the way in which the restructuring of global capital has impacted on the concrete form of particular state formations and the institutional dynamics which link global capital and national, regional and local state ensembles.... [W]e suggest that the concept of risk provides a way of highlighting the concrete processes and dynamics which link the crisis of global capital and the concrete restructuring of the state in post-war Britain.

The conceptual category of *risk* has become an increasingly central element in social scientific discourse over the past decades. Within economics this has taken the form of transaction cost economics and the problem of how capital can most effectively deal with the risks of agency and trust (Williamson, 1975, 1985, 1994). Within the sociology of risk there has been a concern to explore the way in which ecological and financial risks increasingly impinge on human consciousness and identity in the context of an increasingly radicalised modernity (Beck, 1992, 1995; Giddens, 1990, 1991). There can indeed be little doubt that in recent years life has become increasingly risky for both capital and labour: the reproduction of the capital relation faces unprecedented threats and dangers. The abstract theories of economics and sociology merely describe this danger in perverted and fetished ways. An adequate theorisation of risk does not require an abstract theory of risk, but, on the contrary, an analysis of the risks facing the reproduction of the process of abstraction inherent in the capital relation.... [W]e explore the historical decomposition of the British state using the conceptual tools of insurance and risk in order to begin the process of mapping out the changing historical form of the British state. In essence we argue that this takes the form of a restructuring of the state marked by the crisis of the 'law of insurance' on which the Keynesian welfare state was premised to a recomposition of the state according to an emergent 'law of lottery'. These claims require some initial theoretical clarification.

Our argument ... is that the 'law of insurance' and the 'law of lottery' represent changing tendencies within the 'general law of capitalist accumulation' through which the capital relation is produced and reproduced. These laws are not absolute laws for as Marx noted all laws are modified in their working by many circumstances (Marx, 1976: 798). Rather we approach these changes as partial, contradictory and contingent tendencies within the absolute law of capital accumulation. In order to properly periodise the historical and logical development of the state form it is necessary to differentiate between four levels of abstraction: between the liberal state in its most abstract form, through the institutional forms in which working class struggle against the liberal state form become manifest, through the different modes of global integration and finally typologies of the different historically specific modes of state intervention (Clarke, 1992). Thus, the laws mentioned above are explored as modes of state intervention related to a neo-liberal mode of global integration which emerged as a result of organised working class struggles in the era of global Keynesianism. This needs to be related to our later remarks that the National Lottery constitutes an important neo-liberal response to the fiscal crisis of the state. What we are suggesting is *not* that the money raised from the Lottery is sufficient to overcome the fiscal crisis of the state; but, rather, that modes of state intervention are becoming increasingly lottery-like in their forms.

The 'law of lottery' is connected to the increasing problems of assessing risks through *actuarial principles* which is itself a crisis of the planner state. We explore this through an analysis of the workings of the National Lottery and the linkages between the crisis of insurance and the crisis of the state. We conclude ... by pointing to the problems of recent sociological analyses of risk and provide the outlines of an alternative materialist analysis of risk and risk society.

The collapse of the Keynesian planner state has meant that both levels of social welfare and access to employment has increasingly become a game of chance—a lottery. In the UK this national lottery has recently been accompanied by an official version—the *National Lottery*. Risk and chance are thus basic characteristics of the production and reproduction of neo-liberal social formations: positing the economic, political and ideological premises for social reproduction. There is an increasing risk of redundancy or of not being adequately cared for when one is ill, but this is legitimated through a state-sponsored discourse of risk and chance. In other words, the lottery has developed into a social form—a form of social being—which we explore [here] as the 'law of lottery'. In order to pursue these themes we will begin by exploring the basic social form of chance and risk through an analysis of the National Lottery and insurance.

The National Lottery

There is nothing new about national lotteries. In Britain the first national lottery was sanctioned by Elizabeth I, took place in 1569 and consisted of 400,000 lots at 10 shillings each. In the years that followed the lottery became an essential tool of public finance. The profits from lotteries were used to repair harbours and ports and provided funds for expensive military campaigns: £10million between 1710 and 1714 to fund the War of the Spanish Succession and later over £70million for the war against the American colonies. The lottery also provided resources for important infrastructural investment: both Westminster Bridge and the British Museum were established with resources from lotteries.

Later lotteries also benefited members of the 'propertied class' who bought vast quantities of the tickets which, priced at between £10 and £100, were beyond the means of ordinary people, and wealthy agents were able to sell shares in lottery tickets at a premium. This practice was formalised in 1788 when the Treasury sold all tickets to 'lottery contractors', often stockbrokers, who were responsible for generating the feverish excitement around the drawing of the lottery. Alongside this was the underground practice known as 'insurance': with tickets valid for a certain number of draws, individuals could 'hire' a lottery ticket for one of the days in which the lottery was being drawn and were thereby entitled to any prize drawn for that ticket on that day. There was, therefore, both the lottery and a lottery within a lottery: gambling on the outcome of the lottery.

The demise of the lottery is often attributed to the wave of public opposition generated by the new generation of political economists. In the 17th century William Petty described the lottery as a tax on 'unfortunate, self-conceited fools'. Adam Smith, David Ricardo and Henry Thornton all commented on the negative effects of lotteries on both the moral and economic health of the nation. According to a Parliamentary Report of 1808 the results of the lottery were that:

> Idleness, dissipation and poverty were increased: the most sacred and confidential trusts were betrayed, domestic comfort was destroyed, madness was often created, suicide itself was produced and crimes subjecting the perpetrators to death were committed.

This was compounded by the declining proportion of the lottery which contributed to the Exchequer; by 1819 the lottery was contributing less than one per cent to the 'ways and means' account of the Government. Consequently, the lottery was abolished in 1823, and apart from Premium Bonds, which were introduced in 1956, and the football pools (defined as a game of skill rather than chance) it has lain dormant ever since. Indeed, from the Victorian period gambling has been presented by both the state and the Church as a crime and a sin. These attitudes persisted into the 20th century as can be illustrated by the words of Geoffrey Fisher, Archbishop of Canterbury, who fulminating against the introduction of Premium Bonds argued that gambling:

> debas(ed) the spiritual coinage of the people (and that) ... the Government knows, as well as the rest of us, that we can regain stability and strength only by unremitting exercise all through the notion of the old fashioned and essential virtue ... honest work honestly rewarded (quoted in *Financial Times* 9/1/95).

Harold Wilson labelled Premium Bonds a 'squalid little raffle'. However, in 1994 the National Lottery was re-introduced following an absence of over 170 years with the support of all the political parties and only stifled murmurs of discontent from the established Church. The new National Lottery began operating in the UK in November 1994. In its first full year of operation the lottery operated under licence by the Camelot company had achieved sales of £5.2billion, raised £1.4billion for various 'good causes' and contributed £677 million to the exchequer (Camelot, 1996; Fitzherbert et al., 1996). The Lottery in the UK claims to be the largest and most efficient lottery in the world: when assessed in terms of the level of sales and as the relationship between sales and contributions to the Government and 'good causes'. Despite odds of 14,000,000 to 1 of winning the jackpot, the Lottery attracts 30 million regular players to both a twice-weekly draw and to a variety of scratch cards. Camelot have made great strides to appear as the 'people's lottery' and have invested in extensive 'market research' in order to assess the views of players and to engender a sense of 'ownership' amongst lottery players. Camelot itself has become an important corporate actor: in 1995–6 the company achieved an operating profit of £66.7million, employed 600 staff and allowed retail agents to earn at least £265million in extra sales (Camelot, 1996).

The 'good causes' which benefit from the Lottery come under five headings: arts, charities, heritage, millennium and sport. Money is distributed through the Arts Council, the National Lottery Charities Board, the National Heritage Memorial Fund, the Millennium Commission and the Sports Council. In deciding on the eligibility of projects for Lottery funds these bodies have to take into account the financial viability of projects, particularly as money is only contributed to capital expenditure costs rather than running costs. With the exception of charities, most grants are dependent on 'partnership' funding from the applicant. Together with the restrictions on local authority capital spending this has resulted in Lottery funds being disproportionately aimed at 'flagship' projects in London and the South East of England, whilst the 5% of the population living in the most disadvantaged areas fail even to get a 5% share of funds. In 1995–6 this percentage of money awarded amounted to 1.7% to the arts, 1.4% to heritage and 3.9% to sport. An exception was made to charities which are directly aimed at disadvantaged sections of the population, but they still only managed to attract 13% of the total share of the funds available (see Fitzherbert et al., 1996).

As a social form the Lottery clearly articulates the contradictions of the capital relation: mediating real human needs through the perverted abstract forms of money and the law. What however have been the key historical and logical factors behind its development and increasing importance at the present juncture? Lotteries have become popular in all advanced societies: indeed, a key argument in supporting the development of a lottery in the UK was that apart from Albania the UK was the only European society not to have some type of lottery. The National Lottery has played an important role in resolving the fiscal crisis of the state: it represents an ideological form which makes the payment of taxation into a leisure pursuit. The Lottery is a clear form of voluntary taxation: taxation that is, moreover, highly regressive with lower earners spending an average of £4 per head as against £1.20 by the better off (*Financial Times, 28/6/95*). In a clear link to the past, the fastest sales of lottery tickets have been in poorest and richest parts of the UK: the devastated council estates of Sunderland and in the Lombard Street Post Office in the City of London (*Financial Times, 15/7/95*). The state has, in essence, encouraged the expansion of gambling from 74% of the population prior to the Lottery to 89% following the introduction of the Lottery (*Financial Times, 5/6/95*).

The introduction of the Lottery reveals important insights into the way in which the neo-liberal state has been reconstituted in the UK. The Lottery is a new form of *nationalisation*. An intensification of state power which attempts to colonise the worlds of gambling, charity and culture and make them increasingly functional for the neo-liberal accumulation of capital. Casualties of this process have been capitals within the UK gambling sector. Following the introduction of the Lottery, the football pool industry suffered a loss in turnover of between 10% and 15% and Vernons, the second biggest pools operator, suffered a £230million pre-tax loss in 1994 (*Financial Times*, 11/3/95). Similarly, spending in the UK's 900 bingo halls has dropped by 20% and the cash pouring into the UK's 210,000 one-arm bandits is £8million a week less than before the introduction of the Lottery. Related to this has been a 17% increase in calls to 'Gamblers Anonymous'. There is also an important sense in which the Lottery amounts to an important step towards the nationalisation of culture. While the Lottery has been presented as part of a 'new cultural golden age' it also will mean the death of many arts organisations which fail to attract Lottery funding because either they are not financially viable or because they fail to generate partnership funding. Arts groups will be increasingly dependent on private sector sponsorship to attract partnership finance and this will obviously favour large, commercially-viable and mainstream arts groups and projects.

Using the UK as an example we argue that the regulation of societies through the 'law of lottery' has become increasingly important as the crises and contradictions of the Keynesian planner state have intensified. In order to understand this process we will explore the actuarial principles underlying insurance, the way in which these principles underpinned the social form of the Keynesian planner state and how the crises and contradictions of the planner state is simultaneously a crisis of insurance which has resulted in the development and increasing importance of the Lottery as a social form. Insurance was the form of state invention manifested by the modes of social integration which emerged from the struggles in and against the liberal state in the Keynesian period. We will now explore the way in which the Lottery and lottery-like forms of state intervention are increasingly manifested by the modes of integration emerging from struggles in and against the liberal state in the era of global monetarism. In order to understand the institutional principles of the planner state we need to first explore the logic of insurance as a social form.

The Economics of Risk

The category of risk is the fundamental concept underlying the actuarial principles of insurance. The concept of risk was a central concern of classical political economy. According to Adam Smith it is an intrinsic human failing to over-value the chance of gain and hold risk in presumptuous contempt (Smith, 1970: 210–11). This was evident, Smith argued, in the universal success of lotteries through which individuals were systematically encouraged to pay over-inflated prices for tickets when the prospective prize was worth only a fraction of the money paid by the total number of subscribers. Conversely, despite the moderate profits and premiums of insurance companies many individuals held risk in contempt and chose not to insure themselves against potential injury. For Smith, the value of risk amounted to the compensation of common losses and the expenses of management: the profits of insurance being no greater than in other common trades. The level of risk was intimately connected with the level of return to labour and capital (ibid: 213): levels of wages and returns on stock being proportionate to the hazards faced in their employment in particular sectors. Risk becomes, therefore, the original contribution made by capital in the process of production, the level of reward accruing to labour being a derivative of the level of risk taken by capital (Clarke, 1991a: 27).

The unplanned nature of capitalism makes risk a central feature and dynamic in both the reproduction of capitalist social relations and the continual crisis which threatens the reproduction of these relations. In neo-classical economic theory the category of risk is analysed in terms of the way in which uncertainty is a disutility to marginal maximising individuals. It is a commonplace assumption that the return to capital varies proportionately with the degree of risk to which it exposed. Uncertainty imposes a cost on 'society' and the removal of uncertainty will be a source of gain (Willett, 1951: 8). Uncertainty is a disutility and will only be borne if something can be gained from doing so. The assumption of risk, therefore, attracts a special economic reward which varies with the degree of uncertainty. Risk is objectified uncertainty and the degree of risk is ascertained by applying the laws of probability to the accumulated results of past events. In this way the utility and disutility of uncertainty allow economic actors to choose between the avoidance, prevention or assumption of risk in particular circumstances.

Insurance is an important means through which uncertainty and the costs which it imposes on capital can be prevented or reduced. Insurance is the 'transfer' of risk to a specialised undertaker of risks in the form of an insurance company. Insurance companies combine and concentrate risks in order to reduce uncertainty and thereby reduce the cost of risk to wider 'society'. The risk carried by an insurance company is less than the sum of the risks of the insured. The insurance premium makes the incalculable calculable. Insurance constitutes a cost to capital and labour in the sphere of circulation. In the long-run insurance is constituted by a 'mutual' insurance fund out of which losses and the costs involved in the provision of insurance are paid by the insured.

> [I]nsurance companies divide the losses of individual capitalists among the capitalist class. But that does not prevent these

equalised losses from remaining losses so far as the aggregate social capital is concerned (Marx, 1956: 140).

Insurance is the social form through which the losses resulting from the non-valorisation of capital are socialised.

> This is a question of the distribution of the surplus value amongst the different sorts of capitalist and of the deductions which are consequently made from (the surplus value accruing to) the individual capitalists. It has nothing to do with either the nature or the magnitude of the surplus ... Instead of each capitalist insuring himself, it is safer as well as cheaper for him if one section of capital is entrusted with this (Marx, 1971: 357–8).

Insurance constitutes the alienated form in which unexpected losses are socialised in capitalist society. Insurance projects future configurations of time and space on the basis of the past. As time and space are increasingly subordinated to the abstract logic of capital accumulation so they reflect the contradictory determination of all social forms in capitalist society. In capitalist society time and space increasingly imply both the possibility and development of not-time and not-space: configurations of time-space outside the circuit of capital. The riskiness of the reproductive cycle of capital accumulation is thus reflected in the social, spatial and temporal representation of insurance as a social form. The crisis of insurance is ultimately a crisis of the rational ordering of time and space on the basis of the capital relation and this crisis of insurance underpins the development and crisis of the institutional form of the Keynesian planner state.

The 'Law of Insurance' and the Crisis of the Planner State

In this section we trace the historical processes which link the crisis of insurance to the crisis of the state and the way in which this has resulted in the subordination of the state by the 'law of lottery'. We will approach this through an exploration of the origins, development and crisis of state insurance in the UK. The origins of social insurance are to be found in the administrative moment of the state. In capitalist society law and money are the abstract social forms through which the capital relation is produced and reproduced: the creation of formal equivalence through generalised commodity production and exchange by 'free' and 'equal' legal subjects. The state appears as a separate authority to represent the 'impersonal' interests of the system. Capitalist commodity production, however, requires the substantive domination of labour within the labour process and hence the contradictions of capitalism as a social form cannot be totally formalised within the legal and money forms. Alongside formal regulation, therefore, emerges substantive *administration*. The historically specific form of the state is a result of class struggle: the struggle of labour to achieve 'political' gains through the state by avoiding commodification precipitates a process of state restructuring which attempts to re-impose commodification on the production and reproduction of the capital relation.

The problem of unemployment has thus always posed a problem that required *administration*. Administration is necessary owing to the possibility of labour escaping the absolute poverty of wage labour and confirming the possibility of abundance outside the capital relation (Kay and Mott, 1982). In the early development of capitalism, marked by the underdevelopment of the socialised worker, the problem could be administered through punitive measures such as the workhouse and poor relief. These forms of administration, however, denied the equality of labour as both workers and citizens, and as the working class developed as a political force these forms of administration provided the basis for alternative social arrangements based on the possibility of real equality and freedom outside capital (communism). It is necessary, therefore, to explore the way in which these developments resulted in the reconstitution of the state on the basis of the 'law of insurance'.

In the work of classical political economists, such as David Ricardo, civil society was conceptualised as a 'natural' and self-regulating order of independent labourers. In this approach, the circumstances of the worker were a result of individual decisions taken in the context of natural laws. The conceptualisation of workers as independent labourers was, however, increasingly punctured by the inequality and domination faced by workers in the sphere of production. The abstract regulation of labour needed, therefore, to be increasingly supplemented by the direct and unmediated administration of labour. An attempt to grasp the importance of these changes, albeit in a partial and fetished way, is provided by the work of William Beveridge on unemployment and insurance.

The work of Beveridge on social insurance was an important moment in the re-definition of poverty and the role of the state in the amelioration of poverty. Beveridge recognised the way in which the development of the working class shattered the apparent naturality of the economy and attempted to demonstrate empirically the factors which constantly forced the labour market away from a condition of equilibrium. The imperfections of the market undermined the independence of the worker. In other words, the market needed administration. An important focus of Beveridge's investigations were, therefore, the causes of unemployment. Beveridge's investigations sought to explore why the laws of political economy had failed to operate and to uncover ways of making them work. The notion of 'independent labourer' could be upheld only if workers were rewarded for behaviour and character congruent with the morality of money. Beveridge was thus concerned to create administratively the conditions in which the morality of the 'independent labourer' could be rewarded. Beveridge deepened the concerns of classical political economy through the way in which the 'independent labourer' was made both a premise and a goal of political economy. In policy terms the labour exchange was to administer the relationship between the supply and demand of labour. In the context of a socialised working class the surplus population could not be simply discarded, political economy needed to administratively create and maintain the conditions for the existence of the 'independent labourer' and to adequately differentiate between these independent workers and dependent workers.

The 'discovery' of poverty and unemployment was inextricably tied to the potential for socialism. This is the context in which social insurance was developed. Insurance recognised the potential of the working class to exist in a state other than in and through capital, and attempted to re-incorporate the working class through the administrative reconstruction of the 'independent labourer'. The system of social insurance established by the Beveridge reforms was premised on a state-administered compulsory insurance scheme which *socialised* the risk posed to the integrity of the 'independent labourer' by the poverty associated with unemployment, and thus a state-administered 'collective wage' replaced the individual wage. The efficient administration of this process was premised on the accurate calculation of the likely levels of unemployment and thereby politicised aggregate levels of unemployment through their transformation into an administrative category. The discretion inherent to the administrative moment of the state, therefore, posed both a threat to the actuarial soundness of the system and threatened to deepen the crisis of the liberal form of the state.

The 'law of insurance' was necessarily mediated by the abstract social forms of money and the law. The monetary relationship was premised on the contributions paid by the worker and the asymmetrical relationship between benefit and the wage. The system was to be 'policed' through making benefits dependent on genuine 'need' and the punishment of malingerers and fraudulent claimants. In order for social insurance to work it was necessary for the state to accurately calculate the level of unemployment in order to balance contributions and benefits. The administrative discretion inherent in state insurance as a social form, however, allowed the state to cover higher than expected levels of unemployment through general taxation. Social insurance, therefore, linked aggregate levels of unemployment to the fiscal crisis of the state. In other words, insurance became a form of class struggle. Throughout the 1920s and 1930s the working class in the UK struggled over the form of insurance: a struggle for ad hoc benefits, against the means test for higher levels of benefit. Where it was politically expedient—as in 1919 when ex-servicemen and munitions workers were granted extra benefits in order to quell potential revolt—levels of benefit were indeed increased through administrative intervention.

The development of the welfare state thus resulted in the Ricardian 'law of nature' being replaced by the 'law of insurance'. The abstract premises of the actuary were, however, constantly ruptured by the concrete development and movement of the working class, and Beveridge himself conceded that during the 1920s the actuarial basis of the state insurance system was never adhered to (Beveridge, 1930: 277 quoted in Dixon, 1996). The development of the 'social worker' forced the organising principle of the insurance scheme from contract to status: benefit linked to classes of claimants rather than to the contribution of benefits. The crisis of insurance was ultimately addressed by Keynes who devised a way of setting levels of unemployment by the state.

As we mentioned above the insurance makes the incalculable calculable through the way in which it projects future configurations of time-space on the basis of the past. Through the political establishment of an aggregate level of unemployment Keynes allowed the future to be projected on the basis of a recognition that the working class could be maintained only if the subjectivity of labour could be tied inextricably to the development of capital in its most abstract and inscrutable form—*money*. This required the further administration of money through fiscal and monetary policies which regulated the money supply in order to provide levels of benefits and services demanded by labour through the representative channels of the Keynesian planner state. The law of insurance was thus dependent on the monetary stability provided at the global level by the Bretton Woods agreement and the subsequent global hegemony of the dollar and the stable administration of money domestically by the nation-state.

Keynesianism thus provided a way of socialising and thus controlling risks inherent to capital accumulation at the global level. Paradoxically, however, this was a highly contradictory and risky strategy for capital to undertake. The law of value cannot be suspended through administrative intervention because the capital relation on which the law of value is premised is not a thing but a *social relation*. The state is a political form of this relation and is thus unable to resolve the contradictions on which it is premised as a social form. The state is premised on the co-existence of the circuits C-M-C and M-C-M′ and the provision of administrative goods and services through the circuit C-M-C is necessarily mediated by the forms of abstraction inherent to the circuit M-C-M′. The crisis of the capital relation, therefore, became increasingly manifest as a crisis of the state. The state provided welfare and social insurance but in alienating and oppressive forms designed to contain the costs of administration within the socialised valorisation imperatives of capital. The working class demanded reforms to the social welfare system through the extension of benefits and the reform of provision. The 'law of insurance' was thus the historical manifestation of class struggle in the post-war period.

The internal decomposition of Keynesianism was eventually compounded by a global crisis of over-accumulation engendered by the contradictions inherent in the administration of global money by the IMF [International Monetary Fund] and the World Bank (Clarke, 1988). The crisis was contained through the restructuring of capital and the state through the ways in which the administrative and political forms of Keynesianism were (re)subordinated to the abstract power of money and law. The temporal and spatial configuration of capital became liberated from place and the result was a global intensification of capital accumulation and the neo-liberal restructuring of the nation-state (Burnham, 1996). The intensification and globalisation of capital has made the actuarial calculation of risk increasingly problematic. The state no longer has the *dirigiste* mechanisms to maintain aggregate levels of employment and the spatial and temporal impact of unemployment has, therefore, become a matter of *chance*: a lottery. The 'law of insurance' has thus been supplanted by the '*law of lottery*'.

The neo-liberal restructuring has involved the simultaneous restructuring of the economic, political and ideological aspects of the capital relation. The political deconstruction of the institutions of the welfare state and the economic deregulation of the market has thus been accompanied by the development of an ideological focus on chance and risk and the political and economic recomposition of new modes of state intervention premised on these principles. The National Lottery is the most developed institutional form of this process. The crisis of state insurance is thus part of a wider crisis of insurance as the intensity of change and the increasingly massive risks faced by humanity make the calculability of the future increasingly problematic.

Materialities of Risk

As we mentioned earlier risk has become an increasingly central concept within mainstream social science discourse. To take sociology in both its neo-Kantian (Beck, 1992, 1995; Giddens, 1990, 1991) and post-structuralist (Lash and Urry, 1994) forms risk is presented as an abstract theory of being and there has been no consideration of the role that risk plays in the reproduction of abstract material forms. We will conclude ... through the elaboration of an alternative materialist analysis of risk. We need to approach this with reference to the reproduction schema presented by Marx in *Capital: Volume Two*. The dynamism and the contradictions underlying the development of the modern condition is premised on the contradictory coexistence of the circuits C-M-C and M-C-M′. The latter is an inherently risky process as far as capital is concerned. In the metamorphosis of capital through its successive forms—money, capital, productive capital, commodity capital, (more) money capital (M-P ... C-M′)—time and space are constantly ruptured and there is constant risk and uncertainty with respect to the (re)structuring of time and space in a way which permits the successful accumulation of capital. The process is ruptured by the necessary social reproduction of labour through the wage (money) form (Marx, 1956: 35). The unfettered subjectivity of labour is denied by its necessary reproduction through the wage form: money advanced through the wage to enable labour access to commodities necessary for its own reproduction (L-M-P). Hence:

> *The risk faced by individuals in everyday life is thus the alienated and fetished form in which the risks attendant on the reproduction of capital appear.*

In the (post)modern world 'risk fetishism' is the sociological accompaniment of commodity fetishism. The 'actuarialisation' of society is the ideological expression of the risks faced by capital in the neo-liberal process of global capital accumulation. While the crisis appears as a crisis of insurance, this is simply the institutional expression of a more fundamental crisis of the neo-liberal modes of social integration and regulation on a global scale. The crisis of insurance is thus a *crisis of private property*. A crisis of private property becomes a crisis of the most concrete form of private property: *money*. A crisis of money becomes a crisis of money's most abstract form: *capital*. A crisis of capital becomes a crisis of the law and its enforcement: the *state*. A crisis of state demands a more concrete imposition of capital through its most concrete form: the enforcement of the law of money through poverty (monetarism) in an attempt moralise the demoralised, and through bigger risk to offset bigger disaster. The imposition of poverty and bigger risk becomes a crisis of insurance (more crime, bigger disaster). The state can no longer protect the social relationship out of which it is derived and expressed as private property. Bigger risk lies beyond the world of quantifiable redemption.

Insurance makes the world a safer place for capital. Insurance predicts the risks to future patterns of spatial and temporal development on the basis of the past. The increasingly intense and globalised circuits through which capital flows has made prediction increasingly problematic. Indeed, the rational, capitalistic ordering of time-space has reached the limits of its contradictory form. The increasingly uncertain nature of the future makes the quantification of risk increasingly difficult. It is important to recognise however that capital is not a 'thing' or a 'symbol' but a *social relation*: a relation premised on the subordination of living labour power to the abstract power of money capital. The crisis of insurance is thus a crisis of the reproduction of labour as labour power in the circuit of capital accumulation. The crisis is manifested in many forms: crime, unemployment, ecological disaster, nuclear armageddon.... The material manifestation of the risk society is thus a generalised crisis of capital expressed as *uninsurability* through the 'law of lottery'. The death of the future—how soon is now?

Acknowledgment

We would like to thank our friend William Dixon for providing historical and theoretical insights into the significance of William Beveridge to the development of state welfare insurance.

References

Beck, U. (1992) *Risk Society: Towards a New Modernity*, Sage, London.
_____ (1995) *Ecological Politics in the Age of Risk*, Sage, London.
Bonefeld, W. (1992) 'Social Constitution and the Social Form of the Capitalist State' in W. Bonefeld, R. Gunn and K. Pyschopedis (eds) (1991a) *Open Marxism: Dialectics and History*, Pluto Press, London.
Bonefeld, W., R. Gunn and K. Pyschopedis (eds) (1992a) *Open Marxism: Dialectics and History*, Pluto Press, London.
_____ (1992b) *Open Marxism: Theory and Practice*, Pluto Press, London.
Bonefeld, W., R. Gunn, J. Holloway and K. Pyschopedis (eds) (1995) *Open Marxism: Emancipating Marx*, Pluto Press, London.
Burnham, P. (1996) 'Capital Crisis and the International State System' in W. Bonefeld and J. Holloway (eds.) *Global Capital, National State and the Politics of Money*, Macmillan, London.

Camelot (1996) *Annual Report and Accounts 1996* Camelot Group plc, Tolpits Lane, Watford, WD1 8RN.

Clarke, S. (1988) *Keynesianism, Monetarism and the Crisis of the State*, Edward Elgar, Aldershot.

_____ (1991a) *Marx, Marginalism and Modern Sociology: From Adam Smith to Max Weber*, Macmillan, London.

_____ (ed.) (1991b) *The State Debate*, Macmillan, London.

_____ (1992) 'The Global Accumulation of Capital and the Periodisation of the Capitalist State Form' in W. Bonefeld et al. (eds) *Open Marxism: Dialectics and History*, Pluto Press, London.

Dixon, W. (1996) *The Development of the Concept of Unemployment Leading to Keynes's General Theory*, Unpublished PhD Thesis, City University, London.

Fitzherbert, L., C. Giussani and H. Hurd (eds.) (1996) *The National Lottery Year Book*. Directory of Social Change, London.

Giddens, A. (1990) *The Consequences of Modernity*, Polity, Cambridge.

Giddens, A. (1991) *Modernity and Self-Identity: Self and Society in the Late Modern Age,* Polity, Cambridge.

Kay, G. and J. Mott (1982) *Political Order and the Law of Labour*, Macmillan, London.

Lash, S. and J. Urry (1994) *Economics of Signs and Space*, Sage, London.

Marx, K. (1956) *Capital Volume Two: The Process of Circulation of Capital*, Lawrence & Wishart, London.

_____ (1972) *Theories of Surplus Value*: Vol. III, Lawrence & Wishart, London.

_____ (1976) *Capital: A Critique of Political Economy* Vol. I, Penguin, Harmondsworth.

Smith, A. (1970) *The Wealth of Nations*, Penguin, Harmondsworth.

Willett, A.H. (1951) *The Economic Theory of Risk and Insurance*, University of Pennsylvania Press, Philadelphia.

Williamson, O.E. (1975) *Market and Hierarchies: Analysis and Anti-Trust Implications*, Free Press, New York.

_____ (1985) *The Economic Institutions of Capitalism*, Free Press, New York.

_____ (1994) 'Transaction Cost Economics and Organization Theory' in N.J. Smelser and R. Swedberg (eds.) *The Handbook of Economic Sociology*, Princeton University Press, Princeton.

CHAPTER 17

The Pathological Gambler and the Government of Gambling

ALAN F. COLLINS

The pathological gambler is with us. In the psy sciences of the late 20th century the figure of a person addicted to gambling is well established. He or she is not limited to the pages of academic publications or to the consulting-room but is to be found in self-help groups, the courts, TV soaps, chat shows, radio phone-ins, news items, the racing press, the policy of casino chains and, perhaps most ironically of all, in the character of a forensic psychologist in a popular TV series. As I write, *The Times* of 15 June 1995 has an article on its front page proclaiming the identification of 'lotto-mania', a 'delusional illness triggered by publicity' surrounding the UK's national lottery.[1] The article goes on to quote Dr Harry Doyle, a consultant psychiatrist, as believing that 'plenty of people are addicted' (presumably to the lottery or to the delusion of winning).

Today the pathological gambler lurks not only in the pages of the psy literature but in every casino, fruit-machine hall, racetrack and betting office. One does not have to look back far for the picture to be very different: in the psychiatric and psychological writings of the 1970s, the 1960s, the 1950s and before, the pathological gambler was a rare figure and one almost always denied the recognition afforded by an entry in the nosologies of mental illness. In 1980 this changed when the condition was listed in the American Psychiatric Association's *Diagnostic and Statistical Manual,*

3rd edition (DSM-III) and since then there has been a rapid expansion of research on pathological gambling and it has achieved a higher profile in everyday life. [Here] I explore the emergence of the category of pathological gambler and, in particular, I focus on the apparently late construction of that figure.

There is a rich literature on gambling and within that literature stories of gambling too much and too often are commonplace (Ashton, 1898; Cotton, 1674; Lucas, 1714). What is new today is not the idea of excessive gambling but the way in which particular patterns of gambling and feelings about it have become constructed as a distinctive mental disorder. This is not to say that the terms 'compulsive gambler' or 'pathological gambler' had *never* been used before 1980—they most certainly had. However, I claim that interest from the psy professions was minimal prior to the 1980s but has mushroomed since; the construction of excessive gambling as an issue of mental health has been sharpened and much more widely touted since 1980.

There have been previous histories of the category of pathological gambler which have documented the shift from conceiving excessive gambling as a moral concern to seeing it as an essentially medical and psychological problem (Dixon, 1980, 1991; Nelson Rose, 1988; Rosecrance, 1985). My aim is not to attack those histories but to offer a different one. This history is concerned with the role of psychiatry and psychology in the construction of gambling as pathology; it takes as the central issue the conditions which have allowed some gamblers to be seen as mentally ill. It is not a history which looks at the interplay of pressure groups and the law in the government of gambling or which simply regards the pathological gambling as another instance of the medicalization of deviance.

The framework for the present account is provided by Foucault's concepts of government and governmentality (Foucault, 1979). For Foucault, government was a set of practices around 'How to govern oneself, how to be governed, how to govern others, by whom the people will accept being governed, how to become the best possible governor' (Foucault, 1979: 7 [1991: 87]). Central to this programme is the maximizing of 'the forces of the population and each individual within it' (Nikolas Rose, 1989: 5). The practices of government geared towards such maximization are concerned with grand themes such as mortality and poverty but they are also concerned with less obviously major issues such as bad habits, minor ailments and whatever other irritants might prevent a population or an individual from realizing some potential. Government in the senses used by Foucault is fundamentally dependent upon knowledge: knowledge is needed to create ways of seeing people that enable the project of maximization, and knowledge must be given a material form which allows activities such as collation, comparison and the identification of differences in individuals. Knowledge in these forms makes various domains governable, that is, certain sociopolitical aims become possible, certain forms of conduct can be conducted. The particular contribution of psychology, psychiatry and psychoanalysis in this concept of government is that they have invented new ways of talking about the person and new means of inspecting the population and the individual. These new ways claim to reveal deficiencies, differences, problems and deviations from the norm which have made new domains both visible and calculable. By creating and inspecting things such as 'mental ability', the psy sciences provide new ways of effecting education: they claim to bring the mental abilities of populations and individuals into the realm of the governable. The influence becomes even wider as the psy sciences provide us with new means of construing our own subjectivity (these themes are explored in far more depth elsewhere especially by Nikolas Rose, 1985, 1988, 1989).

The history of the pathological gambler is one small example of how the psy sciences produce new means of governing populations. Those sciences now offer a view of gambling not simply as a bad habit, a vice, or a moral failing but as a pursuit which is potentially addictive. They offer a view of the gambler as someone who may be compared with the population of gamblers and whose gambling may be inspected in a way that allows a judgment to be made as to whether or not the individual's gambling is a form of mental disorder. The psy sciences provide ways of constructing ourselves and promise means of maximizing ourselves by offering techniques for overcoming personal difficulties and so becoming happier, more fulfilled and, ultimately, more efficient citizens. The claim that the psy sciences are now enmeshed in the project of governing gambling is hardly surprising. What is much more surprising in this history is that many of the apparent conditions for the emergence of the pathological gambler were in place well before the end of the 19th century, let alone 1980. In this sense the present history is rather a strange one in that it is as much concerned with silence about the pathological gambler as with what has been said, and towards the end of the [chapter] I offer some speculations on the odd silence concerning gambling as mental illness or maladapted personality.[2] Like Hacking (1986), I take the view that the history of the pathological gambler is a history of 'making up people', of inventing a new category. I also take Hacking's point that each of these categories has its own history to be explored and debated. As a first step in this history, I wish to talk a little more about the conceptualization of the pathological gambler in contemporary psychology and psychiatry.

The Pathological Gambler since 1980

The first classifications of the pathological gambler as a distinct disorder appeared in 1980 in the third edition of the American Psychiatric Association's *Diagnostic and Statistical Manual* (DSM-III) and in the 10th edition of the international classification of disorders (ICD-10) published by the World Health Organisation (1992). Both schemes have considerable importance in the psychiatric profession. The ICD scheme has particular relevance in Britain as it provides the recommended nosology to be used when assigning a diagnosis to patients. This also means that psychiatric admission forms and official statistics on mental disorders for the UK are based upon the ICD classification. As one might expect, following its appearance in the official nosologies of the psychiatric profession, pathological gambling has made its way into psychiatric texts. For example, the *Comprehensive Textbook of Psychiatry*, published in 1989, contains a separate chapter on the 'Impulse Control Disorders Not Elsewhere Classified', with pathological gambling occupying an important place within it (Popkin, 1989). This is not to say that the impulse control disorders are regarded as a central or critical category within psychiatry; it is clear that they occupy a small and marginal niche but they are recognized as a legitimate area of concern for the profession. The sanction offered by DSM and ICD has given pathological gambling a visibility it previously lacked, something that members of Gamblers Anonymous had realized when that organization argued for the recognition of gambling as a form of mental illness (McGurrin, 1992: 9).

In the revision of DSM-III, known as DSM-III-R (1987), pathological gambling was classified as a type of 'Impulse control disorder' along with kleptomania, pyromania, trichtillomania, intermittent explosive disorder, and the recursively entitled 'impulse control disorders not otherwise specified'. The features taken to be common to this group are: a failure to resist an impulse where the resistance may or may not be conscious and the act itself may or may not be premeditated; increased tension or arousal before committing the act; and pleasure, gratification, or release following the act (Popkin, 1989).

The characterization of the impulse control disorders as a group is similar to ideas of compulsion, a term that has also been applied as a description of pathological gambling. However, in the psychiatric view of compulsion, the person experiencing the urge sees it as alien and something to be dreaded and resisted, a characterization which, it is claimed, rarely fits with the experience of the pathological gambler (Moran, 1970). Pathological gambling is also frequently portrayed as an addiction because it satisfies the three key requirements for an addiction: some form of dependence, progression, and withdrawal symptoms in the absence of the drug or behaviour. Although writings on excessive gambling use both the ideas of impulse disorder and addiction they are rarely brought into opposition and the most obvious implication of this is that all of the features listed above may coexist in the pathological gambler, allowing the labels 'impulse control disorder' and 'addiction' both to be used.

There is an important distinction in the psychiatric literature between excessive behaviour as a cause of mental illness and excessive behaviour as a mental illness in and of itself. Levine (1978) points out that it is the latter view which most closely fits with modern conceptions of addiction (though this does not preclude accounts of how addictions can lead to all kinds of other mental illnesses or can be associated with other forms of disturbed behaviour). There is now a considerable literature on the extent to which pathological gambling co-occurs with other addictions or compulsive behaviours such as substance misuse, sexual addictions, overeating and overspending (for a brief review, see Lesieur and Rosenthal, 1991). Behind all of these efforts is the idea of some general mechanism or process that has a causal role in different addictions or compulsions. There are also literatures on the co-occurrence of pathological gambling with other psychiatric disorders, such as depression, and with crime (Lesieur and Rosenthal, 1991). These literatures bind pathological gambling to existing disorders and social problems in a way that makes it more difficult to attack the category of pathological gambler. Apart from literatures, there are also explicit efforts to develop treatment programmes aimed at multiple addictions and co-occurring psychiatric problems (Blume, 1986). Both the literatures and treatment programmes ensnare pathological gambling in a web of pathologies so that should one doubt its status as a mental illness one has to unravel a whole web of relationships that are now part of the understanding of pathological gambling. The consolidation of a psychiatric category is made more certain by such intertwining.

The particular criteria for pathological gambling were revised for DSM-III-R (American Psychiatric Association, 1987) and were in the form of a checklist with a range of possible combinations allowing the diagnosis. Further revisions of the diagnostic criteria were introduced for DSM-IV but the checklist approach was retained (Lesieur and Rosenthal, 1991). The thrust of the revisions for DSM-IV produced a compromise between DSM-III and DSM-III-R. For the diagnosis of pathological gambling, at least four of the following must be exhibited:

1. As gambling progressed, became more and more preoccupied with reliving past gambling experiences, studying a gambling system, planning the next gambling venture, or thinking of ways to get money
2. Needed to gamble with more and more money in order to achieve the desired excitement
3. Became restless or irritable when attempting to cut down or stop gambling
4. Gambled as a way of escaping from problems or intolerable feeling states
5. After losing money gambling, would often return another day in order to get even ('chasing' one's losses)
6. Lied to family, employer, or therapist to protect and conceal the extent of involvement with gambling
7. Committed illegal acts such as forgery, fraud, theft, or embezzlement, in order to finance gambling
8. Jeopardized or lost significant relationship, marriage, education, job, or career because of gambling
9. Needed another individual to provide money to relieve a desperate financial situation produced by gambling (a 'bailout'). (Lesieur and Rosenthal, 1991: 10)

However well specified such criteria may be, they must still leave considerable room for interpretation and clinical judgment. Presumably someone who gambles only once in a while yet is preoccupied with ways of making money (1), who sometimes visits the bookies or racetrack to take his or her mind off other things (4) and who is in a relationship with someone whose religious convictions would mean that knowledge of any gambling by their partner would lead to considerable difficulties (6 and 8) would not qualify as a pathological gambler.

The psychiatric diagnosis is a key means of examining the individual and making individuality visible (Nikolas Rose, 1989). More than this the diagnosis leads to written records and with written records come the possibility of making various calculations about the population of gamblers and all that implies about locating individuals within that population. Alongside the clinical judgments required in a diagnosis based on the DSM criteria listed above, psychological tests for identifying the pathological gambler have been developed and refined since the emergence of the pathological gambler category. The most widely known of these tests is the South Oaks Gambling Screen (SOGS) developed by Lesieur and Blume (1987, 1993). The SOGS is a questionnaire and scores obtained from it claim to distinguish between those with 'no gambling problem', those with 'some problem' and someone who is 'the probable pathological gambler'. In so doing the instrument objectifies and quantifies and renders the pathological gambler calculable but requires little by way of clinical judgment or expertise to administer. It allows individuals to be located on a continuum of gambling and it is argued that at some point on this continuum an individual's life and mental health are sufficiently damaged for them to be said to be mentally ill or to be demonstrating a maladaptive personality. The SOGS is intended to be used in both research and clinical work and it can be used for self-diagnosis; it is a means of inscription that does not simply provide a transient piece of knowledge about a person, it also 'makes persons amenable to having things done to them—and doing things to themselves' (Nikolas Rose, 1985: 7–8).

It is clear that the study of gambling in the contemporary psy sci ences is dominated by gambling as pathology. For example, a search of the PSYCLIT database for the years 1987–93 revealed that of 438 papers referring to gambling or gamblers, 90 per cent discussed pathology in some form.[3] Not only this but the concern with pathology has increased markedly in recent times as the same search of the PSYCLIT database for the years 1974–86 reveals a much lower figure of 45 per cent. In line with these developments a journal explicitly devoted to the study of gambling behaviour began in 1985 (then the *Journal of Gambling Behaviour*, now the *Journal of Gambling Studies*—a journal which has links with the National Council on Gambling); the behaviour is listed in dictionaries of psychiatry (e.g. Stone, 1988; Walton, 1985), is covered in major texts (e.g. Kaplan and Sadock, 1989; Halgin and Whitbourne, 1993) and is the subject of specialist texts (e.g. Dickerson, 1984; Eadington and Cornelius, 1993; Galski, 1987; Lesieur, 1984) and of numerous articles in general psychiatry journals as well as journals devoted to the study of addiction such as the *British Journal of Addiction* and the *International Journal of Addiction*.

The idea of pathological gambling has a presence well beyond the psychiatric and psychological literatures. The self-help organization Gamblers Anonymous (GA) was founded in the 1950s in the USA and its emergence is often quoted as a key moment in the recognition of gambling as pathology, something to which I shall return (Dixon, 1980; Dixon, 1991: 318). GA adopted many of the practices of Alcoholics Anonymous though there were and are some differences (Browne, 1993; Lesieur, 1990). It was introduced to the UK in 1964 largely through the efforts of the Rev. Gordon Moody of the Churches Council on Gambling and still represents a major resource for those seeking support for the problems they experience (Moody, 1990).

A network of self-help GA groups now exists in the UK and it represents a major resource for those seeking help.

The view of excessive gambling as mental illness obtained sufficient grip for 'compulsive gambling' to be offered as a form of insanity defence in the USA (Nelson Rose, 1988), although most of these cases took place prior to the tightening of the insanity defence, which involved a return to the stricter M'Naghten Rules, and now compulsive gambling is rarely used as a defence in the USA. However, it has been used in mitigation and in other ways; Rose provides the example of a defendant able to convince the California Supreme Court that his conviction for murder should be squashed because his original defence had been ineffectively handled by a trial attorney who was a compulsive gambler. Nelson Rose (1988) points out that the law prefers the term 'compulsive gambling' to the term 'pathological gambling' because the latter already presumes illness; in psychiatry the reverse is the modern preference because, it is claimed, excessive gambling does not involve compulsion as usually understood by psychiatrists. Such a difference highlights a tension in medico-legal approaches to the gambler and competing constructions of that person and his or her behaviour, the repeated struggle between notions of free will versus mental disorder.

Pathological gambling is now surrounded by the trappings of professionalization: there are movements dedicated to its study, there are researchers and journals whose primary concern is with gambling as pathology, there are debates between different theoretical accounts and therapies, self-help networks have emerged, and the figure has a place in the psychiatric and psychological literatures. Pathological gambling has become a further imperative when we reflect on how we gamble: gamblers must exercise self-regulation not just because gambling is something that has a dubious moral basis or because of the money they might lose or because of the time it might occupy. We need to guard against gambling taking hold of our minds and our lives, against our becoming mentally ill.

Of course, the story so far will come as no surprise: the entry of psychiatric and psychological knowledge into everyday life has been rigorously explored (Nikolas Rose, 1985, 1988). What is a surprise in this particular domain of mental health is that it should have been accepted so late: addictions of various forms have been with us since the 19th century as have a variety of what are now known as impulse control disorders (in particular, kleptomania and pyromania). However, before one can confidently assert that pathological gambling was largely absent from the 19th and early 20th centuries and go on to speculate on some of the reasons for this, one first needs to consider the extent of gambling in 19th-century Britain.

Gambling in 19th-Century Britain

During the 19th century, gambling was a reasonably common pursuit but despite the 'avalanche of numbers' associated with this century, there were no reliable statistics on the extent of gambling or on the amounts of money involved (Clapson, 1992).[4] However, it is generally agreed that there was an expansion in gambling in the late 19th and early 20th centuries, an expansion which is attributable to increasing working-class affluence and the development of important technologies such as the telegraph (McKibbon, 1979). Whilst acknowledging this expansion, it would be wrong to think that gambling was either absent from earlier times or that it had previously been restricted to the upper classes. There is substantial evidence that gambling was endemic in British society during the 19th century and before. It is impossible to present anything other than a smattering of this evidence here but it is explored more fully in recent histories of gambling, all of which have something to say of the 19th century (Chinn, 1991; Clapson, 1992; Dixon, 1991). What emerges from this literature is that gambling was not simply a benign presence in the social fabric; gambling was viewed as a social problem attracting attention from a variety of sources including Parliament, pressure groups, social commentators, the law and the legal machinery.

The mid-19th century saw the emergence of a considerable number of social commentaries that included gambling as a behaviour to be condemned. A variety of moral objections to gambling were offered in such texts, the most frequent being: obtaining money from others without giving anything in return, the rejection of rationality and divine purpose, and effectively gaining money for oneself at the expense of others (Perkins, 1950). Clearly a central aim of these moral writings was not only to discourage gambling but to encourage gamblers and those tempted to gamble to develop their own sense of its immorality, to put in place a better set of habits. Part of the moral aspects of the condemnation of gambling stemmed from deeper longstanding concerns of Protestantism with ideas such as Fortune, Destiny and Providence (Thomas, 1971). However, it would be too great a generalization to claim that all moral commentaries were solely concerned with the gambler himself as the wrongdoer. For example, the social explorer James Greenwood in his book *The Seven Curses of London* has a chapter on 'Advertising Tipsters and Betting Commissioners', which, after a few opening remarks about the 'vice of gambling ... amongst the English working classes', berates the 19th-century equivalent of the modern tipping service (and those enamoured of present-day tipsters would find many of his comments still to the mark). Likewise many pieces of anti-gambling writing were not solely concerned with morality but also paid attention to what they viewed as the potentially dire social costs of excessive gambling (Dixon, 1991). The notion of danger was a theme in all of these writings: gambling and gamblers were dangerous because they threatened to bring about moral decay, inefficiency and poverty.

Regular publications concerned with sport and betting, particularly on horse-racing, began to increase in number during the mid-19th century and by 1883 the interest and enthusiasm for horse-racing was such that it allowed the *Sporting Life* to become a daily paper (Clapson, 1992). Other forms of gambling, such as betting on the tossing of coins, were also common (Chinn, 1991: 63). In histories of Victorian leisure and accounts of Victorian crime, gambling is frequently mentioned (Bailey, 1987; Chesney, 1970; Reader, 1964; Storch, 1977). Gambling challenged concepts of rational leisure and so became a target in moves towards governing the leisure of the working class (Bailey, 1987). It also became the focus of various political arguments where both the contention that gambling was a means of controlling the masses and the contrary view that it represented the masses out of control were voiced (Dixon, 1991). So, in a variety of 19th-century discourses and in detailed commentaries on the era, one can hardly miss gambling; it is, to adapt the cliche, woven into the rich tapestry of the times.

In the 19th century, gambling was seen as a threat, albeit a minor one, which required intervention and government. Perhaps the two most obvious examples of attempts to govern it were the passing of a number of pieces of legislation and, late in the 19th century, the emergence of a social movement called the National Anti-Gambling League. There were several 19th-century Acts that had some major concern with gambling and betting, of which five were specifically concerned with these activities:

1818 The Disorderly Houses Act 58, Geo. III, c. 70
1845 Gaming Act, 'An Act to Amend the Law concerning Games and Wagers', 8 & 9 Vict., c. 109
1849 Quarter Sessions Act, 12 & 13 Vict., c. 45
1853 Betting Act, 'An Act for the Suppression of Betting Houses', 16 & 17 Vict., c. 119, 995-1000
1854 The Gaming Houses Act, 'An Act for the Suppression of Gaming Houses', 17 & 18 Vict., c. 38
1869 The Prevention of Gaming (Scotland) Act, 32 & 33 Vict., c. 87
1874 Betting Act, 'An Act to amend ... [the 1853 Act]', 37 & 38 Vict., c. 15

In addition, there were two select committees (1808 on lotteries, 1844 on gaming) as well as two early in the 20th century (1901 and 1902, both

House of Lords Select Committees on betting). The 1808 reports are shot through with concerns over the poverty and crime associated with participation in lotteries and presaged the abandonment of the state lottery in 1826. Not all the legislation of the period was prohibitive; the 1845 Act simply reinforced the point that debts relating to gambling wages were not—and they still are not—legally enforceable. In other words the integrity of the gamblers and the free play of the market were to govern and the Act is often presumed to have been aimed primarily at the middle class (Clapson, 1992). In general, however, both the title and the opening sentence of the 1853 legislation can represent much of the tone of debate in this period: 'Act for the Suppression of Betting Houses. Whereas a kind of Gaming has of late sprung up tending to the Injury and Demoralization of improvident persons by the opening of Places called Betting Houses or Offices.… For the suppression thereof be it enacted.…'

Even a cursory glance at quarter session records from the 19th century reveals that gambling and gamblers made reasonably frequent contact with the law. Clapson (1992) reviewed the Manchester police returns for the 1840s and 1850s, and in 1847, a typical year, he identified 73 arrests related to gambling. The records of the forms of employment show that most of those arrested were clients of betting shops and were mainly working-class. As Clapson notes, this is a minor problem when compared with drink: arrests for illegal gambling amounted to approximately 25 per cent of the total for drunkenness. What these statistics mask, of course, are those instances of offences such as fraud and theft which are committed in order to sustain gambling. The thorny issues surrounding both the will to enforce the laws and the means of doing so also mean that statistics from quarter session records tell us little about the true extent of gambling. What they do tell us is that gambling was seen as a legitimate target for the law and law enforcement; gambling was not ignored.

The National Anti-Gambling League (NAGL) was founded in 1890 and finally folded in 1946 (what follows draws heavily on Dixon, 1991). It campaigned for anti-gambling legislation and for educating people into forms of leisure that did not involve gambling. In the late 19th and early 20th centuries, the NAGL succeeded in bringing gambling into the public forum and it played some part in the introduction of the 1906 Street Betting Act which prohibited off-course gambling. The 1906 Act has been seen as legislation by a paternalistic liberalism and as a law that strongly discriminated against the working-class gambler (Chinn, 1991; Clapson, 1992). If the 1906 Act represented the NAGL at its peak, its subsequent story is one of decline and disorganization. The NAGL's hardline arguments for the prohibition of gambling, which had seemed so much in tune with the other moral reform movements of the late 19th century and the demands of wartime, jarred against the spirit of post-First World War Britain and eventually its extreme moral stance became an anachronism.

The general view in recent histories of gambling is that it was a common activity in 19th-century Britain and was a focus for both legislation and moral pleading (Clapson, 1992; Dixon, 1991). However, the moves against gambling seem not to have stopped gambling continuing among both the working and middle classes. Does all this mean that the 19th-century government of gambling by legislative restriction and more or less organized campaigns to imbue the population with a sense of its inherent evil and abundant dangers were largely unsuccessful? Yes.

The Absence of Gambling as Pathology in the 19th Century

I have argued that gambling was widespread in the 19th century and, far from being ignored as an activity, was identified both as a social problem in itself and as one which could lead to a variety of further difficulties. The problem was largely constructed in terms of threats to moral well-being, health, wealth and happiness. An ordered society and the means of achieving it were preoccupations of the 19th century when order was regarded as the basis of civilization and disorder as something threatened by all kinds of urgent irrationalities in human nature (Smith, 1992). In line with this, the writings of 19th-century psychiatrists are run through with concerns about the regulation and control of our mental life and of our behaviour. Consequently, any mental states or behaviours that could be interpreted as loss of control were prime candidates for the label insanity. As Roger Smith notes in his history of inhibition, the example *par excellence* of loss of control was drunkenness but other behaviours also challenged the ideas of rationality and control. For example, both pyromania and kleptomania are frequently listed as forms of insanity in 19th-century texts.[5] However, in my researches, gambling is not explicitly discussed as a *form* of mental illness until the late 19th century and so for much of that century the pathological gambler simply does not exist.[6]

The most obvious source of information on the categories of 19th-century psychiatry is the texts of that period. It would be both impossible and dull to review all of those consulted.... However, to give a brief flavour of 19th-century writings about madness and to highlight how close these sometimes come to a concept of the pathological gambler without constructing that figure, I will look at some of the more important 19th-century texts on insanity. In particular, I focus on those sections of their work apparently most closely related to the modern conceptualization of impulse disorder.

Pinel (1806), in a key early psychiatric text, talks of five species of insanity: melancholia, mania without delirium, mania with delirium, dementia, and idiotism. Within his discussion of different forms of mania he describes how some of the mad are 'actuated by an instinctual propensity to commit to the flames everything of a combustible nature' (1806: 21) a description bearing a crude resemblance to the modern classification of the impulse disorder pyromania. In what is generally viewed as the most influential nosology of the 19th century, Esquirol (1845) talks of incendiary monomania (Marc's pyromania) and though he admits to having not encountered it himself, this does not prevent its being given a separate category within his list of monomanias, a list which also includes monomania from drunkenness, erotic monomania and reasoning monomania. Despite monomania being a broad and frequently debated category, I have found only one instance of monomania of gambling which is an illustration of Géricault for an unpublished work by Georget in the early 1820s (see Gilman, 1982).

Apart from monomania, 19th-century psychiatry is littered with other apparently catch-all categories, perhaps the most well-known of which was 'moral insanity' (Prichard, 1835). Prichard himself stated that 'the varieties of moral insanity are perhaps as numerous as the modifications of feeling or passion in the human mind', though he went on to say that most were characterized by extreme excitement or extreme melancholy (Prichard, 1835). While most attention was paid to instances of moral insanity associated with violent criminal acts, other behaviours were also embraced by the category. For example, Duncan (1853) discusses cleptomania (*sic*) as a manifestation of moral insanity and Prichard himself saw 'propensity to theft' as a common feature of moral insanity. Because of the breadth of the category, it is possible that gambling may have been subsumed under it and so obscured from casual scrutiny. Moral insanity was seen as a disturbance of the feelings rather than of the intellect and partly because of this it threw into high relief some of the main points at issue between medical and legal views of lunacy in the 19th century (Smith, 1981). Gambling activities certainly brushed with the law but the alienists of the time did not regard such acts as deserving of the label insanity and I have not found gambling discussed as a form of mania under any of the more general headings I have mentioned.

It is not only in discussions of manias or other states explicitly labelled as examples of loss of control that alienists provide frameworks apparently conducive to seeing gambling as madness. Connolly (1830) is riddled with moments when the explicit mention of gambling as madness seems a whisker away. In his 1830 work, his main thesis is that the mad have lost the ability to compare; that is, a madman has a long-lasting inability to distinguish, for example, between the real and the unreal, between the reasonable and the unreasonable. Lack of control is at times added to this central concept and produces characterizations sufficiently broad to put almost any behaviour within the scope of madness. As Connolly states:

> Seeing that any feeling in excess—the love of pleasure, or of ease, or of money, or of expense, or of applause; or that self-denial, or anger, or jealousy, or hope too sanguine, or sorrow too much indulged, may become independent of the restraint of the comparing powers, and thus impair or disorder the understanding; we cannot but remark the importance of cherishing that governing and protecting action of the mind ... by careful cultivation and exercise. (Connolly, 1830: 231)

Connolly is careful to point out that in his scheme eccentricities do not count as insanity because the object of attention is 'deliberately and well chosen' and the eccentric has not lost 'the power of transferring his attention from one object to another'. On these criteria, given the numerous 19th-century misgivings about gambling and testimonies to its power to preoccupy, excessive gambling might easily have crossed from eccentricity to madness.

Gambling is not entirely without mention in the writings of the 19th-century alienists. Moseley (1838) in talking of the possible exciting causes of madness lists '24thly Gambling'. Maudsley (1868), ever resistant to nosologies, presents a series of cases at the end of a chapter on 'Causes of Insanity' and for case 22 writes: 'Gambling, betting, drinking, and sexual intemperance. General paralysis.' Seguin (1870) presents a list of four 'new causes' of idiocy, the fourth of which is gambling (it is the gambling of the husband that is the problem: it induces dread in the pregnant woman, a dread which affects the mental wellbeing of the unborn child).[7] Like several other alienists of his time, Neville (1836) talks about how sudden changes in fortune may trigger the onset of madness:

> It is, in fact, the gradual conversion of healthy action into diseased activity that explains the change so frequently observed in the mind both of the gamester and the mercantile speculator, long before absolute insanity occurs: in the outset, before organisation has suffered, all the powers of the mind are healthy, efficient, and under control, and a certain degree of prudence, foresight, and arrangement is manifest in every venture. After a time, however,

whether of success or mishap, the organs of acquisitiveness, self-esteem, and control, from excessive stimulation become permanently and uncontrollably excited, and assume the mastery. (Neville, 1836: 83)

Finally, in the minutes of the 1808 Select Committee set up to consider the 'Evils attending lotteries' and how far they had been remedied, the unwanted effects of such gambling are listed as 'the most sacred and confidential truths are betrayed, domestic comfort is destroyed, *madness often created*, crimes, subjecting the perpetrators of them to the punishment of death, are committed, and even suicide itself is produced' (SC, 1808, Appendix A: 157; my italics). What is significant in all these references to gambling is that it is viewed as a cause or manifestation of insanity rather than as insanity in itself.

Apart from the unpublished work by Georget mentioned above, in my researches the first appearance of gambling as a possible form of mental illness occurs in Clouston (1883) who referred to a group of disorders collectively known as 'states of defective inhibition' of which the 'commoner and more typical varieties' were: general psychokinesia; epileptiform impulse; animal and organic impulse; homicidal impulse; suicidal impulse; destructive impulse; moral insanity; dipsomania; kleptomania and pyromania. In a section on dipsomania, Clouston advances the idea of 'neurine stimulant craving' which is associated with 'impulses or weaknesses of control', states which he describes in the following way:

> ... all the faculties and powers that we call moral are gone, at all events for the time the craving is on. The patients lie; they have no self-respect or honour; they are mean and fawning; they cannot resist temptation in any form; they are morbidly erotic, especially at the beginning of an attack; they will steal; the affection for those formerly dearest is suspended; they have no resolution and no rudiments of conscience in any direction. (Clouston, 1887: 342)

Clouston goes on to argue that:

> We cannot regard the drink-craving alone. We must also be prepared to deal with the opium eater, insane smoker, chloral taker, gambler, and even many insane speculators. (Clouston, 1887: 343)

It is clear from Clouston's account that he saw all of these problems as arising from a brain dysfunction that impaired the operation of a physically realized moral faculty. In a later paper, Clouston (1890) developed his ideas about dipsomania and went on to discuss morphinomania, chloralism and cocainism in similar terms. Clouston's descriptions clearly fit with the ideas about addiction that had been developed around that time by Levinstein (1878) and Kerr (1894). I shall return to the concept of addiction later, it is sufficient to note here that ideas about morphinomania, cocainism and opium addiction were all present in the late 19th century and that these ideas were challenged, worked upon and transformed—the concern with these excesses as mental illness did not disappear. For gambling, however, the occasional mentions remained just that and apart from psychoanalytic writings there was no discussion of it as mental illness.

Psychiatric texts provide only a limited insight into psychiatric practice. Anyone studying such texts alongside asylum records can hardly fail to notice the mismatch between them in their use of diagnostic categories; in asylum records 'medical labelling of patients seems to have been observed more in the breach than in the observance' (Digby, 1985; Scull, 1993). This gap raises the possibility that while gambling may not have entered the nosologies, it may have been used in the institutions as a reason for admission; a diagnostic category in practice if not in name. Searching every record for every asylum in Britain is simply not feasible, one can engage only in the admittedly rather dangerous strategy of taking a sample of such records and making a rather bold generalization.[8] Lancaster Moor Hospital opened in 1816 and became one of the biggest asylums in Britain taking in patients from all over the north-west of England, including Manchester, Liverpool, the cotton towns of East Lancashire and rural Lancashire, as well as from elsewhere within Britain (J. K. Walton, 1979). I examined the complete case-records from the Lancaster Moor for five years (1823, 1845, 1888, 1904, 1912) and this revealed only two mentions of gambling: one an instance of a young man who boasted that he could earn a good deal of money from matches at billiards (it is clear from the case-notes that this was viewed as one among several delusions) and the other where a patient saw people in his bed gambling (this patient was diagnosed as suffering from delirium tremens). This absence is set alongside frequent mentions of problems caused by excessive drinking and, by 1912, fairly frequent mentions of alcoholism and addiction to drink. As might be expected from the mismatch between asylums and texts described above, other behaviours listed in the nosologies of the times, such as kleptomania, were also absent from the asylum records I consulted. It remains a possibility that for all of these behaviours it is simply their rarity that is responsible for their non-appearance in the sample of records consulted. It is impossible to refute such an argument but it can be looked at from another angle: rarity in practice did not prevent the appearance of categories such as kleptomania and pyromania in texts and, similarly, lack of personal encounters with people suffering from such problems did not seem a barrier to their inclusion in a nosology (for example, Esquirol discusses several cases of pyromania but all are drawn from Marc). In conclusion, my overwhelming impression is that the psychiatrists of the 19th century not only did not encounter the excessive gambler, they did not seek him out.

The Pathological Gambler in the Early 20th Century

Most references to the emergence of the idea of gambling as mental pathology refer to the psychoanalytic literature as being the earliest reasonably extensive literature in the area (Fenichel, 1945; Freud, 1961; Simmel, 1920; von Hattingberg, 1914). The literature continued into the middle of the 20th century particularly in the work of Bergler (Bergler, 1936, 1958) and there continues to be a literature in this vein (Rosenthal, 1985, 1987). Although there are variations in the accounts, the most important and most popularized theory, developed by Bergler, is that underpinning the excessive gambling is some form of unconscious desire to lose; the pathological gambler engages in a form of psychic masochism. Since Bergler, there have been a number of attempts to rework his specific theory but overall, even within the psychoanalytic literature, gambling receives little attention: Bergler was the only thorough-going specialist and the topic was frequently absent from texts on neuroses.

Outside the psychoanalytic literature I have located two early 20th-century references to gambling by major figures in the psychiatric literatures: Kraepelin, the so-called 'father of psychiatric nosology', referred to 'gambling mania', and the same term is also used by Bleuler in his work, which is based upon that of Kraepelin (1913, English translation 1924).[9] In 20th-century psychiatric texts, pathological gambling as a category was not described in a wide range of standard works prior to the 1980s.... When pathological gambling did receive a mention, this was usually brief and often served to deny it as a psychiatric problem by reinforcing the view of excessive gambling as an everyday problem rather than as a mental illness or by seeing it as simply indicative of a more serious malaise. Forrest (1977) mentions excessive gambling but only as part of his discussion of the nature of sociopathy. Kolb (1973) has no entry for gambling but has separate chapters for alcoholism, drug dependence and personality disorders, the latter including discussion of both compulsive and hysterical personalities. Slater and Roth (1969) likewise devote chapters to 'Alcoholism, Drug Addiction and Other Intoxicants' and 'Personality Deviations and Neurotic Reactions' but nowhere mention excessive gambling as an illness. The *American Handbook of Psychiatry* published between 1959 and

1966 has only the briefest of mentions of gambling in its chapter on alcoholism (where it is remarked that 'Even excessive gambling has been seen as another form of addiction in alcoholics'; Arieti, 1959: 1204). In a later version of the same handbook, published between 1974 and 1981, there are two references to gambling: the first of these is as an instance of antisocial behaviour (Volume III) though the second gives it fuller consideration as a subcategory of the group of impulse disorders (Volume VII). What is significant about this second mention and this shift in status is that the publication date of Volume VII was 1981, a year after pathological gambling gained recognition in DSM-III.

There has been no paucity of labels for mental disorders in 20th-century psychiatry. For example, in Slater and Roth's text quoted above, the chapter on 'Personality Deviations and Neurotic Reactions' includes discussions of such fringe figures as the 'unstable drifter', or 'the cold and emotionally callous' and of states such as 'irritability'. In Chambers' *Dictionary of Psychiatry* (1967 edition) there is no listing for pathological gambling yet it contains a plethora of compulsive or impulsive disorders: erotomania, dromonomania (compulsive wandering), dipsomania (compulsive drinking), pyromania, kleptomania, emetomania (compulsive vomiting), mono- or hypolepsiomania, nostomania (intensive homesickness), toxicomania (driven to take toxic substances), trichtillomania (impulse to pull out one's own hair), bibliomania (common in the academic community), and bibliokleptomania (one hopes not so common) to name but some of those listed and not to consider the category of addiction at all. The absence of gambling from these lists can hardly be attributed to a shy or reticent psychiatry.

Excessive gambling is now construed as an addiction and the concept of addiction dominates psychological and psychiatric thinking about 'excess'. Addiction as a psychological concept began when looking at excessive intake of alcohol but in the late 19th and early 20th centuries it was extended to drug addiction (Berridge and Edwards, 1981). The central features of addiction were progression, lack of control, and the inability to abstain from the activity. Frequently added to these core features was the idea of unpleasant effects if the object of addiction was withdrawn. It is claimed that these concepts were in place for alcohol addiction as early as the 18th century but were extended to opium and some other substances in the late 19th century (Berridge and Edwards, 1981; Harding, 1988; Parssinen, 1983; Porter, 1985). All of these core concepts persist in present day views of addictions and are contained in the criteria for pathological gambling described earlier.

Despite these apparent continuities, there have been changes in how addiction is conceptualized. Levine (1978) describes the switch from Temperance thought, where it was alcohol itself that was addictive (so if *any* person take too much, beware), to later thinking, where the source of the addiction is in the individual. However, it is more difficult to maintain that 19th-century alienists viewed addiction as simply the inevitable end of taking too much of a substance. Instead they attributed part of the problem to some deficiency in the individual, particularly the will (see, for example, Clouston), and not just to the drug, so that characterizations of addiction were frequently described in a way that made them a heady mix of attributions implicating the deficient morality of the person, hereditary weakness, and/or some form of lesion to the nervous system.

Since the late 19th century there has been a specialist literature on drug addiction (for examples, see Adams, 1937; Armstrong-Jones, 1902; Clouston, 1890; Crothers, 1902; Kerr, 1894; Levinstein, 1878; Light, 1929; Nyswander, 1956; Sainsbury, 1909). Also from the 1880s on there were promptings for some form of provision for both alcoholics and drug addicts. In particular, the Society for the Study and Cure of Inebriety, founded in 1884, pushed hard for the recognition of both excessive inebriety and drug-taking as diseases, for legislation allowing hospitalization and for provision of specialist facilities such as retreats (this is not to say that the disease view was regarded as unproblematic either within the Society or more widely).

The dominant theory of addiction in the 1880s was that the symptoms of craving and of withdrawal had some underlying physical cause which resulted in a weakened will or in a greater susceptibility to the effects of the drug (either in terms of its effects in general or its effect upon some form of moral faculty). Treatment typically involved withdrawal of the drug and working on the willpower or moral fibre of the addict. Harding (1988) refers to this as the moral-pathological view of addiction. However, by the time the Rolleston Report was published in 1926 there had been a marked shift towards a view of addiction that retained the idea of an underlying physical cause, a disease state, but did not draw on the idea of a diseased will. Instead there was a shift to focusing on the effects of the drug on physical well being. The new conceptualization allowed treatments that sought to restore or maintain the physical health of the addict and, in practice, this led to recommendations that addicts could be given a maintenance dose of the drug if that did not impinge on their physical health.

Harding speculates on the conditions of possibility for these differing views of addiction. He maintains that the idea of addiction as a deficient or diseased will relied heavily on Quaker ideas of the will or moral faculty as a physical entity that could be damaged. The later more medical view demanded upon the emerging unity of the medical profession from the mid-19th century, upon how the concept of disease was interpreted and how the relationship between symptoms and diagnosis was conceived. Stemming from the work of Bernard in 1867, Harding argues that diseased and normal states came to be defined in the same terms—as physiological phenomena. Diseases led to physiological change, to a different state of the tissues. Adapting this view to addiction, the claim in the Rolleston Report was that the addict's physiology was altered and he or she simply needed the drug to maintain usual physiological functioning: without it there would be intense craving followed by much worse and potentially lethal consequences. Morality or vice was not such a key issue. Detecting this underlying physiological change required close observation of symptoms produced by a lack of the drug. Harding is not arguing that the moral dimension was no longer alive in medical attitudes to addiction—such a position would be untenable both then and now—but he is pointing to how it was possible both to conceive of addiction as a disease and for shifts to occur within this conception. Unfortunately, Harding's analysis ends in the mid-1930s, implying that there have been no further significant changes in the conceptualization of the disease model of addiction or the idea of addiction more generally. One of the claims I shall make later is that there *have* been such changes and ones which have made it easier for gambling to be accepted as addiction in the 1980s.

As writing on gambling began to increase within psychology, major perspectives such as behaviourism and cognitive psychology had an impact and they continue in writings about gambling as pathology as they do in writings about other addictions (for modern examples see Dickerson, 1979, 1984; Orford, 1985). Despite the impact of these other perspectives, up until the 1970s the amount of psychological or psychiatric research on gambling was small with only some of that smattering of research being dedicated to the study of pathology so that the literature on pathological gambling was little more than a trickle for much of the 20th century. The thin stream of writing on pathological gambling within academic journals and texts was not countered by a clamour in the press or other media for recognition of excessive gambling by individuals as a problem be it social or individual. Nor was there pressure from the legal profession for excessive gambling to be adopted by the psy professions. While the dangers of gambling, particularly excessive gambling, were continually emphasized by the National Anti-Gambling League (NAGL) and later the Churches' Council on Gambling (CCG) their writings reached a relatively small circle (though their importance in pushing the idea of gambling as pathology has been discussed by Dixon, 1980, 1991). Additionally, occasional moral panics on the topic of excessive gambling and articles on gambling as an addiction, often prompted by the CCG, did appear sporadically in newspapers (Dixon, 1980).

Governmental reviews have continued to lock horns with gambling; Select Committee Reports or Royal Commissions on gambling and betting occurred in 1901, 1902, 1908, 1918, 1923, 1933, 1951 and 1978. However, the discussion of gambling as an individual pathology was relatively limited within these. For example, Cornish's review for the 1978 commission devotes a chapter to 'Excessive Gambling' and reinforces the view of the 1951 commission that gambling is a danger only when immoderate. Despite the recognition that it is only in excess that gambling can be viewed as problematic, Cornish does not emphasize the idea of gambling as a pathology but focuses more on the bad effects of excess, and when discussing excessive gambling as a concern for future policy, his main emphasis is on the regulation of gambling opportunities and environments, not upon provision of support services or therapy. The focus was more on the actions of gamblers than on an identity.

The Pathological Gambler in the Late 20th Century: Governing Gambling through Pathology

The problem of the late emergence of the pathological gambler resists any simple, unitary factor account and instead requires consideration of a range of factors; none of these is sufficient on its own but when compared with factors operating in the 19th and early 20th centuries they make it clearer why the pathological gambler became established only in 1980. In their history of drug addiction, Parssinen and Kerner (1980) reflect on a similar problem: 'If medical men had been aware that opium produced patient dependence, tolerance and withdrawal as early as the eighteenth century, why was it not until the 1870s and 1880s that they began to consider opium addiction as a disease?' Their response is that the answer is 'multilayered' and they invoke five main ideas to explain the delay in the creation of the disease model: the emergence of a new technology (the hypodermic needle); the reaction to sanguine beliefs about morphia in the 1850s and 1860s; fears that the medical profession was losing control of therapy; the cheapness of opium as a 'cure'; wider changes in the role and status of the medical profession. My response to the delay in the emergence of gambling as pathology is similarly multilayered but it is more concerned with the conditions that allow gambling to be constructed as mental disorder.

I will offer some speculations on the following as critical in understanding what seems the late emergence of the pathological gambler: the decline in the moral and causal arguments against gambling as a social problem,

including the lack of statistics on its size and extent; the apparent liberalization of the laws on gambling and the increase in opportunities to gamble; the changes in technology around gambling; the increasing affluence
of the working class; changes in conceptions of addiction in psychiatry
and psychology; the emergence of self-help groups; some speculations on
the history of gambling and gamblers as domains of government.

The tone of debate surrounding gambling in the 1990s is substantially
different from that in the 1890s. As Dixon makes clear in his excellent
analysis of the interplay between the law and social pressure groups in
the history of gambling legislation, the 19th-century arguments against
gambling were largely moral and causal: gambling destroyed the moral
fibre and it led to considerable social problems (Dixon, 1991). The most
extreme view, such as that peddled by the NAGL in its early years, was that
gambling should be banned. However, the moral and causal arguments
for complete prohibition floundered and that case was lost well before the
1920s. Although arguments over the moral and social dangers of gambling
have not disappeared (for example, the vociferous objections from the
Methodist Church to the new national lottery), the continuation of widespread gambling through the 19th and 20th centuries with little apparent
moral or social cost has made it increasingly difficult to sustain the case
that gambling per se is a major evil.

The case against gambling has not been helped by the almost complete
lack of accurate statistics on gambling, not just in the 19th century but
right through into the late 20th century. Even in 1978 the Royal Commission on Gambling concluded that 'There is ... a serious lack of quantitative information about certain classes of gambling' (Royal Commission
on Gambling, 1978). Without such statistics the claims about the extent of
gambling and its dire consequences became seen as mere speculation and
often worse: speculation driven by some outmoded moral agenda rather
than careful, 'rational' gathering of evidence (Cornish, 1978; Dixon, 1991).
In line with previous commissions the Royal Commission of 1978 also
concluded that there was inadequate evidence on the extent of excessive
gambling by individuals. The absence of statistics taken together with laws
that made much gambling a rather secretive activity until the early 1960s
meant that problems resulting from gambling were simply not visible.

In the UK, the laws on gambling have become more liberal over the last
150 years and continue to do so with the very recent introduction of laws
allowing horse-race betting on Sundays. Those laws that placed very strict
restrictions on gambling had an unhappy history: not only did they not
prevent gambling from taking place but they were frequently 'defied and
ignored' because they were seen as transgressing some kind of 'right to

flutter' (Clapson, 1992: 209). The impractical nature of the gambling laws up to 1960, their conflict with notions of harmless leisure and their subsequent liberalization are evidence of the awkward relationship between gambling and the law. The story is one of shift from attempts at authoritarian prohibition in the late 19th and early 20th centuries through to administrative regulation of betting after the Second World War (Dixon, 1991). The Royal Commissions of 1949–50 and 1978 both recognized the shortcomings of prohibition and they both embraced the philosophy that legislation should interfere as little as possible with individual freedom to gamble whilst at the same time providing restrictions to discourage excess. In particular, the 1978 commission argued that legislative control was most necessary for 'those [forms of gambling] which are most likely to be addictive'. That is, there was an explicit construction of government of gambling as requiring attention to the psychology of the gambler. What the demise of the hard-line anti-gambling stance and the repeal of the prohibitive laws had provided was a *space* for the emergence of the pathological gambler.

As has already been noted, law enforcement agencies and much of the populace had a rather mixed view of gambling: it may have been illegal but the activity was perceived by many as a minor misdemeanour or more positively as a 'right'. The crimes of the excessive gambler—fraud and theft, for example—were not immediate products of the impulse to gamble unlike the acts of the pyromaniac or the kleptomaniac where the impulse itself was manifested in crimes. Similarly, other disorders such as moral insanity and partial insanity were described as leading directly to violent acts or thefts (Prichard, 1835; Smith, 1981). Where someone commits a crime to support their gambling, however, the gambling 'craving' itself is not so transparently related to the criminal act. Nikolas Rose (1986) has highlighted how the interplay between psychiatry and the law has been important in how a range of social problems have been constructed and governed. For gambling the deficiencies of the law as a means of controlling it and the distance between associated crimes and any underlying 'impulse disorder' were such that this productive interplay did not occur in the 19th and early 20th centuries.

Along with the liberalization of laws of gambling, there has been an increasing recognition of gambling as a legitimate form of leisure. There has also been an increase in the opportunities to gamble. For example, only in the last few years legislation has been passed in the UK that allows betting shops to open in the evenings and on Sundays, the national lottery has been reintroduced along with a national system of instant win scratchcards, new forms of betting, such as spread betting, have been given wider publicity and gamblers are increasingly bombarded with offers of credit and deposit account betting. In neo-liberalism not only is prohibition unacceptable but so is over-rigorous regulation: the market must hold sway. Gambling has now reached a point where it can be seen as a market and it has been analysed as such (Dowie, 1976; Gandar, Zuber and Rosso, 1993). As in most market systems there will be casualties and the concept of pathological gambling provides a particular way of regarding such casualties and brings with it the possibility of various actions that attempt to manage those casualties. In other words, the free play of the market and the constructions and techniques of the psy sciences together allow for gambling to be governed through means other than prohibition or regulation.

One aspect of the psy sciences is that they render visible what would otherwise be invisible, their expertise and practices allow them to scrutinize populations and individuals in a way that reveals problems that have gone unnoticed and untreated. This promise of discovery becomes all the more compelling when there is a case to be made that the problem is one surrounded by secrecy and surreptitious behaviour as was the case for gambling. Tests such as the South Oaks Gambling Screen (SOGS) could use the instrument to inspect the gambling behaviour of populations and, as with most psychological tests, do so in a way that immediately connects conduct and the psyche without the intervention of the body: one can inspect the questionnaire responses and say something of the person's psyche without ever seeing or touching them (Nikolas Rose, 1988). In line with the work of scholars such as Foucault and Hacking, such claims to expertise and the projects to which they lead can be seen not as discovery but as the psy sciences being an integral part of producing the object, of rendering something visible. In short, the psy sciences produce new ways of seeing gamblers.

As I have already argued, much of the conceptual apparatus necessary to construe gambling as a pathology was in place in the 19th century: there was a pervasive concern with the regulation and control of impulsive tendencies, there were models akin to addiction and impulse control, and there were apparently closely related syndromes in the baroque nosologies of psychiatry. Like addiction, a central concept in the concern over control of behaviour was inhibition. Ideas about inhibition and its role in behaviour gradually became incorporated into psychological and psychiatric writings through the 19th century and produced models couched in terms of both physiology and psychology (Smith, 1992). For the complex social, physiological and psychological models of concepts like addiction and inhibition, the case *par excellence* of addiction and the failure of inhibition was behaviour following consumption of alcohol. In this climate, the combination of an activity which visibly and dramatically led to loss of control and which involved the intake of a substance was almost an ideal. In the early 20th century, the emerging view of addiction as a physiological change was again well tailored to accounting for both excessive drinking and drug-taking. Gambling was not so ideal: no substance was taken and so physical change and physical dependence were less obviously involved and the excess and its effects were far less easily discerned. The first of these points is hardly a complete explanation of the absence of excessive gambling as a candidate for mental illness because many other recognized forms, such as kleptomania and pyromania, also lacked a substance.

In the 20th century, behavioural and social criteria have been increasingly used when making judgments about whether or not a behaviour represents an addiction (perhaps the best-known account of 'excess in behaviour' is Orford, 1985). However, the criteria are rarely simply couched in terms of amount or frequency of the addictive behaviour. The SOGS introduced earlier is a classic example of this where the respondent's answers to questions about the amount and frequency with which s/he gambles do *not* form part of the critical score. Instead the key questions on SOGS refer to things such as hiding one's gambling behaviour from others, borrowing money for gambling and not repaying it, losing time from work or school because of gambling, borrowing money to pay gambling debts, gambling more than you intended to do and so on (Lesieur and Blume, 1993). For this psychological inspection what matters more than the excess itself is the effect that that excess has in other spheres of the person's everyday life and the internal states associated with the activity. By making these the points of attention a huge range of behaviours can be constructed as coming within the scope of the psy professions; with such criteria one can be addicted to almost anything—from frozen peas to shopping, from the internet to lip balm. Instruments like SOGS allow one to gather information about individuals' gambling and to locate an individual in relation to the population: it is a technique for the 'disciplining of human difference' (Nikolas Rose, 1988).

In the 20th century, psychology and psychiatry have laid claim to a knowledge of treatments that promises the return to a well-regulated life through a well-regulated self. However, it can be too easy to ascribe therapies to professions and their expansion whilst neglecting the importance of groups such as Gamblers Anonymous (GA). Of course, the view of gambling addiction touted by GA is not and never was independent of previous ideas on addiction—it hardly could be, given GA's deliberate close modelling of AA's practices. Nevertheless, GA was a force that asserted the existence of pathological gambling, construed it in a particular way and thrust it in the face of the professions that claimed an expertise most obviously relevant to the problem: medicine and the psy sciences. In other words, by its very nature as a group, GA made visible the gambler and partly through the kinds of model of the gambler that it adopted made that figure amenable to inclusion in the psychiatry and psychology of the late 20th century. In Ian Hacking's terms, the member of GA is a labelled individual whose behaviour creates 'a reality ... [the] expert must face' and in this way individual gamblers are a force in the construction of their own gambling as pathology (Hacking, 1986).

The focus on the gambling of individuals means that extent becomes even more clearly a matter for the gambler to monitor: he or she must ask themselves: 'Do I gamble excessively?' and 'Am I in control of my gambling?' The moral pleadings of the anti-gamblers of the 19th century would have approved of such self-scrutiny. What has changed is the urgency behind the questions. Why must one curb one's gambling? Why must it be under control? The urgency no longer comes solely from the dangers of moral degeneracy or from the financial and social costs, it also comes from the threat to one's own psychological health. More and more of our activities are understood within psychological frameworks, so much so that psychology and psychiatry not only provide definitions and interventions for mental disturbance, they also offer us a way of seeing problems in ourselves, for ourselves. As Nikolas Rose argues, 'citizens of a liberal democracy are to govern themselves'; the psy sciences are now an important component of that self-government.[10]

So far the account that I have given is in line with the recent literature discussing the psychologization or psychiatrization of everyday problems, and in this sense gambling is simply one more site for the practice of psychiatry (Nikolas Rose, 1985). It is also consistent with the idea that the psy sciences are intimately bound up with new ways of seeing individuals and populations, ways that allow government to embrace new domains. In the story of the pathological gambler the psy sciences did not introduce the domain of gambling to government and became part of the government of gambling only late in the 20th century. However, it is worth pausing to consider whether or not the lateness of the pathological gambler was in fact due partly to gambling itself only becoming constructed as a fully fledged object of government rather late on. Despite the history of legislation in the 19th century, gambling may not have been governable in the strictest sense. For example, Nikolas Rose argues that for a domain to be governable 'one not only needs the terms in which to speak and think about it, one also needs to be able to assess its condition' (Nikolas Rose, 1988: 184). In the 19th century there was no problem with talking or thinking about gambling nor in gathering some kinds of information about it (see, for example, the witnesses to the Select Committees). What was missing, as I have already noted, were numbers, statistics, charts, graphs and other physical inscriptions of the gambling population. Until the late 20th century the means of assessing extent of gambling were not in place: its illegality made much of it hidden, the informal and secretive nature of many gambling forums made them extremely difficult to assess, there were the thorny issues of defining gambling, and, perhaps most importantly of all, there was the technical problem of distinguishing money new to the gambling market from money being recycled within the market. Most of these problems remained well into the 20th century (Cornish, 1978).

The continued liberalization of gambling laws has had the effect of making gambling more truly governable in the sense described by Rose. This was especially true of the 1960 legislation that made off-course betting legal and led to the opening of legalized betting offices. The records of betting offices, and of the bookmakers who run them, provide a detailed account of betting transactions from which statistics can be gathered on critical things such as number of bets and turnover. I cannot argue that gambling was not governed before 1960 but on a stricter reading of the term 'governable' one could contend that it was a domain always on the fringes of government, a form of conduct that could be talked of and acted upon but which was not easily transcribed into the material form of numbers. The difficulty of embracing gambling within government would be consistent with the delay in the construction of the pathological gambler.

We are left with no single answer as to why gambling was pathologized so late; instead a constellation of factors ranges from the place of gambling in society to the more familiar tale of the psychologization of everyday problems and a speculative claim about gambling's status as a domain for government. If there is to be a moral to the story, it is that the psychologization of a problem need not be viewed as the result of an avaricious and expanding discipline gathering to itself whatever it can, whenever it can; such a story would accord too much to the psy professions and too little to their own place in a wider context.

Notes

This [chapter] is a longer version of papers given to the History and Philosophy Section of the British Psychological Society, York, April 1994 and the History of the Human Sciences conference in Melbourne, September 1994. I would like to thank the Faculty of Social Sciences at Lancaster University for providing financial support for the work reported. I would also like to thank my colleagues at

Lancaster—Susan Condor, Gavin Kendall, Mike Michael, and Roger Smith—for comments on an earlier draft....

1. The UK reinstated a national lottery in 1994 after a break of 168 years, the closure of the previous lottery having related in part to claims of excessive gambling, particularly among the working classes; see below.

2. The rarity of something is not in itself worthy of historical scrutiny, such a programme would promise a scholarly exercise of infinite scope. However, when that absence is juxtaposed with conditions that render the rarity surprising and when set in a project that is concerned with the emergence of an idea, the questions of 'Why not earlier?' or 'Why not more widely?' become more sustainable. In what follows, remarks apply mainly to Britain though inevitably they draw on work from other European countries and the USA just as the psychiatries of the 19th and early 20th centuries were not independent.

3. The search included the terms 'pathological' and 'compulsive'. There is some dispute as to the most appropriate term for gambling behaviour judged to qualify as some form of psychiatric problem but for this [chapter] the term 'pathological gambler' is preferred because it is the most commonly used in contemporary research.

4. I plead guilty, in advance, of treating the 19th century in an undifferentiated way. Of course, such a treatment glosses over huge changes in the social, political, religious and scientific arenas as well as significant changes within psychiatry and psychology. However, the aims of this part of the [chapter] and the following section are simply to establish that gambling was prevalent in the 19th century, that it was constructed as a problem yet not as mental illness. With such simple aims, I hope that my playing fast and loose with the complexities of the 19th century can be tolerated.

5. Caution should be exercised here, however, in equating current constructions of these terms with those of the past. It is clear from descriptions of cases in sources such as Esquirol (he takes his examples from Marc) that pyromania often included burning things in fits of temper or disappointment, acts that would be unlikely to be considered sufficient indicators of pyromania in the late 20th century. However, the core feature of not retaining control over some impulse remains at the heart of both characterizations.

6. Of course, the claim here and throughout the [chapter] is not that people did not gamble to excess before the late 20th century, clearly some did, but that such gambling was not constructed as a form of insanity. In the same way other behaviours may have existed but a designation or class of person did not. For example, Halperin argues that homosexual acts occurred prior to the 19th century but that the homosexual as a person, a designation, did not (Halperin, 1990).

7. I would like to thank Ian Bishop for directing me to this reference.

8. The advantage of generalizations about absence, of course, is that they are so easily refuted by subsequent research.

9. It is notable, however, that gambling mania is listed in neither the admittedly partial English translation of the seventh edition of Kraepelin's *Clinical Psychiatry: a Textbook for Students and Physicians* nor in his *Lectures in Clinical Psychiatry* (Kraepelin, 1912) despite many instances of compulsive insanity being listed in both—such as 'grumbling mania' (Kraepelin, 1918: 408).

10. This is not saying that individuals who gamble 'excessively' always accept it as a problem or as a form of mental illness. However, gamblers *can* now see themselves in this way and, according to some therapeutic regimes, *must* see themselves in this way before change is possible.

References

Adams, E. W. (1937) *Drug Addiction*. London: Oxford University Press.

American Psychiatric Association (1980) *Diagnostic and Statistical Manual*, 3rd edn., Washington, DC: APA.

American Psychiatric Association (1987) *Diagnostic and Statistical Manual*, 3rd edn., revised. Washington, DC: APA.

Arieti, S. (1959) *American Handbook of Psychiatry*. New York: Basic Books.

Armstrong-Jones, R. (1902) 'Notes on Some Cases of Morphinomania', *Journal of Mental Science* 48: 478–95.

Ashton, J. (1898) *The History of Gambling in England*. London: Duckworth.

Bailey, P. (1987) *Leisure and Class in Victorian England: Rational Recreation and the Contest for Control, 1830–1885*, 2nd edn. London: RKP.

Bergler, E. (1936) 'Zur Psychologie des Hasardspielers', *Imago* 22: 409–41.

Bergler, E. (1958) *The Psychology of Gambling*. New York: International Universities Press.

Berridge, V. and Edwards, G. (1981) *Opium and the People*. London: Allen Lane.

Bleuler, E. (1924[1913]) *Textbook of Psychiatry*, trans. A. A. Brill. New York: Macmillan.

Blume, S. B. (1986) 'Treatment for the Addictions: Alcoholism, Drug Dependence and Compulsive Gambling in a Psychiatric Setting', *Journal of Substance Abuse Treatment* 3: 131–3.

Browne, B. R. (1993) 'The Selective Adaptation of the Alcoholics Anonymous Program by Gamblers Anonymous', in W. R. Eadington and J. A. Cornelius (eds) *Gambling Behavior and Problem Gambling*. Reno: Institute for the Study of Gambling and Commercial Gaming, University of Nevada.

Chesney, K. (1970) *The Victorian Underworld*. London: Maurice Temple Smith.

Chinn, C. (1991) *Better Betting with a Decent Feller: Bookmakers, Betting and the British Working Class, 1750–1990*. Hemel Hempstead, Herts: Harvester Wheatsheaf.

Clapson, M. (1992) *A Bit of a Flutter: Popular Gambling and English Society, 1823–1961*. Manchester: Manchester University Press.

Clouston, T. S. (1883) *Clinical Lectures on Mental Diseases*, 1st edn. London: Churchill.

Clouston, T. S. (1890) 'Diseased Cravings and Paralysed Control: Dipsomania, Morphinomania, Chloralism, Cocainism', *Edinburgh Medical Journal* 35: 508–21, 689–705, 793–809, 985–96.

Connolly, J. (1830) *An Inquiry Concerning the Indications of Insanity, with Suggestions for the Better Protection and Care of the Insane.* London: J. Taylor.

Cornish, D. B. (1978) *Gambling: A Review of the Literature and its Implications for Policy and Research.* Home Office Research Study no. 42. London: HMSO.

Cotton, C. (1674) *The Compleat Gamester.* London: R. Cutler. Reprinted in C. H. Hartmann (1930) *Games and Gamesters of the Restoration.* London: Routledge & Sons.

Crothers, T. D. (1902) *Morphinism and Narcomanias from Other Drugs. Their Etiology, Treatment and Medico-legal Relations.* London: W. B. Saunders.

Dickerson, M. (1979) 'FI Schedules and Persistence at Gambling in the UK Betting Office', *Journal of Behavioural Analysis* 12: 315–23.

Dickerson, M. (1984) *Compulsive Gamblers.* London: Longman.

Digby, A. (1985) *Madness, Morality and Medicine: A Study of the York Retreat, 1796–1914.* Cambridge: Cambridge University Press.

Dixon, D. (1980) 'The Discovery of the Compulsive Gambler', in Z. Bankowski and G. Mungham (eds) *Essays in Law and Society.* London: RKP.

Dixon, D. (1991) *From Prohibition to Regulation: Bookmaking, Anti-Gambling and the Law.* Oxford: Clarendon Press.

Dowie, J. A. (1976) 'On the Efficiency and Equity of Betting Markets', *Economica* 43: 139–50.

Duncan, J. F. (1853) *Popular Errors on the Subject of Insanity Examined and Exposed.* Dublin: McGlashan.

Eadington, W. and Cornelius, J. A., eds (1993) *Gambling Behavior and Problem Gambling.* Reno: Institute for the Study of Gaming and Commercial Gambling, University of Nevada.

Esquirol, J. E. D. (1845) *Mental Maladies: A Treatise on Insanity*, trans. E. K. Hunt from the French edn of 1817, with additions. Philadelphia, PA: Lee & Blanchard.

Fenichel, O. (1945) *The Psychoanalytic Theory of Neurosis.* New York: W. W. Norton.

Forrest, A., ed. (1977) *Companion to Psychiatric Studies*, 2 vols. London: Churchill Livingstone.

Foucault, M. (1979) 'On Governmentality', *I & C* 6: 5–22. Also in G. Burchell, C. Gordon and P. Miller, eds (1991) *The Foucault Effect: Studies in Governmentality.* Hemel Hampstead, Herts: Harvester Wheatsheaf.

Freud, S. (1961[1928]) 'Dosteovsky and Parricide', in *The Standard Edition of the Complete Psychological Works of Sigmund Freud*, ed. and trans. J. H. Strachey, Vol. XXI. London: Hogarth Press, pp. 175–96.

Galski, T. (1987) *The Handbook of Pathological Gambling.* Springfield, IL: Charles C. Thomas.

Gandar, J. M., Zuber, R. A. and Rosso, B. (1993) 'Testing Efficiency in Gambling Markets: a Comment', *Applied Economics* 25(7): 937–43.

Gilman, S. L. (1982) *Seeing the Insane.* New York: Wiley.

Greenwood, J. (1869) *The Seven Curses of London.* London: Stanley Rivers.

Hacking, I. (1986) 'Making up People', in P. Heller et al. (eds) *Reconstructing Individualism*. Stanford, CA: Stanford University Press, pp. 222–36.

Halgin, R. P. and Whitbourne, S. K. (1993) *Abnormal Psychology: The Human Experience of Psychological Disorders*. New York: Harcourt Brace.

Halperin, D. M. (1990) *One Hundred Years of Homosexuality*. London: Routledge.

Harding, G. (1988) *Opiate Addiction, Morality and Medicine*. New York: St. Martin's Press.

Kaplan, H. I. and Sadock, B. J. (1989) *Comprehensive Textbook of Psychiatry*, 5th edn. Baltimore, MD: Williams & Wilkins.

Kerr, N. (1894) *Inebriety or Narcomania*. London: H. K. Lewis.

Kolb, L. C. (1973) *Modern Clinical Psychiatry*, 8th edn. Philadelphia, PA: W. B. Saunders.

Kraepelin, E. (1912) *Lectures on Clinical Psychiatry*. London: Balliere, Tindall & Cox.

Kraepelin, E. (1918[1907]) *Clinical Psychiatry: A Textbook for Students and Physicians*, trans. A. Ross Diefendorf from the 7th German edn. London: Macmillan.

Lesieur, H. R. (1984) *The Chase: Career of the Compulsive Gambler*. Cambridge, MA: Schenkman Books.

Lesieur, H. R. (1990) 'Working with and Understanding Gamblers Anonymous', in T. J. Powell (ed.) *Working with Self-Help*. Silver Spring, MD: NASW Press.

Lesieur, H. R. and Blume, S. B. (1987) 'The South Oaks Gambling Screen (the SOGS): a New Instrument for the Identification of Pathological Gamblers', *American Journal of Psychiatry* 144: 1184–8.

Lesieur, H. R. and Blume, S. B. (1993) 'Revising the South Oaks Gambling Screen in Different Settings', *Journal of Gambling Studies* 9(3): 213–23.

Lesieur, H. R. and Rosenthal, R. J. (1991) 'Pathological Gambling: a Review of the Literature' (prepared for the American Psychiatric Association taskforce on DSM-IV Committee on Disorders of Impulse Control Not Elsewhere Classified), *Journal of Gambling Studies* 7: 5–39.

Levine, H. (1978) 'The Discovery of Addiction: Changing Conceptions of Habitual Drunkenness in America', *Journal of Studies on Alcohol* 39: 143–76.

Levinstein, E. (1878) *Morbid Craving for Morphia*. London: Smith, Elder.

Light, A. B. et al. (1929) *Opium Addiction*. Chicago, IL: American Medical Association.

Lucas, T. (1714) *Memoirs of the Lives, Intrigues, and Comical Adventures of the Most Famous Gamesters and Celebrated Sharpers in the Reigns of Charles II, James II, William II and Queen Anne*. London: Jonas Brown. Reprinted in C.H. Hartmann (1930) *Games and Gamester of the Restoration*. London: Routledge & Sons.

McGurrin, M. C. (1992) *Pathological Gambling: Conceptual, Diagnostic, and Treatment Issues*. Sarasota, FL: Professional Resource Exchange Inc.

McKibbin, R. (1979) 'Working-class Gambling in Britain, 1880–1939', *Past and Present* 82: 147–78.

Maudsley, H. (1868) *The Physiology and Pathology of Mind*, 2nd edn. London: Macmillan.

Moody, G. (1990) *Quit Compulsive Gambling: The Action Plan for Gamblers and Their Families*. London: Thorson.

Moran, E. (1970) 'Gambling as a Form of Dependence', *British Journal of Addiction* 64: 419–28.

Moseley, W. W. (1838) *Eleven Chapters on Nervous or Mental Complaints, and on Two Great Discoveries, by which Hundreds have been, and All may be Cured.* London: Simpkin, Marshall.

Murray, J. (1992) 'Review of Research on Pathological Gambling', *Psychological Reports* 72: 791–810.

Neville, W. B. (1836) *On Insanity: It's Nature, Causes and Cures.* London: Longman, Rees, Orme, Brown, Green & Longman.

Nyswander, M. E. (1956) *The Drug Addict as Patient.* London: Grune & Stratton.

Orford, J. (1985) *Excessive Appetites: A Psychological View of Addictions.* London: Wiley.

Parssinen, T. M. (1983) *Secret Passions, Secret Remedies: Narcotic Drugs in British Society, 1820–1930.* Philadelphia, PA: Institute for the Study of Human Issues.

Parssinen, T. M. and Kerner, K. (1980) 'Development of the Disease Model of Drug Addiction in Britain, 1870–1926', *Medical History* 24: 275–96.

Perkins, Rev. E. B. (1950 [1919]) *The Problem of Gambling.* London: Epworth Press.

Pinel, P. (1806) *A Treatise on Insanity*, trans. D. D. Davis from the French edn of 1801. Sheffield: Cadell & Davies.

Popkin, M. K. (1989) 'Impulse Control Disorders Not Elsewhere Classified', in H. I. Kaplan and B. J. Sadock (eds) *Comprehensive Textbook of Psychiatry*, 5th edn. London: Williams & Wilkins.

Porter, R. (1985) 'The Drinking Man's Disease: the Prehistory of Alcoholism in Georgian Britain', *British Journal of Addiction* 80: 385–96.

Prichard, J. C. (1835) *A Treatise on Insanity and Other Disorders Affecting the Mind.* London: Sherwood, Gilbert & Piper.

Reader, W. J. (1964) *Life in Victorian England.* London: Batsford.

Rose, I. Nelson (1988) 'Compulsive Gambling and the Law: From Sin to Vice to Disease', *Journal of Gambling Behavior* 4: 240–60.

Rose, Nikolas (1985) *The Psychological Complex: Psychology, Politics and Society in England, 1869–1939.* London: Routledge.

Rose, Nikolas (1986) 'Psychiatry: The Discipline of Mental Health', in P. Miller and N. Rose (eds) *The Power of Psychiatry.* Cambridge: Polity.

Rose, Nikolas (1988) 'Calculable Minds and Manageable Individuals', *History of the Human Sciences* 1(2): 179–200.

Rose, Nikolas (1989) *Governing the Soul: The Shaping of the Private Self.* London: Routledge.

Rosecrance, J. (1985) 'Compulsive Gambling and the Medicalization of Deviance', *Social Problems* 32(3): 275–84.

Rosenthal, R. (1985) 'The Pathological Gambler's System for Self-Deception', in W. R. Eadington (ed.) *The Gambling Papers: Proceedings of the Sixth National Conference on Gambling and Risk-taking.* Reno: University of Nevada.

Rosenthal, R. (1987) 'The Psychodynamics of Pathological Gambling: a Review of the Literature', in T. Galski (ed.) *Handbook of Pathological Gambling.* Springfield, IL: C. C. Thomas.

Sainsbury, H. (1909) *Drugs and the Drug Habit.* London: Methuen.

Scull, A. (1993) *The Most Solitary of Afflictions: Madness and Society in Britain, 1700–1900*. New Haven, CT: Yale University Press.

Seguin, E. (1870) *New Facts and Remarks Concerning Idiocy*. New York: W. M. Wood.

Simmel, E. (1920) 'Psychoanalysis of the Gambler', *International Journal of Psychoanalysis* 1: 352–3.

Slater, E. and Roth, M. (1969) *Clinical Psychiatry*, 3rd edn. London: Balliere, Tindall & Cassell.

Smith, R. (1981) *Trial by Medicine: Insanity and Responsibility in Victorian Trials*. Edinburgh: Edinburgh University Press.

Smith, R. (1992) *Inhibition: History and Meaning in the Sciences of Mind and Brain*. London: Free Association Books.

Stone, E. M. (1988) *American Psychiatric Glossary*, 6th edn. Washington, DC: American Psychiatric Press.

Storch, R. D. (1977) 'The Problem of Working-class Leisure. Some Roots of Middle-class Moral Reform in the Industrial North: 1825–1850', in A.P. Donajgrodski (ed.) *Social Control in Nineteenth-Century Britain*. London: Croom Helm.

Thomas, K. (1971) *Religion and the Decline of Magic*. London: Weidenfeld & Nicolson.

von Hattingberg, H. (1914) 'Analerotik, Angstlust und Eigensinn', *Int Zür Psychoanalysis* 2:244–58.

Walton, H. (1985) *Dictionary of Psychiatry*. Oxford: Blackwell.

Walton, J. K. (1979) 'Lunacy in the Industrial Revolution: a Study of Asylum Admissions in Lancashire, 1848–1850', *Journal of Social History* 13: 1–22.

World Health Organisation (1992) *The ICD-10 Classification of Mental and Behavioural Disorders: Clinical Descriptions and Diagnostic Guidelines*. Geneva: WHO.

19th-Century Texts Consulted

Allen, M. (1837) *Essay on the Classification of the Insane*. London: J. Taylor.

Blandford, G.F. (1892) *Insanity and its Treatment: Lectures on the Treatment, Medical and Legal, of Insane Patients*, 4th edn. London: Simpkin, Marshall, Hamilton, Kent.

Bucknill, J.C. and Tuke, D.H. (1879) *A Manual of Psychological Medicine, Containing the Lunacy Laws: the Nosology, Aetiology, Statistics, Description, Diagnosis Pathology, and Treatment of Insanity, with an Appendix of Cases*, 4th edn. London: J. & A. Churchill.

Burrows, G.M. (1828) *Commentaries on the Causes, Forms, Symptoms, and Treatment, Moral and Medical, of Insanity*. London: T. & G. Underwood.

Clouston, T.S. (1883) *Clinical Lectures on Mental Diseases*, 1st edn. London: Churchill.

Clouston, T.S. (1887) *Clinical Lectures on Mental Diseases*, 2nd edn. London: Churchill.

Clouston, T.S. (1890) 'Diseased Cravings and Paralysed Control: Dipsomania, Morphinomania, Chloralism, Cocainism', *Edinburgh Medical Journal* 35:508–21, 689–705, 793–809, 985–96.

Conolly, J. (1830) *An Inquiry Concerning the Indications of Insanity, with Suggestions for the Better Protection and Care of the Insane*. London: J. Taylor.

Duncan, J.F. (1853) *Popular Errors on the Subject of Insanity Examined and Exposed*. Dublin: McGlashan.

Esquirol, J.E.D. (1845) *Mental Maladies: A Treatise on Insanity*, trans. E.K. Hunt, from the French edn. of 1817, with additions. Philadelphia, PA: Lee & Blanchard.

Knight, P.S. (1827) *Observations on the Causes, Symptoms and Treatment of Derangement of the Mind*. London: Longman, Rees, Orme, Brown & Green.

Maudsley, H. (1868) *The Physiology and Pathology of Mind*, 2nd edn. London: Macmillan.

Maudsley, H. (1895) *The Pathology of Mind*, 2nd edn. London: Macmillan.

Morison, A. (1826) *Outlines of Lectures on Mental Diseases*, 2nd edn. London: Longman, Rees, Orme, Brown & Green.

Moseley, W.W. (1838) *Eleven Chapters on Nervous or Mental Complaints, and on Two Great Discoveries, by which Hundreds have been, and All may be Cured*. London: Simpkin, Marshall.

Neville, W.B. (1836) *On Insanity: Its Nature, Causes and Cure*. London: Longman, Rees, Orme, Brown, Green & Longman.

Pinel, P. (1806) *A Treatise on Insanity*. trans. D.D. Davis from the French edn. of 1801. Sheffield: Cadell & Davies.

Prichard, J.C. (1835) *A Treatise on Insanity and Other Disorders Affecting the Mind*. London: Sherwood, Gilbert & Piper.

Prichard, J.C. (1842) *On the Different Forms of Insanity in Relation to Jurisprudence*. London: Balliere.

Tuke, D.H., ed. (1892) *Dictionary of Psychological Medicine*. London: J. & A. Churchill.

Upham, T.C. (1840) *Outlines of Imperfect and Disordered Mental Action*. New York: Harper.

Uwins, D. (1833) *A Treatise on those Disorders of the Brain and Nervous System Which Are Usually Considered and Called Mental*. London: Renshaw & Rush.

20th-Century Texts Consulted

Arieti, S. (1959) *American Handbook of Psychiatry*. New York: Basic Books.

Berg, C. (1948) *Clinical Psychology: A Case Book of the Neuroses and their Treatment*. London: Allen & Unwin.

Binger, C. (1951) *More about Psychiatry*. London: Allen & Unwin.

Bleuler, E. (1924[1913]) *Textbook of Psychiatry*, trans. A.A. Brill. New York: Macmillan.

Braude, M. (1937) *The Principles and Practice of Clinical Psychiatry*. Philadelphia, PA: P. Blakiston's Son.

Cobb, S. (1943) *Borderlands of Psychiatry*. Cambridge, MA: Harvard University Press.

Cole, R.H. (1913) *Mental Diseases: A Text-Book of Psychiatry for Medical Students and Practitioners*. London: University of London Press.

Conklin, E.S. (1935) *Principles of Abnormal Psychology*. London: Allen & Unwin.

Coriat, I.H. (1910) *Abnormal Psychology*. London: William Rider.

Davis, D.R. (1957) *An Introduction to Psychopathology*. London: Oxford University Press.

Dayton, N.A. (1940) *New Facts on Mental Disorders: Study of 89,190 Cases*. Springfield, IL/Baltimore, MD: Charles C. Thomas.

Dicks, H.V. (1939) *Clinical Studies in Psychopathology: A Contribution to the Aetiology of Neurotic Illness*. London: Edward Arnold.

Elkes, A. and Thorpe, J.G. (1967) *A Summary of Psychiatry*. London: Faber.

Ewen, J.H. (1933) *A Handbook of Psychiatry*. London: Balliere, Tindall & Cox.

Ewen, J.H. (1947) *Mental Health: A Practical Guide to Disorders of the Mind*. London: E. Arnold.

Fenichel, O. (1945) *The Psychoanalytic Theory of Neurosis*. New York: W.W. Norton.

Fisher, V.E. (1937) *An Introduction to Abnormal Psychology*. New York: Macmillan.

Forrest, A., ed. (1977) *Companion to Psychiatric Studies*, 2 vols. London: Churchill Linvingstone.

Henderson, D. and Gillespie, R.D. (1956) *A Textbook of Psychiatry for Students and Practitioners*, 8th edn. London: Oxford University Press.

Jaspers, K. (1963[1946]) *General Psychology*, 7th edn. Manchester: Manchester University Press.

Kolb, L.C. (1973) *Modern Clinical Psychiatry*, 8th edn. Philadelphia, PA: W.B. Saunders

Kraepelin, E. (1912) *Lectures on Clinical Psychiatry*, London: Balliere, Tindall & Cox.

Kraepelin, E. (1918 [1907]) *Clinical Psychiatry: A Textbook for Students and Physicians*, trans. A. Ross Diefendorf from the 7th German edn. London: Macmillan.

Lydston, G. F. (1904) *The Diseases of Society: The Vice and Crime Problem*, London: J.B. Lippincott.

Slater, E. and Roth, M. (1969) *Clinical Psychiatry*, 3rd edn. London: Balliere, Tindall & Cassell.

Stoddart, W.H.B. (1912) *Mind and its Disorders: A Textbook for Students and Practitioners*, London: H.K. Lewis.

CHAPTER 18

Busted Flush

South Carolina's Video-Poker Operators
Run a Political Machine

DAVID PLOTZ

"If you're not playing at Treasures, you're taking a chance," warns the billboard towering above Broad River Road on the outskirts of Columbia, South Carolina. I don't like to take chances, so I pull into the parking lot, beneath Treasures' glowing, glowering pirate sign, and find a space next to a black Mustang, license plate: HNG OVR.

Treasures is suburban-strip architecture as funhouse. The building, a low slung, cheap-looking structure the size of a tennis court, is covered with mirrors from rooftop to asphalt. The walls are mirrors, the roof is mirrors, the doors are mirrored glass. It's as though the building is trying to pretend it doesn't exist. I enter through the mirrored doors and find myself in a fifteen-year-old boy's dream room: floor-to-ceiling mirrors, a carpet the color of dried blood, black lights, a choking fog of cigarette smoke, a plastic bowl filled with Tootsie Rolls, and all the gambling one's heart desires.

In any other spot on the planet Treasures would be called a casino, but because Treasures is in South Carolina, and because South Carolina likes to make believe it doesn't have legal gambling, Treasures goes by a cheerful euphemism: "video mall," or, if you prefer, "video parlor." Whatever you want to call it, it's a warren. I wander through a dozen "game rooms" sardined back-to-back off a central corridor. Each is a dark narrow cleft the size of a large closet, with just enough space for five stools, the five people perched on those stools, and the five machines those five people are glued to. The machines are "Pot-O-Golds," and they are video-gambling devices. South Carolina, naturally, prefers the euphemism "video games." The game rooms hold about sixty video-poker machines among them, even though South Carolina law states with blinding clarity that no business can have more than five machines. This is possible because Treasures is not one business but many: technically—and only technically—each closet is its own independent enterprise.

It's past eleven P.M. on a Thursday evening. Even so, every machine is occupied. About half the gamblers are elderly white women, about a third are young black women, and there's a smattering of young redneck men. The manufactured good cheer of Las Vegas is absent here. The gamblers gaze transfixed at their terminals and tap the touchscreens with a kind of Stepford intensity. An eerie silence envelops the place: the only noises are the bells ringing on the Pot-O-Golds, signaling gamblers that someone else just won a few bucks, so you will too. I settle into the only empty stool I can find and watch the woman next to me. She is chainsmoking Vantages with her left hand and jabbing the screen rapidly with her right. She's playing Shamrock Sevens, a poker game that rewards a hand of three sevens with a din of electronic Irish music, a digital leprechaun who announces, "Aye, a pot o' gold for ye!" and a mingy bonus. She occasionally interrupts poking and puffing long enough to gulp down handfuls of Tootsie Rolls and Styrofoam cups of water. These are the only food and drink Treasures offers, unless you count breath mints as food. I intrude on her during one of these refueling breaks. Her name is Joyce, she tells me, and she's a grandmother in her fifties. She has been playing Shamrock Sevens on this Pot-O-Gold since four P.M., she thinks. Joyce is betting twenty-five cents a hand, six hands a minute, 360 hands an hour. If she is at the odds,[1] she has lost sixty dollars in her seven and a half hours of wagering.

Treasures is one of more than 7,000 places to gamble in South Carolina, which means that the Palmetto State—which you probably didn't even know had legal gambling—has more places to wager than any state, and about three times as many as Nevada. South Carolina has 36,000 gambling machines, more than any state but Nevada, New Jersey, and Mississippi—and nearly one device for every hundred residents. South Carolina offers gambling without rules: the state collects no taxes, imposes virtually no regulations, does not restrict who can own machines, does not require that the machines be honest, does not forbid children from playing them.

South Carolina's video-poker millionaires call this "convenience gaming." (And indeed it must be convenient to gross $2.5 billion annually, net $728 million, pay no taxes, and have your profits climb 20 percent a year.) Gambling experts, on the other hand, call it the worst gambling industry in America, economically useless and socially devastating.

How South Carolina wound up in this mess is a cautionary tale about money and politics, but it's not one of the money-and-politics stories you've heard a thousand times before. It is not a story about how big businesses bent politicians to their will, or a story about how some megacorporation invaded South Carolina and corrupted it, or a story of how an industry lobbied and bribed politicians to lower burdensome taxes and abolish burdensome regulations. No, video poker's conquest of South Carolina is a tale of the sinister power of *small* business. It is a tale of how, in almost no time at all, a bunch of gas-station owners, jukebox operators, and barkeeps used lawsuits, strong-arm lobbying, dead-of-night legislation, and just plain deception to transform a small-time illegal gambling business into a multi-billion-dollar legal one; how these folks fought to *increase* regulation and taxation; and how, in the process of all this, they resurrected the state Democratic Party, battered the state legislature, wiggled out of campaign-finance restrictions, made common cause with white supremacists, and, in a remarkable and demoralizing 1998 election, deposed one government and bought themselves a new one. And this, in the grandest euphemism of all, they call just politics.

Video poker is South Carolina's white noise, so pervasive that you stop noticing its ugliness. The first building outside the Columbia airport is a dingy warehouse, dressed up with eight video-poker machines, a fresh carpet, and a sign reading AIRPORT GAMES. Video-poker casinos form a stockade around the state. At the northeast tip the ramshackle fishing village of Little River now has sixteen video-poker casinos and a new nickname, "Little Reno." At the southern tip, the State Line Casino guards the Savannah River crossing from Georgia. (It was here, in the summer of 1997, that Army Sgt. Gail Baker left her ten-day-old baby, Joy, in the car while she went inside to play a few hands. When she exited the casino seven and a half hours later, Joy was dead of dehydration.) In the north the first exit off I-77, even before the state welcome center, delivers you to a strip of shabby double-wides and stucco prefabs, halfheartedly decorated with bunting and hopeful names: Golden Touch, Treasure Chest, Lady Luck, Slots of Fun (CHECK CASHING, CASH ADVANCES, CAR TITLE LOANS, says the sign above the door). Each one is a maze of snaking corridors, sardine closets, and countless Pot-O-Golds.[2]

Some 339 cities and towns in South Carolina now have video-poker machines. Columbia, a city of barely 100,000, has 483 places to gamble and more than 2,000 machines. "There is not a place in South Carolina where there could be a machine and there isn't one," says Glenn Stanton, who runs the anti-gambling Palmetto Family Council. Vegas has The Strip. South Carolina has the gambling strip mall: Babylon in the shopping center. Almost any business with a steady flow of customers has a machine or two or five in the corner and a red neon GAMES sign in the window. L'il Cricket, a convenience-store chain, is among the state's biggest gambling companies. So is R.L. Jordan Oil, which owns gas stations. An astonishing one-quarter of South Carolina's retail businesses offer video poker. Sometimes it feels as if all of them do.

As an experiment, I try driving west out of Columbia on a rural road and stopping at every business I pass. The Locker Room, a down-at-the-heels pool club, has two machines at the back. The Hot Spot, the convenience store next door, owns five machines, a bettor parked at every one. Half a mile up the road at Kelly's, you can buy pickled pigs' lips, then drop a few bucks in the five poker machines along the sidewall. Judy's advertises BEER, POOL, GAMES. Club 76 Game Room is a cinderblock shack: its windows are boarded up, but it's open for gambling. At long last, I pass a building where I can't play video poker: The Prayer Bible Study Church.

How South Carolina got this way—a Pot-O-Gold on every corner, a gambler in every home—is a tale that best begins in a handsome office in downtown Columbia with a man known as "Lucifer." His real name is Dick Harpootlian, and he loves his nickname. He loves that the minions of David Beasley—that is, former Republican governor David Beasley, the man whom Harpootlian destroyed in 1998—coined the moniker. "Beasley is an opportunistic, insincere scalawag. An Elmer Gantry," says Harpootlian. "I think his Christianity is his business, but you know it would be very like them to somehow depict an enemy as being sponsored by or somehow inspired by the devil. As a practical matter, my ancestors were worshiping Christ while his people were scraping bark off a tree and worshiping it, okay? So why do they call me Satan or Lucifer? Because it's convenient for them to think of me as being sponsored by the forces of darkness, I suppose. That's how they have to convince themselves that they lost—rather than accepting the fact that they're full of shit and the people finally figured them out!"

Harpootlian unleashes this torrent with undisguised joy. Fiftyish and boyish, he has the air of the Greatest Frat Brother Ever: smarter than you, wittier than you, louder than you, and as much fun as a barrel of monkeys. In the first few minutes of our talk, he fields calls from a lobbyist, a lawyer, and an old friend. All are supplicants. The lobbyist wants to know what happened at an important conference in the statehouse. Can Dick tell him? Hell, yes. The lawyer wants Dick's client to behave himself. Can Dick make it happen? Hell, yes. The old friend wants the new governor to appoint him to a commission. Can Dick arrange a meeting? Hell, yes. When he finally gets off the phone he reaches into his desk, grabs a hazelnut, tosses it to me, and swings into a story about a lawsuit that has something to do with a hazelnut orchard contaminated by runoff from a latex factory. "But these nuts are good! Crack that nut open. You'll be amazed!" he shouts. He grabs the nut, smashes a book on it, brushes away the shattered shell, and reveals a bright pink condom. He laughs uproariously, then pockets the condom.

Harpootlian has the irrepressible glee of a man who has gotten exactly what he wants. He is the epicenter of South Carolina, the intersection of money and politics, of gambling and the Democratic Party. As the leading lawyer for the video-poker industry, Harpootlian has done more than anyone to make gambling prosperous, legal, and mighty. As the chairman of the state Democratic Party, he has revived an institution long ago left for dead. In 1998, when both video poker and the party seemed to face extinction, Harpootlian married his vocation and his avocation. He harvested the profits of video poker to save his party and harnessed the power of his party to save his industry.

At rock bottom, South Carolina has a gambling mess because it can't decide if it's a puritanical state or a libertarian one. The interior of the state is severe, religious, and conservative, but coastal Carolina is high-spirited and honky-tonk. The state beverage is milk, but the state university mascot is a gamecock. State law frowns on gambling, but law enforcement has long tolerated illegal wagering on cockfights, dogfights, and golf. In the late 1980s and early 1990s, when states and tribes staked their prosperity on lotteries and casinos, puritanical South Carolina resisted. It abjured a lottery and rejected Vegas mogul Steve Wynn's 1994 proposal to build six dockside casinos. Meanwhile, libertarian South Carolina embraced video poker, a form of wagering that seemed innocent, mild-mannered, and hardly to be gambling at all.

Video poker arrived in South Carolina as a fluke, a spin-off of the jukebox-and-pinball business. The father of the industry is Fred Collins, who bought his first pinball machine fifty years ago, when he was thirteen, and then built a "route" operation for distributing jukeboxes, pinball machines, pool tables, and video games to arcades and stores throughout the state. Collins brought the first video-poker game to South Carolina in the early 1970s—a "kit" that he added to the video game Pong. When stand-alone video-poker games were perfected a decade later, Collins and other route operators began installing terminals all over the state, splitting profits with restaurants, shops, and bars.

Here it's worth noting two critical oddities of South Carolina's gambling industry: it is rinky-dink and it is homegrown. Elsewhere in the United States, megacorporations such as Harrah's, Mirage, and IGT monopolize casinos, machine distribution, and lotteries. In South Carolina, there are more than 400 video-poker companies, all are local, and most came to gambling by chance. The names of the state's biggest video-poker companies—Darlington Music, Tim's Amusement, McDonald Amusement, Rosemary Coin Machines, Harrison & King Music—betray their origins as jukebox route operations and arcades. (Many still like to pretend they're in their old business: Collins, who owns 4,000 video-poker machines—more than anyone—and grossed $90 million off of them last year, insists, "I am in the amusement business, not the gambling business.") Most video-poker operators are small-timers with just a handful of employees, local companies knitted into the fabric of South Carolina.

Video poker began as an afterthought, but as profits surged through the 1980s, operators longed for legitimacy. South Carolina law forbade games of chance, so at first the operators relied on linguistic chicanery: Poker, they said, equals pinball. Play pinball well enough and you win a free game. Same thing in video poker. Suppose it costs twenty-five cents to play a game of pinball or poker. Well, then each skillfully won free game must be worth twenty-five cents. And if each game is worth twenty-five cents, surely you ought to be able to collect a quarter for it. And if you can collect a quarter for one free game, surely you should be able to collect 4,000 quarters for drawing a royal flush.

This pinball wizardry was not quite enough to make poker legal, so the industry turned to a more traditional political tactic: backdoor legislation. In 1986, State Senator Jack Lindsay silently dropped a tiny technical amendment into a distant corner of a 1,000-page budget bill that struck the words "or property" from a law banning any game from distributing "money or property to a player." Lindsay did this at the behest of Alan Schafer, owner of the massive roadside attraction South of the Border. At the time, no one except Schafer and Lindsay seemed to notice this picayune change or understand its significance. But in 1988, the state arrested a convenience store owner and charged him with illegally paying out hundreds of thousands of dollars to video-poker customers. Harpootlian, once a county prosecutor, was hired for the defense, thus beginning his brilliant service to the industry. By striking "or property," Harpootlian argued, the legislature clearly permitted machines to distribute credit slips, which could, in turn, be redeemed for cash. In 1991, the state supreme court agreed. Without a debate, without an open vote, without a public referendum, South Carolina had legalized gambling.

The supreme court decision opened the way for poker's expansion, but it also galvanized poker opponents. Many of the anti-poker activists were conservative Christian Republicans, but perhaps the most fervent was a Democratic state legislator named Jim Hodges. Hodges, serious-minded and liberal, had grown alarmed at poker's explosion in his district and viewed the machines as a scourge on the poor and vulnerable. He lobbied feverishly to ban poker "payouts" (as the credit slips are called), and in 1991 and 1992 the legislature came up just short. When Hodges and his allies went after payouts again, the industry conceded to a county-by-county referendum, and in 1994 twelve counties voted to abolish them. Although the poker industry had agreed to the referendum, it immediately sabotaged it. Operators in those twelve counties hired Harpootlian, who persuaded a court to overturn the ban on the grounds that it violated the state constitution by applying criminal law inconsistently.

In that same 1994 election, South Carolina narrowly elected Republican David Beasley as its new governor. Then a thirty-seven-year-old state legislator, Beasley had abandoned the Democratic Party and shaken a playboy reputation by becoming a born-again Christian. (He had squired around Donna Rice during his days as a ladies man.) Blow-dried to Ken-doll perfection and oozing ambition, Beasley was elected chairman of the Republican Governors Association and was discussed as a potential vice-presidential candidate for 2000.

Beasley opposed video poker, but he chose a curious way to fight it: he ignored it, believing that if poker were taxed and regulated, the state would get hooked on the gambling revenues. "We felt it was immoral to enter a profit-sharing plan with an industry whose lifeblood was the peril of the unwitting," says former Beasley adviser Larry Huff. Beasley chose anarchy instead, and the industry mushroomed. "We had a governor who would not admit he had a gambling industry," Harpootlian says. "David Beasley was a narcoleptic when it came to gambling."

It's true that Beasley didn't do much to control video poker, but it's equally true that Harpootlian & Co. squelched what few efforts Beasley and others did make. In 1996, when Beasley and the state legislature attempted to reinstate the twelve-county ban by imposing only *civil* penalties, Harpootlian persuaded a judge to stay the new law. When a class-action lawsuit on behalf of compulsive gamblers tried to end video gambling on the grounds that it was a lottery, Harpootlian convinced the supreme court that video poker was not a lottery because it does not "involve a drawing."

A year before Beasley took office, the legislature had managed to pass a few anti-poker laws, regulations limiting one location to eight machines (later five), capping winnings at $125 per day, forbidding most advertising, and banning inducements. The industry spent the Beasley administration ignoring some of these regulations and mangling the rest beyond recognition. Consider the $125 cap, designed to ensure that video poker is played for low stakes. Every machine advertises its jackpot: The smallest I saw was $251.04. The largest was more than $7,000. In 1998 lawyers in a class-action suit against the industry sent a private investigator with a camera hidden in his watch to photograph thousands of poker machines; none of them had a jackpot of less than $125. Operators circumvent the law by long division: if someone hits a $500 jackpot, the machine prints out four $125 slips that players must cash on four different days. "The industry said it would just be low-stakes gambling—$125," says Richard Gergel, the lawsuit's lead attorney. "But these people were criminals. They never obeyed the law. They decided they were going to engage in high-stakes illegal gambling until someone stopped them, and no one did."

When Beasley tried to impose a statewide computer-monitoring program that could automatically prevent payouts of more than $125, Harpootlian went to court and delayed it. As for the advertising ban, you can't drive down a highway in South Carolina without seeing a billboard directing you to VIDEO GAMES. The legislature forbade inducements, but operators ply gamblers with free food, free booze, free massages, free taxi rides, even free film development.

During Beasley's term, the industry also managed to weasel out of the five-machine limit that legislators had imposed to prevent casinos. A video-poker entrepreneur named Mickey Stacks noticed that the law simply restricted operators to five machines on one "premises." According to the State Department of Revenue, a "premises" has to have firewalls, a business license, a power meter, and an attendant. Stacks realized that as long as he met those specs, he could cram as many "premises" as he wanted into a single building. So in 1995 he built Treasures, the original warren-casino. Soon scores of these subdivided monstrosities were sprouting across the state. Video malls now house 45 percent of the state's poker machines.

What's remarkable about South Carolina is not simply the few (flouted) regulations it does have but the many regulations it doesn't have. Unlike virtually every other state with gambling, South Carolina has no gambling commission and no rules about who can own a gambling license (two of the state's leading video-poker operators are convicted felons). South Carolina does not forbid children from gambling (though an adult must collect their winnings). Nor does the state require that machines be honest or fair, so operators can set poker terminals to pay out as little as they want. The half-dozen other states with video poker harvest up to 50 percent of revenues in taxes. South Carolina collects only a piddling $2,000 annual license fee on each machine. South Carolina, says University of Nevada gambling economist William Thompson, is "the Wild West" of gambling.

On Friday morning, twelve hours after my first visit, I return to Treasures. It is a gorgeous day, 75 degrees in the middle of February, but Treasures is as packed and gloomy as it had been when I left at midnight. I turn into the game room where I played the night before, and Joyce is sitting there, right where I left her. She is still playing Shamrock Sevens. She is still clutching a cigarette in one hand and pinging the screen with the other. She is wearing the same green sweat suit she had on last night. She claims she went home and has come back "just for an hour" because she won't be able to play all weekend. She'll be too busy babysitting her grandchildren. "Oh, that's going to be a real treat," she told me. "We are going to have a real party."

I play the machine next to her for a few minutes, lose a couple of dollars, then stroll among the game rooms. I spot another woman I had seen playing the night before. She too is wearing the clothes she had on last night. I fall into conversation with Chris, a game room attendant. He delivers the candy and water to gamblers and wipes down the machines with Windex. For this, Chris makes $5.50 an hour "plus tips," of which there are exactly none. He took the Treasures job three days ago because he got fired from a dog food factory.

I have gambled in Vegas casinos, Indian casinos, Mississippi dockside casino, bingo parlors, horse tracks, and dog tracks, but if there is a gambling house one-tenth as depressing as a South Carolina video parlor, I have not seen it. America's vision of gambling is Las Vegas, a fantasyland where the air is—or so goes the myth—perfumed and oxygenated so that customers bet more, where there are cigarette girls and slick dealers and free drinks and sparkling lights. Vegas shellacs gambling with so much glamour that you forget it's gambling. South Carolina has done the reverse. It has distilled gambling to its purest essence: an icy transaction between man and machine. No liquor, no food, no dealers, no glamour, no perfume, no neon, no cigarette girls, only cigarettes. (Forget oxygenated air—there's barely air.) All that remains is the grind: the machine, a few Tootsie Rolls, and a whole lot of people who don't have too much money squandering it.[3]

"You wouldn't really call it entertainment. It's more like a peep show," says Glenn Stanton, "Why do so many people play it?" he asks. "Why do so few people exercise? People don't do what they should. And on this issue, it is clear that the state has a compelling interest in keeping people from behaving in a way that is detrimental to them."

Video-poker supporters recast Stanton's stop-them-for-their-own-good views as overblown and puritanical. "Are we going to ban Ben & Jerry's?" Harpootlian asks. "I mean, more people are going to die from cardiac arrest stuffing their fat faces with Ben & Jerry's ice cream than they are from the perils of betting. It's a little paternalistic." But there is a flaw in Harpootlian's practiced libertarian creed, and that flaw is video poker. As poker metastacized during Beasley's administration, South Carolinians began to realize that it was not simply an irritant but a menace. Video poker is not Ben & Jerry's. It is the crack cocaine of gambling, gambling at its most addictive and virulent, producing few economic benefits and high social costs. If there were ever a case for government restriction of gambling, South Carolina is it.

Video poker is dangerous for the same reason it is popular. It combines the speed of slots and the skill of table games but avoids their bad features. Gamblers dislike slots because they're dull: a random-number generator determines whether you win or lose. Table games are slow and intimidating to novices. But video poker is as fast as slots: I clocked myself playing eight games of video poker a minute, nearly 500 chances for a jackpot in an hour. And video poker requires (minimal) skill: you *can* make decisions that will improve your likelihood of winning—there's an entire library of books and videos devoted to strategy, such as *Fundamentals of Video Poker, Video Poker Mania! Video Poker for Winners*—though not decisions that will ever let you beat the house. Unlike table games, video poker doesn't scare novices, because "you can sit down and play the games without being worried about other people judging your competence," says Fred Preston, a sociology professor at University of Nevada at Las Vegas. (Preston adds that this makes video poker especially enticing to women, who rarely play table games.) But video poker is devastatingly addictive to the susceptible. According to compulsive-gambling expert Robert Hunter, gamblers hooked on the horses or table games take twenty years from first bet to bottoming out. Video-poker addicts take only two and a half years. Unlike other forms of gambling, video poker does not excite players. It numbs them. "There is an ability to block out external stimuli while you are playing the games. Almost without exception, my video-poker patients report not excitement but anesthetized nothingness. It is a twilight-zone experience for them," says Hunter. In hours and hours of South Carolina gambling, I saw only one display of emotion. A woman dropped to her knees and prayed for four of a kind: "Give me a king," she implored, "a king for my birthday." She drew a jack. More typical was the middle-aged man seated next to me who hit a $208 jackpot on a quarter bet. I heard the celebratory bells and looked over. He was expressionless, already playing his next hand.

South Carolina does not collect data on gambling addiction, but during the Beasley years the number of Gamblers' Anonymous chapters in the state tripled. Last year Columbia psychologist Frank Quinn conducted the first statewide survey of gamblers and found that some 20 percent of the 553 poker players he quizzed met the criteria for a problem-gambling diagnosis—a compulsive gambling rate twice as high as Las Vegas's.

The economics of video poker are just as devastating. University of Nevada at Reno Professor William Eadington ranks different sorts of gambling by their economic benefits. Topping his list are "destination casinos," such as those in Las Vegas, which draw tourists, support hotels, restaurants, shops, and theaters, and provide tons of new jobs, many of them at union wages. Since tourists take their addictions and bankruptcies home with them, destination casinos "export the social impacts of gambling." Next on Eadington's list are rural casinos, such as most Indian casinos, which bring jobs to undeveloped areas, "export" most social impacts, but don't generate much ancillary development. Large urban casinos rank next. They may attract some tourists and spark a little ancillary development, but because most gamblers are local, the surrounding community bears the social costs.

At rock bottom, says Eadington, is the South Carolina model. The low-density, low-glamour gambling draws few tourists and no development. The jobs are McJobs, such as convenience-store clerks and game-room attendants. Most gamblers are locals, so little out-of-state money flows into the economy, and the state absorbs the social costs, which are particularly high, because video poker is so addictive and the machines are so ubiquitous. Other gambling models limit addiction by requiring gamblers to travel some inconvenient distance to bet. But in South Carolina nothing stops the vulnerable from gambling all the time.

"There is no pretense that this is about tourism or this is about a nice night out or that this is about entertainment," says Tom Grey, head of the National Coalition Against Gambling Expansion. "This is hard-core, grab-the-paycheck gambling."

For several months last year, this sign greeted drivers crossing from Georgia into South Carolina: GOV. DAVID BEESLAY WELKUMS YOU TOO SOUTH CAROLINA. WE BE GOTS DE WURSTEST SKOOLS IN DE UNITED STATE. WE BEES NUMBUH 50TH.

The sign was the inspiration of Henry Ingram, one of the state's largest video-poker operators, who, like virtually everyone in the industry, detests

David Beasley. Ingram detests Beasley so much that he spent his own money last year—no one knows how much, since such expenditures go unreported—attacking Beasley's education record. Ingram detests Beasley so much that he placed a covenant on his own property: it cannot be sold to a Yankee or "anyone named Beasley." Ingram and his fellow video-poker tycoons detest Beasley so much, in fact, that Beasley is no longer governor.

Now, let's make something clear. Beasley is a shameless political opportunist. He wields his religion like a club. He was caught lying to schoolchildren about his athletic exploits. His fellow Republicans don't trust him. South Carolinians, who loathe Bill Clinton, compare Beasley unfavorably to the President. I had to struggle to find anyone in the state who actually likes Beasley. So it is a testament to the crushing power of the video-poker industry that it actually makes people feel sorry for David Beasley.

In early 1998, Beasley was coasting toward reelection. All good Republican things—incomes, prison populations, executions—were way up. All bad things—unemployment, crime, taxes—were way down. The Christian right, which all but owned the state Republican Party, was thriving, and the party coffers were full of cash. The Democratic Party was battered by twelve years of defeat, its treasury empty, its staff skeletal, its poll numbers dismally low. "They appeared," says State Republican Party Chairman Henry McMaster, "headed for extinction." Early polls gave Beasley a twenty-point lead, and no wonder. His Democratic opponent was the anti-gambling legislator Jim Hodges, who seemed a sure loser: little-known, uncharismatic, and a bit gloomy.

Then Beasley did something that was simultaneously incredibly courageous and cravenly opportunistic. He declared video poker a "cancer," and in his January 1998 State of the State address he proposed to ban it immediately. Almost the entire audience, which included all 168 state legislators, rose in a standing ovation. "The industry was gaining political clout, and if they were not stopped then, a couple of years down the road they would have too much political clout to reverse," Beasley says now. "In your heart you know that *this* is the time to do it, no matter the political consequences, no matter the cost."

This kind of talk makes Beasley's critics gag. "He decided that he was going to ratchet himself up to the next level. He could be the Governor That Killed Gambling," mocks Harpootlian. "This was all a calculated move on his part, not sincerely based on a hatred of video poker or gambling but to ratchet himself into a V.P. candidacy in 2000. Huge miscalculation."

The move may have been heartfelt and it may have been calculated, but it was undoubtedly disastrous. Beasley prodded the state legislature to outlaw video gambling, and within weeks of his speech the Republican-controlled house overwhelmingly passed a ban. A majority of the Democratic-controlled senate also favored the ban, but anti-gambling senators successfully filibustered. "I stood on the floor and said video poker owns this senate, and no one disagreed with me," says Senator Wes Hayes, who led the legislative campaign to ban poker.

The bill died in April, and in essence so did Beasley. Every machine owner, every owner of a convenience store, truck stop, gas station, bar, or restaurant that depended on video poker, and all their employees were now out for Beasley's scalp. As the new chairman of the Democratic Party, Harpootlian was perfectly positioned to solicit contributions from the disgruntled pokerites.

Harpootlian found a surprisingly cooperative partner in Hodges, who, as the Democratic gubernatorial candidate, conveniently discarded his ferocious anti-poker stance. Hodges says he decided after the 1994 referendum that voters, not politicians, should determine whether poker was to be legal. Republicans contend that he cynically dropped his objections to poker in order to fund his run. In any case, as the gubernatorial race began, Hodges announced that although he disliked video poker personally, he favored a voter referendum to decide whether to keep it. If voters approved poker, he would regulate and tax it. This declaration of neutrality, coupled with Harpootlian's presence in the Democratic Party headquarters, signaled to poker operators that Hodges was their candidate.

"Look, Hodges had a history of being opposed to video poker," says John Crangle, who runs the state's chapter of Common Cause. "But I think he saw an opportunity to knock Beasley off, and he thought the price was worth paying. He thought that as governor, he could do things for education and corrections and race relations that would counterbalance whatever evil video poker was."

In previous elections Democratic gubernatorial candidates had managed to raise only $1–2.5 million, half what their Republican opponents collected. But in 1998 the Democratic Party and Hodges's campaign found themselves awash in money. Hodges estimates that "less than 10 percent" of the $3.7 million he raised came from video-poker sources. This is laughable. The Republican Party analyzed Hodges's large donations and concluded that more than 70 percent of his contributions of $1,000 or more came from people tied to video poker. (For example, one video-poker operator told me she gave the $3,500 maximum to Hodges and enlisted family members to give $20,000 more.) And although campaign-disclosure laws don't require parties to report their soft-money receipts, educated guessers hazard that video poker also supplied a million dollars or more to the Democratic Party. "David Beasley is the best friend the South

Carolina Democratic Party has had in the last several years. David Beasley, through his own stupidity, funded the statewide Democratic ticket," says Crangle. (If this seems to be an odd statement from a good-government type, it's worth noting that Harpootlian served on Common Cause's board till he became the Democratic Party chairman.)

Harpootlian and Hodges put the money to good use. Hodges, who had also long opposed a state lottery, reversed himself and made the introduction of a lottery the cornerstone of his campaign. He promised to earmark the revenues for public education, as Georgia had done with great success. The lottery notion polled more than 70 percent of voter's support, and it massacred Beasley. The Democratic Party spent a fortune on ads showing a Georgian "Bubba" thanking Beasley for the millions of dollars South Carolinians had contributed to Georgia schools via the Georgia lottery. "Hodges just took the lottery, turned it into a blunt instrument, and clubbed Beasley senseless with it," says Stanton.

The poker moguls were not satisfied with simply writing checks to Hodges and Harpootlian, however. Several launched their own independent anti-Beasley crusades. Fred Collins had loathed Beasley ever since state agents had conducted a Christmastime raid on one of his warehouses in a fruitless search for illegal gambling devices. "What would you do if someone called your business a cancer?!" Collins shouts at me. Collins ran thousands of anti-Beasley radio ads; erected 110 BAN BEASLEY billboards; distributed BAN BEASLEY bumper sticks, hats, and T-shirts; and bought full-page ads in twenty-six state newspapers urging an anti-Beasley vote. Collins staffed an anti-Beasley war room in Greenville and funded anti-Beasley phone banks. He refuses to divulge how much he spent, but even the most cautious estimates peg it at more than $500,000; a good guess is more like $1 million.

Meanwhile, Henry Ingram spent thousands on ads in southern South Carolina, and South of the Border's Alan Schafer is estimated to have dropped more than $50,000 on 4,300 radio ads in the northeast of the state. The L'il Cricket chain sponsored its own dump-Beasley campaign. (The private spending of Collins, Ingram, and Schafer so shocked South Carolinians that one of the first bills the general assembly passed in 1999 requires disclosure of independent expenditures.)

Video poker's money also spilled into other strange corners of the campaign. "Republicans for Hodges," a handful of Republicans who detested Beasley for screwing over a local party operative, received more than $35,000 from poker interests; the Black Community Developer Program is thought to have received more than $25,000 for its grass-roots, anti-Beasley work. And in what must be the most peculiar episode of the race, poker operators underwrote the Palmetto League, a coalition of "heritage" groups. These groups—Sons of Confederate Veterans, Heritage Preservation, the Conservative Alliance, and the like—ostensibly espouse "Southern pride." In practice, they are essentially white supremacists with mailing lists and a veneer of mainstream respectability. The Palmetto League's founder, Jerry Creech, used to run South Carolina's chapter of the racist Council of Conservative Citizens. ("We believe America was founded by Christians who believe in Jesus Christ. Not Muslims. Not Hindus," Creech tells me in one of his milder moments.)

The heritage groups constitute a small but vocal bloc whose greatest passion is to keep the Confederate battle flag flying over the state capitol. In 1994, Beasley courted the heritage vote by promising to protect the flag, but two years later he announced a revelation: his reading of the Bible convinced him the flag should come down. Beasley fought briefly for his epiphany, the legislature smashed him on it, he dropped the issue, and the flag stayed. But the heritage groups never forgot his betrayal.

Hodges had been one of the few white legislators who opposed the Confederate flag, but when Creech called on Hodges early in the campaign, he said that he wouldn't try to remove it. Satisfied that Hodges wasn't a threat, the Palmetto League set about savaging Beasley, mailing fliers, establishing a "Dump Beasley" Web site, and buying ads on cable TV and country-radio stations. At least half of the money the Palmetto League spent, which by Creech's account was more than $100,000, came from video poker.

Beasley's twenty-point lead narrowed and then vanished under the universal ambush. Everything went sour. He was forced to call a press conference to deny that he had had an affair with his former spokeswoman, a rumor reportedly linked to Harpootlian's opposition research machine. With Hodges killing him on the lottery, Beasley abandoned his resistance to it, infuriating his conservative base. Whenever Beasley complained that video poker was buying the election, Hodges countered effectively by blaming gambling's explosive growth on Beasley's inaction. On Election Day, the poker moguls delivered the coup de grace. Collins gave his 370 employees the day off, and they ferried more than 8,000 voters to the polls. Collins's phone banks called 20,000 voters in Columbia and Greenville alone. Other video-poker companies shuttled voters directly from their game rooms to voting booths.

Hodges beat Beasley convincingly, 53–45 percent, and Democrats also snatched four GOP seats in the statehouse and two statewide offices held by Republicans. L'il Cricket celebrated Beasley's defeat by awarding employees a dollar-an-hour raise. Beasley fled to Harvard University's Institute of Politics to teach a seminar about "political figures risking it all."

Hodges and Harpootlian insist that video poker did not win them the election. They note that voters loved Hodges's lottery/education twofer and that Beasley had infuriated his base by flipflopping on the lottery and the Confederate flag. Harpootlian claims that the million-dollar interference by Collins actually harmed Hodges because it was so heavy-handed ("one ignorant schmuck," is what Harpootlian calls Collins).

But it's undeniable that without video-poker money, Hodges wouldn't have reached so many voters with his lottery message. He couldn't have afforded enough TV time, polling, opposition research, and get-out-the-vote drives to overcome Beasley's incumbency. "Democrats have been sucking on the hind tit here for so long. This was the first time in decades Democrats were able to raise money," says Common Cause's Crangle. *USA Today*, which in January made the first systematic attempt to calculate the video-poker contribution, conservatively estimates that the industry spent at least $3 million in its varied efforts to topple Beasley. This translates into about $6 for every Hodges vote.

To which Democrats and video-poker operators say: no big deal. Video poker is just another special interest, $3 million is just free speech, and the gang-tackle of Beasley was just old-fashioned politics. "Are those people equally disturbed by the money David Beasley raised from people who had ties to state government? Were they worried about the health-insurance and life-insurance and auto-insurance companies that gave substantial dollars to David Beasley?" asks Hodges. "The truth is that, sadly, people who have interest in state government contribute to campaigns.... That happens to be the way the system works."

But this is a weak rationalization. No special interest gave Beasley anything like what video poker gave Hodges. A "special interest" is an industry whose contributions may total 5 percent of a candidate's war chest or a corporation that spends $25,000 in an election cycle. Put the $3 million in context: In 1997 and 1998 the entire gambling industry, an industry notorious for its muscle, gave $2.8 million in PAC money, soft money, and direct contributions to *all* candidates in *all* congressional elections—less than $3 million for 468 races. And here is video poker spending more than $3 million for a single candidate in a single election in a single state. When 70 percent of your big contributions come from a single industry, when the head of your party is the leading advocate for that industry, when a tycoon from that industry spends $1 million on your behalf, that industry is no longer a special interest, it is a parent company.

"Had the video-poker industry not been involved in my campaign, I probably would have won 65–35 percent," says Beasley. "The video-poker industry is buying the leadership in our state. They have shown they can unduly influence elections and there is no consequence to that. They intimidated the media. And they own the governor's office."

"Own" may be an exaggeration, but you can see Beasley's point. The Democratic Party, which seemed dead and buried, is alive and flourishing. The poker industry, which Beasley tried to kill, is alive and flourishing. And Beasley himself is dead and buried, virtually renounced by his own party. "David Beasley is a non-person," says Harpootlian gleefully. "I am here. And he is not!"

I don't believe in the journalistic trope that the office represents the man, but I'm willing to make an exception for Jim Hodges. Governor Hodges's office is cavernous and dark. Thick curtains block the sunlight. A portrait of a grand old South Carolinian—John C. Calhoun, perhaps—sneers at the far end of the room. The principal illumination is the screen saver on Hodges's computer, an endlessly scrolling message: "It's all about South Carolina schools." This somber atmosphere seems suited to the dolorous Hodges. He suffers from a case of Al Gore disease: too earnest to have a common touch.

It's clear from the moment we meet that Hodges would rather talk about anything than what I have come to discuss. He has spent the first months of his administration deflecting allegation after allegation that video poker bought him. And here he is, compelled to deflect another one. "I certainly wasn't advocating for the business," he says. "I'm sure the people that had connection to the industry looked at the options that they had and felt like they had a choice between a guy who said, 'Look, I don't like the business and I'd vote against it personally if it came up for referendum again, but I think people ought to have a choice,' and a guy who was basically blaming them for everything that was wrong in South Carolina."

"We have the worst of both worlds. We have unregulated and untaxed video gaming," Hodges continues. "I've made it very clear that if I had my druthers, South Carolina would not have video gaming. But up to this point the people in the state have said they do want it, and until the people of the state say they don't want it, then I think our obligation as leaders is to regulate it as effectively as we can and police it as effectively as we can."

As soon as he took office, Hodges and Democratic legislators introduced a regulatory package: drop the $125-a-day winnings cap, which Hodges calls "unenforceable," and impose a $500 "per-sitting" winnings limit instead; bar felons from owning video-poker machines; tighten the advertising ban; place a moratorium on casinos; and tax wagers to raise $200 million a year. As promised, Hodges is also pushing for a statewide referendum on video poker, which is likely to be held this fall.

Hodges is proud of the strictness of these proposed regulations, and he honestly considers himself a foe of the industry. And it's true that video poker did not buy a governor in 1998. Video poker bought something more valuable than a governor. It bought the right to be taxed and regulated; that is, the right to survive forever. Taxation and regulation are anathema to most businesses. But to a rogue industry they are priceless—guaranteed legitimacy. The poker operators are happy to pay $130 million in taxes. They know that once cash starts flowing into the treasury, the state will grow hooked on the money. And poker operators will still have $600 million in profits to take to the bank. (Collins, with a calculation so blatant that it's almost charming, proposes that poker tax funds be spent on college tuition for South Carolina high school graduates. "Palmetto Promise Scholarships," he calls this proposal. What state legislator would dare to cut "Palmetto Promise Scholarships"?)

John Crangle of Common Cause says he doesn't worry about video poker's 1998 flood of political spending, because it will never happen again. "The magnitude of the spending is a one-time thing." He's right. Collins and his poker partners won't spend millions in the 2002 election to re-elect Hodges. They won't need to. In slaughtering Beasley, they warned every politician in the state: Challenge us and die. The state Republican Party still officially opposes gambling and is pushing for tougher regulations than the ones Hodges has proposed, but the party has faint hope of winning the statewide referendum. "It's over," one GOP staffer tells me. "You aren't going to do something when you just know you are going to take an old-fashioned butt whipping if you try."

On my last night in South Carolina, a Saturday, I return to Treasures. I am starting to feel like a regular. I immediately see Joyce. She is wearing different clothes than when I saw her on Friday, thank God. And she is betting on a different machine. She's planted at the terminal right next to the one she had been playing for the past two days. The first thing she says to me is, "I hit it. I hit it this afternoon." I don't have to ask what she means: she won the $700 jackpot on the other machine. "My grandkids got sick, so I didn't have to baby-sit. So I came in around three, and I hit it." It is now seven P.M. She says all this matter-of-factly, her eyes still on her machine, one hand clawing for a Vantage, the other automatically tapping the screen.

She has me sit down next to her, but not at the machine she hit. After all, she says, "What are the chances of getting another jackpot on that one?" Joyce believes in clusters: because she hit one machine in this room, she's confident (if not quite sure) that one of us is going to hit a jackpot on another. We play Shamrock Sevens, twenty-five cents a hand. After an hour or so, I run out for some dinner. She is still there when I get back. I take my seat next to her, and we keep playing, till nine P.M., ten P.M., eleven P.M.

We don't talk at all, except once when Joyce interrupts the silence to say, "There was a guy down in the other room. He was playing blackjack—300 bucks a hand. I couldn't believe it. He just kept sliding twenties into the bill collector. And he was winning too." We are playing for a quarter a hand, and neither of us is winning much of anything. I am up thirty dollars for a while, then down ten, then back up twenty. A woman ducks her head in, looking for a hot machine. "Any bells ringing in your office tonight?" she asks. We shake our heads no. At about 11:15 my right arm starts to ache from all the tapping. It will hurt for the next three days. I go to the bathroom and see that my eyes have turned bright red, a reaction to the smoke and the screen. When I get back to my machine I notice that Joyce's eyes, too, are bright red. Everyone's eyes, in fact, are bright red.

Joyce asks me for the time. "I have no conception of time when I get in here," she says. I tell her it's 11:30. She laughs. "My dog has probably peed in the house by now. I wouldn't blame him if he did. It's my fault. I left him there." She says she has to go. She ups her bet from twenty-five cents to fifty cents, to lose faster.

Actually we all have to go, because the poker machines go dark at midnight on Saturday and stay dark till Monday morning. This is a tiny nod to South Carolina's churches, and it is just about the only law that video-poker operators always obey. At 11:45, Joyce finally stops in earnest. She has lost all that she was playing. ("Just a twenty," she says.) She grabs her pack of Vantages and wishes me goodnight. Then she turns to the attendant and points at her Pot-O-Gold. "Put that machine aside for me for Monday, would you, honey? Eight-thirty A.M., okay?"

Notes

1. On average, gamblers lose about twice as much—10 percent—on every video-poker bet as they do on every table game or slots bet.
2. Five-card-draw poker is the basic video-gambling game, but "multigame" machines also offer blackjack, bingo, keno, and curiosities such as Pieces of Eight Criss Cross, an inexplicable combination of poker and ticktacktoe.
3. No one has studied the demographics of video-poker players, but a cursory look around any venue reveals that it is an activity for the lower middle class: elderly women, blacks, hicks. Not a single one of the prosperous pro-poker lawyers, lobbyists, politicians, and machine owners I talked to plays video poker. It is a game for other, poorer people.

Suggestions for Further Reading

Aasved, Mikal (2003) *The Sociology of Gambling*. Springfield, IL: Charles C Thomas.

Abt, Vicki, James F. Smith, and Eugene Martin Christiansen (1985) *The Business of Risk: Commercial Gambling in Mainstream America*. Lawrence: University Press of Kansas.

Adam, Barbara, Ulrich Beck, and Joost Van Loon, eds. (2000) *The Risk Society and Beyond: Critical Issues for Social Theory*. London: Sage.

Alexander, Jeffrey C. (1996) "Critical Reflections on 'Reflexive Modernization,'" *Theory, Culture and Society*, 13(4): 133–38.

Alvarez, A. (1983) *The Biggest Game in Town*. Boston: Houghton Mifflin.

Alvarez, A. (2001) *Poker: Bets, Bluffs, and Bad Beats*. San Francisco: Chronicle Books.

Austrin, Terry and Jackie West (2004) "New Deals In Gambling: Global Markets and Local Regimes of Regulation," *Globalism/Localism at Work: Research in the Sociology of Work* (13): 143–158.

Balint, Michael (1959) *Thrills and Regressions*. New York: International Universities Press.

Barker, Thomas, and Marjie Britz (2000) *Jokers Wild: Legalized Gambling in the Twenty-First Century*, Wesport, CT: Praeger Publishers.

Beck, Ulrich (1997) *The Reinvention of Politics: Rethinking Modernity in the Global Social Order*, trans. Mark Ritter. Oxford: Polity Press.

Beck, Ulrich (2000) *The Brave New World of Work*, trans. Patrick Camiller. Oxford: Polity Press.

Beck, Ulrich (2002) "The Terrorist Threat: World Risk Society Revisited," *Theory, Culture & Society* 19(4): 39–55.

Bellin, Andy (2001) *Poker Nation*. New York: HarperCollins.

Bernhard, Bo. J and Frederick W. Preston (2004) "On the Shoulders of Merton: Potentially Sobering Consequences of Problem Gambling Policy," *American Behavioural Scientist* 47 (11): 1395–1405.

Brenner, Reuven, and Gabrielle A. Brenner (1990) *Gambling and Speculation: A Theory, a History and a Future of Some Human Decisions*. Cambridge: Cambridge University Press.

Buck-Morss, Susan (1990) *The Dialectics of Seeing: Walter Benjamin and the Arcades Project*. Cambridge, MA: MIT Press.

Burchell, Graham, Colin Gordon, and Peter Miller, eds. (1991) *The Foucault Effect: Studies in Governmentality*. Chicago: University of Chicago Press.

Casey, Emma (2003) "Gambling and Consumption: Working-Class Women and UK National Lottery play," *Journal of Consumer Culture* 3(2): 245–63.

Castellani, Brian (2000) *Pathological Gambling: The Making of a Medical Problem*. Albany: State University of New York Press.

Clotfelter, Charles T., and Phillip J. Cook (1989) *Selling Hope: State Lotteries in America*. Cambridge: Harvard University Press.

Cornish, David (1978) *Gambling: A Review of the Literature and Its Implications for Policy and Research*. London: HMSO.

David, Florence N. (1962) *Games, Gods and Gambling: The Origins and History of Probability and Statistical Ideas from the Earliest Times to the Newtonian Era*, New York: Hafner.

de Goede, Marieke (2005) *Virtue, Fortune, and Faith: A Genealogy of Finance*. Minneapolis: University of Minnesota Press.

Dean, Mitchell (1999) "Risk, calculable and incalculable," in *Risk and Sociocultural Theory: New Directions and Perspectives*, ed. Deborah Lupton, 131–59. Cambridge: Cambridge University Press.

Devereux, Edward C. (1949) "Gambling and the Social Structure: A Sociological Study of Lotteries and Horse Racing in Contemporary America," Ph.D. diss., Harvard University.

Devereux, Edward C. (1968) "Gambling in a psychological and sociological perspective," *International Encyclopedia of the Social Sciences* 6: 53–68.

Dixon, David (1991) *From Prohibition to Regulation: Bookmaking, Anti-Gambling and the Law*. Oxford: Clarendon Press.

Dodd, Nigel (1994) *The Sociology of Money: Economics, Reason and Contemporary Society*. Cambridge: Polity Press.

Elliot, Anthony (2002) "Beck's Sociology of Risk: A Critical Assessment," *Sociology* 36(2): 293–315.

Ericson, Richard V., and Aaron Doyle, eds. (2003) *Risk and Morality*. Toronto: University of Toronto Press.

Ewald, Francois (1991) "Insurance and risks," in *The Foucault Effect: Studies in Governmentality*, ed. Graham Burchell, Colin Gordon, and Peter Miller, 197–210. Chicago: University of Chicago Press.

Ewen, C. L'Estrange (1932) *Lotteries and Sweepstakes*. London: Heath Cranton.

Ezell, John Samuel (1960) *Fortune's Merry Wheel: The Lottery in America*. Cambridge, MA: Harvard University Press.

Falk, Pasi, and Pasi Maenpaa (1999) *Hitting the Lottery Jackpot: Lives of Lottery Millionaires*. Oxford: Berg.

Findlay, John M. (1986) *People of Chance: Gambling in American Society from Jamestown to Las Vegas*. New York: Oxford University Press.

Gabriel, Kathryn (1996) *Gambler Way: Indian Gaming in Mythology, History, and Archaeology in North America.* Boulder: Johnson Books.

Giddens, Anthony (1990) *The Consequences of Modernity.* Cambridge: Polity Press.

Goffman, Erving (1961) *Encounters: Two Studies in the Sociology of Interaction.* Indianapolis: Bobbs-Merrill.

Goffman, Erving (1963) *Stigma: Notes on the Management of Spoiled Identity.* Englewood Cliffs, NJ: Prentice-Hall.

Goodman, Robert (1995) *The Luck Business: The Devastating Consequences and Broken Promises of America's Gambling Explosion.* New York: The Free Press.

Gottdenier, Mark, Claudia C. Collins, and David R. Dickens (1999) *Las Vegas: The Social Production of an All-American City.* Oxford: Blackwell.

Goux, Jean-Joseph (1990) *Symbolic Economies: After Marx and Freud,* trans. Jennifer Curtiss Gage. Ithaca: Cornell University Press.

Habermas, Jurgen (1975) *Legitimation Crisis.* Boston: Beacon Press.

Habermas, Jurgen (1984) *The Theory of Communicative Action, Volume One: Reason and the Rationalization of Society,* trans. John McCarthy. Boston: Beacon Press.

Hacking, Ian (1975) *The Emergence of Probability.* Cambridge: Cambridge University Press.

Hacking, Ian (1990) *The Taming of Chance.* Cambridge: Cambridge University Press.

Hannigan, John (1999) *Fantasy City: Pleasure and Profit in the Postmodern Metropolis.* New York: Routledge.

Hayano, David (1977) "The Professional Poker Player: Career Contingencies and the Problem of Respectability," *Social Problems* 24: 556–64.

Hayano, David (1982) *Poker Face: The Life and Work of Professional Card Players.* Berkeley, CA: University of California Press.

Herman, Robert D. (1967) *Gambling.* London: Harper & Row.

Herman, Robert D. (1976) *Gamblers and Gambling: Motives, Institutions, and Controls.* Lexington, MA: Lexington Books.

Hoggart, Richard (1962) *The Uses of Literacy: Aspects of Working-Class Life with Special Reference to Publications and Amusements.* Harmondsworth: Pelican Books.

Huizinga, Johan (1955) *Homo Ludens: A Study of the Play Element in Culture.* Boston: Beacon Press.

Hutchinson, Brian (1999) *Betting the House: Winners, Losers and the Politics of Canada's Gambling Obsession.* Toronto: Viking.

Kavanaugh, Thomas M. (1993) *Enlightenment and the Shadows of Chance: The Novel and the Culture of Gambling in Eighteenth-Century France.* Baltimore: Johns Hopkins University Press.

Knapp, Bettina (2000) *Gambling, Game, and Psyche.* Albany: State University of New York Press.

Knorr-Cetina, Karin (2005) *The Sociology of Financial Markets.* Oxford: Oxford University Press.

Kusyszyn, Igor (1977) "How Gambling Save Me From A Misspent Sabbatical," *Journal of Humanistic Psychology* 17(3): 19–34.

Lash, Scott, and John Urry (1994) *Economies of Signs and Space.* London: Sage.

Lears, Jackson (2003) *Something for Nothing: Luck in America*. New York: Viking.

Luhmann, Niklas (1993) *Risk: A Sociological Theory*, trans. R. Barnet. Berlin: Walter de Gruyter.

Luhmann, Niklas (1998) *Observations on Modernity*, trans. William Whobrey. Stanford: Stanford University Press.

Lupton, Deborah (1999) *Risk*. London: Sage.

Lupton, Deborah, ed. (1999) *Risk and Sociocultural Theory: New Directions and Perspectives*. Cambridge: Cambridge University Press.

M@n@gement 4(3), (2001) Special Issue: Deconstructing Las Vegas.

Marx, Karl (1977) *Capital*, Vol. 1, trans. Ben Fowkes. New York: Vintage Books.

Mason, W. Dale (2000) *Indian Gaming: Tribal Sovereignty and American Politics*. Norman, Oklahoma: University of Oklahoma Press.

Mason, John Lyman, and Michael Nelson (2001) *Governing Gambling*. New York: Century Foundation Press.

McManus, James (2000) "Fortune's Smile: Betting Big at the World Series of Poker," *Harper's Magazine* (December) 39–57.

McManus, James (2003) *Positively 5th Street: Murderers, Cheetahs, and Binion's World Series of Poker*. New York: Farrar, Straus, Giroux.

Mestrovic, Stjepan G. (1991) *The Coming Fin de Siecle: An Application of Durkheim's Sociology to Modernity and Postmodernity*. London: Routledge.

Mestrovic Stjepan G. (1998) *Anthony Giddens: The Last Modernist*. London: Routledge.

Morton, Suzanne (2002) *At Odds: Gambling and Canadians, 1919–1969*. Toronto: University of Toronto Press.

Mullis, Angela, and David Kemper, eds. (2000) *Indian Gaming: Who Wins?* Los Angeles: UCLA American Indian Studies Center.

Munting, Roger (1996) *An Economic and Social History of Gambling in Britain and the U.S.A.* Manchester: Manchester University Press.

Newman, Otto (1972) *Gambling: Hazard and Reward*. London: Athlone Press.

Nietzsche, Friedrich (1982) *Daybreak*. trans. R.J. Hollingdale. Cambridge: Cambridge University Press.

Nietzsche, Friedrich (1993) *The Birth of Tragedy: Out of the Spirit of Music*, trans. Shaun Whiteside and Michael Tanner. Harmondsworth: Penguin.

Nussbaum, Martha C. (1986) *The Fragility of Goodness: Luck and Ethics in Greek Tragedy and Philosophy*. Cambridge: Cambridge University Press.

O'Brien, Timothy (1998). *Bad Bet: The Inside Story of the Glamour, Glitz and Danger of America's Gambling Industry*. New York: Random House.

Pascal, Blaise (1984) *Pensees*, trans. and introduction, A. J. Krailsheimer. New York: Penguin.

Peele, Stanton (1985) *The Meaning of Addiction: Compulsive Experience and Its Interpretation*. Lexington, MA: Lexington Books.

Prus, Robert (2004) "Gambling as Activity: Subcultural Life-Worlds, Personal Intrigues and Persistent Involvements," *eGambling: The Electronic Journal of Gambling Issues* 10 (February: A festschrift in honour of Henry R. Lesieur).

Rose, Nicolas (1993) "Government, Authority and Expertise in Advanced Liberalism," *Economy and Society* 22(3): 282–300.

Rose, Nicolas (1996) "The Death of the Social? Re-figuring the Territory of Government," *Economy and Society* 25(3): 327–56.

Rosencrance, John (1985) "Compulsive Gambling and the Medicalization of Deviance," *Social Problems* 3(2): 275–84.

Schwartz, David G. (2003) *Suburban Xanadu: The Casino Resort on the Las Vegas Strip and Beyond*. New York: Routledge.

Scimecca, Joseph A. (1971) "A Typology of the Gambler," *International Journal of Contemporary Sociology* 8(1): 56–71.

Scott, Marvin (1968) *The Racing Game*. Chicago: Aldine.

Simmel, Georg (1971) "The Miser and the Spendthrift," in *On Individuality and Social Forms,* ed. Donald N. Levine. Chicago: University of Chicago Press.

Simmel, Georg (1978) *The Philosophy of Money,* trans. Tom Bottomore and David Frisby. London: Routledge and Kegan Paul.

Sjoberg, Gideon (2005) "Intellectual Risk Taking, Organizations, and Academic Freedom and Tenure," in *Edgework: The Sociology of Risk-Taking,* ed. Stephen Lyng, 247–71. New York: Routledge.

Strange, Susan (1986) *Casino Capitalism*. Oxford: Blackwell.

Stranger, Mark (1999) "The Aesthetics of Risk: A Study of Surfing," *International Review for the Sociology of Sport* 34(3): 265–76.

Sullivan, George (1972) *By Chance a Winner: The History of Lotteries*. New York: Dodd, Mead.

Thackrey, Ted, Jr. (1968) *Gambling Secrets of Nick the Greek*. New York: Rand McNally & Co.

Walker, Jonathan (1999) "Gambling and Venetian Noblemen c.1500–1700," *Past & Present* 162: 28–69.

Weber, Max (1958) *The Protestant Ethic and the Spirit of Capitalism,* trans. Talcott Parsons. New York: Charles Scribner's Sons.

Academic Journals

Gambling Research—Journal of the National Association of Gambling Studies (Australia)

Gaming Law Review (U.S.)

International Gambling Studies (Australia)

Journal of Gambling Issues (Internet journal—Canada)

Journal of Gambling Studies (U.S.)

National Association for Gambling Studies Journal (U.S.)

Permissions

Index

A

abstract systems 31, 33, 45, 51, 53, 54, 55, 57
  and trust 52
action 106, 208, 209, 225, 246, 247, 248, 280
  and irrationality 107
  pit 247
actor-networks 74
actuarial
  calculation 68, 93
    actuarialisation of society 325
  principles 341, 345
Adam, Barbara 71, 72
addiction 256, 358, 370
  conceptions of 359, 376
  disease model of 375
  drug 372, 373, 375
  and excess 372
  history of drug 375
  and impulse control 378
  moral-pathological view of 373
Adelphia 14
Adorno, Theodor 74
adventure 143, 207, 215–224, 245, 314
  "dreamlike" quality of 216
    as *form of experiencing* 223
adventurer
  fatalism of 221
  and gambler 218
  professional 217
  and symbolism 219

agon and alea 102, 103
aleatory principle 103
  of heredity 104
    and agonistic 118
Alcoholics Anonymous (AA) 361, 379
alienated labour 8
alienation 334
Althusserian structuralism 341
Alvarez, A. 278
American Handbook of Psychiatry 371
American National Academy of Sciences 41
American National Crime Prevention Institute 92
American Psychiatric Association 355, 358
  Diagnostic and Statistical Manual-DSM III 355, 372
    DSM-III-R 358, 359
    DSM-IV 359
amusement centers 106
animism 110
aristocracy 144, 190
  gambling orgies of 281
aristocratic
  display 281
  ethic 283
  excess 283
  play 281
art
  work of 217, 219
Arthur Anderson accounting firm 14